GLOBALIZATION AND BEYOND

New Examinations of Global Power and Its Alternatives

Jon Shefner
and
Patricia Fernández-Kelly

THE PENNSYLVANIA STATE UNIVERSITY PRESS
UNIVERSITY PARK, PENNSYLVANIA

Library of Congress Cataloging-in-Publication Data

Globalization and beyond : new examinations of global power
and its alternatives / [edited by] Jon Shefner and Patricia
Fernandez-Kelly.
    p. cm.
Includes bibliographical references and index.
Summary: "Explores the origins and the reciprocal influences of
globalization and the recent economic crisis, and suggests what
new ideological foundations and geographic regions will be
ascendant"—Provided by publisher.
ISBN 978-0-271-04885-7 (cloth : alk. paper)
1. Globalization.
2. International economic relations.
3. Economic development—Political aspects.
4. International cooperation.
I. Shefner, Jon, 1958– .
II. Fernández-Kelly, María Patricia, 1948–   .
III. Title.
JZ1318.G5786245   2011
337—dc22
2011009651

Contents

Part I: Declining and Emerging Hegemons?

Part II: Alternative Expressions of Global Power

Figures

Tables

Acknowledgments

This volume is the fruit of a conference organized by Patricia Fernández-Kelly and Jon Shefner, held in December 2005 at Princeton University. The conference, NAFTA and Beyond: Alternative Disciplinary Perspectives in the Study of Global Trade and Development, was both a discussion of academic research, much of which is included in this volume, and an effort to think about what might be coming with the progression of globalization.

As the authors and editors worked on the papers that constitute this volume, vast changes, and the potential for even wider changes, emerged with the global financial crisis. In response to that crisis, the authors and editors revised their chapters in a process that delayed publication but reflected the reality of dramatically changing times. Shefner and Fernández-Kelly are deeply grateful to the authors for their willingness to change their chapters in response not just to editorial needs and referee comments but also to the very different world that developed during the crisis.

The NAFTA and Beyond conference was wide-ranging in its concern and coverage. No less wide-ranging were its sponsors at Princeton University. We would like to thank the following conference sponsors for their generosity: the Center for Migration and Development; the Center for Human Values; the Center for Globalization and Governance; the Dean of Campus Life; the International Economics section of the Woodrow Wilson School; the Mexican Migration Program; the Office of the Provost; the Office of the President; the Princeton Institute for International and Regional Studies; the Program in Latin American Studies; the Program in Urbanization and Migration; the Woodrow Wilson School for Public and International Affairs; and the Department of Sociology.

In addition to the researchers whose work is presented in this volume, we would like to recognize and thank the following researchers for participating in the conference: Rina Agarwala, Sarah Babb, Miguel Angel Centeno, James Galbraith, David Harvey, David Kyle, Donald Light, Douglas Massey, Dani Rodrik, Saskia Sassen, and Barbara Stallings.

Finally, we are deeply grateful to Sandy Thatcher, former director of The Pennsylvania State University Press, and two anonymous reviewers, all of whom helped usher this volume into being. We also greatly appreciate the help of Aaron Rowland and Katie Morris. Julie Schoelles provided great aid as well.

During the preparation of this volume, a dear friend and deeply admired colleague passed away. Much has been said about the contributions of Giovanni Arrighi. Much more could and will be said. In memory of his contribution as a friend, a colleague, and a scholar, we dedicate this book to Giovanni Arrighi.

Abbreviations

ABM	Asociación de Bancos de México/Mexican Bankers Association
ADB	Asian Development Bank
AFTA	ASEAN Free Trade Area
AICO	ASEAN Industrial Complementation
AIP	ASEAN Industrial Projects
ALBA	Alternativa Bolivariana para las Américas/Bolivarian Alternative for the Americas
ALCA	Área de Libre Comércio das Américas/Free Trade Area of the Americas
APEC	Asia Pacific Economic Cooperation
ASEAN	Association of Southeast Asian Nations
CCE	Consejo Coordinador Empresarial/Business Coordinating Council
CCP	Chinese Communist Party
CEMAI	Consejo Empresarial Mexicano para Asuntos Internacionales/Mexican Business Council for International Affairs
CIBS	China, India, Brazil, and South Africa
CIEP	Comparative Immigrant Entrepreneurship Project
CMHN	Consejo Mexicano de Hombres de Negocios/Council of Mexican Businessmen
COECE	Coordinadora de Organismos Empresariales de Comercio Exterior/Business Coordinating Council for International Trade
CONAIE	La Confederación de Nacionalidades Indígenas del Ecuador/Confederation of Indigenous Nationalities of Ecuador
COPARMEX	Confederación Patronal de la República Mexicana/Mexican Business Owners Confederation
ECUARUNARI	Ecuador Runakunapak Rikcharimuy/Confederation of Peoples of Kichwa Nationality
EPZ	Export processing zone
FDI	Foreign direct investment
FIRE	Finance, insurance, and real estate

FMLN	Frente Farabundo Martí para la Liberación Nacional/ Farabundo Martí National Liberation Front
FTA	Free trade agreement
FUNGLODE	Fundación Global Democracia y Desarrollo/Global Foundation for Democracy and Development
GATT	General Agreement on Tariffs and Trade
HIPC	Heavily Indebted Poor Countries
IFI	International financial institutions
IME	Instituto de los Mexicanos en el Exterior/Institute of Mexicans Abroad
IMF	International Monetary Fund
ISI	Import-substituting industrialization
MNC	Multinational corporation
NAFTA	North American Free Trade Agreement
NGO	Nongovernmental organization
OECD	Organisation for Economic Co-operation and Development
PAN	Partido Acción Nacional/National Action Party
PLD	Partido de la Liberación Dominicana/Dominican Liberation Party
PRD	Partido Revolucionario Dominicano/Dominican Revolutionary Party
PRI	Partido Revolucionario Institucional/Institutional Revolutionary Party
PTA	People's Trade Agreement/El Tratado de Comercio entre Pueblos
SECOFI	Secretaria de Comercio y Fomento Industrial/Secretariat of Trade and Industrial Promotion
SEIU	Service Employees International Union
SITC	Standard International Trade Classification
SOE	State-owned enterprise
TCC	Transnational capitalist class
TINA	"There is no alternative"
TNC	Transnational corporation
TNS	Transnational state
TVE	Township and village enterprise

INTRODUCTION:
HEGEMONS, STATES, AND ALTERNATIVES

Jon Shefner and Patricia Fernández-Kelly

This book is about recent global changes and how they have affected states and citizens in Latin America and Asia. Early in the millennium, scholars began to examine the shift in power that emerged with the decline of the Washington Consensus, the diminishing political and economic power of the United States, and the rising power of other nations and regions. The current global economic crisis has accelerated some of those trends while introducing new complexities in ways that few foresaw.

The authors included in this book came together at a conference held at Princeton University with the purpose of discussing questions regarding the current moment in globalization.[1] The conference took place just as understandings of worldwide economic integration had begun to shift dramatically. Increasingly, the expectation that globalization would continue to be defined by the hegemonic presence of the United States—and U.S.-linked multinational corporations backed by international financial institutions (IFIs)—was being shaken. For some time, scholars and activists had argued about the potential for *alternative globalizations* (Cavanagh and Mander 2004; McLaren and Jaramillo 2005; Sklair 2002; Stiglitz 2003) and about the factors necessary for them to emerge and be nurtured. The events that occurred around the time of the Princeton conference, and those that have occurred since then, further emphasize the importance of these discussions.

The economic recession spurred by the plunge in housing values and the stock market in the United States has leveled severe damage on people and nations across the globe. Unemployment has risen and production decreased; welfare state provision has been strained and savings devastated. Prior to the crisis, the authors of this book examined how state policy trajectories differed during a period of uneven application of neoliberal orthodoxy, and how this process posed obstacles and opportunities for different states. Equally important to the discussion was how globalization posed obstacles and opportunities for citizens to act collectively in pursuit of their interests, participating in social movements and playing active roles in states and regions, and what implications this activity holds for the further evolution of globalization.

The stunning economic ascent of China and India, the decreasing ability of the U.S. military to resolve political crises, the growing impotence of IFIs and the Washington Consensus to determine economic schemes, and political challenges from Latin America offered an opportunity to rethink the direction of trends that seemed unstoppable less than a decade earlier. The current crisis makes the questions of state and citizen action and interaction all the more pertinent. The authors of this volume examine those issues.

A Declining Hegemon?

Reasons to investigate a possible reconfiguration in the distribution of power at the world level fall into two categories: First, economic developments in the United States raise doubts about whether that country will be able to maintain its preeminence in the international scene. Second, political activity, including foreign policies enacted by the George W. Bush administration, has increasingly isolated the United States and reduced its capacity to establish alliances with other countries.[2] Below, we discuss the two phenomena further.

The U.S. economy is still the largest and most technologically vibrant in the world, with a per capita GDP of $46,000 and a purchasing power parity of $13.78 trillion (Central Intelligence Agency 2007). Yet one indication of the country's declining power is its ballooning national debt. In December 2008, the total outstanding public debt of the United States exceeded $10.6 trillion. This was a substantial increase from the $5.6 trillion reported in December 2000 (U.S. Department of the Treasury 2009). The size of either number is difficult to comprehend, but the rise is clear. So too is the fact that foreign governments own an increasing share of the debt.

A mainstay of Keynesian economics is the principle that incurring national debt is a legitimate government tool when used in pursuit of employment or the production of social goods; government spending can (a) mitigate the market's tendency to concentrate wealth in the hands of a few and (b) lessen the adverse effects of economic recessions, depressions, and booms (Keynes 1936). Keynes, of course, wrote before the age of globalization, and it seems that the recent expansion of government debt has not had the impact he foresaw. Increases in employment following the economic downturn precipitated by the September 11, 2001, attacks on New York and Washington have been significantly smaller than those linked to previous recessions; employment growth in the March 2001–April 2006 period was one-fifth of that in similar periods of economic downturn and recovery. Similarly, unemployment in the aftermath of the 2001 downturn has remained higher than in previous cycles (Mishel, Bernstein, and Allegretto 2007, 214, 222). Judging from the evidence, incurring government debt in the early years of the twenty-first century had more to do with changing tax structures and the cost of military ventures than with securing higher rates of employment or addressing social needs.

Trade data offer further evidence of the weakening U.S. economy. America's international deficit in goods and services increased to $63.1 billion in November 2007. By early 2009, months of global economic paralysis had helped the deficit shrink to $40.4 billion, still a significant rise from $33 billion seven years earlier.[3] This reflects not only debt without employment growth but also increasing imports by comparison to exports. The decline in manufacturing output reported in the 1980s by those who recognized "the deindustrialization of America" (Bluestone and Harrison 1982) has continued to the present day. Services and information have proven no more resilient than smokestack industries; following in the footsteps of older factory production, they too have become vulnerable to outsourcing (Mishel, Bernstein, and Allegretto 2007).[4]

Indications of economic decline are also confirmed by data on U.S. wages, which have been largely stagnant over the past thirty years. After an annual growth rate of 2.8 percent from 1947 to 1973, median family income fell within a range of − 0.5 to 1 percent between 1973 and 2005, interrupted only by a short stretch of higher growth (2.2 percent) in the period 1995–2000 (Lawrence 2008). In addition, the period 1973–2005 was defined by increasing inequality in wage earnings. After 1973, the proportion of income going to 80 percent of families declined while the income share of the highest-earning 20 percent of families increased. During the past thirty years, income disparities have grown, and the United States now ranks as the country with the highest levels of inequality among the nations of the Organisation for Economic Co-operation and Development (OECD) (Dicken 2007; Sassen 2001; OECD 2008).

Income decline in the United States is partially related to the shifts in occupational sectors resulting from deindustrialization. Services are characterized by great variation in wages, from lower-paying retail to the much-vaunted and remunerative FIRE (finance, insurance, and real estate) sector. Yet America generates five times more jobs for janitors and cleaners than for computer software engineers (Dohm and Shniper 2007, table 3). The thirty occupations with the largest job growth in 2006 employed roughly 46.5 million people, of whom nearly 27 million—58 percent of the total—received low or very low wages.[5] Thus, despite expansion of the FIRE sector, the erosion of the industrial backbone has resulted in lower wages for many Americans. Occupations that have contracted in the past three decades paid between $5,000 and $15,000 more than occupations that expanded during the same period (Mishel, Bernstein, and Allegretto 2007, 169–70). Of course, the current crisis demonstrates that a crucial segment of the FIRE sector, although extremely rewarding for individuals, has had a devastating impact on the U.S. economy.[6]

Other short-term trends provide additional evidence of economic weakening in America. The subprime housing scandal of 2007 led to the precipitous drop in housing prices and stock market values. Home sales that year declined more than in the previous four decades (Grynbaum 2007). Given the extended period of this decline, there are reasons to be wary. First, with declining savings in the United States, the top family investment has been home ownership and many homes are rapidly losing value. Second, every recovery from succeeding recessions since the 1960s has been more modest (Mishel, Bernstein, and Allegretto 2007). Thus, while home buying and housing prices may go up again at the end of the current downturn, those increases are unlikely to recover lost wealth while debt will remain in place. Both phenomena have long-term implications for economic well-being.

In addition to economic indicators, political factors must be considered in any assessment of diminishing U.S. hegemony. Over the last decade, the country has retrenched into greater isolation and unilateral decision making on issues ranging from military intervention to environmental policy. Alliances formed by the United States during the Cold War—aided by coercive interventions and economic rewards—have largely faded in the wake of one-sided military undertakings, the latest of which was the war in Iraq. America's few allies left the field as that disaster unfolded. Decisions to flout international bans on torture and illegal detentions exacerbated U.S. isolation. Intransigence toward multilateral efforts to address environmental concerns, including the unwillingness of the Bush administration to join the Kyoto Protocol on greenhouse gas emissions, provided allies with an additional reason to criticize the United States (McGuirk 2007).

There are still countervailing trends, however, that demand care in the assessment of hegemonic change. That the United States can pursue military action independently reflects its strength as the sole superpower in the world, as measured by expenditures and technological capacity. As Harvey (2003) and Piven (2004) point out, the United States increasingly uses its military capability to address aspects of its economic and political decline. Moreover, a focus on war has proven to be an effective tool to galvanize the patriotic fervor of the American public, at least in the short term, effectively shifting attention away from troubling domestic issues.

At one point, another manifestation of ongoing American power was the surging profits of U.S.-linked corporations. As of March 2006, these profits had increased by 21.3 percent over the preceding year, thus accounting for the largest share of national income in four decades (Nutting 2006). Prior to the current economic meltdown, corporate profits appeared to be solid, with evidence coming from a variety of governmental, academic, and journalistic sources.[7] Initially, of course, with the stock market plunge, corporate fortunes similarly declined—with the notable exception of the oil industry. Even during times of corporate profit increases, however, they proved an imperfect measure of economic strength and viability. Favorable governmental policies diminish corporate contributions to the national troth, while outsourcing further limits employment and wages in certain sectors of the U.S. economy. The gains of corporations nominally based in the United States add to the wealth and income of the U.S. public in ever decreasing and polarized amounts. Record corporate profits in 2010, concurrent with high unemployment, demonstrate the increasingly tenuous link between corporate and societal well-being.

Examinations of the potential decline of U.S. hegemony are incomplete without reference to the Bretton Woods IFIs. The Washington Consensus is fastened not only to the overwhelming power of the U.S. Treasury and U.S.-linked corporations but also to American control of the World Bank, the International Monetary Fund (IMF), and the World Trade Organization (WTO). The early moments of the crisis provided indications that the influence of these entities may be weakening.

IMF influence during the neoliberal era was based on its ability to impose conditions on nations that were taking out new loans or restructuring old ones. Beginning in the mid-1970s, the IMF's structural adjustment policies were among the most potent tools available to neoliberal reformers. Nation after nation was subjected to external policy designs that reduced the ability of governments to regulate their own economies. Privatization took away much governmental regulatory power and imposed limits on spending in areas like education, housing, and medical care. Signature policies of structural adjustment also included increased interest rates, currency devaluations, and wage freezes, which devastated much of the developing world (Abouharb and Cingranelli 2008; Jones 2004; Morley 1995; Schydlowsky 1995).

IMF loan programs contracted in the early 2000s, indicating the organization's waning influence. According to Naomi Klein, from 2004 to 2007, "the IMF's worldwide lending portfolio shrunk from $81 billion to $11.8 billion" (2007, 30). Part of that decline is explained by the movement of several nations from the Heavily Indebted Poor Countries (HIPC) program into the Multilateral Debt Relief Initiative. Participants able to survive six years under the harsh HIPC regime found their debts cancelled under the new initiative (Ambrose 2007).

In addition, since the 1997 East Asian financial crisis, the IMF has been subjected to increasing condemnation and decreasing participation (Helleiner and Momani 2007). Astoundingly, the wave of criticism included a 2005 speech by U.S. Under Secretary of the Treasury for International Affairs Tim Adams, who attacked the organization for its undemocratic governance and destructive policies. High officials in the United Kingdom and South Africa, among others, echoed his displeasure after years of denunciation from social movements such as Jubilee and the European Network on Debt and Development (Eurodad).

Perhaps the most significant pressure on the IMF came from middle-income debtors. Argentina, Brazil, and Bolivia paid back all of their IMF loans; Georgia, Uzbekistan, Indonesia, Thailand, South Korea, Serbia, Russia, Uruguay, Bulgaria, Algeria, Zimbabwe, and Armenia began to pay off their loans ahead of schedule (Eurodad 2006). Although loan repayments impose hardships on former debtors, those nations' governments concluded that being rid of IMF policy prescriptions was worth the pain. Another national strategy has been to increase monetary reserves in order to avoid relying on the IMF. By August 2006, early repayments had escalated and, for the first time, the IMF faced the possibility of monetary losses. In an ironic turnaround, top officials of the organization considered internal austerity measures, including layoffs (Ambrose 2007).

Later moments in the economic crisis have reinvigorated the IMF, however. The institution has begun lending to nations hard hit by the drying up of global capital markets, such as Iceland, Ukraine, Belarus, Hungary, and Pakistan. Additionally, various developing nations are turning to the IMF for short-term credit in order to cover high fuel costs.[8] The "resurgence" of the IMF has resulted in some policy changes. First, some recent loans appear to come with fewer of the conditions that were so damaging to recipient nations. The IMF has not given up on conditionality, as reports have suggested that "Pakistan's recent interest rate hikes were a result of IMF pressure. Ukraine is expected to balance its budget in 2009 and tighten monetary policy as part of an IMF agreement, as well as float its currency" (Center for Economic and Policy Research [CEPR] 2008; see also Eurodad 2008a, 2008b). The widely applied structural adjustment conditions do not now appear to be as consistent a part of the negotiations for loans as they were previously. Second, recent IMF actions came about during a period when rich and poor nations alike were calling for a conference that would redefine the roles and activities of the IFIs. This conference, held in November 2008, changed little as the world awaited the transition in U.S. administrations. Currently, a recapitalized IMF is regaining prominence, with some ambivalence in its policy-making ranks toward policies of conditionality. The resurgence of the IMF is even more apparent in its partnering with the European Union (EU) in the 2010 bailout of Greece and Ireland; notably, these bailouts show some increased flexibility in IMF adjustment policies.

The WTO's declining influence is clearer, as illustrated by the ongoing failure of the Doha negotiations round. The Doha Round, begun in 2001 and currently suspended, was intended to address the competitiveness and growth needs of developing nations. After several free trade successes, developing nations argued that the time had come to increase access to Northern markets by reducing import tariffs and diminishing domestic and export subsidies. The 2001 meetings were shut down amid the "Battle in Seattle," one of the most incendiary demonstrations against globalization of the last decade. In 2003, the Fifth WTO Ministerial Conference was held in Cancún, Mexico. During its proceedings, the Group of 22 forcefully opposed WTO policy dominated by the United States, Western Europe, and Japan regarding intellectual property rights, agricultural subsidies, and capital movement.[9] Despite earlier promises, the United States, Japan, and the EU refused to remove protection and support from key farming sectors. As negotiations went on, other problems emerged. New analyses assessing potential agreements found that advanced nations would benefit much more than those that the round had allegedly targeted, and that much of the limited benefits to the developing world would go to only eight nations: Brazil, Argentina, China, India, Thailand, Vietnam, Mexico, and Turkey (Wise and Gallagher 2005). Developing nations responded by attempting to maintain protection for agricultural production (Gallagher and Wise 2006). Unable to address the concerns of the Group of 22, the conference ended in frustration.

In 2006, the Doha Round reconvened in Geneva but collapsed when countries could not agree on key issues about the reciprocal opening of markets. Talks were suspended largely as a result of the refusal of the United States and other industrialized nations to eliminate farm subsidies (Wise and Gallagher 2005; Cho 2007; Furtan, Güzel, and Karantininis 2007). The current suspension entails the cancellation of various agreements regarding substantial cuts in tariffs and subsidies, the elimination of export funding programs, and tariff- and quota-free market access of exports by the least-developed countries. The most recent efforts to revive the Doha Round focused on "mini-ministerial talks" in Geneva, where the WTO has tried to work through the diverging demands of rich and poor nations. As the economic crisis pointed out the failure of global financial deregulation and as ongoing disadvantages of trade among rich and poor nations continued, positions hardened on market access and agricultural subsidies. Efforts to revive the talks in December 2008 failed (CEPR 2008).

The diminishing power of IFIs is important in its own right, as is the capacity of nations from the Global South to play a decisive role in the changing world hierarchy. If developing nations coalesced, their unity would present a significant potential for resistance to the rules currently framing the world economy. Assuming that institutions that have defined decades of global power are declining, what kinds of expressions appear to be poised to supplant them? One of the potential sources of opposition may lie in Latin America, where electoral shifts popularly labeled the "pink tide" are challenging neoliberal authority (Birns 2006; Rouaux 2006; Carlsen 2006; Campbell 2006). Neoliberalism began to dominate Latin American policy as early as the mid-1970s and accelerated during the "lost decade" of the 1980s (Portes 1997; Stiglitz 2002; George 2000). Across the hemisphere, nations acceded to IMF austerity regimes and were forced to endure structural adjustment programs that increased the cost of living while decreasing wages, eliminating consumer subsidies and industrial protection regulations, and gutting social services. Similar measures imposed by national governments in response to international pressure for debt renegotiations continued into the 1990s under the guise of debt recovery, or increasingly defined as the cost of playing on the world market (Portes and Hoffman 2003; Harvey 2007).

Across Latin America, protestors contested the savage effects of neoliberal policies (Walton 1989; Walton and Ragin 1990; Shefner 2004; Shefner, Pasdirtz, and Blad 2006). Such protests ushered in the election of leftist governments. New leaders in Argentina, Brazil, Bolivia, Chile, Ecuador, Nicaragua, Paraguay, Uruguay, and Venezuela have relied on rhetoric that characterizes national problems as the result of neoliberal reform. The number and scale of changes advocated by those leaders vary significantly. So too does the support for leftist governance, as demonstrated by the recent presidential election of a rightist candidate in Chile. Nevertheless, political shifts throughout Latin America suggest the potential for a unified regional response to neoliberalism. Earlier efforts to resist IMF-imposed policies came from nations like Jamaica and Peru, whose political resources were few. By contrast, countries currently opposing the IMF, like Brazil, Argentina, Venezuela, and Ecuador, have significant economic power, including large oil reserves. Finally, although slow, the emergence of the Bank of the South and the Bolivarian Alternative for the Americas (ALBA) provides both rhetorical means for opposition and an institutionalized asset reserve that imposes fewer conditions than weakening IFIs of the past (Strautman 2008). It is important to recognize the popular roots of the new leftist governments. The authors of this volume help us understand not only the emergence of new constituencies but also the different levels at which they resist and pursue expressions of power.

State Power and the Incomplete and Uneven Application of Neoliberalism

We attribute a great portion of the decline in the U.S. economy to this nation's version of neoliberal policy, carried through by both the state and its corporate allies. Deregulation of various financial instruments facilitated profit accumulation in industries that employed relatively few workers compared to the industrial base that was left to decay. Loosening capital restrictions further eased the way for U.S. investment dollars to seek higher returns elsewhere. National trade policy weakened U.S. labor's efforts to maintain wages and pensions, while the threat of exit further strengthened corporate power. Finally, decades of union-busting policy weakened labor to the point that its resistance to the flight of U.S.-based industry proved ineffective. In effect, the U.S. neoliberal state offered more opportunities for short-term corporate profits, even as capital broke the post–World War II accord with labor. However, the economic decline of the United States is but one manifestation of state changes under neoliberalism.

For the past thirty-five years, Keynesianism has been under assault by neoliberal economists and IFIs. Neoliberal theory sees state intervention in the "free market" as the predominant obstacle to economic growth. Neoliberals argued that government interventions slow economic growth in wealthy and poor nations alike and perpetuate poverty by eliminating incentives to competition.[10] The neoliberal critique extended beyond its earlier attack on Keynesian use of debt, attacking government provision of public services, state-owned enterprises (SOEs), and state regulation of all kinds. Ignoring state contributions to economic growth during the years of import substitution industrialization, and the growth of Asian developmental states, not to mention the social welfare provision that forestalls the savagery of capitalism (Polanyi [1944] 2001), neoliberals effectively captured the ideological and policy high ground and demonized the state (Harvey 2005). The power of the ideological argument, added to the pressure exerted by IFIs, resulted in the activities of what many called the "neoliberal state." Scholars increasingly employed the notion of the neoliberal state, whether their research centered on development, resistance, trade union activity, gender, surveillance, disaster management, or numerous other topics.

Despite the overall condemnation of state interventions in the economy—Keynesian, socialist, or otherwise—the application of neoliberal policy in an effort to shrink the state and its influence in economies has been uneven. Nations made vulnerable by debt were forced to substantially redesign their national economies. IFIs used the tools of structural adjustment to shrink welfare state provisions, privatize government-owned industries, and change trade policies in ways that benefited external and internal elites at the expense of working people in indebted nations. Much of Latin America has fallen prey to these influences from the 1980s to the current day (Portes and Hoffman 2003; Portes 1997). Elsewhere, the application of neoliberal orthodoxy was less severe, and states thus continued to push development and regulate some economic excesses. Some nations won more flexibility because they were frontline states during the Cold War, while other national economies

were either too large or too vibrant to be forced to replicate neoliberal orthodoxy. Many Asian states, especially before the 1997 financial crisis, forestalled
the wider attacks on the state suffered in Latin America.

In short, despite the efforts of neoliberal policy makers, there has been no
single neoliberal state. There has instead been a range of state interventions
and policies, which are uneven in their allegiance to neoliberalism. The variation in how neoliberalism has been applied by states may be explained by
different histories, economic dynamism, indebtedness and subsequent vulnerability, national investment and disinvestment choices, and citizen response. State responses within a wide rubric of neoliberalism help us
understand both how hegemony is shifting and how different nations and
organized citizens are prepared to manage those changes.

Within the context of shifting hegemonies, the authors of this volume
address a series of questions regarding state policies under neoliberalism:
How have different states responded to global economic pressures on state
policy? What state strategies have proven effective in coping with economic
shifts? How evenly have neoliberal policies been applied, and what have been
the results of those different policy formulations? In what ways has other
nations' power risen, and how has the United States kept from sinking even
further?

In chapter 1, Giovanni Arrighi and Lu Zhang find reason for optimism in
their analysis of China's ascent, especially in that nation's tailoring of neoliberal orthodoxy. After showing how U.S.-driven neoliberal reform generated
the most pressure on labor in recent decades, they ask why China has been
able to take such great advantage of global economic change. The answer is
that in China the state remained a crucial force in shaping the economy despite hewing to some elements of neoliberalism, like spurring competition
among SOEs and between domestic and foreign corporations. On the whole,
however, the Chinese state played a decisive role in planning, regulating, and
directing industrialization and infrastructural modernization, all actions that
deviate from neoliberal prescriptions. Gradual reforms were implemented at
the same time that state-driven diversification polices expanded high-tech and
labor-intensive manufacturing.

Other elements that differentiated China's path from the neoliberal dictum included the expansion of domestic markets (partly because of the size
of the economy), the will to improve rural living conditions, and the transfer
of large numbers of rural workers from agriculture to the manufacturing
sector through state-sponsored programs such as the Township and Village
Enterprise (TVE) program. Key to the success of these reforms were the
maintenance of a large peasantry only partially separated from the means to
produce its own subsistence, and a blend of industrious and socialist
revolutions.

According to Arrighi and Zhang, China's industrious revolution offered an alternative to Western development strategies by increasing the utility of labor-intensive production and strengthening workers' roots in the household and village rather than in the factory. In turn, the improved standards of living that resulted from China's socialist revolution heightened workers' loyalty and diligence. Industrialization in that country continues to successfully rely more on labor productivity than capital investment. Revolutionary ideology gave priority to Chinese peasants and workers as the engine of industrial growth and legitimized their claims for expanded rights. Recent unrest—by government count, up to 87,000 public demonstrations in 2006—has occurred in response to violations of the social contract implicit in the "iron rice bowl." An emergent labor movement is now contesting exploitive labor policies in China. In Arrighi and Zhang's view, despite its flaws, the Chinese example may provide an alternative path to Western-defined globalization and the neoliberal state. Whether this new example will lead to regional solidarity based on higher levels of general welfare, or to abuses of Southern nations, is yet to be determined.

If China's policy defies neoliberal state theory regarding internal production, its international economic relations suggest that the nation has taken greater cues from neoliberal trade policy. In chapter 2, Walden Bello examines how China's emerging hegemony may not be accompanied by progressive political alternatives to globalization. China has looked to the Association of Southeast Asian Nations (ASEAN) to broaden its consumer exports and to increase imports as its food and raw materials production prove insufficient. Such efforts do not require the re-creation of unequal exchanges like those marking North-South trade relations of the past. Yet recently negotiated trade agreements, Bello finds, follow historical trends by benefiting China at the expense of its trading partners. One example is the harm inflicted on Thai farmers who have not received agreed-upon tariff reductions in China. China may be poised to merge its advantage as an emerging hegemon with its developing nation status; it might thus combine its massive consumer market with its cheap labor to gain access to foreign markets and simultaneously limit imports. Such an approach bears similarity to that followed by the United States and other developed nations that control domestic market access while retaining the capacity to transfer cheap products abroad.

China's new hegemony wavers between the repetition of past trajectories of power and new regional possibilities. Bello points out that the country's ability to profit above the average levels of ASEAN trading partners has much to do with the limited regional integration of that economic bloc. Greater ASEAN amalgamation might provide more negotiating capacity vis-à-vis China, an important difference from past trade relations. Bello also finds that China is much less likely to use military might in the way that nations of the North have done to maintain dominance. Powerful nations of the future may try to imitate their predecessors, but the changed global environment may provide greater resources for weaker regions to resist intrusions.

In chapter 3, Gary Gereffi similarly examines China as an emerging dominant power whose state policy has challenged neoliberal orthodoxy. China's impressive ascent is all the more dramatic when compared to the developmental trajectory of Mexico, a nation whose economic vulnerability has led it to structure state policy along neoliberal lines for close to three decades. Between 1940 and 1975, Mexico pursued an import substitution industrialization model of development that entailed a salient role for the state in economic regulation and production. The government invested in and protected industry, attempting to attract foreign capital to pay for enterprise creation and infrastructure building. This focus on foreign investment in large part resulted in Mexico's high accumulation of debt and its subsequent vulnerability to the imposition of neoliberal measures (Fernández-Kelly and Massey 2007).

In Mexico, neoliberal policy led to periods of stagnation interspersed with stretches of moderate growth, always accompanied by increased inequality. China, by contrast, has enjoyed much greater success with its economic reforms, as also noted by Arrighi and Zhang (chapter 1). Attracting capital investment, opening domestic markets, and using low-wage labor were the hallmarks of China's developmental approach. The application of those strategies led to economic growth, although they contradicted the socialist ideology promoted by the Chinese state. Gereffi cites current concerns that opening China to foreign investments will choke domestic firms, as has been the case in other countries implementing similar policies. For Gereffi, the most important question is how to understand the efficacy levels of different economic interventions. Will one developmental strategy or another have more or less success at moving a country from low-value to high-value production?

International trade data demonstrate that Mexico moved more quickly and intensively to high-value exports, with China following close behind and then surpassing Mexico by 2000. Both nations experienced significant success in the diversification of their economies, but China won a greater market share for exports to the United States. Lower labor costs, huge economies of scale, and a coherent industrial plan—the product of heightened state intervention—help explain China's advantage. The combined effect of those factors has been yet another benefit: "supply chain cities" that build on low labor and other input costs, and favorable governmental policies, to increase production. Gereffi shows that, amid China's success, questions remain, especially with respect to a resulting context of increasing inequality and environmental degradation. In Mexico and China, the costs of growth strategies may have to be addressed by increasing state welfare expenditures. In both cases, national economic policy demonstrates the failure of the neoliberal model, and the implications for the near future suggest a further retreat from "thinning" the state.

China's trade relations are instructive not only in the implications they hold for its neighbors but also in how global power is pursued and maintained through dependent trade and production. In chapter 4, James Cypher and Raúl Delgado Wise demonstrate how the United States has similarly benefited from such relations with Mexico, showing that the United States' ongoing strength is a product of that relationship. Far from laying the basis for free trade, the negotiations preceding and instituting the North American Free Trade Agreement (NAFTA) established new arrangements to maintain America's economic viability in ways that suggest that China's ASEAN trading partners have reason to be wary. NAFTA and the subsequent restructuring of the Mexican economy owe much to the increasing autonomy of Mexican capitalists who made strategic choices to ally themselves with U.S.-based multinationals, thereby greatly benefiting comparatively few sectors in each nation.

The pre-NAFTA era was marked by increasing coordination between Mexican government officials and investors, in contrast to the previous phase of import substitution industrialization, during which the Mexican state actively intervened in economic matters (Fernández-Kelly and Massey 2007). One of the main goals of increasingly autonomous Mexican capital was the capture of new foreign direct investment (FDI). The heightened involvement of Mexican elites helped keep the plan focused on long-term investment at the expense of national control over foreign capital. Contrary to other analyses on the subject (Cuevas, Messmacher, and Werner 2005; Monge-Naranjo 2002), Cypher and Delgado Wise present evidence to support the claim that NAFTA did not lead to increased foreign investment in Mexico. Instead, its most significant results were the restructuring of the Mexican economy and its increasing dependency on the United States.

Cypher and Delgado Wise argue that in the post-NAFTA period, Mexico's development strategy has increasingly entailed the sale of cheap labor for the manufacture of exportable goods. The consequence of this maquiladora model is that few jobs in the formal sector have been created, wages for assembly workers continue to sink, and more and more people emigrate to the United States in search of opportunity. Mexico's comparative advantage as a provider of low-cost labor does little to build its economy. Instead, U.S. interests have won control of Mexican markets, allowed firms to avoid legal obligations toward the protection of labor and the environment, and increased profits along the way. The unequal relationship between the United States and Mexico has been reinforced and may be understood as an outcome of a wide application of neoliberal policy.

New Expressions of Global Power

We argue that current shifts in the distribution of global power indicate that the neoliberal project may be wearing out, thus opening space for alternative models. Harvey (2007), Centeno (1998), Babb (2001), and George (2000), among others, document how neoliberalism evolved from a theoretical critique of Keynesianism to an economic policy with practical ramifications. Think tanks, universities, IFIs, and national governments worked to turn neoliberalism from an academic exercise into a development strategy that was subsequently discredited by the widespread damage it caused. Alternative development models, however, have not been coherently articulated yet, partly because many scholars have been forced into defensive postures as they attack neoliberalism. National and local governments, as well as actors included in what some authors call "civil society"—small businesses, class-based groups, professional associations, indigenous peoples, social movements, and nongovernmental organizations—have all fought neoliberal policies. In other words, neoliberalism has been notable in its capacity to create solidarity compacts against harm.[11]

Oppositional coalitions have brought together agents previously segregated by state actions such as corporatism and clientelism, on the one hand, and vicious repression, on the other. But strong resistance to the neoliberal scheme may become an obstacle for the creation of alternative approaches. Northern unions and anarchists who spoke out in 2001 in Seattle share outrage with indigenous groups in the Andes, but they are unlikely to advance common solutions. They may share a commitment to social justice but have a different definition of it. Certain strands of new design have come into view, from new ways of life and politics proposed by World Social Forums, to critiques inherent in the Fair Trade movement, to the rationale behind the creation of institutions such as ALBA and the Bank of the South (Barnett 2007; Strautman 2008). Forging alternatives to neoliberalism is a work in progress.

The authors in the second part of this book recognize that new configurations of power require an intellectual project analogous to the one that activated neoliberalism and brought it to its pinnacle. If new nations or regions are to exercise power with greater attention to social justice, they must have clear options at their disposal. Resistance to neoliberalism has led emerging actors to support new definitions of property, class, and environment, but declining hegemons are also reexamining priorities in response to the changing global environment.

What political opportunities are generated by globalization? How can citizens work in and through their national states to increase the scope of their influence? In chapter 5, William I. Robinson addresses these questions by focusing on the transnational character of global processes. He directs us to look beyond the nation-state to fully understand class and social relations. The emergence of globalization, Robinson argues, generates a transnational capitalist class (TCC) that organizes production and accumulation on a global scale. Analysts who focus exclusively on the nation-state are likely to ignore the political relevance of transnational actors. National states are not disappearing, but they continue to be transformed and absorbed by transnational entities. It is through the transnational state (TNS) that the ideology and practice of market liberalization work to integrate national economies, freeing capital to move rapidly. The current moment of globalization is increasingly being defined by a crisis of legitimacy and authority, which has elicited global collective action.

Robinson does not discuss regional possibilities of resistance. But the emergence of new transnational solidarities, and new transnational institutions, logically follows from his argument. On the one hand, political decentralization gives some power to smaller actors. At the same time, the capacity of Latin American states, among others, to contest transnational power has weakened the IMF and the World Bank. This allows us to consider the emergence of a multipolar globalization (Ellner 2005). The movement from resistance to creation of alternatives requires mobilization at multiple levels. Robinson's research reminds us that a new understanding of capitalist expansion is as crucial to those opposing the prevailing system as to those benefiting from it.

In chapter 6, Frances Fox Piven refuses to cede all power to those whom Robinson labels the TCC. Global production may limit the actions of working people, and electoral choices may be the prerogative of those with greater access to resources, but globalization requires the cooperation and participation of ordinary people. Class interdependence remains an important feature of worldwide capitalism: just as workers have withdrawn cooperation and disrupted national stages in the past, so too can popular power operate on a global terrain. According to Piven, increased world integration implies the potential for coordinated action among those targeting oppressive states and enterprises. National bonds among firms may break, but new ties among workers in production chains can be forged. Whether it is in labor struggles, contested claims over farmland, or efforts to protect natural resources, Piven finds examples of popular power across the globe.

Piven also recognizes that states and corporations still have the means to stifle resistance. Furthermore, global interdependence does not necessarily breed capable disruptors. On the other hand, opposition to neoliberal reforms has engendered new strategies for collective action. Fragmented production can complicate the expression of popular power, but Piven looks to nascent cross-border efforts, new union structures, and the energy of street mobs for clues about the character of new mobilizing efforts. Even the social bonds that deter individuals from participating in protest may offer resources for disruption when their allegiance is contested or justice is violated.

In chapter 7, Alejandro Portes, Cristina Escobar, and Alexandria Walton Radford turn our attention to immigrant transnational organizations as an example of new forms of globalization put in place from the bottom up. They examine ninety Colombian, Dominican, and Mexican organizations pursuing philanthropic projects across borders, noting that organizational efforts on the part of transnational immigrants differ in terms of the immigrants' mode of exit from sending countries and type of reception in areas of destination. All the evidence indicates that economic, political, and sociocultural activities linking immigrants with their communities of origin emerge as an initiative of the immigrants themselves, with governments joining in after the importance and economic potential of those activities become evident. Across the hemisphere, immigrants in the developed world have come to rely on bonds of solidarity and a shared sense of obligation to those left behind, not only for the survival of families but also for the implementation of civic initiatives in sending nations and localities. The bulk of remittances sent by immigrants to their home countries easily surpasses foreign aid to those nations and even matches their hard currency earnings from exports. In 2004, the worth of remittances was assessed at $2–3 billion for both Guatemala and El Salvador, $5 billion for Colombia, and a staggering $16 billion for Mexico. Remittances reached $23 billion for the whole continent (Cortina and de la Garza 2004).

The interconnections forged by transnational immigrant organizations reach beyond the economic realm, producing unexpected but increasingly visible effects in the politics of hometowns and home countries. In the case of Mexico, this has taken the form of matching programs for immigrant contributions and the creation of a government agency, the Institute of Mexicans Abroad (IME), which is housed in the Federal Secretariat of Foreign Relations. Although the capacity of immigrants to influence large political apparatuses is not new, it signals innovative forms of political mobilization that stand in clear contrast to previous policies imposed from the top down. Yielding to pressure from their expatriate populations, national states now seek to demonstrate their interest in immigrant welfare with concrete actions, while trying to attract the loyalty and contributions of immigrants.

Focusing on the fissures of market fundamentalism, Fred Block suggests in chapter 8 that the new global environment provides a variety of new possibilities for the United States, not the least of which is the formation of a new post-imperial foreign policy. The failures of economic orthodoxy and the fracture of traditional bases of authority in the United States offer opportunities to design new relationships between state and market. In addition, growing concerns among U.S. citizens about global climate change, the high cost of health care, and declining prosperity provide an opening to consider new solutions to political problems. Block proposes innovative arrangements rooted in a moral economy that upholds social justice while at the same time promoting efficient social and economic practices. He suggests five specific criteria to guide the creation of the new economy: (a) ethical corporations with limits to executive compensation, and substantial employee representation; (b) social inclusion through redistributive policies; (c) democratic development to reinvest and engage in public dialogue about basic research; (d) design and production adhering to environmentally friendly standards; and (e) the prioritization of human services.

A moral economy would have momentous implications for foreign policy. According to Block, it would provide opportunities for the United States to help repair failed states that pose hazards ranging from terrorism to health emergencies. It would also send a very different message than the one associated with the Washington Consensus—making human rights the center of foreign policy is diametrically opposed to the neoliberal position of economic efficiency as the central social good.

New standards of operation in the global economy are consistent with many of the objections voiced by the representatives of developing nations at the failed Doha negotiations. A global regulatory regime must articulate labor, environmental, and human rights standards and design mechanisms for enforcement. Furthermore, a crucial element of any new regulatory regime must be the recognition that consumption does not constitute a route out of environmental degradation. Block argues that global sustainability requires measures that focus not just on production but on conservation as well.

Above all, a new U.S. foreign policy must have as a foundation the respect of human rights, an objective that will require the replacement or drastic reform of IFIs. Entities with the material resources and political clout to enforce human rights and standards will be needed, whether goals are set by the Universal Declaration of Human Rights, the Millennium Development Goals, or the Convention on the Prevention and Punishment of the Crime of Genocide. From Block's point of view, pursuing ethical globalization will require that the United States abandon claims to hegemony, pursuing instead the kind of foreign policy that may restore its leadership role in the world scene. Such state policy would provide deep challenges to the global inequalities that neoliberalism has exacerbated and maintained.

Finally, in chapter 9, Catherine Walsh offers a pointed analysis of colonialism and knowledge, concluding that one of the most important sectors articulating alternatives to corporate-driven globalization comprises those who have endured conquest, subjugation, imperialism, and, finally, globalization. Indigenous peoples and nations have responded to free trade negotiations with a critique that links recent abuses to older forms of oppression, while simultaneously proposing alternatives. It is not a coincidence that resistance has emerged in the Andean region, a critical U.S. outpost in protecting national security and exploiting scarce natural resources. Resistance to such intrusions has been embraced by labor unions, indigenous social movements, and national governments.

Walsh finds the United States advancing policies to reshape Latin America along political lines congruent with the analysis of Cypher and Delgado Wise (chapter 4). It is not just to the economic and political project of neoliberalism that indigenous peoples are responding, but also to cultural definitions of progress, development, and knowledge. In the region studied by Walsh, the most recent attempt to pursue colonial advantage has been the North American–Andean Free Trade Agreement. Despite the agreement's regional focus, U.S. negotiators have sought to forge accords nation by nation, thus diminishing the possibility of a multilateral coalition that would oppose American interests. Such efforts seek to perpetuate the "coloniality of power" that has persisted in the region for over five hundred years.

According to Walsh, indigenous resistance to free trade agreements articulates economic options. For example, ancestral forms of knowledge advocate a less extractive relationship to nature; denying the centrality of profit leads to more equitable norms of reciprocity and complementarity; and refusing the institution of Western political structures advances autonomy and self-determination at the local level. Indigenous movements succeeded in halting Ecuadorian entrance into the North American–Andean Free Trade Agreement, not only as a result of their objection to economic subordination but also because such agreements show insufficient respect for nature and humanity. Another example pointing to innovative socioeconomic arrangements is ALBA, which moves beyond critiques of economic and political imperialism to build cooperation, regional integration, and the possibility of multipolar power. The Bank of the South follows a similar path, promoting cooperation, development, and integration instead of the kind of competition characteristic in older financial institutions.

The scholars included in this book agree that the present moment is fraught with opportunities for a movement away from corporate-driven globalization. U.S. hegemony seems to be waning despite fervid military ventures and the pursuit of free trade. China's ascent has ambiguous potential: a new hegemon may recreate policies similar to its predecessor, or it may forge a new stance marked by greater levels of collaboration, egalitarianism, and reciprocity among nations. Under the proper circumstances, the rise of perspectives opposing neoliberalism might eventuate in multipolar power centers.

None of these changes is understandable or possible without examining collective mobilization at multiple levels. Popular power, state resources, and regional coalitions have all been at work in the recent transition. All of these strands of analysis force us to rethink how states and citizens have applied neoliberal theory, and how differing results of this uneven application have implications for the next stage of theories and action on states, development, and citizen action. This book brings together these multiple strands.

NOTES

1. The conference, NAFTA and Beyond: Alternative Disciplinary Perspectives in the Study of Global Trade and Development, took place on December 3–5, 2005, under the sponsorship of the Princeton Center for Migration and Development. The only chapter in this book that did not come out of that gathering is the contribution by Walden Bello.

2. Barack Obama's historic presidential victory has the potential to reintegrate the United States into the global community and rehabilitate its image after the disastrous presidency of George W. Bush. At the time of this writing, it is too early to gauge how the new presidency will address the current global crisis and how other nations will respond.

3. The reduction in the trade deficit demonstrates global weakness rather than U.S. strength. Trade deficit estimates for 2000 and 2007 were taken from the U.S. Census Bureau and Bureau of Economic Analysis (2010). Trade data for 2009 was obtained from Healy (2009). See chapter 5 for a different reading of trade data.

4. In contrast to this clear pattern of declining wages and polarizing family income, hours of work have increased significantly.

5. The U.S. Department of Labor defines low wages as $21,260 to $30,560 and very low wages as up to $21,220.

6. For more on the financial sector, see the concluding chapter of this volume.

7. Some of these sources include OMB Watch (2004) and *The Economist* (2005). Recent estimates by the U.S. Department of Commerce's Bureau of Economic Analysis (2007) show some decline in recent measures of corporate profits.

8. For more on the reemergence of the IMF, including the G-20's commitment to its funding, see the concluding chapter of this volume.

9. The Group of 22 was composed of Argentina, Bolivia, Brazil, Chile, China, Colombia, Costa Rica, Cuba, Ecuador, Egypt, Guatemala, India, Indonesia, Mexico, Nigeria, Pakistan, Paraguay, Peru, the Philippines, South Africa, Thailand, and Venezuela. Importantly, this group coalesced some of the economic giants of the developing world, representing half of the world's population and two-thirds of its farmers.

10. Critiques of the neoliberal position are many. For some of the most coherent, see Harvey (2006); Portes and Hoffman (2003); Panitch et al. (2004); and chapter 1 of this volume.

11. For more on the shared damages of neoliberalism, and a critique of civil society, see Shefner (2008).

REFERENCES

Abouharb, M. Rodwan, and David Cingranelli. 2008. *Human Rights and Structural Adjustment.* Cambridge: Cambridge University Press.

Ambrose, Soren. 2007. "Coming Up Empty: Confidence Crisis at the IMF." *CounterPunch,* April 17.

Babb, Sarah. 2001. *Managing Mexico: Economists from Nationalism to Neoliberalism.* Princeton: Princeton University Press.

Barnett, Anthony. 2007. "The Three Faces of the World Social Forum." Open Democracy. January 30. http://www.opendemocracy.net/globalization-protest/wsf_faces_4297.jsp.

Birns, Larry. 2006. "Latin America—The Path Away from U.S. Domination." Council on Hemispheric Affairs. June 2. http://www.coha.org/latin-america-the-path-away-from-us-domination/.

Bluestone, Barry, and Bennett Harrison. 1982. *The Deindustrialization of America: Plant Closings, Community Abandonment, and the Dismantling of Basic Industry.* New York: Basic Books.

Bureau of Economic Analysis, U.S. Department of Commerce. 2007. "Gross Domestic Product: Third Quarter 2007 (Final); Corporate Profits: Third Quarter 2007 (Revised)." December 20. http://www.bea.gov/newsreleases/national/gdp/2007/gdp 307f.htm.

Campbell, Hartford. 2006. "Argentina's Néstor Kirchner: Peronism Without the Tears." *Panama News,* February 5–18. http://www.thepanamanews.com/pn/v_12/issue_03/opinion_06.html.

Carlsen, Laura. 2006. "Leaders, Parties, and Movements—Latin America's Pink Tide?" *CounterPunch,* December 19.

Cavanagh, John, and Jerry Mander. 2004. *Alternatives to Economic Globalization: A Better World Is Possible.* San Francisco: Berret-Koehler.

Centeno, Miguel A. 1998. "Electoral-Bureaucratic Authoritarianism: The Mexican Case." In *Politics, Society, and Democracy: Latin America,* edited by Scott Mainwaring and Arturo Valenzuela, 27–48. Boulder, Colo.: Westview Press.

Center for Economic and Policy Research (CEPR). 2008. "Attempt to Convene Another Last-Minute WTO 'Mini-Ministerial' Collapses in the Midst of Global Recession." December 12. http://www.cepr.net/index.php/press-releases/press-releases/attempt-to-convene-last-minute-wto-qmini-ministerialq-collapses-in-the-midst-of-global-recession.

Central Intelligence Agency. 2007. "United States." *CIA World Factbook.* http://64.233.169.104/search?q=cache:1XDMEvdhY7sJ:https://www.cia.gov/library/publications/the-world.

Cho, Sungjoon. 2007. "Beyond Doha's Promises: Administrative Barriers as an Obstruction to Development." *Berkeley Journal of International Law* 25 (3): 395–424.

Cortina, Jeronimo, and Rodolfo de la Garza. 2004. *Immigrant Remitting Behavior and Its Developmental Consequences for Mexico and El Salvador.* Los Angeles: Tomás Rivera Policy Institute.

Cuevas, Alfredo, Miguel Messmacher, and Alejandro Werner. 2005. "Foreign Direct Investment in Mexico Since the Approval of NAFTA." *World Bank Economic Review* 19 (3): 473–88.

Dicken, Peter. 2007. *Global Shift: Mapping the Changing Contours of the World Economy.* New York: Guilford Press.

Dohm, Arlene, and Lynn Shniper. 2007. "Occupational Employment Projections to 2016." *Monthly Labor Review,* November.

Economist. 2005. "Corporate Profits: Breaking Records." February 10. http://www.economist.com/node/3645126?story_id=3645126.

Ellner, Steve. 2005. "Venezuela: Defying Globalization's Logic." *NACLA Report on the Americas* 39 (2): 20–24.

European Network on Debt and Development (Eurodad). 2006. "IMF Conditionality in Nicaragua: Interview with Adolfo Acevedo." July 17. http://www.eurodad.org/aid/report.aspx?id=132&item=1294&&LangType=1033.

———. 2008a. "IMF and World Bank Put Best Feet Forward Ahead of Bretton Woods II Summit." *Development Finance Watch,* no. 16 (November 13). http://www.eurodad.org/whatsnew/articles.aspx?id=3092.

———. 2008b. "IMF Back in Business as Bretton Woods II Conference Announced." *Development Finance Watch,* no. 15 (October 23). http://www.eurodad.org/whatsnew/articles.aspx?id=3010.

Fernández-Kelly, Patricia, and Douglas S. Massey. 2007. "Borders for Whom? The Role of NAFTA in Mexico-U.S. Migration." *ANNALS of the American Academy of Political and Social Science* 610 (1): 98–118.

Furtan, W. Hartley, A. Guzel, and Kostas Karantininis. 2007. "The Doha Talks and the Bargaining Surplus in Agriculture." *Estey Centre Journal of International Law and Trade Policy* 8 (2): 138–54.

Gallagher, Kevin P., and Timothy A. Wise. 2006. *Doha and the Developing Countries: Will the Doha Deal Do More Harm than Good?* RIS Policy Brief 22 (April). New Delhi: Research and Information System for Developing Countries.

George, Susan. 2000. "A Short History of Neoliberalism—Twenty Years of Elite Economics and Emerging Opportunities for Structural Change." Revised version of a paper presented at the Conference on Economic Sovereignty in a Globalising World, Bangkok, March 24–26, 1999 (mimeo).

Grynbaum, Michael M. 2007. "Home Sales and Prices Fall Sharply." *New York Times,* September 28.

Harvey, David. 2003. *The New Imperialism.* Oxford: Oxford University Press.

———. 2006. *Spaces of Global Capitalism: Towards a Theory of Uneven Geographical Development.* London: Verso.

———. 2005. *A Brief History of Neoliberalism.* Oxford: Oxford University Press.

Healy, Jack. 2009. "Sharp Drop in Oil Price Helps Shrink Trade Deficit." *New York Times,* January 13. http://www.nytimes.com/2009/01/14/business/economy/14econ.html.

Helleiner, Eric, and Bessma Momani. 2007. "Slipping into Obscurity? Crisis and Reform at the IMF." CIGI Working Paper No. 16 (February), University of Waterloo. http://ssrn.com/abstract=964915.

Jones, Peris S. 2004. "When Development Devastates: Donor Discourses, Access to HIV/AIDS Treatment in Africa, and Rethinking the Landscape of Development." *Third World Quarterly* 25 (2): 385–404.

Keynes, John Maynard. 1936. *The General Theory of Employment, Interest, and Money.* London: Macmillan.

Klein, Naomi. 2007. *The Shock Doctrine: The Rise of Disaster Capitalism.* New York: Metropolitan Books.

Lawrence, Robert Z. 2008. *Blue-Collar Blues: Is Trade to Blame for Rising U.S. Income Inequality?* Washington, D.C.: Peter G. Peterson Institute for International Economics.

McGuirk, Rod. 2007. "Australia Signs Kyoto Protocol; U.S. Now Only Holdout." *National Geographic News,* December 3. http://news.nationalgeographic.com/news/2007/12/071203-AP-aus-kyoto.html (page discontinued).

McLaren, Peter, and Nathalia E. Jaramillo. 2005. "Alternative Globalizations: Toward a Critical Globalization Studies." In *Critical Globalization Studies,* edited by Richard P. Appelbaum and William I. Robinson, 131–40. New York: Routledge.

Mishel, Lawrence, Jared Bernstein, and Sylvia Allegretto. 2007. *The State of Working America, 2006/2007.* New York: International Labor Review.

Monge-Naranjo, Alexander. 2002. "The Impact of NAFTA on Foreign Direct Investment Flows in Mexico and the Excluded Countries." Working paper, Department of Economics, Northwestern University, Evanston, Ill.

Morley, Samuel A. 1995. *Poverty and Inequality in Latin America: The Impact of Adjustment and Recovery in the 1980s.* Baltimore: Johns Hopkins University Press.

Nutting, Rex. 2006. "Profits Surge to 40-Year High—When Will Corporations Spend Some of Their Hoard?" *Market Watch,* March 30. http://www.marketwatch.com/story/corporate-profits-surge-to-40-year-high.

OMB Watch. 2004. "Economy and Jobs Watch: Corporate Profits at Record Highs, While Labor Compensation at 38-Year Lows." May 14. http://www.ombwatch.org/node/1943.

Organisation for Economic Co-operation and Development (OECD). 2008. *Growing Unequal? Income Distribution and Poverty in OECD Countries.* Paris: OECD.

Panitch, Leo, Colin Leys, Alan Zuege, and Martijn Konings, eds. 2004. *The Globalization Decade: A Critical Reader.* London: Merlin Press.

Piven, Frances Fox. 2004. *The War at Home: The Domestic Costs of Bush's Militarism*. New York: New Press.

Polanyi, Karl. [1944] 2001. *The Great Transformation*. Boston: Beacon Press.

Portes, Alejandro. 1997. "Neoliberalism and the Sociology of Development: Emerging Trends and Unanticipated Facts." *Population and Development Review* 23 (2): 229–59.

Portes, Alejandro, and Kelly Hoffman. 2003. "Latin American Class Structures: Their Composition and Change During the Neoliberal Era." *Latin American Research Review* 38 (1): 41–82.

Rouaux, Fernando. 2006. "Kirchner's Argentina—Surfing Latin America's Pink Tide." *Latin America News Review* (blog), November 27. http://lanr.blogspot.com/2006/11/kirchners-argentina.html.

Sassen, Saskia. 2001. *The Global City: New York, London, Tokyo*. Princeton: Princeton University Press.

Schydlowsky, Daniel M., ed. 1995. *Structural Adjustment: Retrospect and Prospect*. Westport, Conn.: Praeger.

Shefner, Jon. 2004. "Global Economic Change, Protest, and Its Implications for U.S. Policymakers." In *Agenda for Social Justice*, edited by Kathleen Ferraro, JoAnn Miller, Robert Perrucci, and Paula Rodriguez Rust, 16–22. Knoxville, Tenn.: Society for the Study of Social Problems.

———. 2008. *The Illusion of Civil Society: Democratization and Community Mobilization in Low-Income Mexico*. University Park: Pennsylvania State University Press.

Shefner, Jon, George Pasditz, and Cory Blad. 2006. "Austerity Protests and Social Immiseration: Evidence from Mexico and Argentina." In *Latin American Social Movements: Globalization, Democratization, and Transnational Networks*, edited by Hank Johnston and Paul Almeida, 19–42. Lanham, Md.: Rowman and Littlefield.

Sklair, Leslie. 2002. *Globalization: Capitalism and Its Alternatives*. Oxford: Oxford University Press.

Stiglitz, Joseph E. 2002. *Globalization and Its Discontents*. New York: W. W. Norton.

Strautman, Gabriel. 2008. "South Bank: 90 Days of Silence." International Development Economics Associates. February 14. http://www.networkideas.org/alt/apr2008/alto2_silence.htm.

U.S. Census Bureau and Bureau of Economic Analysis. 2010. *U.S. International Trade in Goods and Services*. November 10. http://www.census.gov/foreign-trade/Press-Release/current_press_release/press.html.

U.S. Department of the Treasury. 2007. "Monthly Statement of the Public Debt (MSPD)." http://www.treasurydirect.gov/govt/reports/pd/mspd/mspd.htm.

———. 2009. "The Debt to the Penny and Who Holds It." U.S. Treasury Direct. http://www.treasurydirect.gov/NP/BPDLogin?application=np.

Walton, John. 1989. "Debt, Protest, and the State in Latin America." In *Power and Popular Protest: Latin American Social Movements*, edited by Susan Eckstein, 299–328. Berkeley: University of California Press.

Walton, John, and Charles Ragin. 1990. "Global and National Sources of Political Protest: Third World Responses to the Debt Crisis." *American Sociological Review* 55 (6): 876–90.

Wise, Timothy A. 2006. "The WTO's Development Crumbs." Foreign Policy in Focus. January 20. http://www.fpif.org/articles/the_wtos_development_crumbs.

Wise, Timothy A., and Kevin P. Gallagher. 2005. *The Doha Round's Development Impacts: Shrinking Gains and Real Costs*. RIS Policy Brief 19 (November). New Delhi: Research and Information System for Developing Countries.

Part I

DECLINING AND EMERGING HEGEMONS?

1

BEYOND THE WASHINGTON CONSENSUS: A NEW BANDUNG?

Giovanni Arrighi and Lu Zhang

This chapter analyzes what we might call the strange death of the Washington Consensus, with special reference to the economic empowerment of China and a fundamental change in relations between the global North and South.[1] What is strange about this death is that it occurred at a time when the neoliberal doctrines propagated by the Consensus held seemingly undisputed sway. For that very reason, the death went largely unnoticed, and to the extent that it did not, its causes and consequences remain shrouded in great confusion.

Part of the confusion arises from the continuing influence of various aspects of the defunct Consensus on world politics. As Walden Bello (2007) has noted, "Neoliberalism [remains] the default mode for many economists and technocrats that . . . lost confidence in it, simply out of inertia." Moreover, new doctrines are emerging, mostly in the global North, that attempt to revive aspects of the old Consensus in more palatable and realistic forms. Our analysis rules out neither the residual influence by default of neoliberalism nor the possibility of its rebirth in new forms. It simply points out that the neoliberal counterrevolution of the early 1980s, of which the Washington Consensus was an integral component, has backfired, creating the conditions for a reversal of power relations between the global North and South that may well be reshaping world politics as well as the theory and practice of national development.

We begin by sketching the origins and objectives of the neoliberal turn, or counterrevolution, in U.S. policies and ideology of 1979–82. After highlighting the immediate impact of the neoliberal turn on North-South relations, we focus on the Chinese economic ascent as its most important unintended consequence, with deep roots in Chinese traditions, including the revolutionary tradition of the Mao era. We conclude by pointing to the impact of the Chinese ascent on North-South relations, making special reference to the possible emergence of a new Southern alliance with a more solid foundation than the one established at Bandung in the 1950s; we also discuss the challenges and opportunities that the current global economic crisis is creating for China and other developing countries.

The Washington Consensus and the Neoliberal Counterrevolution

The neoliberal turn began in the last year of the Carter administration, when a serious crisis of confidence in the U.S. dollar prompted Paul Volcker, then chairman of the U.S. Federal Reserve, to switch from the highly permissive monetary policies of the 1970s to highly restrictive policies. The turn nonetheless materialized fully only when the Reagan administration, drawing ideological inspiration from Margaret Thatcher's slogan "There is no alternative" (TINA), declared all variants of social Keynesianism obsolete and proceeded to liquidate them through a revival of early twentieth-century beliefs in the magic of allegedly self-regulating markets.[2] Specifically, the liquidation occurred through a drastic contraction in the money supply, an equally drastic increase in interest rates, major reductions in corporate taxation, the elimination of controls on capital, and a sudden switch of U.S. policies toward the Third World from promotion of the development project launched in the late 1940s and early 1950s to promotion of the neoliberal agenda that later came to be known as the Washington Consensus. Directly or through the International Monetary Fund (IMF) and the World Bank, the U.S. government withdrew its support from the statist and inward-looking strategies (such as import substitution industrialization) that most theories of national development had advocated in the 1950s and 1960s, and began to promote capital-friendly shock therapies aimed at transferring assets from public to private hands at bargain prices and at liberalizing foreign trade and capital movements (McMichael 2000; Arrighi 2002).[3]

The change has been widely characterized as a counterrevolution in economic thought and political ideology (see, for example, Toye 1993; Gilpin 2000, 83–84, 227–30; Glyn 2006, 24–26). The neoliberal turn was counterrevolutionary vis-à-vis both labor and the Third World. As Thatcher's advisor Alan Budd publicly admitted in retrospect, "What was engineered . . . in Marxist terms . . . was a crisis of capitalism which re-created a reserve army of labour, and has allowed the capitalists to make high profits ever since" (Harvey 2000, 7). Insofar as the U.S. government was concerned, however, this disempowerment of labor was less an end in itself than a means to the objective of reversing the relative decline in U.S. wealth and power that had gained momentum with the defeat of the United States in Vietnam and culminated at the end of the 1970s in the Iranian Revolution, the Soviet invasion of Afghanistan, and the previously mentioned run on the U.S. dollar.

Although the Washington Consensus was first and foremost a strategy aimed at reestablishing U.S. power, it was presented as a new developmental strategy. Taking this claim at face value, discussions of the neoliberal turn's impact have generally focused on trends since 1980 in world income inequality, as measured by synthetic indicators such as the Gini or the Theil. While a fairly general agreement has emerged that within-country inequality has increased, trends in between-country inequality remain the object of some controversy. Even in this respect, however, the consensus is that, whatever the trends, "improvement in world income inequality and poverty [since 1980] was not broadly based, but rather highly dependent, like the overall growth in world income, on the impressive growth performance of China and the substantial growth of India. When China is excluded from the calculations, inequality increases by most measures. When India is excluded along with China, not only is there a more marked deterioration in the distribution of world income, but poverty incidence remains about constant." In short, sums up Albert Berry, China and India "can be considered to have rescued the world from a dismal overall performance over the [last] two decades" (2005, 17–18). Berry's data also show that the modest decline in the Gini that he detects from 1980 to 2000 did not negatively affect the richest 10 percent of the world population (which has in fact further improved its relative position) but results exclusively from a redistribution of income from middle-income to upper- and lower-income countries.[4]

Table 1.1 provides more details concerning this redistribution. As the table shows, insofar as the overall North-South income divide is concerned, the neoliberal counterrevolution made little difference, resulting at first in a minor decrease and then in a minor increase in the income per capita of the Third World relative to that of the First World. Nonetheless, it did make a big difference for individual regions in both the North and the South. For our present purposes, it is sufficient to focus on three main tendencies. First, in the 1990s, the United States did succeed in reversing its relative decline of the 1960s and 1970s, but the reversal was entirely compensated by a deterioration of the relative position of western and southern Europe and Japan. Second, in the 1980s, sub-Saharan Africa and Latin America both experienced a major relative decline from which they never recovered; this was followed by an equally significant relative decline of the former Soviet Union in the 1990s. Third, the greatest gains were those of East Asia and Japan up to 1990, and of India and China in the 1980s and 1990s, although China's advance was far more substantial than that of India.[5]

Table 1.1   GNP per capita as a percentage of the First World's GNP per capita

Region	1960	1970	1980	1985	1990	1995	2000	2005
Sub-Saharan Africa (w/ South Africa)	5.6	4.7	3.9	3.1	2.7	2.5	2.0	2.3
Latin America	19.7	16.4	17.6	14.4	12.3	12.9	13.4	11.2
West Asia and North Africa	8.7	7.8	8.7	7.9	7.4	7.2	7.7	8.4
South Asia (w/o India)	1.9	1.7	1.3	1.4	1.4	1.5	1.6	1.6
East Asia (w/o China and Japan)	6.0	6.1	8.0	8.6	11.0	13.8	11.5	11.8
China	0.9	0.7	0.8	1.2	1.3	2.1	3.2	4.6
India	1.5	1.3	1.1	1.2	1.2	1.4	1.6	1.9
Third World*	4.5	4.0	4.3	4.1	4.1	4.7	4.9	5.2
Third World (w/o China)*	6.5	5.7	6.1	5.5	5.3	5.9	5.6	5.5
Third World (w/o China and India)*	9.3	8.1	8.8	7.7	7.5	8.2	7.7	7.3
North America	123.7	105.0	100.7	101.6	98.2	98.9	116.4	112.5
Western Europe	111.1	104.6	104.6	101.5	100.5	98.5	92.0	99.7
Southern Europe	51.9	58.2	60.0	57.6	58.6	59.2	61.5	70.2
Australia and New Zealand	94.8	83.5	74.7	73.3	66.4	70.6	68.6	84.5
Japan	78.7	126.4	134.4	140.8	149.8	151.9	121.0	103.1
First World**	100.0	100.0	100.0	100.0	100.0	100.0	100.0	100.0
Eastern Europe	—	—	—	—	11.1	10.6	13.4	18.6
Former USSR w/ Russian Federation	—	—	—	—	10.7	5.9	4.6	8.2
Russian Federation	—	—	—	—	14.1	8.2	6.0	11.8
Former USSR w/o Russian Federation	—	—	—	—	7.1	3.6	3.1	4.6
Eastern Europe and former USSR***	—	—	—	—	10.8	7.1	6.9	11.0

SOURCE: Authors' calculations based on the World Bank's world development indicators for 2001 and 2006 (http://data.worldbank.org/data-catalog/world-development-indicators).

NOTE: The GNP is given in constant 1995 U.S. dollars for 1960–95, and in current U.S. dollars (using the Atlas Method) for 2000 and 2005.

*Countries included in the Third World:
  • Sub-Saharan Africa: Benin, Botswana, Burkina Faso, Burundi, Cameroon, Central African Republic, Chad, Republic of the Congo, Democratic Republic of the Congo, Cote d'Ivoire, Gabon, Ghana, Kenya, Lesotho, Madagascar, Malawi, Mauritania, Mauritius, Niger, Nigeria, Rwanda, Senegal, South Africa, Tanzania, Togo, Uganda, Zambia, Zimbabwe
  • Latin America: Argentina, Bolivia, Brazil, Chile, Colombia, Costa Rica, Dominican Republic, Ecuador, El Salvador, Guatemala, Haiti, Honduras, Jamaica, Mexico, Nicaragua, Panama, Paraguay, Peru, Trinidad and Tobago, Uruguay, Venezuela
  • West Asia and North Africa: Algeria, Arab Republic of Egypt, Morocco, Saudi Arabia (1971 for 1970), Sudan, Syrian Arab Republic, Tunisia (1961 for 1960), Turkey
  • South Asia: Bangladesh, India, Nepal, Pakistan, Sri Lanka
  • East Asia: China, Hong Kong, Indonesia, South Korea, Malaysia, Philippines, Singapore, Taiwan (Taiwan National Statistics), Thailand

**Countries included in the First World:
  • North America: Canada, United States
  • Western Europe: Austria, Belgium, Denmark, Finland, France, Germany, Luxembourg, Netherlands, Norway, Sweden, Switzerland, United Kingdom
  • Southern Europe: Greece, Ireland, Israel, Italy, Portugal, Spain
  • Australia and New Zealand
  • Japan

***Countries included in Eastern Europe and the former USSR:
  • Eastern Europe: Albania, Bulgaria, Czech Republic, Hungary, Poland, Romania, Slovak Republic, Slovenia
  • Former USSR: Armenia, Azerbaijan, Belarus, Estonia, Georgia, Kazakhstan, Kyrgyz Republic, Latvia, Lithuania, Moldova, Russian Federation, Tajikistan, Turkmenistan, Ukraine, Uzbekistan

These tendencies have been widely interpreted as the result of the closer integration of China, India, and the former Soviet Union in the global economy. Richard Freeman, for example, has claimed that this closer integration effectively doubled the labor force producing for the world market without increasing the effective supply of capital. With twice as many workers competing for work with the same amount of capital, not only has the balance of power shifted away from labor toward capital, but the prospects for economic growth of middle-income countries that were already integrated in the global economy have deteriorated (Freeman 2005).

If true, this contention would provide a highly parsimonious explanation of the double redistribution of income noted above: from lower- to higher-income groups within countries and from middle-income to low- and high-income countries. The contention, however, does not stand up to empirical scrutiny primarily because, before and after the United States embraced the TINA doctrine, the predominant feature of the global economy has been a large and expanding supply of surplus capital, as much as (if not more than) an unlimited supply of surplus labor. While in the 1970s this expanding supply of surplus capital flowed primarily from high- to low- and especially middle-income countries, and squeezed profits rather than wages, the neoliberal turn shifted the downward pressure from profits to wages and, above all, brought about a massive rerouting of capital flows toward the United States. This rerouting turned TINA into a self-fulfilling prophecy: whatever alternative to cutthroat competition for increasingly mobile capital might have existed before 1980, it became moot once the world's largest and wealthiest economy led the world down the road of ever more extravagant concessions to capital. This was especially the case for Third and Second Worlds (mostly middle-income) countries, which, as a result of the change in U.S. policies, experienced a sharp contraction both in the demand for their natural resources and in the availability of credit and investment at favorable conditions.

The extent of the rerouting of capital flows can be gauged from the change in the current account of the U.S. balance of payments. Insofar as the United States is concerned, the alleged expansion in the global supply of cheap labor has been accompanied by a virtually unlimited supply of capital from the rest of the world. Moreover, as fig. 1.1 shows, in the 1980s and especially after the East Asian crisis of 1997–98, this unlimited supply of capital has come from the former Third and Second Worlds. Whatever the reason for the shift in the balance of power from labor to capital in the United States—where the shift came earlier and has been more pronounced than in other wealthy countries—it cannot be attributed to an expansion of the global supply of cheap labor unmatched by a proportionate expansion of the global supply of capital, as Freeman, among others, maintains.

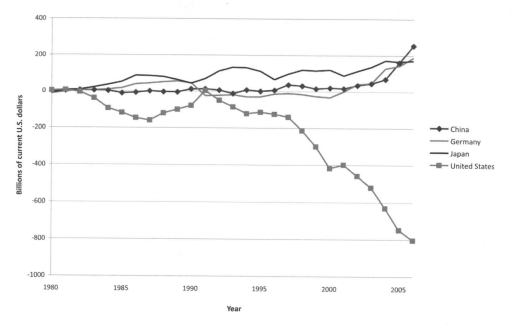

Fig. 1.1   Current account balance, 1980–2005

SOURCE: Data from IMF, World Economic Outlook Database (http://www.imf.org/external/pubs/ft/weo/2010/01/weodata/index.aspx), April 2010.

Low- and middle-income countries have faced an altogether different situation. In these countries, the rerouting of global capital flows toward the United States turned the flood of capital that they had experienced in the 1970s into the sudden drought of the 1980s. First signaled by the Mexican default of 1982, the drought was probably the single most important factor in promoting both an escalation of interstate competition for capital and the major divergence among Southern regions shown in table 1.1. Some regions (most notably East Asia) succeeded in taking advantage of the increase in U.S. demand for cheap industrial products that ensued from U.S. trade liberalization and the escalating U.S. trade deficit. These regions tended to benefit from the redirection of capital flows toward the United States, because the improvement in their balance of payments lessened their need to compete with the United States in world financial markets, and indeed turned some of them into major lenders to the United States. Other regions (most notably Latin America and sub-Saharan Africa), in contrast, did not manage to compete successfully for a share of the North American demand. These regions tended to run into balance-of-payments difficulties that put them in the hopeless position of having to compete directly in world financial markets. The United States' business and governmental agencies were able to take advantage of both outcomes for the South: they were able to mobilize the cheap commodities and credit that Southern winners eagerly supplied, as well as the assets that Southern losers willy-nilly had to alienate at bargain prices. As table 1.1 shows, the overall result was that, while the United States succeeded in reversing its economic decline, the gains and losses of Southern regions relative to the North largely balanced one another.

In short, the prime mover of the intensification of competitive pressures on labor and on Southern countries has not been the integration in world markets of China's and India's allegedly unlimited supplies of labor, but rather the U.S.-sponsored neoliberal counterrevolution. Freeman's emphasis on unlimited supplies of cheap labor does highlight the fact that the Southern regions that have performed best in the competition initiated by the counter-revolution were endowed with large reserves of low-productivity agricultural labor that could be moved into higher-productivity industrial and service jobs. Indeed, Jeffrey Sachs and Wing Thye Woo have contended that the existence of a huge farm sector is the crucial difference that explains the greater success of economic reforms in China in comparison with Russia (1996, 3).

Arguments of this kind can nonetheless be criticized on two grounds. First, as Thomas Rawski has asked with specific reference to Sachs and Woo's interpretation of Chinese achievements, "If millions of ill-educated, over-regulated and under-employed farmers represent 'advantages of backwardness,' why do we see no big growth spurts in Egypt, India, Bangladesh, Pakistan, Nigeria and other nations that have long enjoyed such 'advantages'?" (1999, 141). Second, a large reservoir of low-productivity agricultural labor is not the only source of exploitable labor. Marxists, for example, have long emphasized that capitalist development tends to create an expanding reserve army of labor that can prevent real wages from growing as fast as labor productivity, while they regard the existence of a large reservoir of agricultural labor with access to the means of producing subsistence not as an advantage but as a handicap for economic development (Brenner 1977, 35–36; 1981, 1, 4–6). The question then arises of whether a large peasantry only partially separated from the means of producing its subsistence, like the Chinese, constitutes a greater competitive advantage in attracting capital and promoting economic growth than the urban and semi-urban masses of unemployed and underemployed labor, of which sub-Saharan Africa and Latin America are better endowed than China. If it does, should we revise or altogether reject Marxist theories of the reserve army of labor and of accumulation by dispossession? And if it does not, what other circumstances can account for China's success, in comparison with sub-Saharan Africa and Latin America, in turning to its advantage the world economic conjuncture created by the neoliberal counterrevolution?

China's Reforms and the Washington Consensus

The institutional promoters of the Washington Consensus—the World Bank, the IMF, and the U.S. and U.K. Treasuries, backed by the *Financial Times* and the *Economist*—have boasted that the reduction in world income inequality and poverty, which has accompanied China's economic growth since 1980, can be traced to Chinese adherence to their policy prescriptions.[6] As James Galbraith has underscored, the claim is contradicted as much by the long list of economic disasters that actual adherence to these prescriptions has provoked in sub-Saharan Africa, Latin America, and the former Soviet Union as by the fact that both China and India, first, "steered free from Western banks in the 1970s, and spared themselves the debt crisis;" second, "continue to maintain capital controls to this day, so that hot money cannot flow freely in and out"; and third, "continue to have large state sectors in heavy industry." On the whole, China and India have indeed done well. "But," Galbraith asks, "is this due to their reforms or to the regulations they continued to impose? No doubt, the right answer is: Partly to both" (2004).

With regard to China, Galbraith's claim concurs with Joseph Stiglitz's contention that the success of Chinese reforms—in comparison with the failure of reforms in the former Soviet Union—can be traced to not having given up gradualism in favor of the shock therapies advocated by the Washington Consensus; to having recognized that social stability can only be maintained if job creation goes in tandem with restructuring; and to having sought to ensure the fruitful redeployment of resources displaced by intensifying competition (Stiglitz 2002, 125–26).[7] To be sure, China's reforms did expose state-owned enterprises (SOEs) to competition with one another, with foreign corporations, and especially with a mixed bag of newly created private, semi-private, and community-owned enterprises. Nevertheless, while intensifying competition resulted in a sharp decline in the share of SOEs in employment and production in comparison with the period 1949–79, the role of the Chinese government in promoting development did not subside. On the contrary, it poured huge sums of money into the development of new industries, the establishment of new export processing zones (EPZs), the expansion and modernization of higher education, and major infrastructure projects, to an extent without precedent in any country at comparable levels of per capita income.

Thanks to the continental size and huge population of the country, these policies have enabled the Chinese government to combine the advantages of export-oriented industrialization, largely driven by foreign investment, with the advantages of a self-centered national economy informally protected by language, customs, institutions, and networks accessible to outsiders only through local intermediaries. A good illustration of this combination is the huge EPZs that the Chinese government built from scratch, which now house two-thirds of the world's total EPZ workers. Sheer size has enabled China to build three basic manufacturing clusters, each with its own specialization: the Pearl River Delta, specializing in labor-intensive manufacturing, production of spare parts, and the assembly of those parts; the Yangtze River

Delta, specializing in capital-intensive industry and the production of cars, semiconductors, mobile phones, and computers; and Zhongguancun, Beijing, often called China's Silicon Valley, where the government intervenes directly to foster the collaboration of universities, enterprises, and state banks in the development of information technology (Au 2005, 10–13).

The division of labor among EPZs also illustrates the Chinese government's strategy of promoting the development of knowledge-intensive industries without abandoning labor-intensive industries. In the pursuit of this strategy, the Chinese government has modernized and expanded the educational system at a pace and on a scale without precedent even in East Asia. Building on the exceptional achievements of the Mao era in primary education, the number of annual college graduates has tripled from 2001 through 2005 to over 3 million. As a result, China's state colleges produce graduates in absolute numbers comparable to much wealthier countries. Although the increase in numbers has undoubtedly involved a worsening in the quality of the education offered, the extension by the end of 2002 of the nine-year compulsory education (NYCE) program to an area inhabited by 90 percent of the population is still an impressive achievement. Moreover, China has the largest contingent of foreign students in the United States and rapidly growing contingents in Europe, Australia, Japan, and elsewhere. While the Chinese government has been offering all kinds of incentives to entice Chinese students abroad to return upon completion of their degrees, many of them, including practicing scientists and executives, are lured back by the opportunities afforded by a fast-growing economy (Buckley 2004; French 2005a; Guo 2005, 154–55; Au 2005; Shenkar 2006, 4–5; Aiyar 2006).

In short, the gradualism with which economic reforms have been carried out, as well as the countervailing actions with which the government has sought to promote the synergy between an expanding national market and new social divisions of labor, contrast sharply with the utopian belief of the neoliberal creed in the benefits of shock therapies, minimalist governments, and self-regulating markets. In promoting exports and the import of technological know-how, the Chinese government has sought the assistance of foreign and Chinese diaspora capitalist interests. In these relations, however, the Chinese government has retained the upper hand, becoming one of the main creditors of the dominant capitalist state (the United States) and accepting assistance on terms and at conditions that suit China's national interest. By no stretch of the imagination can it be characterized as the servant of foreign capitalist interests.[8] Even the widespread view that all high-tech industries in China are controlled by foreign capital ignores the large and growing participation of local Chinese companies and joint ventures in the production of high-tech goods, such as mobile phones, personal computers, and "brown" and "white" goods (Popov 2007, 35). Recent changes in China's business tax

code demonstrate that Beijing is far less concerned about importing technological know-how from foreign companies than it was in the past. For nearly
thirty years, foreign direct investment (FDI) was encouraged by taxing foreign
companies as little as 15 percent, whereas domestic firms were taxed up to 33
percent. With some exceptions for high-technology companies and "low-
profit enterprises," within a period of five years all firms will pay the same 25
percent rate. Symbolically, this change signals that foreign priority over China's manufacturing and management has ended (Wolfe 2007).

Intensifying competition among public and private enterprises has undoubtedly resulted in major disruptions in the security of employment that
urban workers enjoyed in the Mao era, as well as in countless episodes of
super-exploitation, especially of migrant workers (Chan 2000; Tang 2003/4;
Lee and Selden 2007). These hardships must nonetheless be put in the context of government policies that did not embrace the key neoliberal prescrip-
tion of sacrificing workers' welfare to profits. David Schweickart has pointed
out that "China entered its reform period without a capitalist class at all. This
was a hugely important fact. Not only [was there no] propertied class that
could block any serious structural change, but the capitalist class that has
been permitted, indeed encouraged, to emerge has been much more entrepreneurial than long-dominant capitalist classes tend to be, and hence more
useful to society in general." Moreover, China's twentieth-century history has
taught its ruling groups that large-scale worker or peasant discontent can
seriously jeopardize the accomplishments of the Chinese Revolution and subsequent reforms, and that repression alone will not do. Schweickart further
observes, "This condition—the real threat of mass disruption and possible
chaos—is absent in the West. It is present to a degree in many parts of the
global South, but there the structure and balance of class forces are quite
different from what they are in China" (2005).

As a result of this balance of class forces, medical, pension, and other
mandatory benefits for workers in joint ventures have remained more generous, and the firing of workers more difficult, in China's formal sector than in
countries at comparable or even higher levels of per capita income. More
important, the expansion of higher education, the rapid increase in alternative employment opportunities in new industries, and rural tax relief and
other reforms, which are encouraging villagers to put more labor into the
rural economy, have combined to create labor shortages that are undermining the foundations of the super-exploitation of migrant labor. "We're seeing
the end of the golden period of extremely low-cost labor in China," declared
a Goldman Sachs economist. "There are plenty of workers, but the supply of
uneducated workers is shrinking. . . . Chinese workers . . . are moving up the
value chain faster than people expected" (quoted in Barboza 2006; see also
Fuller 2005; Montlake 2006; *Economist* 2005).

The gradualism of reforms and state action aimed at expanding and upgrading the social division of labor; the massive expansion of education; the subordination of capitalist interests to the promotion of national development; and the active encouragement of intercapitalist competition have all contributed to this emerging shortage. But the most decisive factor has probably been the expansion of the domestic market and the improvement of living conditions in rural areas associated with the reforms. The key reform was the introduction in 1978–83 of the household responsibility system, which returned decision making and control over agricultural surpluses from communes to rural households. In combination with substantial increases in agricultural procurement prices in 1979 and 1983, the system resulted in a major increase in returns to farm activity, which strengthened the earlier tendency of commune and brigade enterprises to produce nonagricultural goods. Although the government encouraged rural labor to leave the land without leaving the village by imposing various barriers to spatial mobility, in 1983 it gave rural residents permission to engage in long-distance transport and marketing to seek outlets for their products, and in 1984 it further relaxed regulations to allow farmers to work in nearby towns in the emerging collectively owned township and village enterprises (TVEs) (Cai, Park, and Zhao 2004; Unger 2002).

The emergence of TVEs was prompted by two other reforms: fiscal decentralization, which granted autonomy to local governments in the promotion of economic growth and in the use of fiscal residuals for bonuses; and a switch to the evaluation of cadres on the basis of the economic performance of their localities, which provided local governments with strong incentives to support economic growth. TVEs thus became the primary loci of the reorientation of the entrepreneurial energies of party cadres and government officials toward developmental objectives. Mostly self-reliant financially, they also became the main agency of the reallocation of agricultural surpluses to the undertaking of labor-intensive industrial activities capable of absorbing productively rural surplus labor (Oi 1999; Lin 1995; Walder 1995; Whiting 2001; J. Wang 2005, 179; K. Tsai 2004; Lin and Yao n.d.). The result was an explosive growth of the rural labor force engaged in nonagricultural activities, from 28 million in 1978 to 176 million in 2003. Most of the increase occurred in TVEs, which between 1980 and 2004 added almost four times as many jobs as were lost in state and collective urban employment and by the end of the period employed more than twice as many workers as all foreign, private, and jointly owned urban enterprises combined (National Bureau of Statistics of China 2005; China Agricultural Press 2005).

As Deng Xiaoping acknowledged in 1993, the explosive growth of TVEs took Chinese leaders by surprise. Only in 1990 did the government step in to legalize and regulate them by assigning ownership collectively to all inhabitants of the town or village but empowering local governments to appoint and fire managers or to delegate this authority to a governmental agency. The allocation of TVE profits was also regulated, mandating the reinvestment of more than half within the enterprise to modernize and expand production and to increase welfare and bonus funds, while most of what was left was used for the construction of agricultural infrastructure, technology services, public welfare, and investment in new enterprises. In the late 1990s, attempts were made to transform vaguely defined property rights into some form of shareholding or purely private ownership. But all regulations were hard to enforce, so that TVEs came to be characterized by a wide variety of local arrangements that makes their categorization difficult (Woo 1999, 129–37; Bouckaert 2005; Hart-Landsberg and Burkett 2004, 35; Lin and Yao n.d.).

And yet, despite or perhaps because of their organizational variety, the TVEs made key contributions to the success of the reforms. First, their labor-intensive orientation enabled them to absorb rural surplus labor and raise rural incomes without a massive increase in migration to urban areas. Indeed, most labor mobility in the 1980s was the movement of farmers out of farming to work in rural collective enterprises. Second, since TVEs were relatively unregulated, their entry into numerous markets increased competitive pressure across the board, forcing not just SOEs but all urban enterprises to improve their performance (Cai, Park, and Zhao 2004). Third, by becoming a major source of rural tax revenue, TVEs reduced the fiscal burden on peasants and thus contributed to social stability (J. Wang 2005, 177–78; Bernstein and Lü 2003). Fourth, and in key respects most important, by reinvesting profits and rents locally, publicly owned TVEs expanded the size of the domestic market and created the conditions of new rounds of investment, job creation, and division of labor. As Lily Tsai (2007) has observed on the basis of extensive research in rural China, family lineage or affiliation with a particular temple are effective substitutes for formal democratic and bureaucratic institutions of accountability in subjecting local government officials to informal rules and norms that force them to provide the level of public goods needed to maintain social stability (see also Lin and Yao n.d.). The unique position of TVEs as publicly owned enterprises was thus a defining characteristic of China's golden age (1978–96) in the post-Mao reform era. As Barry Naughton writes, "In no other transitional economy did public enterprises play the pivotal role that TVEs played in China" (2007, 287).

To be sure, the entire TVE sector underwent dramatic transformation after the mid-1990s. Faced with a more challenging environment (including a shift of the national government policy toward building regulatory institutions, and increased market integration and competition), the overall growth rate of TVEs slowed significantly. Many TVEs were restructured and transformed into predominantly privately owned business. But some public-owned TVEs were converted into worker-owned joint-stock companies. In

2003, there were 3.7 million workers in joint-stock cooperatives (Naughton 2007, 291). In many localities, the government has retained a stake in the firm and tried to operate a joint venture with private managers. Indeed, it can be hard to determine what constitutes a private firm today among China's TVEs, since local governments may retain stakes ranging from 20 to 50 percent (Naughton 2007, 285–93).

After 1996, TVEs continued to grow, albeit at rates closer to overall GDP growth than in the past. TVE value added as a share of GDP increased from 26 percent in 1996 to 30 percent in 1999, and then leveled off through 2004. More important, even after the restructuring, TVEs continued to be embedded in face-to-face relationships among members of rural communities and contributed to reinvestment in local communities (Naughton 2007, 286). Our own observations in Shandong Province in 2005 support this contention. When one of us asked the manager and owner of a privatized TVE cable factory, which had been one of the major cable producers nationwide since the mid-1990s, what induced his company to keep reinvesting profits locally even after the company was privatized, he pointed out that "although the government encouraged people to get rich first, you cannot ignore your fellow folks if you still want to get along in the village. People here are so close to one another that one simply cannot get along if he is accused of getting rich without thinking of his fellow folks in the village."[9] In addition to such social incentives, we found that political rewards, such as becoming a member of the Communist Party or a representative of the People's Congress, or being appointed as a rural local cadre, constitute major incentives for TVE managers and entrepreneurs to reinvest surpluses in their local communities (see Schweickart 2005).[10]

In summing up the developmental advantages of China in comparison with South Africa—where the African peasantry has long been dispossessed of the means of production without a corresponding creation of the demand conditions for its absorption in wage employment—Gillian Hart has similarly underscored the contribution of TVEs to the reinvestment and redistribution of profits within local circuits, and to their use in schools, clinics, and other forms of collective consumption. Moreover, a relatively egalitarian distribution of land among households enabled the residents of many TVEs to procure their livelihoods through a combination of intensive cultivation of tiny plots and industrial and other forms of nonagricultural work. Indeed, "a key force propelling [TVEs'] growth is that, unlike their urban counterparts, they do not have to provide housing, health, retirement, and other benefits to workers. In effect, much of the cost of reproduction of labor has been deflected from the enterprise." This pattern, Hart goes on to suggest, could be observed not just in China but in Taiwan as well:

> What is distinctive about China and Taiwan—and dramatically different from South Africa—are the redistributive land reforms beginning in

the late 1940s that effectively broke the power of the landlord class. The political forces that drove agrarian reforms in China and Taiwan were closely linked and precisely opposite. Yet in both socialist and post-socialist China, and in "capitalist" Taiwan, the redistributive reforms that defined agrarian transformations were marked by rapid, decentralized industrial accumulation *without* dispossession from the land. . . . That some of the most spectacular instances of industrial production in the second half of the twentieth century have taken place without dispossession of the peasant-workers from the land not only sheds light on the distinctively "non-Western" forms of accumulation that underpin global competition . . . [but should also compel us to] revise the teleological assumptions about "primitive accumulation" through which dispossession is seen as a natural concomitant of capitalist development. (2002, 199–201)

Hart's suggestion that China's economic success may rest on a pattern of accumulation without dispossession brings us back to the question of whether a large peasantry only partially separated from the means of producing its subsistence, like the Chinese, constitutes a greater competitive advantage in promoting economic growth than the urban and semi-urban masses of unemployed and underemployed labor, of which sub-Saharan Africa and Latin America are better endowed than China. The answer that emerges from the foregoing analysis is that it does, provided that government policies succeed in mobilizing the peasantry as a source, not just of abundant supplies of cheap labor but also, and especially, of the entrepreneurial energies and managerial skills necessary to absorb those supplies in ways that expand the national market and the opportunities of new divisions of labor.[11] While Deng's reforms were highly successful in this respect, their success depended critically on two traditions that preceded and shaped the reforms: the tradition of China's eighteenth-century industrious revolution and its more recent tradition of socialist revolution. To these traditions we now turn.

Legacies of China's Industrious and Socialist Revolutions

Kaoru Sugihara has claimed that in the eighteenth and early nineteenth centuries China experienced an "industrious revolution" that established a distinctive East Asian technological and institutional path and shaped East Asian responses to the challenges and opportunities of the Western industrial revolution. Particularly significant in this respect was the development of a labor-absorbing institutional framework centered on the household and, to a lesser extent, the village community. Contrary to the common view that small-scale production cannot sustain economic improvement, this institutional frame-work had important advantages over the class-based, large-scale production that was becoming dominant in England at about the same time. While in England workers were deprived of the opportunities to share in managerial concerns and to develop interpersonal skills needed for flexible specialization, in East Asia

> an ability to perform multiple tasks well, rather than specialization in a particular task, was preferred, and a will to cooperate with other members of the family rather than the furthering of individual talent was encouraged. Above all, it was important for every member of the family to try to fit into the work pattern of the farm, respond flexibly to extra or emergency needs, sympathize with the problems relating to the management of production, and anticipate and prevent potential problems. Managerial skill, with a general background of technical skill, was an ability which was actively sought after at the family level. (Sugihara 2003, 79)

Moreover, the transaction costs of trade were small, and the risk involved in technical innovations was relatively low. Although the East Asian institutional framework left little room for big innovations, or for investment in fixed capital or long-distance trade, it provided excellent opportunities for the development of labor-intensive technologies that increased per capita annual income, even if they did not increase output per day or per hour. The difference between this kind of development and development along the Western path was a strong bias toward the utilization of human rather than nonhuman resources (Sugihara 2003, 87).

Hart's observation that in the TVEs the intensive cultivation of small plots of land is combined with industrial and other forms of nonagricultural work, and with investments in the improvement of the quality of labor, supports Sugihara's contention of the persistence of the legacy of China's industrious revolution. Equally important in this respect is the tendency to utilize human resources as fully as possible and endow such resources with managerial and general technical skills at the family level. Compounded by the educational achievements of the Chinese revolutionary tradition (to be discussed presently), this tendency can be observed even in urban industries, whose chief competitive advantage has been traced to the use of inexpensive educated labor as a substitute for expensive machines and managers. At the Wanfeng automotive factory near Shanghai, for example, not a single robot is in sight. As in many other Chinese factories, the assembly lines are occupied by scores of young men, newly arrived from China's expanding technical schools, working with little more than large electric drills, wrenches, and rubber mallets. Engines and body panels, which in Western factories would move from station to station on automatic conveyors, are hauled by hand and hand truck. By avoiding the use of multimillion-dollar machines, Wanfeng can sell its handmade luxury Jeep Tributes in the Middle East for $8,000 to $10,000 (Fishman 2005, 205–6).[12] Moreover, as one would expect from Sugihara's claim, Chinese businesses substitute inexpensive educated labor not just for expensive machinery but also for expensive managers. As Ted Fishman (2004) also points out, "Despite the enormous numbers of workers in Chinese factories, the ranks of managers who supervise them are remarkably thin by Western standards . . . an indication of how incredibly well self-managed [workers] are."

The legacy of China's industrious revolution might not have survived, let alone produced this kind of developmental effects, had it not been revitalized and transformed by China's socialist revolutionary tradition:

> For all the mistakes, chaos and human suffering of the Maoist years, a stunning transformation had taken place in China over the course of the preceding three decades. In 1949 China was a much poorer country and far less industrialized than was Russia when the Bolsheviks made their revolution thirty-two years earlier. By 1979 China had an industrial base that employed some 50 million workers and accounted for more than half of its GDP. The value of its gross industrial output had grown thirty-eight-fold and that of heavy industry ninety-fold. China was manufacturing jet aircraft, modern ocean-going vessels, nuclear weapons and ballistic missiles. In the countryside mammoth irrigation and water control works had been constructed. A largely illiterate population had been transformed into a mostly literate one. A public health system had been created where none had existed before. Average life expectancy had increased from 35 to 65. All this had been accomplished with virtually no external assistance—which meant that China entered its reform period with zero external debt. (Popov 2007, 25)

Indeed, while China's greatest advances in per capita income have occurred since 1980, the greatest advances in adult life expectancy and, to a lesser extent, in adult literacy (that is, in basic welfare) occurred before 1980 (Research Group for Social Structure in Contemporary China 2005; Shenkar 2006; Unger 2002; H. Wang 2003). This pattern strongly supports the claim that "without the achievements of Mao's regime the market-type reforms of 1979 and beyond would [have] never produce[d] the impressive results that they actually did" (Popov 2007, 26–30).

It is worth underscoring that the success of economic reforms in China, in comparison with the former Soviet Union, should be traced not just or primarily to the existence of a huge farm sector, as Sachs and Woo maintain, or to the gradualism and concern for the welfare of the reforms, as Stiglitz and others maintain. It should be traced also and especially to fundamental differences between the Chinese and Russian revolutionary traditions. These differences originated in the distinct Chinese brand of Marxism-Leninism that first emerged with the formation of the Red Army in the late 1920s and developed fully after Japan took over China's coastal regions in the late 1930s. Unlike the Russian Bolshevik party, the Chinese Communists had to struggle to win the support of the peasantry for a decade and a half before they won power in 1949. In the course of this struggle, they "developed a philosophy of responding to popular needs within the confines of a single party" (Desai 2007, 3).

This ideological innovation had two main components. One was the replacement of the insurrectional aspects of Lenin's theory of the vanguard party with Mao's theory of the "mass line," whereby the party ought to be not just the teacher but also the pupil of the masses. John Fairbank notes that "this from-the-masses-to-the-masses concept was indeed a sort of democracy suited to Chinese tradition, where the upper-class official had governed best when he had the true interests of the local people at heart and so governed on their behalf" (1992, 319). The other innovation was the replacement of Marx's and Lenin's revolutionary class—the urban proletariat—with the peasantry as the main social base of the socialist revolution. Driven ever further from the seats of capitalist expansion by the Western-trained and -equipped Guomindang (GMD) armies, in the 1930s the Chinese Communist Party (CCP) and the Red Army thrust their roots among the peasantry of poor and remote areas. The result was, in Mark Selden's characterization, "a two-way socialization process," whereby the party-army molded the subaltern strata of Chinese rural society into a powerful revolutionary force, and was in turn shaped by the aspirations and values of these strata (1995, 37–38).

The combination of these two features with the modernist thrust of Marxism-Leninism has been the bedrock of the Chinese revolutionary tradition and helps explain key aspects of the Chinese developmental path before and after the reforms. First of all, it helps explain why in Mao's China, in sharp contrast to Stalin's Soviet Union, modernization was pursued through the economic and educational uplifting of the peasantry, not through its destruction. Second, it helps explain why, before and after the reforms, Chinese modernization has been based not just on the internalization of the Western industrial revolution but on the revival of features of the indigenous, rural-based, industrious revolution. Third, it helps explain why under Mao the tendency toward the emergence of an urban bourgeoisie of state-party officials and intellectuals was fought against through a strategy of sending them to rural areas for re-education. Finally, it helps explain why Deng's reforms were launched first in agriculture in the 1980s, a decade that proved to be one of the most vibrant periods of China's reform, while the 1990s policy reversal under Jiang Zemin promoted unbalanced development in favor of urban over rural areas and resulted in the great retraction in real welfare consequences, and why the recent change of policies under Hu Jintao focuses on the expansion of health, education, and welfare benefits in rural areas under the banner of a new socialist countryside (Huang 2008a).

At the roots of this complex tradition lies the crucial problem of how to govern and develop a country with a rural population larger than the entire population of Africa, Latin America, or Europe. No other country, except India, has ever faced a remotely comparable problem. From this standpoint, however painful an experience for urban officials and intellectuals, the Cultural Revolution consolidated the rural foundations of the Chinese Revolution and laid the groundwork for the success of the economic reforms. Suffice it to mention that during its course the disruption of urban industries greatly increased the demand for the products of rural enterprises, leading to a major expansion of the commune and brigade enterprises, out of which many of the TVEs later emerged (Lin and Yao n.d.; Putterman 1997). At the same time, the Cultural Revolution jeopardized not just the power of state-party officials and the political achievements of the Chinese Revolution, but much of the modernist component of the revolutionary tradition as well. Its repudiation in favor of economic reforms was thus considered essential to a revival of that component. By the mid-to late 1990s, however, the very success of the revival began to undermine the revolutionary tradition. Two developments in particular signaled this tendency: a huge increase in income inequality and growing popular discontent with the procedures and outcomes of the reforms.

The huge increase in income inequality within and between urban and rural areas that has accompanied China's switch to a market economy is a well-established fact. China's Gini coefficient, for example, has soared from a very low 0.28 in 1983 to a quite high 0.45 in 2001 and 0.47 in 2007 (Wei 2000; Riskin, Zhao, and Li 2001; Walder 2002; H. Wang 2003; Wu and Perloff 2004; Yi 2005). Up to the early 1990s, this trend could be credibly presented as the result of a strategy of unbalanced development that created opportunities of advancement for most. For one thing, World Bank data suggest that poverty reduction continued unabated; the share of the population living on less than $1 a day dropped from over 60 percent in 1980 to less than 20 percent in 1997. The increase in relative deprivation entailed by increasing inequality was thus accompanied by decreasing absolute deprivation (Davis, Lyons, and Batson 2007). Moreover, the increase in inequality—as measured by synthetic indicators like the Gini—largely reflected an improvement (rather than a deterioration) in the position of middle-income groups. Equally important, increasing inequality was accompanied by an increase in intergenerational (parents' occupation/children's occupation) and intragenerational (first occupation/current occupation) mobility. Individuals in the lower-income occupations thus had greater chances than in the pre-reform period to turn the income gap between occupations into a personal gain by moving to a higher-income occupation (Wu and Perloff 2004; Research Group for Social Structure in Contemporary China 2005).

Under these circumstances, resistance to increasing inequality was limited and could be repressed easily. Over time, however, increasing inequality clashed with the revolutionary tradition and seriously undermined social stability. Although the traditions of the mass line and of the two-way socialization process apparently played a role in the reforms,[13] the more that local and provincial party cadres and officials redirected their entrepreneurial energies to the economic sphere and engaged in acts of accumulation by dispossession, the more the tradition of the mass line became a fiction, and the two-way socialization process between the party-state and the subaltern strata of Chinese society was displaced by a similar process between the party-state and the emerging bourgeoisie. And yet the revolutionary tradition has endowed China's subaltern strata with a self-confidence and combativeness with few parallels elsewhere in the global South, while the party-state's continuing public commitment to that tradition has given some legitimacy to this self-confidence and combativeness (Schweickart 2005; Amin 2005, 268, 274–75; H. Wang 2006, 44–45).

The latest manifestation of this self-confidence and combativeness has been an escalation of social struggles in urban and rural areas alike. Officially reported cases of public order disruptions—protests, riots, and other forms of social unrest—rose from about ten thousand in 1993 to fifty thousand in 2002, fifty-eight thousand in 2003, seventy-four thousand in 2004, and eighty-seven thousand in 2005. In rural areas, until about 2000 the main grievances prompting mass action were taxes, levies, fees, and various other burdens. More recently, diversion of land from farming to industrial, real estate, and infrastructural development; environmental degradation; and the corruption of local party and government officials have become the most incendiary issues. Episodes like the 2005 Dongyang riot over pollution from a pesticide factory, whose operations were suspended, entered Chinese folklore as proof that determined mass action can force the authorities to reverse course and address popular needs (French 2005c, 2005d; Friedman 2005; Muldavin 2006; Ni 2006; Magnier 2006a, 2006b; Lee and Selden 2007).

In the urban areas, the old working class of the SOEs has, since the late 1990s, reacted to mass layoffs with a wave of protests that often appeal to standards of justice of the socialist tradition and to the iron rice bowl social contract between the working class and the state that prevailed during the first four decades of the People's Republic of China (PRC). Initially, a mix of repression and concessions met with some success in containing this wave of protest. More recently, however, an unprecedented series of walkouts has heralded the spread of unrest to the new working class of mostly young migrants, who constitute the backbone of China's export industries. Combined with growing unrest among urban workers in the service sectors, these two waves are putting to rest the Western stereotype that "there is no labor movement in China." "You can go to almost any city in the country now," notes Robin Munro, "and there will be several major collective worker protests going on at the same time." It is a spontaneous and relatively inchoate labor movement, but so was the U.S. labor movement during its golden age of the 1930s (quoted in Smith, Brecher, and Costello 2006).[14]

This upsurge of social unrest in rural and urban areas has prompted the leadership of the CCP to seek a more balanced and sustainable development between rural and urban areas, among regions, and between economy and society, and to introduce new labor legislation aimed at expanding workers' rights (Cody 2005; Yardley 2006; Kahn 2006; Muying 2007). The current Hu-Wen administration is making great efforts to address the rural issues and once again make rural development a priority of the policy agenda. Among other things, the government has abolished agricultural taxes, started to reduce or waive educational charges in the rural areas, and experimented with a basic health insurance program designed to cover the entire rural population (Huang 2008a, 293–94).

In response to the upsurge of social unrest and discontents among the disadvantaged groups in the past decade of the reform, the CCP has also called on its cadres to return to the party's revolutionary tradition of mass line, to listen to ordinary people's requests and complaints, and to help solve their problems. As a result, senior officials of the city, county, and district governments have met with ordinary citizens in person regularly, listening to their requests and complaints. They have also paid more frequent visits at the grassroots level to ease problems that threaten social stability (*Xinhua News* 2008). China has grassroots elections in over 660,000 villages, although these contests are often rigged. There are already small signs of change, with larger cities, such as Nanjing and Guangzhou, opening more important posts to public competition. Most recently, Zhou Tianyong, deputy head of research at the Central Party School, has predicted that by 2020 China will complete its political and institutional reforms with the implementation of a twelve-year plan aimed at establishing "public democratic involvement at all government levels" (Moore 2008).

Whether these changes can rescue the socialist tradition, empower people, and redirect development in a more egalitarian and sustainable direction remains to be seen. But the changes at least signal a shift from the past emphasis on growth for its own sake to a broader focus on quality of life, personal security, and consumption. Moreover, the Chinese ascent is already posing a serious challenge to the increasingly discredited Washington Consensus. To the nature and prospects of this challenge we now turn.[15]

Toward a New Bandung?

Joshua Cooper Ramo, a member of the Council on Foreign Relations in the United States and of the Foreign Policy Centre in Britain, has characterized the emerging Chinese challenge as the displacement of the Washington Consensus by a Beijing Consensus. This new consensus marks the Chinese-led emergence of "a path for other nations around the world" not simply to develop but also "to fit into the international order in a way that allows them to be truly independent, to protect their way of life and political choices." Ramo continues,

> The Washington Consensus . . . left a trail of destroyed economies and bad feelings around the globe. China's new development approach is . . . flexible enough that it is barely classifiable as a doctrine. It does not believe in uniform solutions for every situation. It is defined . . . by a lively defense of national borders and interests, and by the increasingly thoughtful accumulation of tools of asymmetric power projection. . . . While the US is pursuing unilateral policies designed to protect United States interests, China is assembling the resources to eclipse the US in many essential areas of international affairs and constructing an environment that will make US hegemonic action more difficult. . . . China's path to development and power is, of course, unrepeatable by any other nation. It also remains fraught with contradictions, tensions and pitfalls. Yet many elements of the country's rise have engaged the developing world. (2004, 3–5)

Among these elements, Ramo mentions a development model in which "the massive contradictions of Chinese development" make "sustainability and equality . . . first considerations," as well as "a theory of self-determination . . . that stresses using leverage to move big, hegemonic powers that may be tempted to tread on your toes" (2004, 11–12). Ramo's notion of a Beijing Consensus has been criticized for presuming the existence of a consensus where none exists, or for establishing a contrast with the Washington Consensus that some observers consider overdrawn (Kennedy 2008). Neither criticism seems to us appropriate, because Ramo himself emphasizes the variety of developmental paths implicit in the Beijing Consensus, in sharp contrast to the one-size-fits-all doctrine of the Washington Consensus. Ramo nonetheless does not tell us whether the Chinese ascent may actually contribute to a collective empowerment of the global South and not just to the empowerment of one or more of its national components. The relevant question in this connection is under which circumstances the Beijing Consensus can lead to the formation of a new and more effective Bandung—that is, a new version of the Third World alliance of the 1950s and 1960s better suited to counter the economic and political subordination of Southern to Northern states in an age of unprecedented global economic integration (Dirlik n.d., 5–6).

The temptation for China to settle for co-optation in a U.S.- or Northern-dominated world order, and for other Southern countries to seek or accept an alliance with Northern countries, should not be underestimated. But neither should we overestimate the power of the United States, even in collusion with Europe, to succeed once again in rolling back Southern advances, as it did for almost twenty years through the neoliberal counterrevolution. For one thing, the Iraqi debacle has confirmed the limits of coercive means in enforcing the Northern will against Southern resistance. More important in a capitalist world, the financial underpinnings of U.S. and Northern dominance are increasingly shaky. A crucial turning point in this respect has been the Asian financial crisis of 1997–98. Robert Wade and Frank Veneroso have claimed that this crisis confirmed the validity of the dictum that "in a depression assets return to their rightful owners." They note, "The combination of massive devaluations, IMF-pushed financial liberalization, and IMF-facilitated recovery may have precipitated the biggest peacetime transfer of assets from domestic to foreign owners in the past fifty years anywhere in the world, dwarfing the transfers from domestic to US owners in Latin America in the 1980s or in Mexico after 1994" (1998, 18).

By focusing on the immediate effects of the crisis, this diagnosis nonetheless missed its longer-term effects on North-South relations. As fig. 1.2 shows, the 1997–98 crisis was followed by a huge bifurcation between the Northern deficit and the rest of the world's surplus in the current accounts of their respective balances of payments. Much of this surplus still flows to the U.S. financial entrepot, both to finance the escalating U.S. deficit and to be reinvested around the world, including the global South, to the benefit of the United States. But the basic fact underlying the bifurcation is that the North, especially the United States, can produce fewer and fewer goods and services at lower prices than the rest of the world. More important, a significant and growing portion of that surplus is bypassing the U.S. entrepot, instead building up currency reserves and flowing directly to other Southern destinations, thereby weakening the hold of the IMF and other Northern-controlled financial institutions on Southern countries. Flush with cash and eager to regain control over their economic policies, Southern countries voted with their feet and paid off the IMF, thus avoiding the need to take its advice. As market-oriented central bankers began, in effect, to nationalize banks, "Western championing of free markets came in for a good deal of ridicule from states that had resisted the end-of-government enthusiasm of globalizers. Globalization, far from burying the state, now depended on states for rescue" (Malcomson 2008, 12).

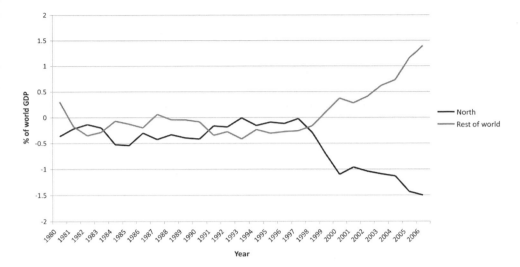

Fig. 1.2   Current account balance as a percentage of world GDP

SOURCE: Data from IMF, World Economic Outlook Database (http://www.imf.org/external/pubs/ft/weo/2010/01/weodata/index.aspx), September 2006.

Notwithstanding its massive purchases of U.S. treasury bonds, China has played a leading role both in rerouting the Southern surplus to Southern destinations and in providing neighboring and distant Southern countries with attractive alternatives to the trade, investment, and assistance of Northern countries and financial institutions. China's extraordinary annual package of $2 billion in loans to the Philippines for three years made the $200 million offered by the World Bank and the Asian Development Bank (ADB) look puny, and it easily outstripped a $1 billion loan under negotiation with Japan. Moreover, China's loans protected the Philippines from Washington's disfavor after President Arroyo pulled the country's troops out of Iraq. This is just one of many deals in which China has been out-competing Northern agencies by offering Southern countries more generous terms for access to their natural resources; larger loans with fewer political strings attached and without expensive consultant fees; and large and complicated infrastructure projects in distant areas at as little as half the cost of Northern competitors (Perlez 2006; Mallet 2006; Carew, Leow, and Areddy 2007).

Supplementing and complementing Chinese initiatives, oil-rich countries have also redirected their surpluses to the South. Of great political and symbolic significance has been Venezuela's use of windfall proceeds from high oil prices to assume the role of new lender of last resort for Latin American countries, thereby reducing Washington's historically enormous influence over economic policy in the region (Weisbrot 2006). Equally important, and potentially more disruptive of Northern financial dominance, has been the

recent interest of West Asian countries in rerouting at least part of their surpluses from the United States and Europe to East and South Asia. This is
partly due to the unpopularity of the Iraqi war and the backlash in the United
States, which forced Dubai's port company to sell off American holdings after
it bought the British port operator P&O. But the most compelling reason is
economic: China and all fast-growing Asian economies want West Asian oil,
and the West Asian capital and liquidity generated by that oil are searching
for investments with higher returns than U.S. Treasury bonds (Timmons
2006).

In May 2006, India's prime minister, Manmohan Singh, urged Asian nations at the annual meeting of the ADB to redirect Asian surpluses toward
Asian development projects. One U.S. observer found his speech "stunning"—"the harbinger of the end of the dollar and of American hegemony"
(Giridharadas 2006). In reality, whether Asian and other Southern countries
continue to use U.S. dollars is not the most important issue. Just as the
pound sterling continued to circulate as an international currency for three
to four decades after the end of British hegemony, so might the dollar. What
really matters for the future of North-South relations is whether Southern
countries will continue to put the surpluses of their balances of payments at
the disposal of U.S.-controlled agencies, to be turned into instruments of
Northern domination, or whether they will instead use them as instruments
of Southern emancipation. From this standpoint, there is nothing stunning
about Singh's statement, which merely lends support to a practice that is
already in place. What is truly stunning is the lack of awareness—in the
South no less than in the North—of the extent to which the neoliberal counterrevolution has backfired, creating highly favorable conditions for the emergence of a new and more powerful Bandung.

The foundations of the old Bandung were strictly political-ideological and,
as such, were easily destroyed by the neoliberal counterrevolution. The foundations of the Bandung that may be emerging now, alongside a political-
ideological component, are primarily economic and, as such, far more solid.
As Yashwant Sinha, a former Indian foreign minister, put it in a 2003 speech,
"In the past, India's engagement with much of Asia . . . was built on an
idealistic conception of Asian brotherhood, based on shared experiences of
colonialism and of cultural ties." The Asian dynamic today, in contrast, "is
determined . . . as much by trade, investment and production as by history
and culture" (quoted in Giridharadas 2005). Sinha's contention applies not
just to Asia but to the global South more generally. Under the old Bandung,
ideologically and politically motivated Third World solidarity had no economic foundation. Indeed, it had to run against the current of world market
processes over which Third World countries had little or no control. Today,
in contrast, a rapidly expanding South-South trade, investment, and cooperation in a growing variety of fields—including regional economic integration,

national security, health, and the environment—rest primarily on the increasing competitiveness of Southern countries in world production. Although idealistic conceptions of Third World solidarity still play a role, they are seldom the only or even the main determinant of South-South cooperation (Deen 2007).

Four countries in particular—China, India, Brazil, and South Africa (CIBS)—are leading the way in this direction. In addition to accounting for 40 percent of the world population, these countries are jointly emerging as major sources of capital, technology, and effective demand for the products of the surrounding regions and the global South at large (Atarah 2007; Aslam 2007). Notwithstanding their leading role in shifting the balance of economic and political power in favor of the global South, the CIBS countries have been criticized for establishing relations with other Southern countries that appear similar in motivation and outcome to traditional North-South relations. China in particular has been taken to task for its relations with commercial partners that reproduce their specialization in primary production at the expense of manufacturing and other high value-added activities.[16]

Insofar as they point to national self-interest rather than idealistic Third World solidarity as the foundation of Southern cooperation, these critiques are largely correct but miss the strengths of the new Bandung in comparison with the old. First of all, they overlook the subversion of the structural foundations of the global hierarchy of wealth and power entailed by the emergence of the CIBS, and especially China, as competitors of the North in world production, trade, and finance. Not only do these countries provide other Southern countries with better terms of trade, aid, and investment than do Northern countries—including substantial cancellations of debt—but by doing so they also intensify competitive pressures on Northern countries to provide Southern countries with better terms than they would otherwise. Critiques that emphasize the specialization of China's and India's trading partners in primary production miss the ongoing reversal of the terms of trade between manufacturing and primary production brought about by the industrial convergence of North and South. Just as industrialization has ceased to be a correlate of development, so specialization in primary production as such may no longer be a correlate of underdevelopment (Arrighi, Silver, and Brewer 2003; Deen 2006).

More important, insofar as the critiques in question point to the socially exploitative practices in which the CIBS may engage at home, or indirectly encourage abroad through their foreign trade and investment, they disregard the fact that exclusion from trade and production, rather than exploitation as such, is more often than not the main cause of Southern underdevelopment. They also disregard the fact that power relations play a crucial role in setting standards of morality in the global political economy. Today these standards

are, for the most part, set by the governments and institutions of the countries that occupy the upper reaches of the global hierarchy of wealth. The
emergence of the CIBS, however, may well be creating a situation in which
the governments and institutions of countries that occupy the middle and
lower reaches might at last have a say. Crucial in this respect is what China
and India, which account for more than one-third of the world population,
will choose to do. Should they choose to cooperate, as Howard French envis-
aged in an *International Herald Tribune* article in response to China and India's huge investments in each other's economies, "the day when a cozy club
of the rich—the United States, the strongest economies of Western Europe
and Japan—sets the pace for the rest of world, passing out instructions and
assigning grades, [would] fast [draw] to a close" (2005b).

The 2008 Wall Street meltdown has sped up the collapse of the Washington Consensus. As neoliberal American-style capitalism—including limited
government, minimal regulation, and the free-market allocation of credit—
lost credibility, many commentators wondered whether China's state-led capitalism could be an alternative. As Yasheng Huang noted, "In contemplating
alternatives to the fallen American model, some looked to China, where markets are tightly regulated and financial institutions controlled by the state. In
the aftermath of Wall Street's meltdown, fretted Francis Fukuyama in *News-
week,* China's state-led capitalism is 'looking more and more attractive.' *Washington Post* columnist David Ignatius hailed the global advent of a Confucian-
inspired 'new interventionism'; invoking Richard Nixon's backhanded tribute
to John Maynard Keynes, Ignatius declared, 'We are all Chinese now'" (2008b).

At the same time, the fact that China's economy was not immune from
the U.S.-centered global economic crisis—especially its slumping exports and
slowdown of economic growth—prompted a reassessment of the export-led
growth model that China had adopted in the 1990s.[17] Indeed, Chinese officials have been aware of the constraints imposed on growth by low levels of
domestic consumption. The current economic crisis may very well be what
was needed to induce them to shift toward a more balanced, domestic consumption–driven development path. Such a shift would inevitably involve a
recession, which is probably also a necessary step toward long-term sustainable development. As Barry Naughton projected in 2006, "Hundreds of firms
will go bankrupt, trade tensions will increase further as failing companies
seek to dump product on world markets, and sentiment toward China will
swing from positive to negative" (2006). But, as should be clear from this
chapter, there are also good reasons to anticipate that the 2008 economic
crisis might eventually lead to the resumption of Chinese growth on more
sustainable long-term foundations and to brighter prospects for a new
Bandung.

NOTES

We would like to thank Astra Bonini, Kevan Harris, and Daniel Pasciuti for assistance in producing the figures for this chapter, and Kevan Harris, Jon Shefner, Beverly Silver, and the graduate students in the Research in International Development seminar at Johns Hopkins University for comments on earlier drafts of the chapter.

1. We borrow the expression "strange death" from George Dangerfield's classic account, first published in 1935, of the dramatic upheaval and political change that overwhelmed liberal England at a time of seemingly undisputed economic and political power. See Dangerfield (1980).

2. On the rise and demise of such beliefs in the late nineteenth and early twentieth centuries, see Polanyi's classic work (1957). For a comparison of the late twentieth-century neoliberal turn and its late nineteenth-century antecedent, see Silver and Arrighi (2003).

3. As Hans Singer (1997) has pointed out, the description of development thinking in the postwar era as statist and inward-looking is correct, but neither characterization had the derogatory implications that it acquired in the 1980s.

4. Thus, while the share of world income of middle-and upper-middle-income groups (deciles 7–9) declined from 42.1 to 36.7 percent, the share of the lower-income groups (deciles 1–6) increased from 11.3 to 14 percent, and that of the high-income groups (decile 10) increased from 46.6 to 49.3 percent. Calculated from data provided by Berry (2005, 18).

5. World Bank data are subject to frequent and unexplained revisions that make them particularly unreliable in measuring short-term variations between specific countries. This unreliability, however, has little effect on the long-term trends among regions shown in table 1.1.

6. For a critical survey of these claims, see Wade (2004). The idea that China has adhered to the neoliberal prescriptions of the Washington Consensus has been as common among left intellectuals as among the promoters of the Consensus. For example, Deng Xiaoping figures prominently, along with Reagan, Pinochet, and Thatcher, on the front cover of David Harvey's *A Brief History of Neoliberalism*, and a whole chapter of the book is dedicated to "Neoliberalism 'with Chinese characteristics.'" More explicitly, Peter Kwong has likened Deng's slogan "Let some get rich first, so others can get rich later" to Reagan's "trickle-down economics." If the two slogans sound the same, we are told, it is because both Reagan and Deng "were great fans of the neoliberal guru Milton Friedman" (Kwong 2006, 1–2). Our critique of the claims of the Washington Consensus's promoters apply also to Harvey's and Kwong's contentions.

7. For similar conclusions reached on the basis of statistical evidence, see Popov (2007).

8. On various aspects of this relationship of the Chinese government to foreign capital, see Arrighi (2007, chap. 12).

9. Interview by Lu Zhang, Qingdao, January 2005.

10. Many studies have shown that the Chinese Communist Party (CCP) and the Chinese state have been able to control the growing number of private entrepreneurs by incorporating them into formal institutions. This has led to widespread claims that Chinese capitalists are not truly autonomous from the state. See, among others, Tsai (2007); Dickson (2003); Pearson (2002); Solinger (1992); and Wank (1999).

11. For a further elaboration on this argument with respect to southern Africa, see Arrighi, Aschoff, and Scully (2010).

12. For other illustrations of substitution of low-cost labor for expensive equipment, see Stalk and Young (2004) and Taylor (2006). As a report in the *Wall Street Journal* points out, statistics showing U.S. workers in capital-intensive factories to be several times more productive than their Chinese counterparts ignore the fact that the higher productivity of U.S. workers is due to the replacement of many factory workers with complex flexible-automation and material-handling systems, which reduces labor costs but raises the costs

of capital and support systems. By saving on capital and reintroducing a greater role for labor, Chinese factories reverse this process. The design of parts to be made, handled, and assembled manually, for example, reduces the total capital required by as much as one-third (Hout and Lebretton 2003).

13. In his dealings with Chinese policy makers as a senior World Bank official, for example, Ramgopal Agarwala "found [that] senior leaders demonstrate greater interest in interaction with various levels of society than in more democratically organized societies such as India's" (2002, 90). See also Rawski (1999, 142).

14. On the earlier wave of unrest, see Lee and Selden (2007). On the contrast between the two waves, see Silver (2003, 64–66; 2005, 445–47).

15. The deepening crisis of U.S. hegemony in the wake of the disastrous Iraqi adventure has played a crucial role both in facilitating the Chinese ascent and in undermining the credibility of the Washington Consensus. This double role of the crisis falls beyond the scope of this chapter. See, however, Arrighi (2007, parts 2 and 3).

16. Among the many critiques of China, see chapter 2 in this volume and the article by Tull (2006). For a critique of South Africa as a "subimperial" power vis-à-vis the rest of Africa, see Bond (2007).

17. According to *Xinhua News* (January 6, 2009), exports in China fell in November 2008 for the first time in seven years. According to the National Bureau of Statistics, in 2007 exports made up 37 percent of Chinese GDP, and exports of cargo and service contributed about 21.5 percent to the growth of the Chinese economy. But in the first half of 2008, only 4.9 percent of the nation's economic growth came from the cargo and service exports—16.8 percentage points lower than the same period in the previous year. Exports of the labor-intensive categories, such as toys, garments, and plastic-made goods, accounted for the bulk of the decline (Yan 2008).

REFERENCES

Agarwala, Ramgopal. 2002. *The Rise of China: Threat or Opportunity?* New Delhi: Bookwell.

Aiyar, P. 2006. "Excellence in Education: The Chinese Way." *Hindu*, February 17.

Amin, Samir. 2005. "China, Market Socialism, and U.S. Hegemony." *Review* 28 (3): 259–79.

Arrighi, Giovanni. 2002. "The African Crisis: World Systemic and Regional Aspects." *New Left Review* II/15 (May–June): 5–36.

———. 2007. *Adam Smith in Beijing: Lineages of the Twenty-First Century*. London: Verso.

Arrighi, Giovanni, Nicole Aschoff, and Benjamin Scully. 2010. "Accumulation by Dispossession and Its Limits: The Southern African Paradigm Revisited." *Studies in Comparative International Development* 45 (4): 410–38.

Arrighi, Giovanni, Beverly J. Silver, and Benjamin D. Brewer. 2003. "Industrial Convergence and the Persistence of the North-South Divide." *Studies in Comparative International Development* 38 (1): 3–31.

Aslam, A. 2007. "U.S., Investors' Favourite, Faces Test from South." *Inter Press Service News Agency*, October 16. http://ipsnews.net/news.asp?idnews=39676.

Atarah, L. 2007. "China, India, Brazil, South Africa Tilt Global Power Balance." *Inter Press Service News Agency*, September 13. http://ipsnews.net/news.asp?idnews=39247.

Au, Loong-Yu. 2005. "The Post MFA Era and the Rise of China." Working paper. http://www.globalmon.org.hk/eng/Post-MFA-era.pdf.

Barboza, David. 2006. "Labor Shortage in China May Lead to Trade Shift." *New York Times*, April 3.

Bello, Walden. 2007. "The Post-Washington Dissensus." *Focus on Trade*, no. 132 (September). http://www.focusweb.org/focus-on-trade.html?Itemid=1 (page discontinued).

Bernstein, Thomas P., and Xiaobo Lü. 2003. *Taxation Without Representation in Contemporary Rural China*. New York: Cambridge University Press.

Berry, Albert. 2005. "Methodological and Data Challenges to Identifying the Impacts of Globalization and Liberalization on Inequality." United Nations Research Institute for Social Development, Overarching Concerns Programme Paper No. 5.

Bond, Patrick. 2007. "South African Subimperial Accumulation." In *The Accumulation of Capital in Southern Africa: Rosa Luxemburg's Contemporary Relevance*, edited by P. Bond, H. Chitonge, and A. Hopfmann, 90–106. Berlin: Rosa Luxemburg Foundation; Durban, South Africa: Centre for Civil Society.

Bouckaert, Boudewijn R. A. 2005. "Bureaupreneurs in China: We Did It Our Way; A Comparative Study of the Explanation of the Economic Successes of Town-Village-Enterprises in China." Paper presented at the EALE Conference, Ljubljana, Slovenia, September 15–17.

Bramall, Chris. 2000. *Sources of Chinese Economic Growth, 1978–1996*. Oxford: Oxford University Press.

Brenner, Robert. 1977. "The Origins of Capitalist Development: A Critique of Neo-Smithian Marxism." *New Left Review* I/104 (July–August): 25–92.

———. 1981. "World System Theory and the Transition to Capitalism: Historical and Theoretical Perspectives." Unpublished English translation of a paper published in *Perspektiven des Weltsystems*, edited by Jochen Blaschke. Frankfurt: Campus Verlag, 1983.

Buckley, C. 2004. "Let a Thousand Ideas Flower: China Is a New Hotbed of Research." *New York Times*, September 13.

Cai, Fang, Albert Park, and Yaohui Zhao. 2004. "The Chinese Labor Market." Paper presented at the Second Conference on China's Economic Transition: Origins, Mechanisms, and Consequences, University of Pittsburgh, November 5–7.

Carew, R., J. Leow, and J. T. Areddy. 2007. "China Makes Splash, Again." *Wall Street Journal*, October 26.

Chan, Anita. 2000. "Globalization, China's Free (Read Bonded) Labour Market, and the Trade Union." *Asia Pacific Business Review* 6 (3–4): 260–79.

China Agricultural Press. 2005. *China Agriculture Yearbook: 2005*. Published in Chinese as *Zhongguo nongye tongji nianjian 2005*. Beijing: China Agricultural Press.

Chomsky, Noam. 2006. "Latin America and Asia Are Breaking Free of Washington's Grip." *Japan Focus*, March 15.

Cody, E. 2005. "China Confronts Contradictions Between Marxism and Markets." *Washington Post*, December 5.

Dangerfield, George. 1980. *The Strange Death of Liberal England*. New York: Putnam.

Davis, B., J. Lyons, and A. Batson. 2007. "Globalization's Gains Come with a Price." *Wall Street Journal*, May 24.

Deen, T. 2006. "South-South Trade Boom Reshapes Global Order." *Inter Press Service News Agency*, December 21. http://ipsnews.net/news.asp?idnews=35931.

———. 2007. "U.N. Backs Rising South-South Cooperation." *Inter Press Service News Agency*, June 5. http://ipsnews.net/news.asp?idnews=38048.

Desai, Meghnad. 2007. "Does the Future Really Belong to China?" *Prospect Magazine*, no. 130 (January). http://www.prospect-magazine.co.uk/pdfarticle.php?id=8174 (page discontinued).

Dickson, Bruce. 2003. *Red Capitalists in China: The Party, Private Entrepreneurs, and the Prospects for Political Change*. Cambridge: Cambridge University Press.

Dirlik, Arif. n.d. "Beijing Consensus: Beijing 'Gongshi.' Who Recognizes Whom and to What End?" *Globalization and Autonomy Online Compendium*. http://www.globalautonomy.ca/global1/position.jsp?index=PP_Dirlik_BeijingConsensus.xml.

The Economist. 2005. "China's People Problem." April 14.

Fairbank, John K. 1992. *China: A New History*. Cambridge, Mass.: Belknap Press.

Fishman, Ted C. 2004. "The Chinese Century." *New York Times*, July 4. http://www.nytimes.com/2004/07/04/magazine/04CHINA.html.

———. 2005. *China, Inc.: How the Rise of the Next Superpower Challenges America and the World*. New York: Scribner.

Freeman, Richard. 2005. "What Really Ails Europe (and America): The Doubling of the Global Workforce." *Globalist,* March 5. http://www.theglobalist.com/storyid .aspx?StoryId = 4542.

French, H. W. 2005a. "China Luring Scholars to Make Universities Great." *New York Times,* October 28. http://www.nytimes.com/2005/10/28/international/asia/ 28universities.html.

———. 2005b. "The Cross-Pollination of India and China." *International Herald Tribune,* November 9. http://www.nytimes.com/2005/11/09/world/asia/09iht-letter.html.

———. 2005c. "Protestors in China Get Angrier and Bolder." *International Herald Tribune,* July 20. http://www.nytimes.com/2005/07/19/world/asia/19iht-china.html.

———. 2005d. "20 Reported Killed as Chinese Unrest Escalates." *New York Times,* December 9. http://www.nytimes.com/2005/12/09/international/asia/09cnd-china.html.

Friedman, T. 2005. "How to Look at China." *International Herald Tribune,* November 10.

Fuller, T. 2005. "Worker Shortage in China: Are Higher Prices Ahead?" *Herald Tribune,* April 20.

Galbraith, James K. 2004. "Debunking *The Economist* Again." March 22. http://www.sa lon.com/opinion/feature/2004/03/22/economist/print.html.

Gilpin, Robert. 2000. *The Challenge of Global Capitalism: The World Economy in the Twenty-First Century.* Princeton: Princeton University Press.

Giridharadas, A. 2005. "India Starts Flexing Economic Muscle." *International Herald Tribune,* May 12. http://www.nytimes.com/2005/05/11/world/asia/11iht-india.html.

———. 2006. "Singh Urges Asian Self-Reliance." *International Herald Tribune,* May 5.

Glyn, Andrew. 2006. *Capitalism Unleashed: Finance, Globalization, and Welfare.* Oxford: Oxford University Press.

Guo, Yugui. 2005. *Asia's Educational Edge: Current Achievements in Japan, Korea, Taiwan, China, and India.* Oxford: Lexington.

Hart, Gillian. 2002. *Disabling Globalization: Places of Power in Post-Apartheid South Africa.* Berkeley: University of California Press.

Hart-Landsberg, Martin, and Paul Burkett. 2004. "China and Socialism: Market Reform and Class Struggle." *Monthly Review* 56 (3): 7–123.

Harvey, David. 2000. *Spaces of Hope.* Berkeley: University of California Press.

———. 2005. *A Brief History of Neoliberalism.* Oxford: Oxford University Press.

Hout, T., and J. Lebretton. 2003. "The Real Contest Between America and China." *Wall Street Journal,* September 16.

Huang, Yasheng. 2008a. *Capitalism with Chinese Characteristics: Entrepreneurship and the State.* Cambridge, Mass.: MIT Press.

———. 2008b. "Private Ownership: The Real Source of China's Economic Miracle." *McKinsey Quarterly,* December. http://www.mckinseyquarterly.com/Private_owner ship_The_real_source_of_Chinas_economic_miracle_2279.

Kahn, J. 2006. "A Sharp Debate Erupts in China over Ideologies." *New York Times,* March 12.

Kempe, F. 2006. "Why Economists Worry About Who Holds Foreign Currency Reserves." *Wall Street Journal,* May 9.

Kennedy, Scott. 2008. "The Myth of the Beijing Consensus." Paper presented at the conference "Washington Consensus" Versus "Beijing Consensus": Sustainability of China's Development Model, University of Denver Center for China-U.S. Cooperation, Denver, Colo., May 30–31.

Korzeniewicz, Roberto Patricio, and Timothy P. Moran. 2005. "Theorizing the Relationship Between Inequality and Economic Growth." *Theory and Society* 34 (3): 277–316.

Kwong, Peter. 2006. "China and the US Are Joined at the Hip: The Chinese Face of Neoliberalism." *CounterPunch,* weekend edition, October 7–8.

Lee, Ching Kwan, and Mark Selden. 2007. "Durable Inequality: The Legacies of China's Revolutions and the Pitfalls of Reforms." In *Revolution in the Making of the Modern*

World: Social Identities, Globalization, and Modernity, edited by J. Foran, D. Lane, and A. Zivkovic, 81–95. London: Routledge.

Lin, Justin Yifu, and Yang Yao. n.d. "Chinese Rural Industrialization in the Context of the East Asian Miracle." Working paper, China Center for Economic Research, Beijing University. http://www.esocialsciences.com/articles/displayArticles.asp?Article_ID =647.

Lin, Nan. 1995. "Local Market Socialism: Local Corporatism in Action in Rural China." *Theory and Society* 24 (3): 301–54.

Magnier, M. 2006a. "As China Spews Pollution, Villagers Rise Up." *Los Angeles Times,* September 3.

———. 2006b. "China Says It's Calmed Down." *Los Angeles Times,* November 8.

Malcomson, S. 2008. "The Higher Globalization." *New York Times,* December 12.

Mallet, V. 2006. "Hunt for Resources in the Developing World." *Financial Times,* December 12.

McMichael, Philip. 2000. *Development and Social Change: A Global Perspective.* 2nd ed. Thousand Oaks, Calif.: Pine Forge.

Meisner, Maurice. 1999. *Mao's China and After: A History of the People's Republic.* New York: Free Press.

Moffett, M., and B. Davis. 2006. "Booming Economy Leaves the IMF Groping for Mission." *Wall Street Journal,* April 21.

Montlake, S. 2006. "China's Factories Hit an Unlikely Shortage: Labor." *Christian Science Monitor,* May 1.

Moore, M. 2008. "China Will Be a Democracy by 2020, Says Senior Party Figure." *Daily Telegraph,* October 15. http://www.telegraph.co.uk/news/worldnews/asia/china/ 3195370/Chin a-will-be-a-democracy-by-2020-says-senior-party-figure.html.

Muldavin, J. 2006. "In Rural China, a Time Bomb Is Ticking." *International Herald Tribune,* January 1.

Muying, Mu. 2007. "Dissenting Voices Within Communist Party Before Seventeenth National Congress." *Cheng Ming Magazine,* August 16.

National Bureau of Statistics of China. 2005. *China Statistical Yearbook: 2005.* Published in Chinese as *Zhongguo tongji nianjian 2005.* Beijing: China Statistics Press.

Naughton, Barry. 2006. "Arguing Against the Motion: Without Significantly Accelerated Reforms and Major New Policy Actions, China's Rapid Growth Will Unravel Before Its Economy Overtakes the U.S." Paper presented at Reframing China Policy: The Carnegie Debates Series 2: China's Economy, Washington, D.C., December 1.

———. 2007. *The Chinese Economy: Transitions and Growth.* Cambridge, Mass.: MIT Press.

Ni, C. 2006. "Wave of Social Unrest Continues Across China." *Los Angeles Times,* August 10.

Oi, Jean. 1999. *Rural China Takes Off: Institutional Foundations of Economic Reform.* Berkeley: University of California Press.

Pearson, Margaret M. 2002. "Entrepreneurs and Democratization in China's Foreign Sector." In *The New Entrepreneurs of Europe and Asia: Patterns of Business Development in Russia, Eastern Europe, and China,* edited by Victoria E. Bonnell and Thomas B. Gold, 130–55. Armonk, N.Y.: M. E. Sharp.

Perlez, J. 2006. "China Competes with West in Aid to Its Neighbors." *New York Times,* September 18.

Polanyi, Karl. 1957. *The Great Transformation: The Political and Economic Origins of Our Time.* Boston: Beacon Press.

Popov, Vladimir. 2007. "China's Rise in the Medium Term Perspective: An Interpretation of Differences in Economic Performance of China and Russia Since 1949." *História e Economia* 3 (1): 13–38.

Porter, E. 2006. "Are Poor Nations Wasting Their Money on Dollars?" *New York Times,* April 30.

Putterman, Louis. 1997. "On the Past and Future of China's Township and Village-Owned Enterprises." *World Development* 25 (10): 1639–55.

Ramo, Joshua Cooper. 2004. *The Beijing Consensus: Notes on the New Physics of Chinese Power*. London: Foreign Policy Centre. http://fpc.org.uk/fsblob/244.pdf.

Rawski, Thomas G. 1999. "Reforming China's Economy: What Have We Learned?" *China Journal* 41 (January): 139–56.

Research Group for Social Structure in Contemporary China, Chinese Academy of Social Sciences. 2005. *Social Mobility in Contemporary China*. Montreal: America Quantum Media.

Riskin, Carl, Renwei Zhao, and Shih Li, eds. 2001. *China's Retreat from Equality: Income Distribution and Economic Transition*. Armonk, N.Y.: M. E. Sharpe.

Sachs, Jeffrey D., and Wing Thye Woo. 1996. "China's Transition Experience, Reexamined." *Transition* 7 (3–4): 1–5.

Schweickart, David. 2005. "You Can't Get There from Here: Reflections on the 'Beijing Consensus.'" Paper for the International Symposium on the China Model or Beijing Consensus for Development, Tianjin Normal University, Tianjin, China, August 8. http://homepages.luc.edu/~dschwei/beijingconsensus.htm.

Selden, Mark. 1995. "Yan'an Communism Reconsidered." *Modern China* 21 (1): 8–44.

Shenkar, Oded. 2006. *The Chinese Century: The Rising Chinese Economy and Its Impact on the Global Economy, the Balance of Power, and Your Job*. Upper Saddle River, N.J.: Wharton School Publishing.

Silver, Beverly J. 2003. *Forces of Labor: Workers' Movements and Globalization Since 1870*. Cambridge: Cambridge University Press.

———. 2005. "Labor Upsurges: From Detroit to Ulsan and Beyond." *Critical Sociology* 31 (3): 439–51.

Silver, Beverly J., and Giovanni Arrighi. 2003. "Polanyi's 'Double Movement': The *Belles Époques* of British and U.S. Hegemony Compared." *Politics and Society* 31 (2): 325–55.

Singer, Hans. 1997. "The Golden Age of the Keynesian Consensus—The Pendulum Swings Back." *World Development* 25 (3): 293–95.

Smith, B., J. Brecher, and T. Costello. 2006. "China's Emerging Labor Movement." October 9. http://www.commondreams.org/views06/1005-30.htm.

Solinger, Dorothy J. 1992. "Urban Entrepreneurs and the State: The Merger of State and Society." In *State and Society in China: The Consequences of Reform*, edited by Arthur Lewis Rosenbaum, 121–41. Boulder, Colo.: Westview Press.

Stalk, G., and D. Young. 2004. "Globalization Cost Advantage." *Washington Times*, August 24.

Stiglitz, Joseph E. 2002. *Globalization and Its Discontents*. New York: W. W. Norton.

Sugihara, Kaoru. 2003. "The East Asian Path of Economic Development: A Long-Term Perspective." In *The Resurgence of East Asia: 500, 150, and 50 Year Perspectives*, edited by G. Arrighi, T. Hamashita, and M. Selden, 78–123. New York: Routledge.

Tang, Jun. 2003/4. "Selections from Report on Poverty and Anti-Poverty in Urban China." *Chinese Sociology and Anthropology* 36, nos. 2–3.

Taylor, A. 2006. "A Tale of Two Factories." *Fortune Magazine*, September 14.

Timmons, H. 2006. "Asia Finding Rich Partner in Mideast." *New York Times*, December 1.

Toye, John. 1993. *Dilemmas of Development: Reflections on the Counter-Revolution in Development Economics*. 2nd ed. Oxford: Blackwell.

Tsai, Kellee S. 2004. "Off Balance: The Unintended Consequences of Fiscal Federalism in China." *Journal of Chinese Political Science* 9 (2): 7–26.

Tsai, Lily. 2007. *Accountability Without Democracy: Solidary Groups and Public Goods Provision in Rural China*. New York: Cambridge University Press.

Tull, Denis. 2006. "China's Engagement in Africa: Scope, Significance, and Consequences." *Journal of Modern African Studies* 44 (3): 459–79.

Unger, Jonathan. 2002. *The Transformation of Rural China*. Armonk, N.Y.: M. E. Sharpe.

Wade, Robert. 2004. "Is Globalization Reducing Poverty and Inequality?" *World Development* 32 (4): 567–89.

Wade, Robert, and Frank Veneroso. 1998. "The Asian Crisis: The High Debt Model Versus the Wall Street-Treasury-IMF Complex." *New Left Review* I/228 (March–April): 3–22.

Walder, Andrew. 1995. "Local Governments as Industrial Firms: An Organizational Analysis of China's Transitional Economy." *American Journal of Sociology* 101 (2): 263–301.

———. 2002. "Markets and Income Inequality in Rural China: Political Advantage in an Expanding Economy." *American Sociological Review* 67 (2): 231–53.

Wang, Hui. 2003. *China's New Order: Society, Politics, and Economy in Transition.* Cambridge: Harvard University Press.

———. 2006. "Depoliticized Politics, From East to West." *New Left Review* II/41 (September–October): 29–45.

Wang, Juan. 2005. "Going Beyond Township and Village Enterprises in Rural China." *Journal of Contemporary China* 14 (42): 177–187.

Wank, David. 1999. *Commodifying Communism: Business, Trust, and Politics in a Chinese City.* Cambridge: Cambridge University Press.

Wei, Yehua D. 2000. *Regional Development in China: States, Globalization, and Inequality.* New York: Routledge.

Weisbrot, M. 2006. "The Failure of Hugo-Bashing." *Los Angeles Times,* March 9.

———. 2007. "IMF Misses Epoch-Making Changes in the Global Economy." *International Herald Tribune,* October 19.

Whiting, Susan H. 2001. *Power and Wealth in Rural China: The Political Economy of Institutional Change.* Cambridge: Cambridge University Press.

Wolfe, A. 2007. "China's Priorities on Display at the National People's Congress." *Power and Interest News Report (PINR),* March 21.

Woo, Wing Thye. 1999. "The Real Reasons for China's Growth." *China Journal* 41 (January): 115–37.

Wu, Ximing, and Jeffrey M. Perloff. 2004. "China's Income Distribution Over Time: Reasons for Rising Inequality." KUDARE Working Paper No. 977 (February), University of California at Berkeley. http://ssrn.com/abstract = 506462.

Xinhua News. 2008. "China Seeks Smooth Communication with Citizens." October 14. http://news.xinhuanet.com/english/2008-10/14/content_10195062.htm.

———. 2009. "Wo waimao zengzhan qinian shouci jian fu" (China's exports drop for first time in seven years). January 6. http://news.xinhuanet.com/fortune/2009-01-06/content_10609747.htm (page discontinued).

Yan, Xinpu. 2008. "China's Exports Need Repairs." *China Daily,* December 22. http://www.chinadaily.com.cn/business/2008-12/22/content_7327205.htm.

Yardley, J. 2006. "China Unveils Plan to Aid Farmers, but Avoids Land Issue." *New York Times,* February 23.

Yi, Li. 2005. *The Structure and Evolution of Chinese Social Stratification.* Lanham, Md.: University Press of America.

2

REGIONALISM AS AN ALTERNATIVE TO GLOBALIZATION: THE EAST ASIAN CASE

Walden Bello

The world remains in the midst of a very deep recession that threatens to turn into a depression. The World Trade Organization (WTO) predicted that world trade would drop by 9 percent in 2009, the first fall in trade flows since 1982. The *Economist* claimed that the "global economic machine has gone into reverse" (2009a) and that "deglobalization" (2009b)—a term that the magazine attributes to the author—may be under way.

The transmogrification of the financial crisis into a global crisis of the real economy is, however, but the latest phase of a process of corporate-driven globalization that was already running into severe problems. Claims that globalization decreased poverty rates were overstated if not false, while there has been substantial agreement that globalization has been accompanied by growing inequality both among and within countries as well as by tremendous instability (Banerjee et al. 2006; Broad 2006). Even before the latest financial crisis, the globalization of finance had spawned some one hundred crises over the last three decades, and given the lack of regulation of the global financial system, it took no particular gift of prescience for former U.S. Secretary of the Treasury Robert Rubin to predict in 2003 that "future financial crises are almost surely inevitable and could be even more severe" (Rubin and Weisberg 2003, 296).

Meanwhile, the multilateral system of global governance that has overseen the institutionalization of neoliberal rules designed to facilitate the free flow of goods and capital has come under severe stress in the last decade. The International Monetary Fund (IMF) never recovered from the Asian financial crisis of 1997; it suffered a rapid erosion of credibility in addition to a budget crisis as its biggest developing country borrowers, on whose repayments the IMF had depended for a large part of its budget, walked away from it. The Doha Round negotiations of the WTO got nowhere. While the World Bank is in less dire straits, its role as the prime lender for development was threatened by China, which offered loans with few strings attached, and by the new Banco del Sur.

With globalization and its institutions in disarray, is participation in regional blocs the way out for countries seeking genuine development? South-South cooperation is now in vogue in development circles, with Latin America occupying center stage due to the dramatic events and initiatives that have occurred there, such as Venezuelan president Hugo Chávez's Bolivarian Alternative for the Americas (ALBA). But there is also talk of an Asian regional bloc coalescing around China, an African bloc led by South Africa, and a South Asian formation anchored by India. How realistic are hopes that regional formations could trigger genuine cooperative relationships? The answer will probably vary by region. In the East Asian region, however, China's moves toward various regional actors have been the focus of attention.

Regional Cooperation in Northeast Asia

In Northeast Asia, there has been much speculation about a Chinese-led regional response to the crisis, which has struck with terrifying swiftness. China's growth in 2008 fell to 9 percent, from 11 percent a year earlier. Japan is now in deep recession, its mighty export-oriented consumer goods industries reeling from plummeting sales. Korea, the hardest hit of Asia's economies so far, has seen its currency collapse by some 30 percent relative to the dollar. The possibility of moves toward a regional response to the crisis has been given substance by a trilateral summit of the leaders of China, Japan, and South Korea, as well as a flurry of bilateral talks between Japan's briefly serving prime minister Taro Aso and South Korean president Lee Myung-bak—all of whom had economic cooperation at the top of their agendas. On the surface, these three countries' coordinated action could be significant: they account for about three-quarters of East Asia's GDP and two-thirds of its trade, and each of them is among the other two's leading trading partners.

There are, however, reasons to be skeptical of recent declarations of cooperation. First of all, the idea of Northeast Asian cooperation in the form of a regional trading area has been kicked around for the last fifteen years in different formulations, with little movement at all in terms of implementation. Second, actual government coordination of economic policies in the face of a crisis does not have a good track record. The United States was not the only country that vetoed the Asian Monetary Fund (AMF) proposed by Japan during the 1997 financial crisis. China also opposed it for fear that it could become a vehicle of Japanese hegemony; and Japan is intent on preserving its much-eroded status as East Asia's economic leader. Third, these meetings have been a case of a mountain giving birth to a mouse. The concrete measures agreed upon—to expand currency swap facilities under the Association of Southeast Asian Nations (ASEAN) +3 arrangement to $120 billion (the Chiang Mai Initiative) and to call for a 200 percent infusion of more capital into the Asian Development Bank (ADB)—were timid compared to the gargantuan task at hand.

Ultimately, there has been little in the recent meetings that suggests that they have departed from the established pattern described by Australian National University's John Ravenhill (2009): "These meetings have aspired to little more than information exchange and establishing a dialogue. They do not involve cooperation as the term is normally understood in international relations. . . . East Asian governments have eschewed measures that would constrain their policy-making autonomy. And there is little in their collaboration that is genuinely regional."

China and Southeast Asia: Regional Cooperation or Domination?

What about China and Southeast Asia? What are we to expect in the coming period? How will the global economic crisis affect the much-vaunted economic initiatives toward the region that have been a feature of Chinese–Southeast Asian relations in the last few years? The past and future trajectory of their relationship is the principal focus of the rest of this chapter.

The nations of Southeast Asia, most of which are formally grouped into ASEAN, constitute the region that is probably most courted by China. At first glance, it seems that the Chinese-ASEAN relationship has been positive. China is currently ASEAN's fifth-largest trading partner, accounting for 7 percent of total ASEAN trade in 2003, after the European Union (EU) (11.6 percent), Japan (13.7 percent), and the United States (14 percent) (Cordenillo 2005). Moreover, demand from a Chinese economy growing at a breakneck pace was a key factor in Southeast Asian growth beginning around 2003, following a period of low growth dependent on domestic demand after the Asian financial crisis of 1997. Indeed, this was also the case for Korea and Japan. For Asia as a whole, in 2003 and at the beginning of 2004, as noted in a United Nations Conference on Trade and Development (UNCTAD) report, "China was a major engine of growth for most of the economies in the region. The country's imports accelerated even more than its exports, with a large proportion of them coming from the rest of Asia" (UNCTAD 2004, 20).

Yet the picture was more complex than that of a Chinese locomotive pulling along the rest of East Asia on a fast track to economic nirvana. There has been widespread concern that China's growth is, in fact, taking place at

Southeast Asia's expense. Many in Southeast Asia fear that China's low wages have encouraged both local and foreign manufacturers to phase out their operations in relatively high-wage Southeast Asia and move them to China. There appears to be some support for this. China's devaluation of the yuan in 1994 diverted some foreign direct investment (FDI) away from Southeast Asia. ASEAN continued to lose ground to China at an accelerated pace after the 1997 financial crisis. In 2000, FDI in ASEAN shrank to 10 percent of all FDI in developing Asia, down from 30 percent in the mid-nineties. The decline continued in 2001 and 2002, with the UN World Investment Report attributing the trend partly to "increased competition from China" (UNCTAD 2003, 41). Since the Japanese have been the most dynamic foreign investors in the region, there was much apprehension in the ASEAN capitals when a Japanese government survey revealed that 57 percent of Japanese manufacturing transnational corporations (TNCs) found China to be more attractive than the ASEAN-4 (Thailand, Malaysia, Indonesia, and the Philippines) (UNCTAD 2002, 44).

Snags in a Free Trade Relationship

Trade was another, perhaps greater, area of concern. In the last few years, China has aggressively sought free trade agreements (FTAs) with the ASEAN governments. This push appears to have met with some success. Thailand and China concluded an "early harvest" free trade pact in 2003. And at the tenth ASEAN Summit held in Vientiane, Laos, in November 2004, the ASEAN countries issued a joint statement expressing agreement with the goal of removing all tariffs between ASEAN and China by the year 2010. At that meeting, a positive spin on the proposed China-ASEAN Free Trade Agreement was provided by Philippine president Gloria Macapagal-Arroyo, who hailed the emergence of a "formidable regional grouping" that would rival the United States and the EU.

Yet things have not proceeded as smoothly as Beijing would have wanted. In the experimental arrangement between Thailand and China, the two countries agreed that tariffs on more than two hundred vegetable and fruit items would be eliminated immediately. Under the agreement, Thailand would export tropical fruits to China while winter fruits from China would be eligible for the zero-tariff deal. The expectations of mutual benefit evaporated after a few months, however, with most Thai commentaries admitting that Thailand got a bad deal. As one assessment put it, "Despite the limited scope of the Thailand-China early harvest agreement, it has had an appreciable impact in the sectors covered. The 'appreciable impact' has been to wipe out northern Thai producers of garlic and red onions and to cripple the sale of temperate fruit and vegetables from the Royal projects" (Chanyapate 2005). An ASEAN

Secretariat report noted that the results were "particularly poignant" for Thailand, "which . . . experienced a surge of 117 percent for apple imports, 346 percent for Chinese pear imports and 4,300 percent for grape shipments" (Cordenillo 2005). Thai newspapers pointed to officials in Southern China who refused to bring down tariffs as stipulated in the agreement while the Thai government brought down the barriers to Chinese products.

Thai fruit and vegetable growers' resentment over the results of the China-Thai early harvest agreement was, in fact, one of the factors that contributed to widespread disillusionment with the broader free trade agenda of the Thaksin government. Opposition to free trade was a prominent feature of the popular mobilizations that culminated in the ouster of that regime in mid-September by a military coup. However, the early harvest experience created consternation not just in Thailand but throughout other Southeast Asian nations as well. It stoked fears that ASEAN might become a dumping ground for China's extremely competitive industrial and agricultural sectors, which could drive down prices due to cheap urban labor that was continually replenished by laborers streaming in from the countryside. People wondered whether FTAs with China would not simply legalize the dumping of Chinese goods, a great deal of which were already being smuggled across their land borders with China or, in the case of the Philippines, across the South China Sea.

For Chinese officials, the benefits to their country of an FTA with ASEAN were clear. The strategy's aim, according to Chinese economist Angang Hu, was to more fully integrate China into the global economy as the "center of the world's manufacturing industry" (2004, 59). A central part of the plan was to open up ASEAN markets to Chinese-manufactured products. In light of growing protectionist sentiment in the United States and EU, Southeast Asia, which absorbed only 7 percent of Chinese exports, was seen as an important market with tremendous potential to absorb more of the country's goods. Also key, noted Hu, was the Chinese government's plan to attract investment in "the western region of China from ASEAN nations, weaving the western region more thoroughly into the fabric of regional and international trade" (2004, 54).

In addition to opening up markets and facilitating investment, there were other important objectives that Chinese officials were less candid about. A major reason for the push into Southeast Asia was the same search for raw materials, fuels, and strategic agricultural commodities that led to a high-profile Chinese presence in Africa and Latin America. The rush with which the Chinese sought to lock up trade and investment agreements with ASEAN and other Southeast Asian countries was also tied to their desire to match, if not beat, the United States, Japan, and the EU in the scramble to conclude free trade deals with ASEAN in response to the stalemate in multilateral negotiations for trade liberalization at the WTO.

ASEAN: A Net Beneficiary?

From the perspective of ASEAN's leaders, China represents both a threat and an opportunity. The threats are clear, but there is some hope in ASEAN that China can revive the regional economy in the aftermath of the collapse and stagnation or weak growth triggered by the Asian financial crisis of 1997. There is also a desire to diversify the region's trade and investment relations among its big trading partners, since at the moment these are heavily skewed toward the United States and Japan. This economic balancing act is consistent with ASEAN's political balancing act, which uses the key regional powers—mainly the United States, Japan, and China—to check one another's ambitions in the region.

However, it is not clear how ASEAN would benefit from the trade agreements being negotiated with China. It is highly doubtful that China will depart from what Hu has characterized as its "half open model," which is marked by "open or free trade on the export side and protectionism on the import side" (2004, 52). Certainly, the benefits would not come in labor-intensive manufacturing, where China enjoyed an unbeatable edge due to the constant downward pressure on wages exerted by migrants from a seemingly inexhaustible rural work force who make an average of $285 a year. The benefits would not lie in high technology either; even the United States and Japan have been scared of China's remarkable ability to move very quickly into high-tech industries, while still consolidating its edge in labor-intensive production. Nor would the benefits be in labor services, since China could produce engineers, nurses, and domestic workers who would perform the same work at lower wages than their ASEAN counterparts. For instance, China's recent deployment of seafarers has threatened the Philippines' premier position as a source of seamen globally.

Would agriculture in ASEAN be a net beneficiary? As the early harvest experience with Thailand showed, China was clearly supercompetitive in a vast array of agricultural products, from temperate crops to semitropical produce, and in agricultural processing. Vietnam and Thailand might be able to hold their own in rice production; Indonesia and Vietnam in coffee; and the Philippines in coconut and coconut products. But there might not be many more products to add to the list. Thus, it is likely that FTAs between the ASEAN countries and China would result in drastic imbalance.

Agro-Imperialism?

However, the Southeast Asian people's fear goes beyond investment diversion and unequal trade agreements. With land and energy scarce in China,

Chinese enterprises, with the blessings of the Chinese government, are seeking deals that would allow them to mine minerals and grow crops in Southeast Asian countries for exclusive export to the Chinese market. Lending some urgency to this new thrust is what Chinese prime minister Wen Jiabao characterizes as the "threat to national food security" posed by falling grain output in China, where cities are encroaching on farmland (Javier 2007).

In a recent deal with the Philippines, to take one example, the Chinese Fuhua Group planned to invest $3.83 billion over five to seven years to develop 1 million hectares of land for the growth of high-yielding strains of corn, rice, and sorghum. The Departments of Environment and Agrarian Reform plan to identify "idle lands" that could be incorporated into the Chinese plantations (Javier 2007). In a country where seven out of ten farmers are landless, this is a formula for real trouble. Such trade and land policies beg the question: Are we seeing here the embryo of a new form of land colonization, one that may be mediated by governments but whose essence is colonial in the classic sense?

Some have called China's international economic policies "imperialistic." However, it is difficult to sustain this label since exploitative relations between China and other developing countries have not congealed structurally. Economic trends in which China emerges as a net beneficiary do not add up to imperialism. Indeed, when African nongovernmental organizations (NGOs), for instance, criticize China's behavior in Africa, they make it a point to say that they are motivated by their desire that China's expanding trade and investment relations do not lead to the same exploitative patterns forged by the European powers (Bello 2007). Yet the element of force and coercion that accompanied the imposition of European and American economic power on weaker societies is absent.

The trade and investment relations that China is building with other developing countries have a tentative, trial-and-error quality. They respond to the overwhelming priority placed by the Chinese leadership on rapid development in order to raise Chinese living standards. The development of these relations, it must be pointed out, is constrained by history. In Africa, for instance, current trade and investment relations have been facilitated and impeded by the old foreign policy of economic assistance based on "proletarian solidarity" of the old Maoist state (Bello 2007).

ASEAN Derailed

In the view of many, the problem lies largely with ASEAN, since despite the rhetoric of regional integration, ASEAN's economies are still primarily ten separate economies. This is indicated by the fact that the percentage of intra-ASEAN trade in ASEAN total trade has remained "relatively constant," at around 25 percent, which is not much more than it was in 1970, when the figure was 20 percent. The vision of creating an integrated market of 450 million consumers that was expressed by the original ASEAN plan for regional import substitution industrialization—a vision that would have been achieved via increasingly freer trade among member countries but with high tariffs and quotas on third-country product—was never implemented. The Southeast Asian nations had over thirty years to build an "ASEAN house," and they squandered that opportunity. Had ASEAN evolved along the lines envisioned by its founders, it would not have displayed the disarray with which its members confronted the rise of China.

It is perhaps worthwhile to examine this history, for it contains lessons on how *not* to carry out regional integration. Founded in 1967, ASEAN's initial economic aspirations were expressed in the Kansu-Robinson Report produced under the auspices of the then Economic Commission for Asia and the Far East (ECAFE), which envisioned an integrated trading zone that would serve as a platform for regional import substitution (Soesastro 2001, 292–93). Cooperative industrialization via coordinated trade policy was the essence of the original ASEAN idea.

During its first two decades, however, the ASEAN economic program was, as noted earlier, derailed by regional politics. The main function that ASEAN played in the 1970s and 1980s was to serve as the frontline formation against "Vietnamese expansionism," in alliance with China and the United States. ASEAN, in fact, indirectly and informally supported the Khmer Rouge in Cambodia. Later, Southeast Asian governments transformed the "ASEAN brotherhood" into a shield against external criticism of human rights abuses. Dominated by strongmen like Suharto in Indonesia, Lee Kwan Yew in Singapore, and Marcos in the Philippines, ASEAN acquired a reputation for being Dictators Inc. in the 1980s.

ASEAN as an economic formation contributed little to the dynamic growth of the Southeast Asian economies in the late 1980s. Regional economic integration was not, however, completely forgotten. The ASEAN Industrial Projects (AIP) scheme aimed at building one capital-intensive industry per country that would service the regional market. The ASEAN Industrial Complementation (AICO) program offered regional incentives for enterprises that built complementary transborder facilities, with each country assigned a particular phase of production. The AIP failed to take off because it involved market sharing, "which ASEAN members were not ready to accept" (Soesastro 2001, 293). As for AICO, it was mainly Japanese automobile and electronic TNCs that took advantage of the plan's incentives, when they split up and relocated different parts of their operations' labor-intensive phases from Japan to other Southeast Asian countries to offset the rising value of the yen in the late 1980s. Thus, some industrial integration took place across borders, but this was not the integration of ASEAN enterprises envisioned by

ASEAN's founders; rather, it was one driven by the logic of profitability of Japanese TNCs.

When the U.S.-backed Asia Pacific Economic Cooperation (APEC) threatened to make the ASEAN economic project irrelevant by creating a trans-Pacific free trade area in the early 1990s, the ASEAN governments set up the ASEAN Free Trade Area (AFTA) to initiate a process of tariff reduction leading to a single market. However, commitment slackened in the mid-1990s, when the APEC project fizzled out and the threat from an alternative regional arrangement disappeared. Later in the decade, governments sought to give new momentum to AFTA by advancing the completion of tariff reductions on products in its "Inclusion List" from 2008 to 2003. There were difficulties in meeting this revised schedule, with Malaysia, for instance, seeking an extension of tariff liberalization for its auto industry. Moreover, some 26 percent of ASEAN tariff lines—those of strategic value to the various countries—are in the "Temporary Exclusion List," "General Exclusion List," or "Sensitive List," meaning that tariff reductions are either deferred indefinitely or permanently. With compliance weakening, the ASEAN leaders who met in Vientiane in November 2004 drew up yet another declaration, this time to abolish tariffs in eleven "priority sectors" by 2007. The end point of the liberalization process is supposed to be 2020, when ASEAN will be a single market and a single, integrated production base. Not surprisingly, the new benchmark has evoked skepticism.

Why has ASEAN regional integration remained so distant after nearly forty years? Aside from its having been overpoliticized, ASEAN as an economic project has suffered from three fundamental flaws. First, the ASEAN governments have had no common vision of the goal of a free trade area. Some governments are guided, perhaps unconsciously, by the vision of the original Kansu-Robinson Report, which promoted the creation of a platform for accelerating and deepening the industrialization of the region by maintaining barriers to the entry of strategic goods and services from third countries. Still others thought of regional free trade in neoliberal terms, along the lines articulated by neoclassical economist Mohamed Ariff: "The long-run goal should be to liberalize trade globally without discrimination. It is important to view AFTA as a transition or stepping stone toward that objective. AFTA can be used as a 'training ground' where the ASEAN countries can learn to compete with one another before they compete in the international market place" (2001, 59). Needless to say, these two different visions of the objective of a trading arrangement are incompatible.

Second, ASEAN has remained principally a project of government leaders and technocrats, with national industrial elites evincing little interest in industrial integration and jealously guarding their markets. Indeed, as late as 2001, intra-ASEAN exports accounted for only 20 percent of ASEAN's total exports—the same proportion as in 1970! Japan and the United States remain, overwhelmingly, the main trading partners of ASEAN's member countries. Third, ASEAN has remained a technocratic project, with little effort given to making it a popular democratic enterprise. Not surprisingly, the "ASEAN brotherhood" (for ASEAN elites do not speak of an "ASEAN sisterhood") has very little resonance, much less name recall at the grassroots level. To build an economic project on a fragile political entity that most Southeast Asians have probably not heard of, much less affectively identify with, is courting failure.

In short, ASEAN remains a very weak economic entity. Moving quickly to conclude an FTA with China is likely to lead to the same consequences that resulted from the early harvest agreement between China and Thailand. Even if China agreed to many ASEAN exemptions from steep tariff reductions, ASEAN would be locked into a process in which agricultural goods would only decrease. At this juncture, an ASEAN-China FTA—or, more likely, separate Chinese FTAs with different ASEAN countries—can only lead to deindustrialization and agricultural crisis in ASEAN. Moreover, China's aggressive effort to lock up multibillion-dollar deals to develop plantations in neighboring countries, thereby producing crops exclusively for the home market, is a disturbing development that could lead to the consolidation of a species of agro-imperialism.

More broadly, big developing countries like China are led by developmentalist elites who are seeking to find their place in a new global capitalist order marked by the loosening economic hegemony of the old capitalist centers, meaning Japan, the United States, and the EU. The pursuit of national economic interest, not regional cooperation for development, is their central concern. By uncritically signing trade and investment agreements or joining a regional formation anchored by these ambitious powers, smaller countries may simply end up being used economically, territorially, and politically to advance these powers' regional and global agendas. Such a course of action might turn out to be a case of jumping from the frying pan into the fire, and in Southeast Asia, there are many who believe that being on the American or Japanese frying pan is better than being consumed by what they fear is the Chinese fire.

Does this mean that trade agreements and regional blocs are to be avoided at all costs? No. It simply means that this might not be the time to conclude an agreement, and that the smaller countries must have a period of careful preparation. In the case of ASEAN, this would probably mean accelerating the process of regional integration. There would need to be a clear sense that integration does not mean free trade, but rather the use of trade policy to create a regional industrial base. Indeed, the current economic crisis might serve as an opportunity to push this process forward. It would also mean bringing the region's citizenries into the process by democratizing decision making on the key issues of economic cooperation.

Once the process of regional integration is well under way, the Southeast Asian countries may enter into negotiations with China. They must see to it that the terms of association are carefully negotiated and that they work closely to offset the dominance of the central power. In this regard, it must be remembered that the relationship between ASEAN and China is not a colonial relationship. As noted earlier, it cannot even be called an exploitative one at this point. But unless considerations of equity are front and center in the negotiation of economic relationships between Beijing and its neighbors, the old structural patterns marking the relations between Southeast Asia and Europe, the United States, and Japan could easily be replicated.

REFERENCES

Ariff, Mohamed. 2001. "Trade, Investment, and Interdependence." In *Reinventing ASEAN*, edited by Simon S. C. Tay, Jesus P. Estanislao, and Hadi Soesastro, 45–66. Singapore: Institute of Southeast Asian Studies.
Banerjee, Abhijit, Angus Deaton, Nora Lustig, and Ken Rogoff. 2006. *An Evaluation of World Bank Research, 1988–2005.* September 24. http://siteresources.worldbank.org/DEC/Resources/84797-1109362238001/726454-1164121166494/RESEARCH-EVAL UATION-2006-Main-Report.pdf.
Bello, Walden. 2007. "China Provokes Debate in Africa." Foreign Policy in Focus. March 5. http://www.fpif.org/fpiftxt/4065 (page discontinued).
Broad, Robin. 2006. "Research, Knowledge, and the Art of 'Paradigm Maintenance': The World Bank's Development Economics Vice Presidency (DEC)." *Review of International Political Economy* 13 (3): 387–419.
Chanyapate, Chanida. 2005. "Dangerous Advice on Free Trade Pacts." *Bangkok Post*, September 20. http://www.bangkokpost.com/News/20Sept2005/opin24.php (page discontinued).
Cordenillo, Raul. 2005. "Economic Benefits to ASEAN of the ASEAN China Free Trade Area (ACFTA)." ASEAN Secretariat, Jakarta. January 18. http://www.aseansec.org/17310.htm.
Economist. 2009a. "The Nuts and Bolts Come Apart." March 28–April 3.
———. 2009b. "Turning Their Backs on the World." February 21–27.
Hu, Angang. 2004. "A Free Trade Agreement Policy for the Northeast Asian Countries and ASEAN: A View from the People's Republic of China." In *Co-Design for a New East Asia After the Crisis*, edited by H. Hirakawa and Y. Kim, 51–66. Nagoya: Economic Research Center, Nagoya University.
Javier, Luzi Ann. 2007. "Chinese Investments Grow in the Philippines." *International Herald Tribune*, January 15. http://www.iht.com/articles/2007/01/15/bloomberg/sxchiag.php (page discontinued).
Park, Howard, and Kamal Saggi. 2006. *The Case for Industrial Policy: A Critical Survey.* London: Department for International Development. www.dfid.gov.uk/pubs/files/itd/industrial-policy.pdf.
Ravenhill, John. 2009. "Seven Myths About East Asian Regionalism." Unpublished manuscript.
Rubin, Robert, and Jacob Weisberg. 2003. *In an Uncertain World: Tough Choices from Wall Street to Washington.* New York: Random House.

Soesastro, Hadi. 2001. "ASEAN in 2030: The Long View." In *Reinventing ASEAN,* edited by Simon S. C. Tay, Jesus P. Estanislao, and Hadi Soesastro, 292–93. Singapore: Institute of Southeast Asian Studies.

United Nations Conference on Trade and Development (UNCTAD). 2002. *World Investment Report 2002: Transnational Corporations and Export Competitiveness.* Geneva: UNCTAD.

———. 2003. *World Investment Report 2003: FDI Policies for Development: National and International Perspectives.* Geneva: UNCTAD.

———. 2004. *Trade and Development Report 2004.* Geneva: UNCTAD.

3

CHINA AND MEXICO IN THE GLOBAL ECONOMY:
COMPARATIVE DEVELOPMENT MODELS IN AN ERA OF NEOLIBERALISM

Gary Gereffi

In recent decades, the role of developing countries in the global economy has evolved in significant ways. In the 1960s and 1970s, Latin America enjoyed the most dynamic economic growth due to its strategy of state-led import-substituting industrialization. In the 1980s, as Latin America became mired in a debilitating debt crisis, attention turned to East Asia and the export growth and industrial diversification of the four tigers (South Korea, Taiwan, Singapore, and Hong Kong), who pursued an export-oriented model of development. The 1990s witnessed a dramatic expansion in the capitalist world economy, as the breakup of the Soviet Union and the economic liberalization of India and China brought 3 billion new workers into the global labor force. By the mid-2000s, China had become the world's workshop for labor-intensive manufactures (especially consumer goods), while India was the world's back office due to the prowess of its offshore business services sector.

Today, the worst international economic crisis since the Great Depression of the 1930s is jeopardizing the prosperity of advanced industrial, emerging, and less developed economies alike. International trade has slowed, domestic consumption is down, and unemployment is skyrocketing in every region of the globe. Fundamental concerns are being raised about the future of global capitalism and its core institutions, as well as the national development models that are straining to adjust to this crisis. This chapter seeks to provide insight into these questions through a comparative analysis of the development trajectories of Mexico and China, two of the most dynamic and rapidly changing economies in the world.

Since the mid-1980s, globalization has been associated with a neoliberal model of development that has produced rapid economic growth and improved standards of living in some parts of the world, most notably East Asia. In other regions, like Latin America, neoliberalism has been marked by slow economic growth, large-scale unemployment, social deterioration, and political protest (Gallagher and Chudnovsky 2009). Development models in both Latin America and East Asia, however, have evolved considerably during this period. Within these regions, Mexico and China present particularly interesting cases because of notable contrasts, as well as similarities, in their development policies and economic trajectories. Mexico is the most diversified and export-oriented economy in Latin America, with a focus on manufactured exports to the United States. China is one of the world's fastest-growing economies, with extensive diversification and growing exports to the rest of the world. Mexico and China compete head-to-head in many product categories in the U.S. market.

This chapter begins by reviewing the main features of the Latin American and Chinese development experiences. It then examines industrial upgrading patterns in both Mexico and China, with an emphasis on their competitive niches in the U.S. market and the reasons why China is surging ahead of Mexico in many industries. I consider the various explanations that might account for China's superior performance, including a distinctive feature of China's industrial upgrading pattern known as supply chain cities. The final section of the chapter situates the experiences of both China and Mexico within the broader trajectory of globalization. In light of the recent economic crisis, we explore what might be expected from the United States and other countries as they struggle to adapt to radical realignments at home and abroad.

The Latin American and Mexican Development Models

The quest to find a common Latin American development model is quixotic for a couple of reasons. First, Latin America as a region is extremely diverse in terms of its geography, demographics, infrastructure, and culture, and its individual economies have diverged since the colonial era. Countries like Mexico have been at the forefront of the region's development, while others have lagged considerably. Second, Latin American development remains a topic of fierce controversy within the region, leading to clashing opinions regarding its future development trajectory (Inter-American Development Bank [IADB] 2006). Consensus is rare. Despite these differences, however, a few clear trends in the history of Latin American development policy can be identified.

Import-Substituting Industrialization

From World War II through the early 1980s, most Latin American countries pursued the import-substitution model, a set of policies that favored state-led industrialization and the protection of domestic industry, using a combination of support for publicly owned enterprises and extensive inflows of foreign investment (Thorp and Lowden 1996). Common features of import-substituting industrialization (ISI) policies in the 1950s and 1960s included high tariff barriers against foreign goods, especially industrial items; overvalued currencies; and provisions for the attraction of foreign capital. In the 1960s and 1970s, the leading Latin American economies moved from a phase of primary ISI, which focused on basic consumer goods (e.g., textiles and apparel), to secondary ISI, which involved using domestic production to substitute for imports of consumer durables (e.g., automobiles), intermediate goods (e.g., petrochemicals), and capital goods (e.g., heavy machinery) (Gereffi 1994; Gereffi and Wyman 1990).

Like its Latin American counterparts, Mexico's ISI experience included a system of high tariff barriers and government involvement in business, largely through state-owned enterprises (SOEs). Under the political hegemony of the Institutional Revolutionary Party (PRI), Mexico posted solid growth from the 1950s to the 1970s, averaging about 6 percent per year while maintaining low levels of inflation (Fourcade-Gourinchas and Babb 2002; Portes 1997). By the 1980s, Latin America's ISI policies had become too heavily dependent on international capital markets, and the debt bubble burst. Changes in the region's economic structure occurred soon after Mexico and other governments publicly announced their inability to meet debt requirements.

Neoliberalism and NAFTA

In the 1980s, a series of economic issues—low growth, widening economic inequality, government balance-of-payments crises, and periodic hyperinflation—led to a more market-oriented approach, which became known in the United States as the Washington Consensus (Gore 2000). This was facilitated by the rise of right-wing dictatorships in countries like Chile, Uruguay, and Brazil. Initially, neoliberal policies focused on reforming current and capital account flows, and controlling volatile inflation rates in the region. Later, reform spread to reshaping the role of the state in the economy (Weyland 2004; Huber and Solt 2004). In nearly every Latin American country, reformers stressed an increased use of market mechanisms and a reduced role for the state. Additionally, national governments sought to adjust their currency valuations and dramatically lower both barriers to free trade (tariffs) and restrictions on foreign private capital.

Within Latin America, the liberalization process spawned three distinct patterns of integration into the world economy (Ocampo 2009). There is a northern regional pattern, shared by Mexico and several Central American and Caribbean countries. It is characterized by manufactured exports mainly geared to the U.S. market; these contain a high portion of imported inputs (this is known as the maquila sector in Mexico and production sharing in the United States), and they generate a substantial number of low-paid assembly-oriented jobs due to the labor-intensive nature of the production process. The Central American economies rely heavily on a combination of traditional and diversified (nontraditional) agricultural exports, while tourism is a significant growth sector in Mexico and the Caribbean. The southern pattern, typical of South America, is characterized by a specialization in primary products and resource-based items, and there is a flourishing intraregional trade in manufactures because of regional trade agreements, such as the Andean Pact and Mercosur. Brazil, like Mexico, exports a broad range of manufactured goods and primary products, but it is less dependent on the United States than Mexico. The third pattern, which applies to Panama and several Caribbean countries, involves a specialization in service exports, such as finance, tourism, and shipping.

Mexico embraced neoliberalism more enthusiastically than any other Latin American country, but these reforms proceeded in stages. The first stage (1982–85) was directly linked to Mexico's negotiations with international monetary authorities following its debt crisis, and introduced new controls on monetary and fiscal policy, including much lower state expenditures. The second stage (1985–93) saw more drastic changes, including widespread privatization, the lowering of trade barriers, and liberalization of the regulations governing foreign investment. The third stage began in 1994 with the passage of the North American Free Trade Agreement (NAFTA), and it resulted in further structural reforms and the continued lowering of trade and investment barriers (Fourcade-Gourinchas and Babb 2002).

The impact of NAFTA on Mexican development is a topic on which opinion is polarized, although the critical evidence is mounting that the trade agreement has fallen far short of its promises and its potential. On the positive side, NAFTA was originally envisioned as a means to increase trade, investment, and jobs in Mexico, and it was assumed that this would promote economic growth and lessen the steady stream of migrants leaving Mexico for more and better jobs north of the border. Indeed, in the first fifteen years of its existence, many of these objectives were realized: exports to the United States increased sevenfold, foreign direct investment (FDI) quadrupled from its pre-NAFTA levels, and Mexico has gained about six hundred thousand jobs in the manufacturing sector since NAFTA took effect (Gallagher and Wise 2008).

However, critics argue that NAFTA's negatives outweigh its presumed gains. Mexico's economy has grown slowly, at an anemic annual rate of 1.6 percent per capita since NAFTA went into effect in 1994, compared with Mexico's robust growth of 3.5 percent per year from 1960 to 1979, the heyday of ISI. Slow growth has limited Mexico's job creation, and consequently Mexico has seen a net loss of employment since NAFTA. While Mexico may have gained six hundred thousand manufacturing jobs under NAFTA, the country lost at least two million jobs in agriculture, as Mexico's peasant farmers were unable to cope with the flood of cheap corn and other commodities that poured into the newly liberalized market from the United States and Canada. With one million young people entering the workforce in Mexico annually, it is not surprising that an estimated half million Mexicans emigrate to the United States in a steady stream every year (Gallagher and Wise 2008). These trends have led to economic and social polarization in Mexico (Dussel Peters 2000), as the wage gap with the United States has gotten bigger, not smaller (U.S. wages are nearly six times those in Mexico). Employment in the maquila sector fell by 9 percent from October 2000 to June 2006, and the value added by maquila plants (their exports minus the value of imported inputs) has been falling from its modest peak of 3.2 percent of GDP in 2000 to less than 3 percent (see chapter 4 of this volume).

These quantitative indicators sidestep an important qualitative discussion on the significance of the maquila sector for industrial upgrading in Mexico. Since it encompasses a panoply of industries, the maquila sector is very heterogeneous. To counter the stereotype that all maquila plants are involved in traditional assembly activities with low-skill workers and low wages, some researchers have argued that we need to distinguish between different generations of maquilas. Carrillo and Hualde (1998) introduced a typology consisting of three generations of companies: the first generation of maquila plants engaged in traditional labor-intensive assembly; the second generation carried out more advanced manufacturing, such as that associated with lean production; and the third generation focused on knowledge-intensive activities, typified by the Delphi–General Motors technical center in Ciudad Juárez, across the border from El Paso, Texas. Carrillo and Lara (2005) have extended this typology to include fourth-generation maquilas that coordinate a range of corporate activities (manufacturing, research, purchasing, and service) from within Mexico for the NAFTA region.

The conception of generations is intended to be an ideal type, and not a strict historical account. Thus, it doesn't imply a linear progression in which one generation fully replaces another, and it recognizes that maquilas of different generations are likely to coexist within specific industries or locales in Mexico. But it does suggest that each successive generation of maquila companies contributes to the advancement of industrial capabilities in Mexico in terms of its technology, value added, knowledge, and organizational complexity (Carrillo and Lara 2005). If these latter generations of maquilas become well established in Mexico, which is a source of controversy, they would indeed enhance the country's industrial upgrading potential.

Given the current economic crisis, many of the debates about Mexico's development are now moot or at least temporarily on hold. The meltdown and restructuring of the U.S. financial sector, the bankruptcies of General Motors and Chrysler, and the downturn in U.S. consumer spending have profound implications for the global economy writ large. But the economic future of the United States is particularly salient to those countries with strong economic ties to the U.S. market: Mexico certainly qualifies, with the United States accounting for over 85 percent of its exports and more than half of its imports, and so does China, a case to which we now turn.

China's Contemporary Development Model

China's reform efforts began in 1978 with the Third Plenum of the Eleventh National Party Congress, and reforms accelerated after Deng Xiaoping's 1992 southern trip and again after China's 2001 accession to the World Trade Organization (WTO) (Wang and Meng 2004; Branstetter and Lardy 2005). The cornerstone of China's economic miracle has been the role of the Chinese government in promoting development. In China's development model, the government established a new reliance on the market and on foreign trade, and it aggressively sought to attract foreign capital (Gao 2006). China has leveraged its domestic advantages, including the size of its potential market and the low cost of its factor inputs (chiefly labor), as well as the cost of land, electricity, and raw materials. It also poured huge sums of money into new industries, the establishment of special economic zones, the expansion and modernization of higher education, and major infrastructure projects, such as airports, shipping terminals, deepwater ports, and highways (see chapter 1 of this volume).

Since 1978, China's economy has expanded at a phenomenal pace. Average annual GDP has increased by 9 percent per year; exports grew by 12.4 percent annually in the 1990s and by more than 20 percent annually since 2000 (IADB 2005). In order to maintain this growth, the Chinese government is seeking to minimize its weaknesses (e.g., bureaucratic red tape, low quality of labor), upgrade its logistics capabilities, and move up the technology value chain. Notwithstanding the significant impact of the current economic crisis, Alexandra Harney, author of *The China Price* (2008) and a close observer of China's business scene, believes that "Beijing's long-term strategy is still to shift the focus of its economy away from reliance on low value-added, labor- and resource-intensive exports toward one that relies more on domestic consumption and higher value-added exports" (Harney 2009, 5).

The Chinese development model is particularly noted for its impressive ability to attract FDI. The annual FDI flows in China jumped from $40 billion in 2000 to $108 billion in 2008 (United Nations Conference on Trade and Development [UNCTAD] 2009, annex, table B.1). The total stock of FDI in China exceeded $378 billion in 2008, compared to Mexico's FDI stock of $295 billion and an FDI inflow of $22 billion in 2008 (see table 3.1). FDI has brought both capital goods and high technology into the country, helped move China's export mix from unskilled to skilled labor-intensive activities, and boosted China's exports in the capital- and technology-intensive sectors (Brandt and Rawski 2005, 23).

From an upgrading perspective, China's openness is beginning to pay off. China has become a top destination for research and development (R&D), due both to its crop of high-quality, low-cost engineers and to the size of its potential market. China's growth of R&D centers has been especially dramatic: whereas in 1997 China registered fewer than fifty multinational R&D centers, by 2004 the Chinese government registered more than six hundred R&D facilities in the country, many from large U.S. multinational corporations (MNCs) (Freeman 2005, 8). Current business reports put the number of MNC R&D centers in China at more than one thousand.

Observers of India, Asia's other emerging economic powerhouse, point out that India's economic growth relies on homegrown entrepreneurs, while China may be tying its export-led manufacturing boom too closely to FDI, since foreign-invested firms account for over 60 percent of China's exports (Huang and Khanna 2003). Given the external contradictions of the Chinese

Table 3.1   Foreign direct investment in China and Mexico, 1990–2008

FDI flows (millions of dollars)	1990–2000 (annual average)	2004	2005	2006	2007	2008
China	30,104	60,630	72,406	72,715	83,521	108,312
Mexico	9,373	22,883	21,922	19,316	27,278	21,950
FDI flows as a % of gross fixed capital formation	1990–2000 (annual average)	2004	2005	2006	2007	2008
China	11.9	8.0	7.7	6.4	6.0	6.0
Mexico	12.4	16.7	12.3	9.1	11.8	8.5

FDI stocks (millions of dollars)	1980	1990	2000	2005	2006	2007	2008
China	1,074	20,691	193,348	272,094	292,559	327,087	378,093
Mexico	—	22,424	97,170	209,564	241,050	272,731	294,680
FDI flows as a % of gross domestic product	1980	1990	2000	2005	2006	2007	2008
China	—	5.1	16.2	13.7	10.5	9.7	8.7
Mexico	—	8.5	16.7	27.3	25.5	25.3	27.1

SOURCE: Data from UNCTAD (2009).

development model, there are calls for a new domestic demand–led development strategy (Palley 2006). The current economic crisis has reinforced the need for a shift of this kind.

China's Supply Chain Cities: A Distinctive Form of Economic Organization

The concept of supply chain cities has been used in media reports and academic literature to highlight the growth of volume production in China and the agglomeration of multiple stages of the value chain in particular locations within China as a key to its upgrading success. Barboza (2004), for example, highlights the incredible specialization and scale that characterize China's export success in the apparel industry, even before the phaseout of the Multifibre Arrangement and apparel quotas by the WTO on January 1, 2005.

The term "supply chain cities" encompasses two distinct but related phenomena in China. The first usage refers to giant vertically integrated firm factories, and the second usage describes horizontally integrated cluster cities (Gereffi 2009, 46–48). Firm factories are company specific and designed to bring together multiple parts of the firm's supply chain—designers, suppliers, and branded manufacturers—so as to minimize transaction costs, take advantage of economies of scale, and foster flexible supply chain management. Many of the largest factories are in Guangdong Province and have been established by firms from Hong Kong and Taiwan. Cluster cities refer to single-product industrial clusters that have sprung up primarily in China's coastal regions. These areas concentrate on the production of specialized items and have attracted related and supporting businesses, including materials and component suppliers, packagers, and freight forwarders. Illustrative examples include Datang (socks) and Shengzhou (neckties) (Wang, Zhu, and Tong 2005; Kusterbeck 2005; Zhang, To, and Cao 2004).

China's supply chain cities have been driven by both market forces and the central government. Originally founded in the 1970s for low-cost manufacturing of export-oriented apparel, foreign-led cluster cities in Guangdong and Fujian are now further along in terms of fostering new, higher-tech industries and building firms with international brands, and they feature a broader export mix in traditional industries. The growth of the electronics industry is a good example (Lüthje 2004). Chinese-led clusters, mainly in Zhejiang and Jiangsu Provinces, were based on so-called township and village enterprises (TVEs), which were a major part of the government's push for economic development in the 1980s and 1990s (Wang, Zhu, and Tong 2005, 12; Zhang, To, and Cao 2004, 7–8; Sonobe, Hu, and Otsuka 2002). These more rural clusters tend to lie at an earlier point on the development trajectory.

Any comparative assessment of the development paths taken by Mexico and China rests heavily on institutional and historical factors. How have these models performed in practice? Has export-oriented development in Mexico and China led to industrial upgrading over the past two decades? How will each country overcome the challenges faced by its current development model? In the next section, we will use international trade data to explore these questions.

Industrial Upgrading in Mexico and China

Industrial upgrading is defined as "the process by which economic actors—nations, firms, and workers—move from low-value to relatively high-value activities in global production networks" (Gereffi 2005, 171). One of the ways that we can assess industrial upgrading for export-oriented economies like China and Mexico is to look at shifts in the technology content of their exports over time. We divide each country's exports into five product groupings, which are listed in ascending levels of technological content: primary products, resource-based manufactures, and low-, medium-, and high-technology manufactures.[1]

In fig. 3.1, we see that in 1988, over 50 percent of Mexico's total exports to the U.S. market were primary products, the most important of which was oil. In 1993, one year prior to the establishment of NAFTA, medium-technology

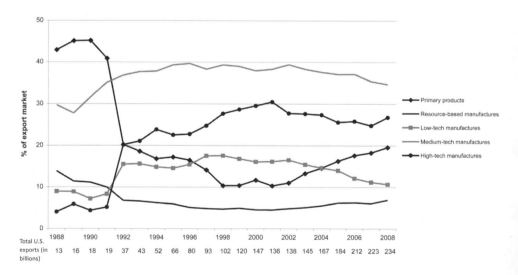

Fig. 3.1   Composition of Mexico's exports to the U.S. market, 1988–2008

SOURCE: Data from UN Comtrade (http://comtrade.un.org/db/dqBasicQuery.aspx), November 2009.

manufactures (mainly automotive products) and high-technology manufactures (largely electronics items) moved ahead of raw materials in Mexico's export mix. By 2008, over 60 percent of Mexico's exports of $234 billion to the U.S. market were in the medium- and high-technology product categories, followed by primary products (which rebounded from their nadir of 10 percent of total exports in 2001) and low-technology manufactures (such as textiles, apparel, and footwear). Thus, in less than twenty years, Mexico's export structure was transformed from one based on raw materials to one dominated by medium- and high-technology manufactured items.

In fig. 3.2, we see the composition of China's exports to the U.S. market during the 1988–2008 period. Unlike Mexico, the leading product category in these exports was low-technology manufactured goods, which primarily consisted of a wide variety of light consumer goods—apparel, footwear, toys, sporting goods, housewares, and so on. These products accounted for about two-thirds of China's overall exports to the United States in the early 1990s. By 2008, however, high-technology exports from China had increased to 35 percent of China's overall exports to the U.S. market, and were poised to pass low-technology exports for the top spot in China's export mix.

Thus, Mexico and China have had a number of commonalities in their export trajectories to the U.S. market during the past two decades. Both are diversified economies, with a range of different types of export products. In both cases, manufactured exports are more important than primary product

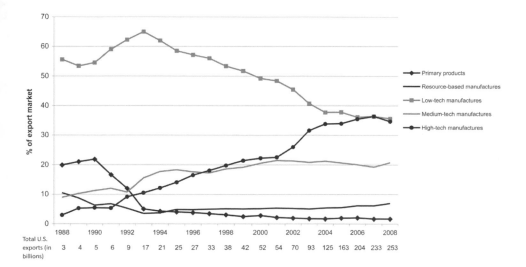

Fig. 3.2 Composition of China's exports to the U.S. market, 1988–2008

SOURCE: Data from UN Comtrade (http://comtrade.un.org/db/dqBasicQuery.aspx), November 2009.

or resource-based exports; within manufacturing, high- and medium-technology exports are displacing low-technology goods. While these export data have limitations as indicators of industrial upgrading, both economies appear to be increasing the sophistication of their export structures.[2]

A more detailed look at the international trade data, however, shows that since 2000, China has been beating Mexico in head-to-head competition in the U.S. market. Table 3.2 identifies six of the leading manufactured products for which China and Mexico are significant U.S. suppliers. Regarding five of these products, Mexico's share of the U.S. market was greater than China's in 2000; by 2009, China had wrested the lead from Mexico in all but one of these items. In automatic data processing machines (SITC 752), for example, China's share of U.S. imports increased more than fivefold from 11.3 percent in 2000 to 59.9 percent in 2009. In telecommunications equipment (SITC 764), China's market share nearly quadrupled from 10.3 to 38.8 percent. And in electrical machinery (SITC 778), it almost tripled from 11.9 to 32.5 percent. Only in auto parts and accessories (SITC 784) did Mexico expand its lead in the U.S. market.[3]

In figs. 3.3 and 3.4, China's superior performance in two industries—automatic data processing machines and telecommunications equipment—is

Table 3.2 Mexico's and China's competing exports to the United States, 2000–2009

SITC category	Product		2000 Value (billions)	2000 Share of U.S. market	2009 Value (billions)	2009 Share of U.S. market	Change in market share (2000–2009)
752	Automatic data processing machines and units	Mexico	6.4	11.5	7.0	13.1	
		China	6.3	11.3	32.0	59.9	
		U.S. total	55.9		53.4		
764	Telecommunications equipment and parts	Mexico	9.1	20.6	12.9	16.3	
		China	4.6	10.3	30.7	38.8	
		U.S. total	44.3		79.1		
778	Electrical machinery and apparatus	Mexico	3.1	18.3	3.8	19.9	
		China	2.0	11.9	6.2	32.5	
		U.S. total	17.1		19.1		
784	Auto parts and accessories	Mexico	4.6	16.3	7.8	26.3	
		China	0.4	1.5	3.1	10.4	
		U.S. total	28.4		29.7		
821	Furniture	Mexico	3.2	16.9	3.0	12.2	
		China	4.5	23.6	12.7	51.6	
		U.S. total	18.9		24.6		
84	Articles of apparel and clothing	Mexico	8.7	13.6	3.6	5.2	
		China	8.5	13.2	27.1	39.1	
		U.S. total	64.3		69.3		

Source: Data from U.S. Department of Commerce (http://dataweb.usitc.gov).

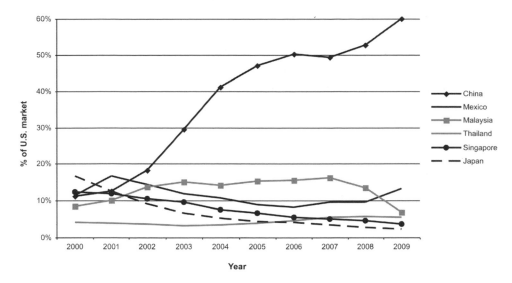

Fig. 3.3   Main competitors in the U.S. market for automatic data processing machines and units (SITC 752)

SOURCE: Data from U.S. International Trade Commission (http://dataweb.usitc.gov/), February 2010.

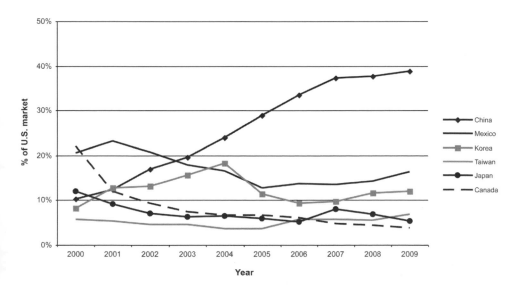

Fig. 3.4   Main competitors in the U.S. market for telecommunications equipment and parts (SITC 764)

SOURCE: Data from U.S. International Trade Commission (http://dataweb.usitc.gov/), February 2010.

examined in greater detail for the 2000–2009 period. China's steep ascent in both high-technology product categories is dramatic. This superior performance also carries over into low-technology products, such as furniture and apparel. Equally notable is the fact that although Mexico is a key competitor in each product market, the other top countries vary considerably in terms of region and overall level of development (Japan, Canada, and Italy are competing for U.S. market share with countries like Vietnam, Malaysia, Thailand, Indonesia, and India). The U.S. market is thus the meeting ground for countries that operate at very different price points and play distinct roles in the global value chains of these respective industries.

Why has China gained U.S. market share over Mexico so rapidly and decisively? There are several factors that account for this. First, Chinese labor costs have traditionally been significantly lower than those of Mexico. However, persistent labor shortages are being reported at hundreds of Chinese factories, a trend that is pushing up wages and leading a number of manufacturers to consider moving their factories to lower-cost countries like Vietnam, Cambodia, and Bangladesh (Barboza 2006; Goodman 2005). It is estimated that 20 million Chinese workers have already lost their jobs as a result of the current economic downturn (Harney 2009).

Second, China has sought to leverage its huge economies of scale, and it has made major investments in infrastructure and logistics to lower transportation costs and to speed time to market for their export products. The growth of China's supply chain cities—led by FDI-driven clusters in Guangdong (including Dongguan and Humen) and single-product clusters in Zhejiang (such as Anji and Datang)—is a perfect illustration of how China's governments and entrepreneurs are turning scale-driven specialization into a persistent competitive advantage for the country. China's sheer size has also allowed it to develop broad manufacturing clusters at the regional level, each with its own specialization: the Pearl River Delta in the southern part of China specializes in labor-intensive manufacturing, including the production of components and their assembly into finished consumer goods in a wide range of industries; the Yangtze River Delta near Shanghai specializes in capital-intensive industry and the production of cars, semiconductors, mobile phones, and computers; and the Zhongguancun technology hub in Beijing is an entrepreneurial high-technology zone, often dubbed China's Silicon Valley (Au 2005).

China's advantage lies not simply in the magnitude of its manufacturing capacity but in the fact that its central government makes its strategic decisions in an authoritarian, top-down manner; once key decisions are reached, often after intense debate in national party congresses, they can be implemented quickly and massively. In its run up to the 2008 Olympics, China spent US$160 billion on airport construction, transportation systems, sports venues, and other infrastructure projects (Ernst and Young 2007, 2). The unprecedented scale of China's development is leading the country to import close to 30 percent of global demand for many hard commodities, including oil, coal, steel, and cement.

Third, China has a coherent and multidimensional upgrading strategy to diversify its industrial mix and to add high-value activities. In their detailed study of China's export performance, Lall and Albaladejo (2004) argue that China and its East Asian neighbors are developing high-technology exports in a regionally integrated fashion, based on complex networks of export production that link leading electronics MNCs to their first-tier suppliers and global contract manufacturers (Sturgeon and Lee 2005; Gereffi, Humphrey, and Sturgeon 2005; Gereffi 1996). The export patterns for high-technology products reveal complementarity rather than confrontation between China and its mature East Asian partners (Japan, South Korea, Taiwan, and Singapore). China's role as a motor of export growth for the region, however, could change as China itself moves up the value chain and takes over activities currently carried out by its regional neighbors. Rodrik (2006) suggests that China is already exporting a wide range of highly sophisticated products, and he calculates that China's export bundle is similar to that of a country whose per capita income is three times higher than China's current level.

Fourth, China is using FDI to promote fast learning in new industries and knowledge spillovers in its domestic market (Zhang and Felmingham 2002; Wang and Meng 2004). Despite restrictions imposed by the WTO against domestic performance requirements for MNCs, China's local market is sufficiently attractive to MNC manufacturers that they are willing to comply with the wishes of local, regional, and national government authorities.

In summary, endowments, productivity, scale, access to foreign capital, and the government's central coordinating role all contribute to making China a formidable economic competitor (Mesquita Moreira 2007). Nonetheless, China has many problems of its own to contend with. Its extremely rapid growth in recent years has heightened expectations for continued prosperity, and a prolonged economic downturn raises the specter of social unrest. Government officials have urged businesses to avoid large-scale layoffs, and investments are being channeled to rural areas to create opportunities for those migrant workers who have already lost their jobs and are returning home to look for work.[4] As its export growth slows, China is striving to rebalance its economy by stimulating domestic consumption and implementing a diversified upgrading strategy that promotes low-technology and high-technology industries simultaneously. Like Mexico, China is trying to move beyond a simple cost-based approach to competitiveness (Farrell, Puron, and Remes 2005). Increasingly, the stakes are defined not as a race to the bottom, but as a quest to push the upgrading model beyond comparative advantages in raw materials, cheap labor, and manufacturing production to high-value niches in a broad range of global industries.

Where Is Globalization Headed?

Even before the current economic crisis, a new governance structure was emerging on the international scene. As argued by Arrighi and Zhang (see chapter 1), the Washington Consensus is dead. The neoliberal turn in global economic ideology in the 1980s, led by the United States and buttressed by the policies of key international organizations like the World Bank, the International Monetary Fund (IMF), and the WTO, was undermined by its failures to deliver on the promise of sustained economic growth and prosperity for developing economies (Ocampo 2009). The relatively successful large emerging economies (such as China, India, Brazil, and Russia) are demanding more clout in the governing institutions of the international economic system, as we see more high-level negotiations involving the G20 countries (nineteen of the world's largest national economies, including many in the developing world, plus the European Union) than the clubby G8 (the United States, United Kingdom, France, Germany, Italy, Russia, Japan, and Canada). While the pre-crisis hegemony of the neoliberal regime is clearly unhinged, the shape of the future is still hard to discern.

The trajectories of the United States and China are likely to define the key features of the new world order in the initial decades of the twenty-first century. For the United States, much will depend on the quality of leadership exercised by President Obama. He has championed multilateralism and the United States' new openness to the poor and excluded regions and populations of the world, as well as a more enlightened stance on the critical environmental and social challenges of the day. However, the financial crisis and mounting unemployment in the United States are leading many to espouse protectionist solutions to America's ills, and China, with its huge bilateral trade deficit with the United States, has received the brunt of the blame for the pain being felt by American workers.

In reality, the U.S.-China trade deficit, which hit a record high of $268 billion in 2008 (U.S. Census Bureau 2009), is not simply a bilateral problem driven by unfair Chinese competition, as is frequently alleged. The United States has a multilateral trade imbalance with one hundred other economies throughout the world. The root cause of this problem is what Stephen Roach, chairman of Morgan Stanley Asia, has called "America's excess consumption model" (Roach 2009). In early 2007, U.S. consumption accounted for 72 percent of real GDP, a record for the United States and for any major economy in the world. While this U.S. consumption binge may seem irresponsible (and even immoral) to some, it has also fueled the export-led growth model of China and much of the rest of Asia for the past two decades. It is precisely for this reason that the post-bubble demise of the U.S. consumer is such a threat: it undermines the external demand on which the Chinese economy and the rest of export-dependent Asia have depended during their boom years.

If the United States consumes too much, then one can say that China exports too much. The two trends have been mutually reinforcing, and a source of vulnerability to both economies. The extent of China's export dependence is extraordinary. Between 2001 and 2007, the export share of China's GDP nearly doubled from 20 to 36 percent, and during the same period developing Asia's export share hit a record of 47 percent of GDP (Roach 2009, figs. 2 and 4). These trends are closely connected because the Asian economy is increasingly China-centric. East Asia's exports to China underpin both Chinese exports to the rest of the world and the economic growth of the entire East Asian region. The complementarity of Asia's China-centric value chains explains why China and its neighbors are raising their high-technology exports in tandem (Lall and Albaladejo 2004). However, this tight pan-regional integration leads to vulnerabilities in tough times, just as it was a virtuous circle when China's exports were booming.

The December 2008 export figures for China's East Asian trade partners are startling. Taiwan's exports plunged 42 percent compared to one year earlier (exports to China fell 56 percent); Japan's exports dropped 35 percent (total and for China); and Korean exports declined by 17 percent (with exports to China down by 35 percent) (Roach 2009). China is now each of these country's leading trading partner (accounting for 28 percent of Taiwan's exports, 23 percent of Korea's exports, and 16 percent in the case of Japan), which explains why Asia is being hit so hard by China's export woes.

Where does the global economy go from here? International trade and FDI will rebound, although economists predict that the impact of the recession on employment and slow domestic growth in the major developed economies of the world will continue to be felt for another three to five years. What will change, however, is the infatuation with export-oriented industrialization stoked during the Washington Consensus years. This model was deemed successful when the large advanced industrial economies of North America and Europe were willing to subsidize the export growth of developing economies via high levels of consumption and burgeoning trade deficits. But as we have seen, this model is unsustainable in the long run.

National development strategies in China, Mexico, and other relatively large export-oriented economies are likely to place much more emphasis on domestic consumption, job creation, and social safety nets for the most vulnerable groups in society. China announced a stimulus package of US$585 billion in November 2008 to boost domestic spending, ease the burden in rural areas, and retrain migrant workers (Harney 2009). Mexico has also been under pressure to redress the social and economic inequalities generated by the neoliberal policies that created gains for a fortunate few but also spurred a general pattern of slow growth, declining productivity, and minimal backward linkages and economic spillovers from its exports and FDI (see chapter 4 of this volume; Gallagher, Moreno-Brid, and Porzecanski 2008; Dussel Peters 2000). As national development strategies become more inwardly oriented, the role of the state will expand. Industrial policy will reemerge, and social programs will seek to provide both skills and services needed by dislocated workers.

Global value chains are becoming more consolidated. Large multinational manufacturers, retailers, and marketers who manage global sourcing networks are proclaiming that they want fewer, larger, and more capable suppliers, and that they will operate in a reduced number of strategic locations around the world. This is likely to promote a higher degree of regional sourcing, with suppliers located close to the major consumer markets in North America, Western Europe, and East Asia.

Globalization is not going to disappear, but it is likely to become more decentralized. Globalization's benefits will continue to be unevenly distributed, with its gains going to those with more education, skills, wealth, and power. However, the inclusion of large emerging economies like China, Mexico, and India among those who are benefiting, at least in part, is a qualitative shift in the process. But it does not necessarily improve the chances for smaller countries in the global economy unless they devise policies to enhance their own capabilities to foster development.

NOTES

I would like to thank Amy Tsai for her excellent research assistance on this chapter.

1. Sanjaya Lall (2000) developed this technological classification of exports based on three-digit Standard International Trade Classification (SITC) categories. His article provides a detailed list of products within each category.

2. The main problem with these export data is that they are not sufficiently detailed to tell us about the process by which products are made. Auto parts or electronic components, for example, could still be made in labor-intensive ways by relatively unskilled workers. Thus, industrial upgrading cannot be assured just by moving in the direction of medium- or high-technology finished products. However, it is probably true that the relative proportion of high-value activities goes up as we move from low-technology to medium- and high-technology export categories.

3. These findings are consistent with the results of Gallagher, Moreno-Brid, and Porzecanski (2008, 1370), which show that in the 2000–2005 period, over half (53 percent) of Mexico's exports were under direct threat (occurring when Chinese exports in the same sector grow and Mexican exports decline) or partial threat (occurring when Chinese exports grow faster than their Mexican counterpart) from China.

4. The manufacturing sector employs many of China's 150 million migrant workers, who journeyed from inland provinces to seek jobs in the dynamic export factories that sprang up in the country's coastal regions. The remittances they send home to their families in the countryside are estimated to represent as much as 40 percent of household income in rural areas (Harney 2009).

REFERENCES

Au, Loong-Yu. 2005. "The Post MFA Era and the Rise of China." Working paper. http:// www.asienhaus.de/public/archiv/post-mfa-era-china.pdf.

Barboza, David. 2004. "In Roaring China, Sweaters Are West of Sock City." *New York Times,* December 24.

———. 2006. "Labor Shortage in China May Lead to Trade Shift." *New York Times,* April 3.

Brandt, Loren, and Thomas G. Rawski. 2005. "Chinese Industry After 25 Years of Reform." In *China's Economy: Retrospect and Prospect,* edited by Loren Brandt, Thomas G. Rawski, and Gang Lin, 20–25. Asia Program Special Report No. 129. Washington, D.C.: Woodrow Wilson International Institute for Scholars.

Branstetter, Lee, and Nicholas Lardy. 2005. "China's Embrace of Globalization." In *China's Economy: Retrospect and Prospect,* edited by Loren Brandt, Thomas G. Rawski, and Gang Lin, 6–12. Asia Program Special Report No. 129. Washington, D.C.: Woodrow Wilson International Institute for Scholars.

Carrillo, Jorge, and Antonio Hualde. 1998. "Third Generation *Maquiladoras?* The Delphi-General Motors Case." *Journal of Borderland Studies* 13 (1): 79–97.

Carrillo, Jorge, and Arturo Lara. 2005. "Mexican Maquiladoras: New Capabilities of Coordination and the Emergence of a New Generation of Companies." *Innovation: Management, Policy, and Practice* 7 (2–3): 256–73.

Dussel Peters, Enrique. 2000. *Polarizing Mexico: The Impact of Liberalization Strategy.* Boulder, Colo.: Lynne Rienner.

Ernst and Young. 2007. "Cross-Border Transactions: Spotlight on China." http://www .imaa-institute.org/docs/m&a/ernst&young_02_cross-border%20transactions%20-%20spotlight%20on%20china%202006.pdf.

Farrell, Diana, Antonio Puron, and Jaana K. Remes. 2005. "Beyond Cheap Labor: Lessons for Developing Economies." *McKinsey Quarterly,* no. 1:99–109.

Fourcade-Gourinchas, Marion, and Sarah L. Babb. 2002. "The Rebirth of the Liberal Creed: Paths to Neoliberalism in Four Countries." *American Journal of Sociology* 108 (3): 533–79.

Freeman, Richard B. 2005. "Does Globalization of the Scientific/Engineering Workforce Threaten U.S. Economic Leadership?" National Bureau of Economic Research (NBER) Working Paper No. 11457. http://www.nber.org/papers/w11457.

Gallagher, Kevin P., and Daniel Chudnovsky, eds. 2009. *Rethinking Foreign Investment for Sustainable Development: Lessons from Latin America.* New York: Anthem Press.

Gallagher, Kevin P., Juan Carlos Moreno-Brid, and Roberto Porzecanski. 2008. "The Dynamism of Mexican Exports: Lost in (Chinese) Translation?" *World Development* 36 (8): 1365–80.

Gallagher, Kevin P., and Timothy Wise. 2008. "Nafta's Unhappy Anniversary." *Guardian,* January 1.

Gao, Bai. 2006. "Neoliberal Versus Classical: Chinese and Japanese Developmentalisms in Comparison." *Social Science Research (She hui ke xue yan jiu)* 1 (January): 116–41.

Gereffi, Gary. 1994. "Rethinking Development Theory: Insights from East Asia and Latin America." In *Comparative National Development: Society and Economy in the New Global Order,* edited by A. Douglas Kincaid and Alejandro Portes, 26–56. Chapel Hill: University of North Carolina Press.

———. 1996. "Commodity Chains and Regional Divisions of Labor in East Asia." *Journal of Asian Business* 12 (1): 75–112.

———. 2005. "The Global Economy: Organization, Governance, and Development." In *The Handbook of Economic Sociology,* edited by Neil J. Smelser and Richard Swedberg, 160–82. 2nd ed. Princeton: Princeton University Press and Russell Sage Foundation.

———. 2009. "Development Models and Industrial Upgrading in China and Mexico." *European Sociological Review* 25 (1): 37–51.

Gereffi, Gary, John Humphrey, and Timothy Sturgeon. 2005. "The Governance of Global Value Chains." *Review of International Political Economy* 12 (1): 78–104.

Gereffi, Gary, and Donald L. Wyman, eds. 1990. *Manufacturing Miracles: Paths of Industrialization in Latin America and East Asia*. Princeton: Princeton University Press.

Goodman, Peter S. 2005. "China Ventures Southward: In Search of Cheaper Labor, Firms Invest in Vietnam." *Washington Post*, December 6.

Gore, Charles. 2000. "The Rise and Fall of the Washington Consensus as a Paradigm for Developing Countries." *World Development* 28 (5): 789–804.

Harney, Alexandra. 2008. *The China Price: The True Cost of Chinese Competitive Advantage*. New York: Penguin.

———. 2009. Testimony before the U.S.-China Economic and Security Review Commission. Hearing on *China's Role in the Origins and Response to the Global Recession*. 111th Cong., 1st sess., February 17.

Huang, Yasheng, and Tarun Khanna. 2003. "Can India Overtake China?" *Foreign Policy*, July–August.

Huber, Evelyne, and Fred Solt. 2004. "Success and Failures of Neoliberalism." *Latin American Research Review* 39 (3): 150–64.

Inter-American Development Bank (IADB). 2005. *The Emergence of China: Opportunities and Challenges for Latin America and the Caribbean Basin*. Washington, D.C.: IADB.

———. 2006. *The Politics of Policies: Social and Economic Progress in Latin America, 2006 Report*. Washington, D.C.: IADB.

Kusterbeck, Staci. 2005. "China Appeals to U.S. Buyers with 'Supply Chain Cities.'" *Apparel Magazine*, August 1.

Lall, Sanjaya. 2000. "The Technological Structure and Performance of Developing Country Manufactured Exports, 1985–98." *Oxford Development Studies* 28 (3): 337–69.

Lall, Sanjaya, and Manuel Albaladejo. 2004. "China's Competitive Performance: A Threat to East Asian Manufactured Exports?" *World Development* 32 (9): 1441–66.

Lüthje, Boy. 2004. "Global Production Networks and Industrial Upgrading in China: The Case of Electronics Contract Manufacturing." East-West Center Working Paper No. 74. http://www.eastwestcenter.org/stored/pdfs/ECONwp074.pdf.

Mesquita Moreira, Mauricio. 2007. "Fear of China: Is There a Future for Manufacturing in Latin America?" *World Development* 35 (3): 355–76.

Ocampo, José Antonio. 2009. Foreword to *Rethinking Foreign Investment for Sustainable Development: Lessons from Latin America*, edited by Kevin P. Gallagher and Daniel Chudnovsky, xiii–xx. New York: Anthem Press.

Palley, Thomas I. 2006. "External Contradictions of the Chinese Development Model: Export-Led Growth and the Dangers of Global Economic Contraction." *Journal of Contemporary China* 15 (46): 69–88.

Portes, Alejandro. 1997. "Neoliberalism and the Sociology of Development: Emerging Trends and Unanticipated Facts." *Population and Development Review* 23 (2): 229–59.

Roach, Stephen S. 2009. "A Wake-Up Call for the US and China: Stress Testing a Symbiotic Relationship." Testimony before the U.S.-China Economic and Security Review Commission. Hearing on *China's Role in the Origins and Response to the Global Recession*. 111th Cong., 1st sess., February 17.

Rodrik, Dani. 2006. "What's So Special About China's Exports?" *China and World Economy* 14 (5): 1–19.

Sonobe, Tetsushi, Dinghuan Hu, and Keijiro Otsuka. 2002. "Process of Cluster Formation in China: A Case Study of a Garment Town." *Journal of Development Studies* 39 (1): 118–39.

Sturgeon, Timothy, and Ji-Ren Lee. 2005. "Industry Co-evolution: A Comparison of Taiwan and North American Electronics Contract Manufacturers." In *Global Taiwan: Building Competitive Strengths in a New International Economy*, edited by Suzanne Berger and Richard K. Lester, 33–75. Armonk, N.Y.: M. E. Sharpe.

Thorp, Rosemary, and Pamela Lowden. 1996. "Latin America's Development Models: A Political Economy Perspective." *Oxford Development Studies* 24 (2): 133–44.

United Nations Conference on Trade and Development (UNCTAD). 2009. *World Investment Report 2009: Transnational Corporations, Agricultural Production, and Development.* Geneva: UNCTAD.

———. 2008. *World Investment Report 2008: Transnational Corporations, and the Infrastructure Challenge.* Geneva: UNCTAD.

U.S. Census Bureau. 2009. "Foreign Trade Statistics: Trade in Goods (Imports, Exports, and Trade Balance) with China." http://www.census.gov/foreign-trade/balance/c5700.html.

Wang, Jici, Huasheng Zhu, and Xin Tong. 2005. "Industrial Districts in a Transitional Economy: The Case of Datang Sock and Stocking Industry in Zhejiang, China." In *Proximity, Distance, and Diversity: Issues on Economic Interaction and Local Development,* edited by Arnoud Lagendijk and Päivi Oinas, 47–69. Burlington, Vt.: Ashgate.

Wang, Mark Yaolin, and Xiaochen Meng. 2004. "Global-Local Initiatives in FDI: The Experience of Shenzhen, China." *Asia Pacific Viewpoint* 45 (2): 181–96.

Weyland, Kurt. 2004. "Assessing Latin American Neoliberalism: Introduction to a Debate." *Latin American Research Review* 39 (3): 143–49.

Zhang, Qing, and Bruce Felmingham. 2002. "The Role of FDI, Exports, and Spillover Effects in the Regional Development of China." *Journal of Development Studies* 38 (4): 157–78.

Zhang, Zhiming, Chester To, and Ning Cao. 2004. "How Do Industry Clusters Succeed? A Case Study in China's Textiles and Apparel Industries." *Journal of Textile and Apparel Technology and Management* 4 (2): 1–10.

4

RESTRUCTURING MEXICO, REALIGNING DEPENDENCY: HARNESSING MEXICAN LABOR POWER IN THE NAFTA ERA

James M. Cypher and Raúl Delgado Wise

In this chapter, we focus on the economic effects of the new structure of investment and production arising from the North American Free Trade Agreement (NAFTA)/neoliberal policy changes. A key component of this new national project has been not just direct investment leading to increased exports, as neoliberal analysts have suggested, but the export of labor. We present a new theoretical formulation of the Mexican economy under NAFTA: the cheap-labor export-led model. We maintain that, in one guise or another, Mexico's new role consists of exporting its cheap labor, not achieving new high value-added forms of production through enhanced specialization.

Our analysis is organized in seven sections. First, we briefly review the background of the NAFTA "framework," highlighting a series of events and processes that have not received their due in most interpretations of Mexico since 1982. Second, we locate the general framework of NAFTA in terms of both its portrayal by the Mexican government and its actual impact, as demonstrated by a less selective use of data. Third, we focus on the maquiladora sector and the disembodied export of cheap labor in its export products. Fourth, we analyze the "disguised maquila" sector and the ways in which it corresponds to and can be differentiated from the maquiladora industry, as commonly understood. Fifth, we briefly review some of the more salient characteristics of the Mexican emigration process as they directly pertain to the cheap-labor export-led model. Sixth, we explicate the processes pertaining to the model that have served to facilitate a restructuring of the U.S. production system. Seventh, we explain the impacts of all of the above processes on Mexico and the reasons why—despite these adverse effects—the Mexican political class and the business elite have been stalwart advocates of Mexico's neoliberal restructuring. Further, we show why the positive effects anticipated by neoclassical economic theorists have failed to appear. Finally, we offer our conclusions based on the research presented in the foregoing sections.

NAFTA in Historical Context

We refer to NAFTA as part of a series of agreements, informal accords, and economic policy changes largely initiated by the United States to confront the new structural forces arising from the present era of intense international economic rivalry among the Northern (first-tier) nations. It is well documented that U.S. policy makers at the state level and U.S.-based transnational corporations (TNCs), particularly through a powerful lobbying organization known as USA*NAFTA, were the propelling forces in the creation and consummation of NAFTA, while the important role realized by both state and capital within Mexico has received less attention (Cypher 1993; Faux 2006). As serious negotiations commenced in March 1990 and proceeded through the approval of NAFTA in late 1993, a little-noticed but momentous change occurred among the peak organizations of Mexican business, such as the Business Coordinating Council (CCE), that reversed decades of corporatist practices wherein the owners of Mexico's dominant conglomerates (known as the *grupos*) accepted the state's lead in matters of economic policy making (Puga 2004). State-led developmentalist strategies had driven Mexico forward from 1940 to 1982, a period sometimes referred to as "the Mexican miracle." During this period, as new business groups were nurtured by multiple forms of state assistance and as older business groups likewise flourished, the interests of large business groups increasingly diverged from many of the initiatives originating at the state level.

The rising tension among the large business groups reached a critical level during the presidency of Luis Echeverría (1970–76) due to his willingness to build on Mexico's revolutionary tradition of land reform, to lend some support to the corporatist labor unions, and to expand on Mexico's large state-owned industrial sector, and due to his boldness in asserting the dominant role of the state in determining the course of state-capital relations. His intransigence was a major factor in the creation of the CCE in 1975, which brought together the Mexican Bankers Association (ABM), the strongly neoliberal Mexican Business Owners Confederation (COPARMEX), the Council of Mexican Businessmen (CMHN), and several other groups to serve as a counterweight to the state-led economic process. By 1987, the CCE had managed to achieve a new status as the interlocutor of the interests of the Mexican business elite. Crucial components of the CCE's alternative program for

Mexico were the resolution of the crisis through the elimination of regulations over market forces, the end of sectoral development programs that had limited foreign ownership in industry, the opening of Mexico to foreign investment, and a strong emphasis on increasing Mexico's exports (Puga 2004, 59).

As Cristina Puga has demonstrated, during the course of the 1980s and early 1990s, a paradigmatic shift was consolidated in the relationship of the state and capital, wherein economic policy making became a historic act of coordination between the peak business associations and several government entities. Collaboration, coordination, consultation, and consent began to describe this relationship as the peak business associations became autonomous agents of economic policy making, sometimes playing a determinant role, sometimes a dual role, but no longer a subordinate role in the creation of policy (Puga 2004, 7, 9, 13). As Puga documents, the pivotal moment came when serious negotiations over NAFTA commenced and the peak business associations formulated the Mexican conditions for NAFTA through a new, comprehensive organization, the Business Coordinating Council for International Trade (COECE). The COECE brought together representatives from all of the most powerful business associations and some from midsized firms. Overwhelmingly dominated by Mexico's economic elite, COECE constituted the "fourth party" throughout the negotiations among the United States, Mexico, and Canada. Mexican state representatives were always accompanied by COECE's top negotiators, whose approval had to be attained at every step in the negotiations. COECE did not merely frame the negotiating parameters for the Mexican state; it also played an active role in selling NAFTA to the Mexican populace and to the U.S. Congress. COECE contested many of the initiatives advocated by the U.S. negotiators, but it was so anxious to obtain new injections of foreign direct investment (FDI) that it was willing to retreat on almost every major point, save the denationalization of oil, gas, and electricity production.

COECE was, in the context of NAFTA's creation, the embodiment and culmination of a tendency that had begun in 1982 when the Mexican conglomerates reacted strongly and adversely to the nationalization of the banking system. From that moment forward, the peak business associations were determined to maximize their independent political clout. Breaking the mold in the election of 1988, the associations clustered in support of the business-oriented neoliberal political party, the National Action Party (PAN), which had dwelt in obscurity theretofore. Winning a surprising 16.8 percent of the official vote, the PAN then began a long march to power; it eventually destroyed the Institutional Revolutionary Party's (PRI's) seventy-one-year monopoly in 2000, managing to again obtain victory in the disputed 2006 election.[1] In effect, by 1990 (as discussed below) the peak business organizations had achieved power as autonomous agents in setting the course of economic policy and then broadened that power to effective (but contested) control of other state functions with the election of 2000.

The NAFTA accord had a long legacy: significant, at least in retrospect, was the creation in 1986 of the Bilateral Commission on the Future of United States–Mexican Relations, an organization that brought together policy academics on both sides of the border and eventually produced an influential five-volume exploration of all aspects of integrating the two nations under the concept of "interdependence." In November 1987, the Reagan administration signed the Mexico-U.S. Framework Understanding on Bilateral Trade and Investment with Mexico's de la Madrid administration (1982–88), designed in part to recognize "the importance of promoting a more open and predictable environment for international trade and investment" (Glade and Luiselli 1989, 135). In 1986, Mexico had joined the General Agreement on Tariffs and Trade (GATT), a step long resisted by Mexican policy makers who believed that it would undermine the relative autonomy of developmental policy. At that point, Mexico's average tariffs were dropped to an insignificant average of 6.2 percent, and 96 percent of all imports entered free of any tariff (Cameron and Tomlin 2000, 59). The radical step of entering GATT was partly driven by the CCE, which spearheaded a sustained effort advocating a reorientation of economic policy toward an export-led posture (Puga 2004, 115). The council had great access to Miguel de la Madrid and his cabinet, as well as the means to orchestrate a public relations initiative in favor of the export-led strategy (Cypher 1990, 104, 106; Puga 2004, 77).

Prior to the debate over entry into the GATT in 1985, Mexico had experienced its most devastating economic crisis of the twentieth century in 1982. Heavily in debt to foreign creditors, Mexico, like most Latin American nations, received many visits from the "money doctors" at the International Monetary Fund (IMF), the World Bank, and the Interamerican Development Bank—all institutions that were overwhelmingly influenced by the United States. Multilateral loans, especially from the World Bank, flowed heavily and repeatedly into Mexico (which received far more support than any other country in the 1980s and early 1990s), always accompanied by conditions and advice. Mexico was told that it needed to drastically alter the structure of its economy; it had to shift from a state-led developmentalist stance, which had generated great advances for many, to what would eventually be known as a "neoliberal" export-led model, while opening up its economy to foreign capital, particularly from the United States (Cypher 1989, 1990).[2] Throughout de la Madrid's presidency, Mexico responded with a certain degree of truculence to the IMF/World Bank programs of "austerity" and structural adjustment, engaging, for example, in limited and often peripheral privatizations. President de la Madrid, as a creation of the developmentalist state, was unable to overcome the forces of economic entropy as Mexico stumbled in meeting payments on its massive foreign debt due to its weak export sector and to record-high interest rates that had resulted from the adoption of monetarist policies in the creditor nations, particularly the United States.

Yielding to these same pressures, his successor, President Carlos Salinas (1988–94), ushered in a group of young, largely U.S.-trained technocrats— who readily embraced the IMF/World Bank neoliberal economic perspective—to work the levers of state power (Babb 2001). Meanwhile, the Omnibus Trade and Competitiveness Act of 1988, one of the most sweeping pieces of trade legislation in U.S. history, was passed in April. This act included text relating to the Mexico-U.S. bilateral agreement of 1987, urging President Bush "to continue to pursue . . . an expansion of mutually beneficial trade and investment" (Glade and Luiselli 1989, 134). In November 1988, President Salinas traveled to the United States to meet with President Bush, who officially advanced the idea of a bilateral trade agreement for the first time, to which Salinas responded negatively (Cameron and Tomlin 2000). Nonetheless, in October 1989, Mexico and the United States signed a memorandum regarding trade and investment facilitation talks, which included an action plan that specified a period of negotiations from October 1989 through October 1991. The eventual consolidation of NAFTA, on the other hand, was not about trade, as its purpose was to build an investment/production bloc to rival those of Japan/Asia and the European Union (EU). On numerous occasions, the Mexican government made it perfectly clear that enhancing foreign and portfolio investment, not trade, was the motivator for Mexico in entering into what would become the NAFTA negotiations (Cameron and Tomlin 2000).

Regarding this focus on investment rather than trade, it is worth recalling that in the 1980s the long-standing view in development economics that FDI could fill crucial gaps (e.g., the savings gap, the foreign exchange gap) was further enhanced by new theoretical formulations. Known as the new growth theory, an impressive body of work suggested that the old approach, which had given FDI a pivotal role, had nonetheless placed insufficient emphasis on its potential catalytic impact. The new theory focused on what is termed "increasing returns," emphasizing that additional quantities of FDI could have rising qualitative effects in terms of learning, technological spin-offs, acquisition of technological capabilities, transference of entrepreneurial capacities, and so on. The new generation of largely U.S.-trained economists surrounding presidents de la Madrid and Salinas was very cognizant of these recent theoretical developments as well as the older formulations that made FDI a centerpiece in a development strategy under assumed conditions of a capital shortage (Babb 2001). Mexico, however, was not particularly deprived of potential investment funds. Rather, the problem was structural: the large, conglomerate-style business groups that dominated the Mexican economy had a great fondness for quick returns, which were often to be found in real estate speculation, stock market manipulations, and lucrative round-tripping of capital flight funds. The Mexican business elite (or the Mexican state) was rarely willing to finance long-term capital-intensive investments that required commitments to research and development spending and technological advances. Thus, it is important to note that in Mexico and the United States, two autonomous parallel processes were merging in the late 1980s: Mexico's devastating economic slowdown of the 1980s—thought to be overcome by greater levels of investment—neatly coincided with an emerging U.S. strategy to displace production plants and equipment to low-cost sites in order to confront both surging Japanese competition and the organized U.S. labor force.

It is certainly the case that some sections of the business elite sought the NAFTA accord for trade-oriented reasons—because it would give them open access to the largest market in the world. But the Mexican conglomerates' interest in trade has turned out to be a relatively minor consideration for two reasons: First, with the exception of some resource-dependent Mexican firms, such as Cemex (cement), and firms that could exploit the Hispanic market in the United States, Mexican firms were not sufficiently competitive to play a significant role in expanding Mexico's exports to the United States. Second, while Mexico's exports grew at an extremely fast rate from 1993 onward, this was a result of the U.S. project to invest heavily in Mexico in order to export manufacturing products produced with cheap Mexican labor as a major input.

Returning to our historical narrative, it was just prior to the aforementioned October 1989 meeting that Mexico agreed to several provisions that would strengthen the incentives for U.S. investments in Mexico, including dropping a 40 percent tax on the export of profits or the sale of capital assets (Cameron and Tomlin 2000, 60). Two new rulings greatly limiting the reach of Mexico's foreign investment law were passed in 1989, with Mexico's Secretariat of Trade and Industrial Promotion (SECOFI) summing up the new stance as follows: "The development and modernization of the national productive base requires ever increasing investments that cannot likely be financed from traditional sources, for which reason foreign investment should serve to compliment national risk capital to the degree necessary to reactivate the nation's economy" (SECOFI 1990, 41). Despite President Salinas's earlier opposition to a bilateral free trade pact, by 1990 he felt that Mexico's strongest option for attracting foreign investment was through what would become known as NAFTA. His grand project (pursued throughout 1989) to seek investment from Asia and particularly the EU had come to naught. In March 1990, President Salinas publicly declared his intention to negotiate NAFTA in front of the Mexican Business Council for International Affairs (CEMAI), one of several peak business associations that constituted the CCE (Puga 2004, 49, 118). At that moment, Cristine Puga notes, there was "consolidation of a clear alliance between the large economic *grupos*, exporting firms, the business associations and the government" (2004, 122). By September 1990, the Mexican government had opened a negotiating office to handle the bargaining over NAFTA, forming an advisory committee of thirty key individuals wherein the business associations and grupos were overrepresented. The government simultaneously launched COECE, an event that marked, for the first time, the active participation of the peak business associations in the formation of public policy, and the momentous repositioning of the state as a secondary participant. COECE's efforts to improve the bargaining position of Mexican business by forming a united front were unprecedented. Massive sectoral consultations were organized and effectively combined with an organized effort to convey the perspective of Mexican business interests to the negotiating office. Thus, the COECE acted not as a supplicant but rather as the bearer of the dominant business consensus on which the NAFTA bargaining was based, and as the final arbiter of the Mexican state's position in the negotiations.

After many delays and complex turns, final approval of NAFTA came in November 1993; it was followed immediately by the passage of Mexico's new foreign investment law in December. This law eliminated all restrictions governing foreign investment in the manufacturing sector, except in basic petrochemicals. In essence, 91 percent of the economy was now totally open to foreign ownership, with arguably the most important changes being made to the automobile sector. Throughout the negotiations, COECE had sought to maintain Mexico's developmentalist policies with regard to autos, which mandated modest levels of domestic content and prohibited transnational firms from importing more components (in value terms) than they exported. This clashed with the position of the U.S. negotiators, who nevertheless successfully opened up Mexico to the U.S. auto sector without restriction. As can be noted from fig. 4.1, FDI has jumped dramatically since 1993. In the five years preceding the NAFTA accord, FDI ranged between $3.5 and $5 billion, and then increased dramatically from $15 to $22 billion during the NAFTA era—a 400 percent increase before taking inflation into account. Fig. 4.1 highlights an important distinction between FDI and new investment: the latter is one of three components that yield the total FDI, the others being reinvestment of profits and intrafirm financial transactions. These two are extremely weak analytical categories in terms of "investment," because they are essentially default distinctions not clearly linked to the purchase of already existing plant and equipment, or new greenfield plant and equipment.[3] It is assumed that if profits are retained, or if a transnational firm receives a loan from its parent corporation, these funds will be invested in new plant and equipment (or the foreign takeover of already existing assets). In fact, these funds may be used for the purchase of stock or flow into financial markets via other mechanisms, rather than for the expansion of the economy's production base. Hence, we place greater emphasis on the lower line in fig. 4.1, which suggests that actual inflows of FDI could be as low as 60 percent of the total FDI, as reported by the Mexican government. This line represents the actual trend of new investment in the NAFTA period, discounting the anomalous bank purchases of the 2001–2 period. It suggests that FDI inflows rose substantially over the pre-NAFTA trend, roughly doubling, but remained significantly below the levels that are generally cited.

Nevertheless, as considerable as these increases may seem, such flows have fallen well short of the goal sought by COECE, the CCE, and other peak business associations, since in their view the underlying dominant purpose of NAFTA was to attract sufficient FDI to dynamize the Mexican economy. A high-growth economy generally requires investment in the range of 25 percent of GNP; such a rate was last achieved in 1980, when 24.76 percent of GDP was devoted to capital formation (Nacional Financiera 1995, 97, 112). Overall, total gross fixed capital formation (investment) as a share of the GNP stood at 19.41 percent in 1992 and at 19.19 percent in 2003, according to official data (Banco de México 2006). NAFTA failed to raise the overall investment rate even though FDI rose, because in accordance with the neoliberal

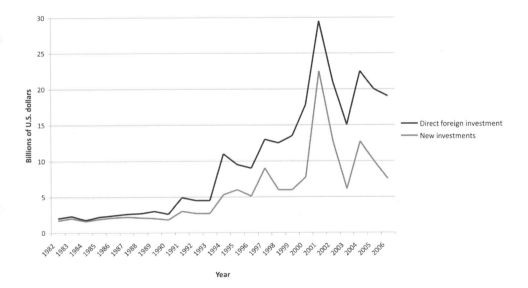

Fig. 4.1   Direct foreign investment in Mexico, 1982–2006

SOURCE: Data from Secretaría de Economía (2007).

strategy, government investment was reduced, and because while foreign investors entered Mexico, Mexican investors left. As Jorge Basave has documented, the grupos have tended to place considerable emphasis on the export
of capital, particularly to the United States and Latin America (2006, 120).
For example, in 2005, the grupos made FDI expenditures of $6.7 billion,
thereby dropping *net* FDI to roughly $12.9 billion (a 34 percent reduction)
from the $19.6 billion level shown in fig. 4.1. Excluding two spectacularly
large bank acquisitions, FDI as a share of GDP has fallen from 3.5 percent in
1994 to less than 2 percent in 2004—a calculation that fails to take the important distinction between gross and net FDI into account (Economist Intelligence Unit 2006, 31).

Thus, Mexico achieved no net gain in total investment over the NAFTA
period even as FDI rose in nominal terms. The level of investment in the
NAFTA era has been anemic—showing a shortfall of roughly 6 percent of
GDP below the level achieved in 1980, for example. Thus, while on a national
level the NAFTA/neoliberal strategy of export-led production, which President Zedillo once termed a new "national project," failed to lift investment
levels, the same policy changes *did* create vast new opportunities to restructure Mexico and realign relationships of dependency with regard to the
United States. Between January 1, 1994, and July 1, 2006, U.S. corporations
attained an accumulated level of investment of $114 billion, steadily account-
ing for one-half to three-quarters of all of the FDI that Mexico acquired in
those years (Secretaría de Economía 2006). President Zedillo was correct in
describing the new policies as a national project, but not for Mexico.

The Cheap-Labor Export-Led Model

The cheap-labor export-led model stands in stark contrast to the vision projected by those who gave shape to NAFTA. Advocates portrayed NAFTA as a
"win-win" proposition for both Mexico and the United States, as well as an
avenue for reducing asymmetries among Mexico, the United States, and Canada. Further, NAFTA was presented as an antidote to emigration. In spite of
the prevailing presumption that the NAFTA model is merely a trade-enhanc-
ing process, we maintain that its underlying objective—its inner rationality—is the export of cheap, largely poorly trained labor through three
interrelated mechanisms: (1) the maquila industry, (2) the disguised maquila
sector, and (3) the emigration of Mexican labor to the United States. The first
two processes constitute the disembodied export of cheap labor, as labor is
represented in the exported products. Emigration, on the other hand, is the
direct (embodied) export of labor. But in all three instances Mexico is not
really exporting goods, because the only Mexican-made value/input in this
complex transnational process is cheap labor. These themes are explored

throughout the rest of this chapter. Our analytical perspective contrasts with Gary Gereffi's considerations of Mexico's export platform under NAFTA, as presented in chapter 3. Although he introduces the concepts of supply chain cities as vertically integrated firm factories and cluster cities in his analysis of China's export-led industrialization model, which diverges from Mexico's manufacturing export strategy, he does not differentiate between the underlying nature of the goods exported by both countries.

We believe that the net result of the cheap-labor export-led model is an economy that lacks continuity, autonomy, and dynamism. It is one in which the productive apparatus has been dismantled and reassembled to fit the structural requirements of the U.S. economy, leaving Mexico only in control of certain low value-added resource-based activities and a range of other rentier pursuits in tourism, finance, and real estate. Instead of advancing its productive apparatus, Mexico is falling further behind because, in essence, the cheap-labor export-led model is structurally designed to transfer Mexico's economic surplus away from its potential positive usage. The process of subordinated integration fails to advance the productive apparatus of the economy through investments in expanded research, development, and technological applications, and through public sector infrastructural investments designed to rapidly improve Mexico's quality of education, public health, and autonomous industrial base. Symbiotically, the Mexican elite (in its economic and political dimensions) coexists with and facilitates the structural dimensions of the restructuring process as delimited by U.S. economic interests. In this process, certain benefits befall the elite, and they carefully maintain their option to engage in devastating capital flight—or deploy the threat of capital flight—to preserve these benefits.

The Apologetic Vision of NAFTA

In Mexico and throughout the world, there is a perception—carefully nurtured by the Mexican government—that Mexico's economic restructuring, in centering the economy on the growth of foreign transactions in accordance with the NAFTA accord, has yielded tremendous results. Authorities frequently cite the following data: first, between 1991 and 2000, exports grew at an annual average rate of 16.3 percent, forming the leading sector of the economy; second, maquiladora exports were the most dynamic of all, growing at an annual average rate of 19.6 percent; third, manufacturing exports rose from less than 25 percent of total exports in 1982 to over 90 percent in the late 1990s; and finally, Mexico has become Latin America's top exporter and has risen to seventh place in the list of trading powers in terms of foreign trade (exports plus imports) (Leon González and Dussel Peters 2001, 653).

Overall, in this new model, the export/GDP ratio rose from less than 10 percent in 1988 to over 25 percent in the late 1990s, with over 90 percent of exports flowing into the United States.

We find, however, that NAFTA has also exhibited detrimental effects. In Mexico, it has been a losing proposition for workers, small and medium-sized businesses, and particularly peasants. In the United States, the impact of NAFTA has been negative for the working class and portions of the middle class, and for some sectors of business (Cypher 2001; Delgado Wise 2006). NAFTA has certainly benefited a small set of interests on both sides of the border, specifically numerous U.S.-based transnational corporations (TNCs) and Mexico's grupos. The sweeping changes in policy have correlated with massive waves of emigration, and this injection of cheap labor has served to indirectly lower the reproduction costs (and hence wages) of U.S. production workers. These results should only be surprising to neoliberal policy makers, and they are entirely consistent with the fact that, for separate reasons, both the Mexican conglomerates and certain sections of the largest U.S. manufacturing TNCs converged on the idea of the subordinated integration of the two distinct national production systems in the late 1980s.

Indeed, the widely disseminated vision portraying Mexico's restructuring as a resounding success stands in sharp contrast to the explosive growth of emigration. Neoliberal restructuring was conceived as the very antidote to emigration, with proponents asserting that the workings of the free trade arrangement would lead Mexico to specialize in labor-intensive activities that would absorb the idle and underutilized labor force. Instead, few jobs in the formal sector, and even fewer decent jobs of a nonprecarious nature, have been created, forcing as many as 89 percent of annual new workers into a scenario wherein the options consist of entering the informal sector as a house servant, a street vendor, or something similar, or emigrating to the United States. While it is generally conceded that Mexico needs to create 1.2 million net new jobs per year to keep the unemployment rate constant and accommodate the youth who are entering the workforce, in President Vicente Fox's *sexenio* (2000–2006) only 40,000 permanent jobs were created per year. This resulted in an annual "jobs deficit" of over 1.1 million, forcing the 6.5 million new entrants who were unable to find permanent jobs into temporary formal jobs (640,000 such jobs were created in six years), the informal sector, or emigration (Cadena 2006a, 21). Of this total, nearly 3 million emigrated. Indeed, emigration has become such a powerful current that 31 percent of the municipalities in Mexico are now suffering from depopulation. In the following analysis, we locate the issue of emigration at the center of our interpretation of the complex economic processes unleashed by the neoliberal restructuring program.

During President Fox's sexenio, the GDP grew at an estimated annual real rate of 2.5 percent. Over the course of the three sexenios during which Mexico embraced the free trade policies that culminated in NAFTA—from 1988 to 2006—the average annual real rate of GDP growth was 3.16 percent, roughly one-half of that achieved in the import substitution era, from 1940 to 1982 (Gutiérrez 2006, 3; Cypher 1990). Manufacturing growth for the 2000–2006 period was roughly 0.6 percent per year, with employment in this sector falling 15.3 percent (Dussel Peters 2006a, 74). In spite of its image as Latin America's most successful case of transformation toward an export-led economy based in manufacturing, the constraints imposed on the weak internal market—due to exploding importation of manufactured products and to low, and falling, wages—have been such that Mexico is actually deindustrializing. The average level of manufacturing expressed as a percent of the GDP in the sexenio of President Ernesto Zedillo (1994–2000) was 19.77, whereas under Fox this coefficient fell to 17.1 percent in 2005 (Becerril 2006b, 18; Dussel Peters 2006a, 69). According to the World Economic Forum's method of calculating competitiveness for 104 nations, Mexico's manufacturing sector fell from thirty-first place in 2000 to fifty-ninth place by 2005 (Becerril 2006b, 18). Most commentators attribute this spectacular fall to Mexico's determined opposition to investments in research and development, and to the virtual absence of anything that could be termed a systemic research and development policy.[4] Meanwhile, throughout Fox's sexenio (and before), overall manufacturing exports proved insufficient to pay for total imports—Mexico encountered a trade deficit of $7 billion for 2005. Thus, even while Mexico's economy enjoyed modest expansion from 2003 to 2006, the manufacturing sector remained stagnant, and its failure to cover the cost of overall imports means that in the highly touted area of the foreign sector, export manufacturing performance has served to reduce Mexico's standard of living and GDP.

Consider, for example, the case of wages for production workers in the manufacturing sector. In relation to real wages received in December 2000, mid-2005 wages were on average 24 percent lower (Bendensky 2005, 25). But real average wages overall in 2000 were only 72.5 percent of their level in 1982 (Unger 2002, 3). If the maquila sector (or more broadly the export sector) had the effect that its proponents pretend, one should anticipate that real wages would correlate positively with the rate of export growth in the 1982–2005 period. Yet the correlation is negative, and it has lasted long enough to negate the perception that it is somehow an anomaly. Instead, the negative correlation is, in fact, the positive expression of the cheap-labor export-led model's underlying premise: Mexico's static comparative advantage rests in the exportation of labor, embodied in the products of the maquilas or transnational firms in the disguised maquila sector (which create and export products by using inputs from the maquilas or directly importing untaxed inputs into their production systems), or in emigration. Thus, the model cannot, and does not, offer development in the most basic sense to its broader population, because all of the benefits of economic growth are being exported. This occurs through repatriation of profits, transfer prices, sumptuous salaries and benefits paid to high-level transnational firm employees, payment of interest on foreign debts, ample profits, and rents and interest payments received by Mexico's technocracy, its political class, and the owners of the giant Mexican conglomerates.

Export of Labor in the Maquiladora Sector

The maquila sector constitutes the starting point in our examination because it has, by definition, been associated with manufacturing exports and in many formulations has been linked to the concept of cheap, unprotected, and essentially nonunionized labor (Cypher 2004). Over 1,200,000 workers are employed in the three thousand maquiladora firms clustered primarily along the U.S.-Mexican border, which generated 55 percent of Mexico's manufactured exports in 2004 (Banco Nacional de Comercio Exterior 2005). Essentially, the maquila industry imports its inputs (such as components, parts, design, and engineering) from the United States and combines these with cheap production labor, with daily pay ranging from $4 to $10. The products are then assembled and re-exported, primarily to the United States.

The maquila sector's role in the national economy reached its upper limit in 2002, and it has since failed to be a leading sector (Banco Nacional de Comercio Exterior 2006). In spite of the overall growth in maquila employment in the NAFTA era (until 2000) and the rise in the total value of Mexico's maquila exports, Mexico retains a decreasing relative share of the economic benefits of these activities, even as the costs in terms of aggregate physical effort rise; the ratio dropped from 18.2 percent in 1988 to only 8.2 percent in 2003, a decline of 55 percent (Capdevielle 2005, 571).

If Mexico had a viable developmental strategy, it could either extract a larger share of the benefits of the maquila industry or engage in a national process of upgrading, which would eventually lead to a viable national development project based in other forms of manufacturing activities. The level of national integration into the maquila sector is essentially static, as indicated by the coefficient of integration (national inputs/gross production). Roughly 60 percent of the national inputs in 2003, for example, derived from the service sector, including cleaning, accounting, packaging, shipping, and similar activities. Only 3 percent of total production value comes from national component/manufacturing inputs (Capdevielle 2005, 570).

Despite the quantitative data, which have repeatedly demonstrated the futility and negative aspects of the maquila industry, a significant cadre of Mexican researchers continues to furnish qualitative studies of so-called second- and third-generation maquila firms that, in their view, have the potential to produce the many externalities posited by the new growth theory (Cypher 2004; Dutrénit and Vera-Cruz 2005; Lara, Arellano, and García 2005; Villavicencio and Casalet 2005). However, none of these studies has presented convincing quantitative data suggesting that, in the aggregate, the maquila sector is anything more than a cheap-labor assembly operation with virtually no backward or forward linkages to Mexico's production system. Nor, in spite of many efforts to do so, have these studies ever established a significant dynamic trend sufficiently large to change the fundamental nature (that is, cheap, dispensable labor) of the maquila industry.

Once thought to be a serious generator of employment, as well as a source of skill upgrading, the maquila sector has ceased to create new jobs. When the maquila sector was growing (in employment terms) between 1994 and 2000, the jobs created paid 52 percent less than nonmaquila manufacturing, while living costs for the maquila workers clustered along the U.S.-Mexican border were considerably higher than in interior states (Cypher 2004, 362). In short, and in spite of the rosy predictions of an indefatigable cadre of Mexican researchers, the maquila project was never a national development strategy, and it is even less so today. Above all, the maquila industry does not represent the exportation of Mexican-manufactured products; rather, it represents merely the export of Mexican labor power, as embodied in the final assembled and exported products.

Disguised Maquiladora Labor in the Export Process

It is common to find a twofold division of Mexico's manufacturing sector, which normally accounts for roughly 85 percent of all exports, into maquila manufacturing and nonmaquila manufacturing. Within the nonmaquila manufacturing sector, 38 percent of all export output in recent years has been undertaken via temporary import incentive programs, such as Pitex and Altex, that largely grant participating firms the same subsidies and fiscal exemptions as those enjoyed by designated maquila plants (Capdevielle 2005, 564–65; Dussel Peters 2006a, 83–85). Thus, a significant and rapidly growing volume of production is handled by maquila firms or other supplier firms that are exempt from certain taxes if they produce inputs for the Pitex or Altex firms. In 2000, according to the Secretariat of the Economy, 3,600 firms produced inputs that were exempt from the value-added tax since they were provided to either the maquilas or the disguised maquila firms. These disguised maquilas are fundamentally large TNCs located throughout the interior of Mexico. They use maquila-made parts and components, or parts and components from the designated Mexican supplier web, to generate finished manufactured products—often of a sophisticated nature, such as autos—which are then exported, primarily to the U.S. market. In another, larger process, parts and components are temporarily imported and then re-exported after they have been processed or assembled in the disguised maquila plants. A third process in this triangulation structure entails exporting maquila products and then re-importing those products as inputs into the disguised maquila sector, where they are then processed and again exported.

In 2006, a total of 3,339 firms were involved in the disguised maquila sector, excluding the supplier base—160 more than were operating in the well-known maquila sector. Together, the maquila and disguised maquila firms accounted for 70 percent of all exports in 2005, as well as an average of 78 percent of all exports during the entire NAFTA period (Becerril 2006a, 18; Dussel Peters 2006a, 75).[5] Furthermore, the movement of inputs from the maquila firms to the larger TNCs frequently constitutes intrafirm transactions, since the TNCs control many maquila supplier firms through joint ventures or direct ownership. U.S. intrafirm transactions for imports in the auto and electronics sectors—Mexico's two largest export sectors—stood at 75.9 percent and 67.5 percent, respectively, in 2002 (Durán Lima and Ventura-Dias 2003, 59).

These disguised maquilization activities employ at minimum five hundred thousand workers, representing approximately 37 percent of all nonmaquila manufacturing workers, who are normally assumed to be working in the national manufacturing sector (Capdevielle 2005, 568). Workers employed in the indirect-labor-export disguised maquila sector have somewhat higher skill levels, and there is some likelihood that their labor rights will be better represented via their unions. Thus, these workers are generally paid at least 50 percent more than maquila workers, because their productivity levels are much higher, they have union representation thanks to the legacy of the import-substituting industrialization (ISI) era, and the major TNCs generally follow a policy of industrial relations wherein payment of subsistence wages is not a goal (Cypher 2004, 363). Nonetheless, workers are paid meager wages given the fact that their productivity often approximates levels found in the (Northern) industrial nations; frequently, the South-North (Mexico–United States) wage differential is in the range of 1:7 in the disguised maquila sector, and nearly double that ratio in the maquila sector. The International Labour Organization (ILO) found that the wage ratio for Mexican manufacturing workers overall in relation to U.S. manufacturing sector workers was 1:11 in 2003 (Howard 2005, 2). Throughout the NAFTA period, wages in the disguised maquila sector have fallen by more than 12 percent, while in the maquila sector, despite some rising productivity, they have increased by only 3 percent or less. Three percent of the lowest-paid maquila workers' daily wage was twelve U.S. cents in 2004 (Cypher 2004, 363).

In the disguised maquila sector, nationally produced inputs/components have fallen from 32 percent in 1993 to 22.6 percent in 2004 (Cadena 2005, 13). In essence, export firms outside of the maquila sector are progressively deindustrializing, leaving only the value of Mexican labor as the determining component of value added, as 77 percent of the inputs into the production process are imported. Once again, we emphasize that in the final analysis for Mexico, the net result in the disguised maquila sector is almost completely reducible to the disembodied export of the Mexican labor force, as represented in the exported products. Furthermore, when Mexican-made inputs are diminished, the impact is not limited to the destruction of supplier firms and jobs, but also entails the destruction of complex socioeconomic relationships and skills that have accumulated over decades. As the giant firms emphasize greater subcontracting, they demand high levels of output with higher quality and performance standards, and production processes that require greater levels of capital intensity, thereby eliminating thousands of Mexican firms while often turning to other TNCs as suppliers. One study estimates that of the 600–800 first-tier suppliers and the 10,000 second-tier suppliers in the auto sector in 2001, only 25–100 first-tier suppliers and 2,000–4,000 second-tier suppliers would remain in 2010 (Mortimore and Barron 2005, 10). Mortimore and Barron (2005) note that in this process, it is increasingly U.S. first-tier suppliers—subsidiaries of U.S. TNCs—that are dominating the autoparts industry. Enhancing outsourcing has collateral benefits in that the U.S. transnational firms can sidestep or fragment unions by shifting significant portions of input production to captive suppliers; this has been well-documented at the giant Volkswagen plant in Puebla, which primarily exports finished autos to the United States (Juárez and Babson 1999).[6]

As these changes continue, the significance of the informal sector has increased. In 2000, based on government data, 24.9 percent of the labor force was relegated to the informal sector; by mid-2005, the percentage had risen to 28.3 percent, indicating that an additional 2.21 million workers had fallen into this category (Fernández-Vega 2005, 28). Those underemployed, unemployed, and working in informal sector activities account for nearly 40 percent of all Mexicans of working age who would normally be counted as part of the labor force in an industrial nation. If anything, these estimates seem to be extremely conservative, given that the Organisation for Economic Co-operation and Development (OECD) maintains that 40 percent of the workforce subsists in the informal sector (Cadena 2006b, 12).

Direct Exportation of the Mexican Labor Force

Given that inputs into the maquila and disguised maquila sectors (aside from labor) are primarily imported or limited to small increases in the value added in the service sector, employment multiplier effects via forward and backward linkages have been minimal. Instead, the institutional policies that undergird the export-led model—neoliberal market fundamentalism, a tax regime that favors the temporary importation of inputs, and subsidies of various types—all tend to narrow the market demands for Mexican labor. This combination of policies has given rise to a near-stagnant economy when viewed from the perspective of the growth rate of per capita income. Between 1980 and 2003, per capita income increased by an average of only 0.5 percent per year, while the average growth rate was an unimpressive 1.4 percent per year between 1988 and 2005—far below the nearly 3 percent rate achieved from 1940 to 1980 under a policy of state-led development (Cypher 1990; Dussel Peters 2006b, 77). Further exacerbating the situation, the growth in productivity in the nonmaquila manufacturing sector (which includes the disguised maquilas, the source of major dynamism in this area) has failed to lift wages (Instituto Nacional de Estadística y Geografía [INEGI] 2006a). In July 2006, manufacturing sector wages (including those paid to nonproduction workers) were 4.6 percent below their 1993 level, adjusted for inflation, while productivity had increased by more than 80 percent over that same period.

Meager wages, in turn, have undermined whatever possibility might exist for growing wage payments to serve as a catalytic factor in the growth of the internal market.[7] Further, viewing the matter from the supply side, the wide range of growing imports in intermediate inputs and capital goods that largely could have been produced within Mexico also undermines the possibility of a growing internal market derived from wages and other forms of income linked to domestic production. This vicious circle can be broken, but only when Mexico marshals the social forces to adopt a vigorous industrial policy similar to those employed by the developing nations of Asia.

All of the above serves to show that the export-led model employed in Mexico is characterized by its low capacity to create national employment, the counterpart of which is the blooming of the informal sector, which has accounted for roughly 50 percent of the growth in employment in recent years. As a direct result of the model's failure, between 1984 and 2004, the number of households registering at either the poverty level or the extreme poverty level rose from 12,970,000 to 15,915,000 (Cypher 2005; Dussel Peters 2006b, 87). Furthermore, this situation has been the nurturing ground for the explosive international emigration process that currently characterizes Mexico.

Under the export-led model, emigration from Mexico to the United States has grown exponentially over the past two decades. This growth was accentuated with the implementation of NAFTA, whereby Mexico became the main source of immigrants to the United States. In terms of sheer numbers, the emigration phenomenon is extremely impressive: in 2006, the population of Mexican origin in the United States was estimated at 27 million, including 11 million immigrants (both documented and undocumented) born in Mexico, as well as U.S. citizens of Mexican descent (Pew Hispanic Center 2008). This is the world's largest diaspora to have settled in a single country. According to UN estimates, between 2000 and 2005, Mexico was the country with the highest number of people annually establishing their place of residence in a foreign country (at 400,000 people, compared to 390,000 for China and 280,000 for India) (United Nations 2006). In line with this dynamic, the country experienced exponential growth in its receipts of remittances, making it the highest-receiving country in the world, together with India. In 2006, total remittances received by Mexico amounted to US$23.7 billion (Banco de México 2007). Indeed, as fig. 4.2 demonstrates, by 2003 remittances reached parity with oil exports and value added by the maquila firms. Practically the entire Mexican territory reports international migration; in 2000, 96.2 percent of the country's municipalities were associated with the phenomenon in some way. This territorial expansion fueled the emergence of new migratory circuits (historic, indigenous-traditional, emerging, etc.) with contrasting dynamics and sets of problems (Zúniga Herrera and Leite 2006). Moreover, the population of Mexican origin—although it remains concentrated in a handful of states—has expanded in recent years throughout most of the United States, including the eastern and north-central states, where some of the country's most dynamic industrial restructuring centers are located (Zúniga and Hernández-León 2005; Champlin and Hake 2006).

In terms of their schooling, 38.9 percent of people aged fifteen years and older who were born in Mexico and now reside in the United States have attained a level of education higher than a basic high school diploma. This

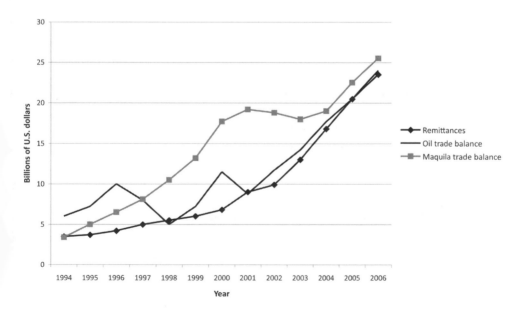

Fig. 4.2   The convergence process in Mexico

SOURCE: Data from Banco de México (2007) and INEGI (2007a).

figure rises to 52.4 percent if the full spectrum of the population of Mexican origin in the United States is taken into consideration. In contrast, the average figure within Mexico is 27.8 percent, which means that more qualified workers are leaving than remaining in the country. It should also be noted, however, that in comparison to other immigrant groups in the United States, the Mexican contingent has the lowest average levels of schooling. Yet one high-profile form of migration that does not fit the stereotypes involves Mexican residents in the United States who have university degrees or postgraduate qualifications. This figure totals slightly more than 385,000 individuals born in Mexico. Of these, 86,000 have postgraduate studies, and 10,000 have doctorates (U.S. Census Bureau 2005). This indicates that "brain drain" is beginning to emerge as a major problem.

All of these changes have been accompanied by a transformation within migration patterns. A predominantly circular migration pattern is evolving into one in which established immigrants prevail; it includes variants such as greater participation by women and entire families (Delgado Wise, Márquez, and Rodríguez 2004). This new pattern, which is associated with the abandonment of productive activities in Mexico, is leading to a growing and worrisome trend toward depopulation: between 2000 and 2005, 832 of the country's 2,435 municipalities (that is, one out of every three) reported a negative rate of growth (INEGI 2006a).

This phenomenon is related to a double movement: the shifting of jobs to Mexico via expansion of the maquila and disguised maquila sectors, and a significant displacement in the United States of native U.S. production workers for Mexican workers. These processes have led to the emergence of a new wave of xenophobia among broad elements of U.S. society, politicizing the immigration issue to a level not seen since the nineteenth century, if ever. Mexican workers have become a major political target, as well-financed and well-organized members of the extreme right have sought to magnify the tensions caused by high levels of immigration for their own political end. Meanwhile, the real forces behind this restructuring process and the prime beneficiaries of it, the corporate elites on both sides of the border, rarely receive serious attention in the public discourse.

The Cheap-Labor Export-Led Model and the U.S. Production System

NAFTA and the general neoliberal restructuring of the Mexican economy that began in the 1980s have had a profound impact on the U.S. production system, notably with the shifting of U.S. investment into Mexico. Without the neoliberal restructuring process in Mexico, in most instances these investments would have been made in the United States, creating jobs, raising the skill level, enhancing productivity, producing spread effects via forward and backward linkages, and stimulating aggregate demand through consumer spending of workers.

However, while increasing capital mobility undermined the rate of capital formation in the United States, a countertendency resulted from the increasing portion of the Mexican economic surplus that was displaced to the United States as profits rose from the Mexican operations of U.S. TNCs. This countertendency was reinforced as Mexican immigrants flowed into the United States and into the industrial sectors, lowering production costs and raising profits. Thus, the impact of capital shifting to Mexico fell on the U.S. labor force, particularly organized labor, while the U.S. restructuring process created two significant avenues to increased profits, with these benefits accruing to a small percentage of owners, managers, and stockholders in manufacturing and finance. At the same time, the U.S. economy receives a certain type of stimulus from Mexican immigration to the degree that new investments occur, derivative of substantially different consumption patterns arising from the 7 million Mexican immigrant workers and their dependents, driving the so-called migration industry (Guarnizo 2003).

Shifting capital to Mexico destroyed jobs in the United States, as did the sizable trade deficit that the United States developed with Mexico once the NAFTA agreement had been consummated. Bringing more of Mexico's economic surplus back to the United States stimulated the economy, and the influx of millions of Mexican immigrants helped push down labor's share of U.S. national income to the lowest levels recorded in the post–World War II era. The net effect was to create a new social structure of accumulation, a leaner and meaner social environment for all workers, and a more contented business elite in the United States, now better positioned to meet foreign competitors by locating production in either the United States or Mexico, as profit maximization strategies indicated.

These resulting macroeconomic relationships, however, were not determinant in the repositioning of U.S. capital in Mexico. Viewing the matter from the standpoint of the restructuring of the U.S. production system, a separate logic—driven by the desire to maximize profits and outperform the competition—prevailed. Under this logic, shifting capital to Mexico could enable U.S. firms to purchase labor processes at as low as 9 percent of the cost in the United States, while accepting that productivity per hour might not be as high as that in the United States.[8] At the microeconomic level of the firm—assuming the stability of final demand for products exported from Mexico to the United States—shifting capital to Mexico to achieve labor efficiencies was a logical step in many instances. In highly oligopolized industries, such as autos, the available research indicates that the cost-saving production processes adopted in Mexico were counted as profits (Cypher 2001). In less capital-intensive industries, such as apparel, where brand identity is strong, similar profit-enhancing results should be anticipated.

Shifting production to Mexico made credible the threat of further production shifts, which would weaken all U.S. labor and particularly organized labor. The stagnation in U.S. production workers' pay is broadly consistent with the increasing tendency of U.S. corporations to move their production operations to Mexico. Thus, in the process of restructuring the U.S. production system—a perceived necessity during the course of the 1980s—a complex, mutually reinforcing, triple movement began. First, significant elements of U.S. capital shifted to Mexico, thereby lowering costs of production, while capital seeking reinvestment in the United States often threatened to also move to Mexico, thereby strengthening its bargaining power over labor. Finally, growing numbers of workers were displaced by the production shifts to Mexico, reducing both the portion of the labor force in unions and the role of union labor in pushing up wages for almost all workers.

By 2003, 1.2 million Mexican immigrants were working in the U.S. manufacturing sector (U.S. Census Bureau 2003). From 1995 through October 2005, the U.S. labor force employed in manufacturing declined by 17 percent, from 17.1 million to 14.2 million (Norris 2005; U.S. Bureau of Labor Statistics 2005). In the manufacturing sector, great numbers of immigrants are to be found in basic wage-goods industries, such as meatpacking, where their low wages serve to cut production costs and, in turn, lower the reproduction costs of workers in general. Immigrants are also well represented in the production of goods that serve as inputs into the production process, such as steel and aluminum and heavy machinery and equipment, as well as in the production of consumer durables such as autos and home appliances.

The role of Mexican labor in U.S. manufacturing, however, is actually much higher than the above figures suggest. If we consider U.S. manufacturing to include not only that which is physically based in the United States but also that based in Mexico in either the maquila or the disguised maquila sector, we find 1.2 million Mexican manufacturing sector workers in the United States, in addition to an estimated 1.2 million in the maquila sector and 0.5 million in the disguised maquila sector as of August 2005, for a total of 2.9 million. Adding the Mexican-based workers into the base number of manufacturing workers (14.2 plus 1.7 million) generates a total of 15.9 million manufacturing workers in the amplified (or globally integrated) U.S.-Mexican production system, of whom an estimated 18 percent are derived from Mexico's cheap-labor export-led model.

Asymmetric Subordinated Integration Under NAFTA

The vast restructuring of the Mexican economy via the NAFTA process could not, and did not, occur without the consent and active participation of Mexico's political class and its industrial elite. The business elite supported the indiscriminate opening of the economy because they had always held a neo-liberal/anti-state view. The stagnation of the 1980s in Mexico had forced many of them to seek growing markets in the international economy, and the vast U.S. market was the closest and cheapest location for the export of goods. But in the 1980s, many of the grupos encountered legal difficulties as U.S. trade authorities accused and convicted them of dumping. In other instances, they faced nontariff trade barriers or other hurdles that the United States had adroitly placed in the way of would-be foreign competitors (Puga 2004). In their struggle to find ways to expand production in the 1980s, the largest conglomerates eventually became convinced that a new bilateral trade agreement (NAFTA) could circumvent the legal obstacles to access to the vast U.S. market. These conglomerates each specialized in the production of one or a few key potential exports, all with a common denominator—low value-added production that demanded low wages and did not result in the transfer of technology or skills. Cement, minerals, beverages, and undifferentiated intermediate goods, specifically industrial products such as steel and plastics, have been their low value-added specialties. Expanding the output of these products has benefited the grupos, but not Mexico. The learning and techno-logical advancements that were expected to accompany expansion have never occurred. Instead, the grupos modernized as they expanded their sales by importing new, cutting-edge machinery and equipment. If there was any learning or technological development, it occurred in Europe, the United States, and Japan, where the new technologies were created.

According to neoliberal/neoclassical economic theory, the spread effects of learning and technological know-how would penetrate to small and me-dium-sized suppliers as giant firms were compelled to share their knowledge, while forcing supplier firms to adopt high quality control standards, just-in-time delivery procedures, and other measures. Such spread effects never occurred in the Mexican production system, partly because Mexican produc-ers have a relatively low level of technological know-how and are not prone to diverting their profits into long-term research on advanced technological processes and products. However, it is primarily the secretive, vertically inte-grated nature of the conglomerates that has nullified the naïve scenarios envi-sioned by neoliberal/neoclassical economists. The grupos do not share their know-how with a large network of suppliers but rather tend to create their own tightly controlled suppliers. They also tend to import inputs of higher technology or buy inputs from other large national grupos. When they do resort to a supplier network, small and medium-sized suppliers are normally incorporated into the web of international production at the lowest possible level; they provide simple, labor-intensive products with low quality levels and production standards. No learning is transmitted, no modern forms of production are needed, and no spread effects occur (Pozas 2002, 226–27).

In a study of one major conglomerate's supplier relationships, María de los Ángeles Pozas found that 60 percent of the value of industrial inputs came from subsidiaries within the vast complex of the grupo itself, while 35 percent of the inputs were supplied either by other grupos or, in the case that inputs had a high degree of technological sophistication, by TNCs. A mere 5 percent of inputs—the least complex and the lowest value-added products— were supplied by small and medium-sized firms (Pozas 2002, 226). In a subsequent study, Pozas emphasized a new structure of dualism wherein foreign firms were increasingly delinked from the domestic grupos due to the decrease in strategic alliances and differing forms of production, implying that the possibility of technology transfers actually declined after the late 1990s. In this dual structure, "the transnationals occupy the high value-added niches, directing their production essentially to the external market while nearly maintaining a monopoly on innovations in the production sector, while the national firms do the opposite by occupying the low value-added niches, producing essentially for the internal market and hardly participating at all in technological developments. . . . The anticipated technological trans- fers into the production chains have not materialized" (Pozas 2006a, 13). Pozas's study showed that in 1992, 21 percent of the national firms were engaged in strategic alliances or joint ventures with transnational firms, while in 2002 the figure had fallen precipitously to only 4.6 percent (Pozas 2006, 84). Pozas attributes this massive shift to increasing patterns of vertical inte- gration within the structures of the TNCs, driven by the need for higher de- grees of complexity with regard to inputs and a greater demand for quality components—criterian that the Mexican firms have been unable or unwilling to meet, particularly in the gigantic auto parts sector (Pozas 2006).

According to Celso Garrido's research, despite the efforts of the CCE and COECE mentioned at the beginning of this chapter, one of the reasons why NAFTA failed to provide the escape from the economic doldrums of the 1980s that the grupos had envisioned is that the terrible crisis of 1994–95 resulted in the renationalization of the banks. Subsequently, the vast majority of banks (with one exception) were sold off to foreign financial interests, thereby depriving the grupos of their historical access to easy credit. This lack of financing has meant that the grupos are no longer as attractive to foreign capital as they may have been in the early 1990s. Certainly, the lack of finan- cial depth has slowed the hoped-for expansion into the U.S. market for most of the grupos; in one broad sample of forty grupos, the number of large firms with foreign sales above 10 percent of total sales fell from twenty-four to twenty-one between 1995 and 2002 (Garrido 2006, 51). Nineteen of these firms showed profit rates in 2002 below those achieved in 1995, once again demonstrating that the NAFTA era failed to produce the economic benefits anticipated by the peak business associations (Garrido 2006, 54). It should be noted that those firms with strong export sales in the NAFTA period achieved them (with rare exception) through their export of very low value-added products, such as beer, steel, corn, wheat, and minerals (Basave 2006, 127).

What are the outcomes of the cheap-labor export-led model for Mexico? This model gives rise to a process of disaccumulation as the economic surplus is transferred abroad, depriving Mexico of potential multiplier effects and spread effects through forward and backward linkages. Surplus transference has taken many forms, including net transference of profits, interest income, licensing fees, and disguised profits through transfer pricing and intrafirm transactions in the maquila and disguised maquila sectors. Net transference also entails the derived benefits from education, health care, and the nurturance of children to maturity, essentially subsidizing inputs into the U.S. transnational production system. An impressively large fund of social capital created in Mexico is then transferred to the United States as immigrants produce in the United States while the costs of their development are paid in Mexico.

Additionally, we must consider the subsidies and lost tax revenues that the Mexican government has permitted to continue. Firms operating in the maquila and disguised maquila sectors pay no tariff charges, are exempt from or able to sidestep most production-related taxes, and pay no income tax. Within the maquila sector in 2000, the value of subsidies received exceeded taxes paid, to the extent that these firms had a net profit tax rate of -7.2 percent (Dussel Peters 2003, 334; Schatan 2002). Finally, the cheap-labor export-led model has involved collateral cost in terms of deindustrialization and rising unemployment, along with deskilling as industrial workers are forced to shift to the informal sector or to underemployment, in effect dismantling much of the productive apparatus of Mexico.

Making matters worse, neoliberal policy makers have imposed very restrictive monetary policies in their single-minded effort to contain inflationary impulses (and to attract and keep liquid, short-term portfolio flows from abroad, in an effort to boost stock values and facilitate financial activities). The result has been a long-term overvaluation of the peso—estimated to be 30 percent—which has undercut the export market for Mexican producers, particularly medium-sized producers who might otherwise be able to generate employment through the export of Mexican-made products. Moreover, as imported inputs are essentially subsidized, it has become difficult for these Mexican producers to play the role of domestic supplier to either the TNCs or the Mexican conglomerates (Dussel Peters 2006b). Finally, these medium-sized firms, as well as numerous small firms, have every incentive to buy imported inputs themselves, further strengthening this vicious circle.

These outcomes define the process of asymmetric subordinated integration in Mexico, a process to a great degree accelerated by NAFTA and the neoliberal policies that formed the framework for the NAFTA accord. At the same time, they capture the passivity and emptiness of the state policy-making process in Mexico. Policy makers have adopted a neoliberal stance prohibiting state intervention or the creation of new forms of dynamic competitive advantage, or even the forestalling of processes that are clearly undermining Mexico's production base. Instead, the Mexican state's posture assumes that the dynamic external effects of new forms of production orientated toward the foreign market will automatically bring about a positive restructuring of Mexico's production system. State policy has been limited to a series of opportunistic maneuvers, including seeking more maquilas, pursuing more FDI, using the boom in oil prices to cover the public sector's debt and to boost the economy through government spending that generally will not build vital skills or infrastructure, and relying on massive inflows of foreign remittances from emigrants.

Conclusion

The theoretical and empirical analysis presented above comprises a large and complex set of elements. Among them, certain components stand out in terms of their sharp contrast with the widely disseminated image of Mexico under NAFTA. First, the actual export-led model deployed by Mexico is not a triumphant example of outward-oriented industrialization, but is rather a very basic form of primarization. Many Latin American nations, most notably Argentina, have taken a step backward into specializing in low value-added exports of commodities or undifferentiated resource-based industrial products. Mexico has taken two steps backward, offering up as its absolute advantage cheap and usually modestly trained labor in an institutional setting where this labor can be deployed with few constraints in terms of unions, benefits, labor rights, legal recourse against adverse health effects, and severance protections. It is possible to argue that Mexico is undergoing a process of subprimarization—a deep regression in its export process in which it specializes neither in value-added activities that transform Mexican national inputs nor in raw material exports, as was the case in the prerevolutionary period with the primarization of exports, but rather in its labor power.

Second, Mexico is undergoing a process of precarization and disaccumulation. Employed Mexican laborers are offered subsistence wages under working conditions that frequently lead to job-related injuries and overwhelming economic insecurity, while the export-led model has failed to create an economic surplus that remains in Mexico for its own use. Instead, this surplus is transferred to the United States, where it serves to expand the production base and assist in the restructuring of the economy. The anticipated external effects of the subordinated integration process—in the form of backward and forward linkages, process upgrading, and technological learning—failed to occur. Instead, a new and nefarious form of profit transfer was centered on the disembodied export of cheap labor, giving rise to the total export of revenues derived from the productive process—discounting wages that constitute an incidental cost. This process reaches far beyond the vitiating relationships described by the dependency writers of the 1960s and 1970s.

Third, we have demonstrated that the NAFTA process was not, in any fundamental sense, a trade-based policy leading to a benign and mutually beneficial process of economic specialization through economic competition on both sides of the border, as portrayed in the textbook models of free trade. Instead, the neoliberal program was constructed to serve the end of oligopoly power by displacing significant portions of the U.S. production system to Mexico. In short, NAFTA was an investment/production restructuring agreement, not a trade agreement, that enabled U.S. firms to shift production to Mexico and to benefit from cheap migrant labor. U.S. firms were allowed to expand their production without domestic content legislation, export quotas or restrictions on the repatriation of profits, technology sharing agreements, or any other constraints on the use of this capital.

For the United States, the potential impact of the cheap-labor export-led model includes lowering production costs in Mexico and/or the United States through the insertion of cheap labor into the production process, which will increase profits. These profits can potentially fund greater research and development spending, leading to greater innovation, as well as fund investment in the modernization of production. Additionally, if the lowering of production costs in Mexico and/or the United States is partially passed on to U.S. consumers via some lower prices, then the cheap-labor export-led model serves to lower the reproduction costs of U.S. labor. In turn, this enables U.S. corporations and businesses to operate with lower wages than would otherwise be necessary, thereby enhancing the competitiveness of the U.S. production system while raising profit margins.

Fourth, rather than promoting convergence in the development levels of Mexico and the United States, economic integration under NAFTA has deepened the asymmetries that exist between the two countries. Whereas in 1994 per capita GDP in the United States was 2.6 times that of Mexico, by 2004 the ratio had increased to 2.9. Similarly, average manufacturing wages in dollars per man-hour in the United States were 5.7 times higher than those reported in Mexico in 1994, and 6.8 times higher in 2004 (Del7do Wise and Márquez 2006, 32). In Mexico, this new form of asymmetric subordinated integration has clearly not been associated with new possibilities for economic development. Stagnating or dropping wages, rising unemployment, and informal activities have contributed to the necessary emigration of millions of people. The lack of linkage effects in the Mexican economy has negated the potential dynamic spillover effects that, according to the new growth theory, were supposed to spread across much of the production system due to enhanced foreign investment under NAFTA. On one hand, this has meant that Mexico has become increasingly dependent on remittances in order to stabilize the macroeconomy and society at large. On the other hand, the uncontrolled leap in emigration has called into question the sustainability of the cheap-labor export-led model, particularly in terms of the depopulation effects in many parts of Mexico. With increasing marginalization and poverty, the pressures to emigrate escalate, and this course of action could very well collide with U.S. policy in the current anti-immigrant climate.

It remains only to add that Mexico is now embedded in a broad process involving an ongoing initiative to restructure the U.S. economy. Central to this process is the cheapening of U.S. labor, be it of a low skill level or any other form, both directly in the United States and indirectly through the establishment of production facilities in Mexico. In order to maintain its competitiveness, or slow its fall, Mexico has played an important role in the strategies of many of the largest U.S. corporations. The U.S. state has also played an integral part in facilitating the restructuring of the economy through the development of policies, the most important of which has been NAFTA. As this process has unfolded, its asymmetrical dynamics have been notable: at one extreme, a smaller and smaller elite on both sides of the border has enjoyed increasing wealth and power, while at the other extreme, the negative impacts have been felt among an ever broader portion of the populace, not only in Mexico but in the United States as well. In the final analysis, socioeconomic development has never been achieved by a nation as a result of exogenous forces. The responsibility for initiating and maintaining a process of economic development fundamentally rests in endogenous social forces; specifically, the state must endeavor to mount and sustain a national project of accumulation (despite its fluctuating ability to do so), rather than adopt policies, such as NAFTA, that generate asymmetric accumulation processes.

NOTES

1. A victory for the PAN was convenient but not necessary, as the PRI had, since 1987, served largely as a willing functionary of the economic elite. The PRI, however, is a complex organization carrying a historical legacy of commitment to the peasantry, organized labor, and nationalism. Hence, while the business elite would have been well served by the PRI had it won once again, a PAN victory constituted a single-minded commitment to the neoliberal corporate agenda.

2. The high growth achieved in the 1940–82 period requires further commentary to avoid misinterpretation of our analysis: Mexico's achievement was impressive, yet increasing degrees of policy weakness were major factors in the crisis of 1982. Among the many weaknesses, we would highlight four elements. First, once the simple stage of easy import substitution was largely completed, wherein Mexico built a capacity to manufacture consumer nondurable products, strategists prematurely pushed for ascendance to the production of capital-intensive durable goods. At this point, the ideal strategy would have been to build export capacity in certain consumer nondurables to gain economies of scale and

foreign exchange earnings. Instead, durable goods production demanded heavy imports of machinery and technology, creating a drain on the balance of payments. Second, to achieve effective state policy, Mexico needed a meritocracy running the many state entities, including the crucial parastate firms. That is, Mexico needed to build state capacity. Third, it needed an embedded reciprocal relationship with large business. Instead, the Mexican state generally failed to enhance economic performance in the private sector, because its many forms of support did not generate reciprocal behavior on the part of business. Finally, and most important to our interpretation, no effort was made to build a national innovation system, either by the business elite or the state, leaving Mexico with no national capacity to autonomously advance its production apparatus, or to achieve dynamic competitive advantage (Evans 1995; Amsden 2001; Delgado Wise and Invernizzi 2005).

3. It is important to note that investment includes the creation of new plant and equipment. In the case of FDI, it also includes the takeover of existing plant and equipment (an international asset swap that adds nothing to production capacity) and investment in structures as well as real estate. Thus, the construction of a golf course or a luxury shopping center by international investors has the same statistical weight (dollar for dollar) as the creation of a new auto plant or a new chemical refinery.

4. In 2005, the share of GDP devoted to all forms of research and development was a mere 0.44 percent; Japan's share was more than seven times greater. Further, according to the Organisation for Economic Co-operation and Development (OECD), nearly two-thirds of Japan's outlays were for development processes (where the private sector searches for innovations), whereas in Mexico 56.5 percent of research and development outlays were basically for theoretical science, with research largely undertaken at government-sponsored universities (Guadarrama 2006, 16)

5. In November 2006, the Mexican government decreed that the juridical difference between the maquila and disguised maquila sectors would cease to exist. In 2007, all former maquila firms and all firms operating under special provisions as temporary importers of inputs (the disguised maquilas) were registered under the same decree, the Decreto para el Fomento de la Industria Manufacturera, Maquiladora y de Servicios de Exportación. The combined sectors are known as the IMMEX sector, and at the official level, the term "maquiladora" is no longer used (Saldana 2006, 19). Aside from eliminating a familiar term, the Decreto appears to impose no substantive changes on either labor or capital.

6. The fragmenting of unions is a transnational tactic employed by the U.S. auto producers who, in the face of an unprecedented crisis of overproduction in 2006, decided to decimate the United Auto Workers—laying off 113,000 workers via buyouts at Delphi–General Motors and 75,000 workers at Ford. Most of these jobs went to Mexico, where wages are $3.50 per hour, versus $27 per hour in the United States. General Motors built a large greenfield plant in San Luis Potosí, employing 1,800 workers; Ford and Daimler-Chrysler similarly expanded their operations in Mexico. Further U.S. investments are likely to flow to the auto parts sector, where 430,000 are already employed (Malkin 2006, C1, C4).

7. In actuality, the situation is even more restrictive, given that 78 percent of maquila activity remains along the U.S. frontier, where a considerable portion of workers' consumption is diverted into the U.S. economy, further undermining whatever potential multiplier effects might be anticipated through rising wage payments.

8. Differences in productivity levels are much narrower than the variation in wages. In the auto sector, it is common to find statements that productivity levels in Mexico are 60–80 percent of those in the United States. However, in some instances, productivity is *higher* than in U.S. plants (Mortimore and Barron 2005, 18).

REFERENCES

Because URLs to publications and Web pages on the extensive websites of the Banco de México, Banco Nacional de Comercio Exterior, CONAPO, and INEGI are both lengthy and subject to change, citations to these sources provide only the URLs to the institutions' home pages.

Amsden, Alice H. 2001. *The Rise of "The Rest": Challenges to the West from Late-Industrializing Economies.* New York: Oxford University Press.

Babb, Sarah. 2001. *Managing Mexico: Economists from Nationalism to Neoliberalism.* Princeton: Princeton University Press.

Banco de México. 2005. "Remesas familiares." http://www.banxico.org.mx.

———. 2006. *Cuentas nacionales.* Consulta de Series. http://www.banxico.org.mx.

———. 2007. "Remesas familiaries." http://www.banxico.org.mx.

Banco Nacional de Comercio Exterior. 2005. *Atlas de comercio exterior.* http://www.banco
mext.com/Bancomext.

———. 2006. Sistema Integral de Información de Comercio Exterior. www.siicex.gob.mx.

Basave, Jorge. 2006. "Desempeno exportador empresarial e impacto económico." In Pozas 2006a, 111–46.

Becerril, Isabel. 2006a. "Marco regulatorio del comerico exterior, un obstáculo." *El Financiero,* September 4.

———. 2006b. "México, reprobado en competitividad." *El Financiero,* September 1.

Bendensky, León. 2005. "La inflación." *La Jornada,* August 15.

Cadena, Guadalupe. 2005. "Manufactura, en la ruta de la 'desindustrialización.'" *El Financiero,* August 16.

———. 2006a. "En la economía informal, 40 por ciento de la PEA en México." *El Financiero,* June 14.

———. 2006b. "Incierto, el panorama laboral mexicano." *El Financiero,* September 1.

Cameron, Maxwell, and Brian Tomlin. 2000. *The Making of NAFTA: How the Deal Was Done.* Ithaca: Cornell University Press.

Capdevielle, Mario. 2005. "Procesos de producción global: ¿Alternativa para el desarrollo mexicano? *Comercio Exterior* 55 (7): 561–73.

Champlin, D., and Hake, E. 2006. "Immigration as Industrial Strategy in American Meatpacking." *Review of Political Economy* 18 (1): 49–70.

Consejo Nacional de Población (CONAPO). 2004. "Migración internacional." http://www.conapo.gob.mx.

Cypher, James. 1989. "The Debt Crisis as 'Opportunity.'" *Latin American Perspectives* 16 (1): 52–78.

———. 1990. *State and Capital in Mexico: Development Policy Since 1940.* Boulder, Colo.: Westview Press.

———. 1993. "The Ideology of Economic Science in the Selling of NAFTA: The Political Economy of Elite Decision-Making." *Review of Radical Political Economics* 25 (4): 146–63.

———. 2001. "Nafta's Lessons: From Economic Mythology to Current Realities." *Labor Studies Journal* 26 (1): 5–21.

———. 2004. "Development Diverted: Socioeconomic Characteristics and Impacts of Mature Maquilization." In *The Social Costs of Industrial Growth in Northern Mexico,* edited by Kathryn Kopinak, 343–82. San Diego: Center for U.S.-Mexico Studies, UCSD.

———. 2005. "Poverty (Mexico)." In *Encyclopedia of Social Welfare History in North America,* edited by John M. Herrick and Paul H. Stuart, 281–83. London: Sage.

Delgado Wise, Raúl. 2006. "Migration and Imperialism: The Mexican Workforce in the Context of NAFTA." *Latin American Perspectives* 33 (2): 33–45.

Delgado Wise, Raúl, and Noela Invernizzi. 2005. "Differences Behind Appearances: Export Growth Technological Capabilities and Development in Mexico and South Korea." *Canadian Journal of Development Studies* 26 (3): 409–24.

Delgado Wise, Raúl, and Humberto Márquez. 2006. "The Mexico–United States Migratory System: Dilemmas of Regional Integration, Development, and Emigration." In *Conference Proceedings: Migration and Development: Perspectives from the South,* 25–45.

Bellagio, Italy (July 10–13). Zacatecas, Mexico: Doctorado en Estudios del Desarrollo, Universidad Autónoma de Zacatecas.

Delgado Wise, Raúl, Humberto Márquez, and Humberto Rodríguez. 2004. "Organizaciones transnacionales de migrantes y desarrollo regional en Zacatecas." *Migraciones Internacionales* 2 (4): 159–81.

Durán Lima, José, and Vivianne Ventura-Dias. 2003. *Comercio intrafirma: Concepto, alcance y magnitud.* Comercio Internacional 44. Santiago: CEPAL.

Dussel Peters, Enrique. 2003. "Ser maquila o no ser maquila, ¿es ésa la pregunta?" *Comerico Exterior* 53 (4): 328–36.

———. 2006a. "Hacia una política de competitividad en México." *Economía UNAM* 3 (9): 65–82.

———. 2006b. "Liberalización comercial en México." In *México en transición: Globalismo neoliberal, estado y sociedad civil,* edited by Gerardo Otero, 69–105. Mexico: Miguel Ángel Porrúa.

Dutrénit, Gabriela, and Alexandre O. Vera-Cruz. 2005. "Acumulación de capacidades tecnológicas en la industria maquiladora." *Comercio Exterior* 55 (6): 574–86.

Economist Intelligence Unit. 2006. "En la cárcel de los monopolios." *La Jornada,* November 28.

Evans, Peter. 1995. *Embedded Autonomy: States and Industrial Transformation.* Princeton: Princeton University Press.

Faux, Jeff. 2006. *The Global Class War: How America's Bipartisan Elite Lost Our Future—and What It Will Take to Win It Back.* Hoboken, N.J.: John Wiley and Sons.

Fernández-Vega, Carlos. 2005. "El gobierno de 'cambio' sigue empecinado en seguir la fiesta." *La Jornada,* August 15.

Garrido, Celso. 2006. "Empresas, economía nacional y sistema financiera en México." In Pozas 2006a, 17–69.

Glade, William, and Cassio Luiselli, eds. 1989. *The Economics of Interdependence: Mexico and the United States.* San Diego: Center for U.S.-Mexico Studies, UCSD.

Guadarrama, José. 2006. "En panales, el desarrollo tecnológico en México." *El Financiero,* June 9.

Guarnizo, Luis. 2003. "The Economics of Transnational Living." *International Migration Review* 37 (3): 666–99.

Gutiérrez, Elvia. 2006. "Bajo crecimiento económico y desempleo." *El Financiero,* September 1.

Howard, Georgina. 2005. "El papel del trabajo: México, empleos, pocos y malos." *La Jornada,* August 9. www.jornada.unam.mx/2004/08/09/004n1sec.html.

Instituto Nacional de Estadística y Geografía (INEGI). 2000. *Censo general de población y vivienda.* Aguascalientes: INEGI. http://www.inegi.gob.mx.

———. 2004. "Encuesta industrial mensual." http://www.inegi.gob.mx.

———. 1996–2007a. "Estadísticas económicas." http://www.inegi.gob.mx.

———. 1996–2007b. "Indicadores económicos de coyuntura." Banco de Información Económica. http://www.inegi.gob.mx.

Instituto Nacional de Estadística y Geografía (INEGI) and Secretaría del Trabajo y Provisión Social (STPS). 1996–2006. "Encuesta industrial mensual." http://www.inegi.gob.mx.

Juárez Núnez, Huberto, and Steve Babson, eds. 1999. *Enfrentando el cambio: Obreros de automovíl y producción esbelta en América del Norte; Confronting Change: Auto Labor and Lean Production in North America.* 2nd ed. Puebla, Mexico: Benemérita Universidad Autónoma de Puebla.

Lara, Arturo, Jaim Arellano, and Alejandro García. 2005. "Coevolución tecnológica entre maquiladoras de autopartes y talleres de maquinado." *Comercio Exterior* 55 (7): 586–600.

Leon González, Alejandra, and Enrique Dussel Peters. 2001. "El comercio intraindustrial en México, 1990–1999." *Comercio Exterior* 51 (7): 652–64.

Malkin, Elisabeth. 2006. "Detroit, Far South." *New York Times,* July 21.

Mortimore, Michael, and Faustino Barron. 2005. *Informe sobre la industria automotriz mexicana.* Serie Desarrollo Productivo 162. Santiago: United Nations.

Mortimore, Michael, and Wilson Peres. 2001. "La competitividad empresarial en América Latina." *Revista de la CEPAL* 74:37–59.

Nacional Financiera. 1995. *La economía mexicana en cifras 1995.* Mexico City: Nafinsa.

Norris, Floyd. 2005. "Proof, Near and Far, That It's Not 1950 Anymore." *New York Times,* October 15. http://www.nytimes.com/2005/10/15/business/15charts.ready.html.

Pew Hispanic Center. 2008. "A Statistical Portrait of the Foreign-Born Population at Mid-Decade." January 23. http://pewhispanic.org/factsheets/factsheet.php?Factsheet ID=36.

Pozas, María de los Ángeles. 2002. *Estrategia internacional de la gran empresa mexicana en la década de los noventa.* Mexico City: El Colegio de México.

———, ed. 2006a. *Estructura y dinámica de la gran empresa en México: Cinco estudios sobre su realidad reciente.* Mexico City: El Colegio de México.

———. 2006b. "Tecnología y desarrollo en las cadenas productivas de las grandes empresas en México." In Pozas 2006a, 71–110.

Puga, Cristina. 2004. *Los empresarios organizados y el tratado de libre comercio de América del Norte.* Mexico City: Miguel Ángel Porrúa.

Rocha, Lourdes. 2006. "Across the Board Reduction of 53 Percent in Tariff Rates." *Review of the Economic Situation in Mexico* 82:382–86.

Rodríguez, Eleazar. 2006. "Empresas mexicanas consolidan su expansión en LA." *El Financiero,* June 9.

Saldana, Ivette. 2006. "Maquiladoras rompen récord en exportaciones." *El Financiero,* December 1.

Schatan, R. 2002. "Regimen tributario de la industria maquiladora." *Comercio Exterior* 52 (10): 916–26.

Secretaría de Comercio y Fomento Industrial (SECOFI). 1990. *Marco jurídico y administrativo de la inversión extranjera directa en México.* Cuadernos Secofi (Serie Jurídico). Mexico City: SECOFI.

Secretaría de Economía. 2006. "Dirección general de inversión extranjera." www.economia .gob.mx/swb/work/models/economia/Resource/13/1/images /TRAMITESDGIE .pdf.

———. 2007. *Registro nacional de inversión extranjera.* http://www.si-rnie.economia .gob.mx/cgi-bin/repie.sh/reportes/selperiodo (page discontinued).

Tello, Carlos. 1996. "La economía mexicana: Hacia el tercer milenio." *Nexos* 19 (223): 47–55.

Unger, Kart. 2002. *Determinantes de la exportaciones manufactureras mexicanas.* Mexico City: CIDE.

United Nations, Department of Economic and Social Affairs. 2006. *International Migration Report 2006: A Global Assessment.* New York: United Nations.

U.S. Bureau of Labor Statistics. 2005. "Current Employment Statistics (Manufacturing)." www.bls.gov/iag/manufacturing.htm.

U.S. Census Bureau. 2003. *Current Population Survey.* Washington, D.C.: U.S. Government Printing Office.

———. 2005. "Current Population Survey." http://www.census.gov/cps/.

Villavicencio, Daniel, and Mónica Casalet. 2005. "La construcción de un entorno institucional de apoyo a la industria maquiladora." *Comercio Exterior* 55 (7): 600–611.

World Bank. 2006. *Global Economic Prospects 2006: Economic Implications of Remittances and Migration.* Washington D.C.: World Bank.

Zúñiga, Víctor, and Rubén Hernández-León, eds. 2005. *New Destinations: Mexican Immigration in the United States.* New York: Russell Sage Foundation.

Zúñiga Herrera, Elena, and Paul Leite. 2006. "Los procesos contemporáneos de la migración México–Estados Unidos: Una perspectiva regional y municipal." In *Migración México–Estados Unidos: Implicaciones y retos para ambos países,* edited by Elena Zúñiga Herrera, Jesús Arroyo Alejandre, Agustín Escobar Latapí, and Gustavo Verduzco Igartúa, 49–82. Mexico City: CONAPO.

Part II

ALTERNATIVE EXPRESSIONS OF GLOBAL POWER

5

GLOBALIZATION, TRADE, AND DEVELOPMENT:
FROM TERRITORIAL TO SOCIAL CARTOGRAPHIES, FROM NATION-STATE/
INTERSTATE TO TRANSNATIONAL EXPLANATIONS

William I. Robinson

A—perhaps *the*—major area of disagreement in the debate over globalization is the extent to which it involves novel changes in the capitalist system. Some reject the idea that there is anything especially new about world capitalism in the twenty-first century. Those scholars from the world-systems perspective, for instance, see globalization as a process that began in the fifteenth century with the genesis of capitalism and its initial outward expansion. They characterize late twentieth- and early twenty-first-century changes as more of the same, that is, as involving quantitative rather than qualitative changes in the system. In contrast, I have argued (Robinson 1998, 2001, 2004a, 2008) that globalization constitutes a qualitatively new stage in the ongoing evolution of world capitalism, marked by a number of fundamental shifts in the system. Globalization, I have contended, involves the supersession of the nation-state as the organizing principle of capitalist development. This does not mean, of course, the end of the nation-state or that the state is now irrelevant. We need to return to an understanding of the nation-state as a *historical* rather than an immanent category, an institution that came about as a result of the particular form in which capitalism as a historical system developed. The kind of categorical thinking that plagues nation-state paradigms ends up reifying the nation-state, so that, for instance, the categories of core and periphery, as the opposite ends of polarized accumulation, must necessarily correspond to territorially defined nation-states.

Nation-state paradigms are unable to grasp the transnational character of many contemporary processes and events, such as world trade, international conflicts, and uneven development, because they box transnational phenomena into the nation-state/interstate framework and hence fail to capture what Sassen (2006) calls "denationalization" and what I have referred to since I began writing about globalization in the early 1990s as "transnationalization." Theory needs to illuminate reality, not make reality conform to it. The pitfall of theoreticism is the development of analyses and propositions to fit theoretical assumptions. Since received nation-state paradigms establish a frame of an interstate system made up of competing national states, economies, and capitals, then twenty-first-century reality must be interpreted so that it fits this frame one way or another. Such theoreticism in the study of globalization forces many, at best, to follow Harvey's (2005) schizophrenic dualism of economic and political logics: capital is economic and globalizes, while states are political and pursue a territorially based political-state logic.

Nation-state paradigms typically analyzed U.S.-Chinese relations, for instance, by drawing on trade data showing a growing U.S. trade deficit and an inverse accumulation by China of international reserves, and then concluded that the two states were locked in competition over international hegemony. But we cannot possibly understand U.S.-Chinese trade dynamics without observing that between 40 and 70 percent of world trade in the early twenty-first century was intrafirm or associational, that some 40 percent of exports from China came from transnational corporations (TNCs) based in that country, and that much of the remaining 60 percent was accounted for by associational forms involving Chinese and transnational investors. These transnational class and social relations are concealed behind nation-state data. When we focus on the production, ownership structures, and class and social relations that lie behind nation-state trade data, we are in a better position to search for causal explanations for global political and economic dynamics.

These nation-state paradigms see nations as discrete units within a larger system—the world system or the international system—characterized by external exchanges among these units. These approaches reify institutions by substituting them for social forces and then giving them a *fixed* character in causal explanations, so that, for instance, national states are bestowed with agency in explaining global political and economic dynamics. Institutions such as states, however, are not actors with an independent life of their own; they are the products of social forces that reproduce as well as modify them and that are causal in historical explanations. Social forces in complex and shifting webs of conflict and cooperation operate through multiple institutions. We need to focus not on states as fictitious macro-agents but on historically changing constellations of social forces operating through multiple institutions, including state apparatuses that are themselves engaged in a process of transformation as a consequence of collective agencies. As global capitalism now sinks into its most serious crisis in decades, an accurate, more than academic, understanding of the nature of the system has become a burning political matter if we are to respond effectively to the depredations that the crisis has unleashed on broad swaths of humanity.

From Nation-State to Global Capitalism

The world economy experienced a sustained period of growth in the quarter century after World War II—the so-called golden age of capitalism (Marglin and Schor 1990). But the illusion of prosperity burst with the worldwide economic downturn that began in the 1970s and threw national corporate capitalism into crisis (Cox 1987; Kolko 1988). This crisis manifested itself economically in recessions, a decline in labor productivity, profit rates and profitable investment opportunities, stagflation (stagnation plus inflation, resulting from the refusal of workers to shoulder the crisis), unemployment, an energy crisis, widespread fiscal and balance-of-payments crises, rising international debt, and the decision made by the Nixon administration in the United States to end gold convertibility of the dollar. The crisis manifested itself politically in a string of Third World revolutions (between 1974 and 1980, no fewer than fourteen Third World countries fell to national liberation movements; see Hoogvelt 1997, 52). The upsurge in class conflict, social movements, armed liberation struggles, and countercultures reached a crescendo in the tumultuous events of 1968 and seemed to be developing into a system-wide crisis of hegemony and political domination by the 1970s (Robinson 1996).

The social origins of this crisis were to be found in the relative strength that working and popular classes won worldwide in relation to capital after many decades of class and social struggles. Organized labor, increased taxes on profits and income, state regulation, revolutions in the Third World, and the explosion of social movements and counterhegemonic cultural practices everywhere constricted private capital's real or perceived capacity for accumulation. The expansion of collective rights, the institutionalization of Keynesian-Fordist class compromise, and the prevailing norms of a moral economy that imputed to capital and the state a set of reciprocities with labor and citizens and an ethnical obligation to minimal social reproduction—all this burdened capital with social rigidities that had to be reversed for a new phase of capitalist growth. Capital and its political representatives and organic intellectuals organized a broad offensive—economic, political, ideological, and military—that was symbolically spearheaded by the Reagan-Thatcher alliance. In its seminal 1975 report, *The Crisis of Democracy* (Crozier, Huntington, and Watanuki 1975), the Trilateral Commission diagnosed the problem as too much democracy and therefore not enough governability (read: social control and obedience). Emerging transnational elites from the centers of power in the world system launched a global counterrevolution that would be as much political and economic as social, cultural, and ideological; it is still being fought out in manifold arenas in the twenty-first century.

In structural terms, this crisis was not merely cyclical. Mainstream business cycle theories identify periodic swings from expansion to recession in the market economy. But world-system, critical political economy, international relations, and neo-Marxist theories have long pointed to the deeper cycles in world capitalism—the Kondratieff cycles or observed fifty-year swings in the system—in which a period of expansion is followed by a period of contraction. Cyclical crises, in these accounts, eventually accumulate in more generalized crises that involve social and political upheavals and usher in periods of restructuring. Restructuring crises result in novel forms that replace historical patterns of capital accumulation and the institutional arrangements that facilitated them (Aglietta 1979; Kotz, McDonough, and Reich 1994; Arrighi 1994; Harvey 1982). The world capitalist crisis that began in the 1970s is generally identified as the turning point for globalization and, in my view, signaled the transition to a new transnational stage in the system.

For much of the twentieth century, all three models—First World Keynesian capitalism, Second World state socialist/redistributive models, and Third World developmentalist capitalism—shared two common features: state intervention in the economy and a redistributive logic. The crisis that began in the 1970s could not be resolved within the framework of these post–World War II social structures of accumulation. Neither socialism in one country nor Keynesianism in one country was any longer a tenable project as we entered the globalization age. All three models now began to face crises of legitimacy and political authority that evoked massive restructuring and integration in emergent global capitalism. In the First World, there was a progressive breakdown of the Keynesian-Fordist welfare states. In the Second World, the socialist/state redistributive projects experienced crisis and collapse in the 1980s and early 1990s. In the Third World, developmentalist projects became exhausted, as primarily manifested in economic contraction and the debt crisis of the 1980s.

Globalization became a viable strategy as capitalists and state managers searched for new modes of accumulation. It allowed capital to shake off the constraints that nation-state capitalism had placed on accumulation—to break free of the class compromises and concessions that had been imposed by working and popular classes and by national governments in the preceding epoch. New technologies, particularly the communications and information revolution but also revolutions in transportation, marketing, management, automation, robotization, and so on, were globalizing in the sense that they provided capital with the material means to go global. Deregulation, especially financial deregulation, made it possible to use this technology to develop new transnational circuits of accumulation. The U.S. government's decision to abandon the fixed exchange rate system in 1973 effectively did away with the Bretton Woods system and, together with deregulation, opened the floodgate to a cascade of transnational capital movement and the meteoric spread of TNCs. Capital achieved a newfound global mobility, or an ability to operate across borders in new ways, which ushered in the era of global capitalism. The renewed power to discipline labor that this afforded transnational capital altered the worldwide correlation of class and social forces in its favor. What was international capital in the preceding epoch metamorphosed into transnational capital.

Emerging global elites and transnational capitalists set about to dismantle the distinct models associated with national corporate capitalism and to construct a new global "flexible" regime of accumulation. In broad strokes, Keynesianism was replaced by monetarist policies, deregulation, and a "supply side" approach that included regressive taxation and new incentives for capital. The Fordist class compromise was replaced by new capital-labor relations based on deunionization, flexible workers, and deregulated work conditions. And the welfarist social contract was replaced by social austerity and the law of the market in social reproduction. More specifically, during the 1980s and onward, the prospects for capital to accumulate and make profits were restored by four key developments associated with capitalist globalization:

1. A new capital-labor relation based on the deregulation and "flexibilization" of labor.
2. A new round of *extensive* and *intensive* expansion. Extensively, the system expanded through the reincorporation of major areas of the former Third and Second Worlds into the world capitalist economy, so that by the 1990s no region remained outside the system. Intensively, public and community spheres that formerly lay outside (or were buffered from) the logic of market relations (profit making) were commodified and opened up to accumulation through privatization, state deregulation and reregulation, including the extension of intellectual property rights, and so on.
3. The creation of a global legal and regulatory structure to facilitate what were emerging globalized circuits of accumulation, including the creation of the World Trade Organization (WTO).
4. The imposition of the neoliberal model on countries throughout the Third World, as well as the First and former Second Worlds, involving structural adjustment programs that created the conditions for the free operation of capital within and across borders and the harmonization of accumulation conditions worldwide.

By the early twenty-first century, there was no longer anything external to the system—that is, not in the sense that it had become a "closed" system, but in that there were no longer any countries or regions that remained out-side of world capitalism or had yet to be incorporated through original accu-mulation, and in that there was no longer autonomous accumulation outside of the sphere of global capital. Harvard economist Richard Freeman observes,

> The most fundamental economic development in this era of globaliza-tion [is] the doubling of the global labor force. The doubling I am refer-ring to is the increased number of persons in the global economy that results from China, India and the ex-Soviet Union embracing market capitalism. In the 1980s and 1990s, workers from China, India and the former Soviet bloc entered the global labor pool. Of course, these workers had existed before then. The difference, though, was that their economies suddenly joined the global system of production and consumption. . . . The entry of China, India and the former Soviet bloc to the global capitalist economy is a turning point in economic history. For the first time, the vast majority of humans will operate under mar-ket capitalism. (2005, 1, 4)

The emergence of globally mobile transnational capital increasingly di-vorced from specific countries has facilitated the globalization of produc-tion—the fragmentation and decentralization of complex production processes, the worldwide dispersal of the different segments in these chains, and their functional integration into vast global chains of production and distribution. World production is thus reorganized into new transnational, or global, circuits of accumulation through which values move instantaneously. National economies are reorganized and reinserted as component elements of this new global production and financial system (Dicken 1998; McMichael 1996), a world economic structure that is qualitatively distinct from that of previous epochs, when each country had a separate national economy linked externally to the others through trade and financial flows. This constitutes a shift from international market integration to global productive integration. At the same time, an integrated global financial system has replaced the na-tional bank–dominated financial systems of the earlier period, which have all but disappeared. Thus, global financial flows since the 1980s have been qualitatively different from the international financial flows of the earlier period.

This worldwide decentralization and fragmentation of the production process has taken place alongside the centralization of command and control of the global economy in transnational capital. Although real power and con-trol still remain rigidly hierarchal and have actually become more concen-trated under globalization, the actual organizational form of economic activity is characterized by decentralized webs of horizontally interlocked networks, as opposed to the old centralized hierarchies based on vertical integration.

The rise of the global economy has been founded on the phenomenal spread since the late 1970s of diverse new economic arrangements associated with the transition from the Fordist regime of accumulation to new post-Fordist flexible regimes (Harvey 1990; Cox 1987; Dicken 1998; Hoogvelt 1997; Lipietz 1987; Fröbel, Heinrichs, and Kreye 1980). Subcontracting and outsourcing have become extremely widespread and a basic organizational feature of economic activity worldwide. In the earlier epochs of capitalism, firms tended to organize entire sequences of economic production, distribution, and service from within. As the phenomenon of subcontracting and outsourcing spread in the 1970s to the 1990s, it was concentrated at first in low-skill, labor-intensive industries, such as textiles and apparel, toys, and electronics. But by the late 1990s, the move to offshore production had spread to such advanced economic activities as the production of semiconductors, aerospace manufacturing, and network computing. By the twenty-first century, the outsourcing of both low-end and high-end services was well under way and included the decentralized worldwide relocation of such jobs as telephone operating, graphic design, accounting, computer programming, engineering (Iritani 2000), and even Hollywood movie production (Horn 2005).

Subcontracting and outsourcing—along with a host of other new economic arrangements, such as formal and informal transnational business alliances, licensing agreements, local representation, and so on—make new subdivisions and specialization in production possible. It is through such interconnections that small local firms and economic agents in one country may be directly linked to a global production network, even when such firms or agents serve only a very restricted geographic area. The structural properties of these chains or networks are global in character, in that accumulation is embedded in global markets, involving global enterprise organization and sets of global capital-labor relations, especially deregulated and casualized labor pools worldwide. Any analysis of world trade must be predicated on this understanding that "trade partners" are not nation-states but rather transnational economic agents operating through a kaleidoscope of global arrangements.

While some academics continue to reject the notion of a qualitatively new global economy, those who are in a commanding position in that economy are clear on the novel configurations and processes that globalization entails. Among them, IBM's chair and CEO, Samuel Palmisano, affirmed in a 2006 article in *Foreign Affairs* that use of the term "multinational corporation" suggests "how antiquated our thinking about it is." It is worth quoting Palmisano at some length:

> The Multinational corporation (MNC), often seen as a primary agent of globalization, is taking on a new form. . . . This new kind of enterprise is best understood as "global" rather than "multinational.". . . The MNC

of the late twentieth century had little in common with the international firms of a hundred years earlier, and those companies were very different from the great trading enterprises of the 1700s. The type of business organization that is now emerging—the globally integrated enterprise—marks just as big a leap. . . . There were, of course, many recognizably global products throughout the twentieth century. . . . But by and large, corporations continue to organize production market by market, within the traditional boundaries of the nation-state. . . . Starting in the early 1970s, the revolution in information technology (IT) . . . standardized technologies and business operations all over the world, interlinking and facilitating work both within and among companies. This combination of shared technologies and shared business standards, all built on top of a global IT and communications infrastructure, changed the sorts of globalization that companies found possible. . . . Simply put, the emerging globally integrated enterprise is a company that fashions its strategy, its management, and its operations in pursuit of a new goal: the integration of production and value delivery worldwide. State borders define less and less the boundaries of corporate thinking or practice. (2006, 127–29)

Global Class Formation and a Transnational Capitalist Class

It is increasingly difficult to separate local circuits of production and distribution from the globalized circuits that dictate the terms and patterns of accumulation worldwide, even when surface appearance gives the (misleading) impression that local capitals retain their autonomy. There are, of course, still local and national capitalists, and there will be for a long time to come. But they must delocalize and link to transnational capital if they are to survive. Territorially restricted capital cannot compete with its transnationally mobile counterpart. To paraphrase the academic slogan "publish or perish," in the case of global capitalism, capitalists in any part of the world beyond the smallest of scale find that they must globalize or perish. As the global circuit of capital subsumes these local circuits through numerous mechanisms and arrangements, local capitalists who manage the circuits become swept up in the process of transnational class formation.

I have been writing about this process of transnational class formation and the rise of a transnational capitalist class (TCC) since the mid-1990s (Robinson 1996, 2001, 2003, 2004a, 2008). The topic has become part of a collective research agenda, and the empirical evidence demonstrating the transnationalization of leading capitalist groups is now considerable (Sklair 2002; Kentor 2005; Kentor and Jang 2004; Carroll and Carson 2003; Carroll and Fennema 2002). With the rise of transnational production chains and circuits of accumulation, transnationally oriented capitalists in each country are shifting their horizons from national to global markets. Different phases of production, as they are broken down into detachable component sequences and dispersed around the world, can be doled out to distinct economic agents through chains of subcontracting, outsourcing, and other forms of association. These agents become integrated organically into new globalized circuits, so that they are denationalized, in the material if not the cultural sense, and become transnational agents. The vast multilayered networks of outsourcing, subcontracting, and collaboration, among others, increasingly link local and national agents to global networks and structures. In this regard, it is worth citing Samuel Palmisano again:

> Everywhere, economic activity is turning outward by embracing shared business and technology standards that let businesses plug into truly global systems of production. . . . Because new technology and business models are allowing companies to treat their different functions and operations as component pieces, firms can pull those pieces apart and put them back together again in new combinations. These decisions are not simply a matter of offloading noncore activities, nor are they mere labor arbitrage. They are about actively managing different operations, expertise, and capabilities so as to open the enterprise up in multiple ways, allowing it to connect more intimately with partners, suppliers, and customers. New forms of collaboration are everywhere. . . . Small and medium-sized businesses everywhere, particularly, are benefiting: as new services—from back-office administration to sales support— create infrastructures once only affordable to large organizations, these businesses can now participate in the global economy. (2006, 130–33)

The TCC is a class group with subjective consciousness of itself and its interests. Its members socialize together in their private institutions and have developed a transnational class consciousness. In this sense, the TCC is a class for itself, whereas the global working class is a class in itself but not yet for itself. The former director of Kissinger Associates, David Rothkopf, has observed,

> Business leaders in Buenos Aires, Frankfurt, Hong Kong, Johannesburg, Istanbul, Los Angeles, Mexico City, Moscow, New Delhi, New York, Paris, Rome, Santiago, Seoul, Singapore, Tel Aviv, and Tokyo all read the same newspapers, wear the same suits, drive the same cars, eat the same food, fly the same airlines, stay in the same hotels, and listen to the same music. [This integrated elite also includes] international bureaucrats . . . [who] coordinate policy . . . on global issues such

as trade, the environment, health, development, and crisis management. (1997, 44–45)

The TCC has exhibited a global political action capacity and placed itself
on the world scene as a coherent actor. In the same way that business groups
organize to orient national policy planning groups and lobby national governments, transnational business groups have become a powerful lobby able to
impose their will on intergovernmental and supranational institutions. On
the eve of the December 2005 Ministerial Conference of the WTO, for instance, the CEOs and chairs of several dozens of the largest TNCs, at the
initiative of the International Chamber of Commerce, wrote a highly publi-
cized letter presenting their collective demand that the secretariat of the WTO
push for a deeper liberalization of the global economy. Among the signatories
were representatives from France, Sweden, Morocco, the Netherlands, Hong
Kong, India, Spain, Pakistan, Thailand, the United States, Japan, and the
Philippines. (For the letter and full list of signatories, see Fourtou and
Wallenberg 2005.)

Nation-state centric analyses of inter- and transnational relations fail to
appreciate the integrative character of global capitalism. Dominant class relations have shifted worldwide. Both national (or local) and transnational forms
of accumulation exist in differing degrees in all nations and regions. The
struggles, interests, and contradictions among diverse class and social forces
appear in a variety of forms and unfold differently depending on particular
histories and sets of relations unique to each country and region. Transnational fractions of local capitalist classes and bureaucratic elites vied for state
power and in most countries won government in the 1980s and 1990s, or at
least came to capture commanding heights of state policy making via key
ministries such as foreign, finance, and central banks. Here, there is a contradictory logic between national and global accumulation, as well as a tension
between nation-centric class interests and those groups who develop new relationships linked to transnationalized accumulation. Class and social sectors
whose interests are linked to the old state system still attempt to advance their
interests and to shape the world more fully to those interests. But the material
benefits connected to the remnants of the nation-centric system are subject
to challenge from the class and social forces rooted in the new forms of globalized accumulation. Elsewhere, I have traced and documented these conflicts
as they have unfolded in the Philippines, Haiti, Mexico, Central America, the
United States, Iraq, and several South American countries (Robinson 1996,
2001, 2003, 2004a, 2004b). As conflicts arise between descending forms of
national production and rising forms of globalized capital, local and national
struggles should be seen as simultaneously global and internal. Transnational
fractions, as they have captured governments around the world or come to

positions in which they can influence and redirect state policies, have utilized national state apparatuses to advance capitalist globalization.

Transnationalization of the State

To the extent that transnationally oriented elites have been able to influence state policies, they have reoriented these toward serving global, rather than local, capital accumulation; this includes a shift in state-provided subsidies from social reproduction and internal economic agents toward transnational capital. Neoliberal(ized) states perform three essential services: (1) they adopt fiscal and monetary policies that assure macroeconomic stability and a legal system that provides for arbitrage and enforces property rights; (2) they provide the basic infrastructure necessary for global economic activity (air- and seaports, communications networks, educational systems, etc.); and (3) they provide social order (that is, stability), which requires sustaining instruments of social control and coercive and ideological apparatuses. When transnational elites speak of "governance," they are referring to these functions and the capacity to fulfill them. On the one hand, the neoliberal national state now facilitates global accumulation within the boundaries of its jurisdiction, whereas previously it facilitated national accumulation; on the other hand, it has dispensed with social functions associated with the Keynesian state.

However, transnational capitalists require additional conditions for the functioning and reproduction of global capitalism. National states are ill equipped to organize a supranational unification of macroeconomic policies, create a unified field for the operation of transnational capital, impose transnational trade regimes, achieve supranational "transparency," and so forth. The construction of a supranational legal and regulatory system for the global economy in recent years has been the task of various sets of transnational institutions whose policy prescriptions and actions have been synchronized with those of neoliberal national states that have been captured by local, transnationally oriented forces. There is a new transnational institutionality—a new transnational configuration of power—but this is a very incomplete, contradictory, and open-ended process. "One promising trend toward greater global stability is the growth of horizontal, intergovernmental networks among the world's regulators and legislators," observes Palmisano, in allusion to the network among national states and trans- and supranational institutions, which I refer to as a transnational state (TNS). "Built on shared professional standards and relationships among cross-national communities of experts, these networks are interesting analogues to new forms of organizing work in business, such as globally integrated supply chains, commercial 'ecosystems,' and open-source communities" (2006, 135).

Transnational institutions attempt to coordinate global capitalism and impose capitalist domination beyond national borders. For instance, the International Monetary Fund (IMF), by imposing a structural adjustment program
that opens a given country to the penetration of transnational capital, the
subordination of local labor, and the extraction of wealth by transnational
capitalists, is operating as a TNS institution to facilitate the exploitation of
local labor by global capital. We can conceptualize a TNS apparatus as a loose
network comprised of inter- and supranational political and economic institutions together with national state apparatuses that have been penetrated and
transformed by transnational forces, which has not yet (and may never) ac-
quire any centralized form. Capitalism is (and has always been) a globally
constituted social relation. The state is not external to capital and capitalism;
it is constitutive of capitalist social relations, both theoretically (logically) and
historically.

My thesis on the TNS (Robinson 2001, 2004a, 2004b) involves a three-
fold argument:

1. Economic globalization has its counterpart in transnational class formation and in the emergence of a TNS brought into existence to function as a collective authority for a global ruling class.
2. The nation-state is neither retaining primacy nor disappearing, but
   rather becoming transformed and absorbed into this larger structure of
   a TNS.
3. This emergent TNS institutionalizes new class relations between global
   capital and global labor, or new class relations and social practices of
   global capitalism.

Although it is true that nation-state power and autonomy have declined in
relation to transnational power structures, this image is somewhat misleading since these transnational power structures are localized within each nation by concrete social forces that are materially and politically part of a
transnational power bloc that emerged in the late twentieth century. I have
insisted (Robinson 1996, 2001, 2004a, 2004b, 2008) that we must move
beyond the dualist constructs of states and markets and the national and the
global because, far from being mutually exclusive, these are interpenetrated
and constitutive of each other. Here, I want to emphasize that governments
undertake restructuring and serve the needs of transnational capital not simply because they are "powerless" in the face of globalization, but because a
particular historical constellation of social forces came into existence in the
late twentieth century that presents an organic social base for this global restructuring of capitalism. Lest we fall into the trap of reifying the state, we
must focus on how social relations and processes are played out through
institutions—including states—that are created and constantly recreated by

collective agents, even if those institutions have in turn a recursive effect on the development of social forces. The question that those who cling tenaciously to nation-state-centric approaches should be asking is this: How do social relations refract into state processes and interstate and TNS relations, and in what ways does the increasing transnationalization of social forces engender a transnationalization of the state?

The TNS played a key role in imposing the neoliberal model on the old Third World and therefore in reinforcing new capital-labor relations. The IMF, by conditioning its lending on a deregulation and flexibilization of local labor markets, as it has often done, is imposing the new capital-labor relations on countries and in the process is fundamentally transforming local labor markets and class and power relations. When the United States invaded Iraq and imposed a property regime that gave free rein to transnational capital there and promoted integration into global capitalism, it was internalizing global capitalist relations in Iraq. In these ways, the TNS imposes the new class relations and social practices of global capitalism, and the state as a class relation becomes transnationalized. TNS apparatuses are able to apply what Gill and Law (1993), among others, have referred to as the structural power of transnational power over the direct power of states—that is, the coercive discipline of the global market, whose levers can be pulled by the international financial institutions (IFIs) or the core national states of the G8 to open up space within each nation and region for global accumulation. In this way, through a TNS apparatus, global elites attempt to convert the structural power of the global economy into supranational political authority. States are subject to this structural power of transnational capital and the coercive discipline of the global economy even when transnationally oriented groups are unable to directly instrumentalize states.

While I cannot explore this issue further here, suffice it to cite the following examples among the many well-known instances of global elites wielding the structural power of global capital to exercise supranational political authority: the pressures that global financial markets were able to place on the Brazilian state and the Workers' Party to bend them to meet transnational capitalist rather than popular class interests; Washington's ability to contribute in no small way to the defeat of the Farabundo Martí National Liberation Front (FMLN) in the El Salvadoran elections of 2004, by threatening to block the sending home of remittances by several million Salvadoran immigrant workers in the United States should the electorate vote the FMLN into office; and the financial strangulation of Hamas's ability to govern in Palestinian territories, throwing it into a crisis of legitimacy and destabilizing the Palestinian polity.

The continued division of the world into nation-states constitutes a fundamental condition for the power of transnational capital, because nation-states

can only exercise jurisdiction/sovereignty within national borders but transnational capital operates beyond national borders and is thus not regulated
or responsible to any single political authority. This point is crucial: the continued existence of the nation-state system is a central condition for the power
of transnational capital. For instance, during the early 1990s, TNCs were able
to utilize the institutions of different nation-states in order to continuously
dismantle regulatory structures and other state restrictions on the operation
of transnational capital in a process of mutual deregulation. In this process,
core national states, as components of a larger TNS apparatus, play key roles
in global restructuring. Transnational fractions among dominant groups are
able to use these core states to mold transnational structures. This helps us
understand the preponderant role of the U.S. national state in advancing capitalist globalization.

Yet a globalizing economy within a nation-state-based political system remains a fundamental contradiction in the global capitalist system. A TNS
apparatus as an incipient and multilayered network is unable to regulate
global capitalism or to ameliorate many of its crisis tendencies. Although they
do not disappear, national states experience dramatic fracturing and restructuring. As globalization proceeds, internal social cohesion declines along with
national economic integration. The neoliberal state retains essential powers
to facilitate globalization, but it loses the ability to harmonize conflicting social interests within a country, to realize the historic function of sustaining
the internal unity of nationally conceived social formation, and to achieve
legitimacy. Unable to resolve the contradictory problems of legitimacy and
capital accumulation, local states opt simply to abandon whole sectors of national populations. In many instances, they no longer bother to try to attain
legitimacy among the marginalized and supernumeraries, who are isolated
and contained in new ways or subject to repressive social control measures
(such as, for example, the mass incarceration of African Americans in the
United States). States, just like political parties, are not monolithic institutions, in the sense that social forces and political groups struggle within state
institutions. As crisis spreads throughout the global system, states and ruling
parties become battlefields for contending forces and can be pulled in multiple and often contradictory directions.

Neoliberalism and Trade Agreements: The Quintessential Program of Transnational Capital

The model for global restructuring rested on the assumptions of neoclassical
economics that eclipsed Keynesianism and led to the particular set of social
and economic policies known as neoliberalism, capitulated on the world stage
by Reagan and Thatcher and formalized in what came to be known as the

Washington Consensus (Williamson 1990, 1993). It was not so much the ideas or ideology of neoliberalism that made it the dominant model; rather, it was that the concrete program it prescribed was perfectly functional for transnational capital at the particular historic moment in which the major combines of capital worldwide were transnationalizing and seeking to develop new methods of accumulation and to impose new social relations of production. Neoliberalism is a concrete program as well as an ideology, a culture, and a philosophical worldview that takes classical liberalism and individualism to an extreme. It glorifies the detached, isolated individual—a fictitious state of human existence—and his or her creative potential, which is allegedly unleashed when the individual becomes unencumbered by state regulation and other collective constraints on freedom.

But apart from its ideological and philosophical dimensions, neoliberalism seeks to bring about a convergence in economic policies and institutions mandated by the globalization of production and exchange. Programmatically, global neoliberalism involved twin dimensions, rigorously pursued by global elites with the backing of a powerful and well-organized lobby of TNCs. One dimension was worldwide market liberalization and the construction of a new legal and regulatory superstructure for the global economy. The other was the internal restructuring and global integration of each national economy. The combination of the two was intended to create a "liberal world order"—an open global economy and a global policy regime that breaks down all national barriers to the free movement of transnational capital between borders and the free operation of capital within borders in the search for new productive outlets for excess accumulated capital.

It is in this context that we can understand global trade policies. Worldwide market liberalization accelerated dramatically with the Uruguay Round of General Agreement on Tariffs and Trade (GATT) negotiations in the 1980s, which established a sweeping new set of world trade rules to regulate the new global economy. These rules were based on (1) freedom of investment and capital movements; (2) the liberalization of services, including banks; (3) intellectual property rights; and (4) a free movement of goods. Transnational elites also promoted regional integration processes, including the North American Free Trade Agreement (NAFTA), the European Union (EU), and the Asia Pacific Economic Cooperation (APEC), and the creation of the WTO in 1995 following the Uruguay Round. Economic restructuring programs, designed in the 1970s and 1980s by the IFIs and the think tanks of emerging transnational elites (Fishlow et al. 1978; Cox 1987; Williamson 1993), were accompanied by a new neoliberal development discourse (Robinson 2002, 2003). These programs sought to achieve within each country the macroeconomic equilibrium and liberalization required by transnationally mobile capital and to integrate each nation and region into globalized circuits of accumulation. The model attempted to harmonize a wide range of fiscal, monetary, industrial, labor, and commercial policies among multiple nations, as a requirement for mobile transnational capital to function simultaneously, and often instantaneously, among numerous national borders. The programs called for the elimination of state intervention in the economy and individual nation-states' regulation of the activities of capital in their territories. Between 1978 and 1992, more than seventy countries adopted 566 stabilization and structural adjustment programs imposed by the IMF and the World Bank (George 1992). These programs become the major mechanism of adjusting local economies to the global economy. Through these programs, there was a massive restructuring of the countries' productive apparatus, and the reintegration of vast zones of the former Third and Second Worlds into global capitalism (Overbeek 1993; Chossudovsky 1997; Robinson 2001).

The neoliberal program is rational vis-à-vis the logic of global capital accumulation, which is why the works of well-known economists who explain and defend neoliberalism from a neoclassical theoretical perspective are not merely wrong or ideological in the narrow sense. The model generates the overall conditions for the profitable renewal of capital accumulation. Internal conditions of profitability are determined by compatibility of the local with the global environment. Adjustment creates the policy environment and the market signals for a shift in resources to external sectors. Economic reactivation in each adjusted country is achieved through the introduction or expansion of activities linked to the global economy and the integration of national accumulation circuits into globalized circuits. Greased by neoliberalism, global capitalism tears down all nonmarket structures that have in the past placed limits on, or acted as a protective layer against, the accumulation of capital. Deregulation made new zones available for resource exploitation; privatization opened up public and community spheres, ranging from health care and education to police and prison systems, to profit making. Nonmarket spheres of human activity—public spheres managed by states and private spheres linked to community and family—are broken up, commodified, and transferred to capital. As countries in the South are integrated into global capitalism through neoliberal restructuring, they become emerging markets that provide new market segments, pools of labor, and opportunities for transnational investors to unload excess capital, whether in productive or financial investment.

From a Territorial to a Social Conception of Development, and an International to a Global Social Division of Labor

Class, racial, and gender inequalities have in many respects been aggravated by globalization, and new social cleavages are emerging. One major new axis of inequality is that of citizen versus noncitizen in the face of a massive up-surge in transnational migration and the increasing use of ethnic immigrant labor pools around the world (Robinson 2006a, 2006b). On the one hand, global society appears stratified ever less along national and territorial lines and more across transnational social and class lines (Castells 2000; Cox 1987; Hoogvelt 1997; Robinson 1998, 2002, 2003, 2008). Yet, on the other hand, the dominant discourse on global inequality is still territorial, that is, focusing on inequality among nations in a world system.

For instance, Hurricane Katrina ravaged New Orleans in 2005, lifting the veil on race, class, poverty, and inequality in the United States. The storm disproportionately devastated poor black communities that lacked the re-sources to protect themselves, and their Third World social conditions be-came apparent. A UN report released in the immediate aftermath of the hurricane observed that the infant mortality rate in the United States had been rising for the previous five years and was the same as that of Malaysia; that black children were twice as likely as whites to die before their first birth-day; and that blacks in Washington, D.C., had a higher infant mortality rate than people in the Indian state of Kerala (UNDP 2005). These observations make it clear that a sociology of national development is no longer tenable. In earlier epochs, core and periphery referred to specific territories and the populations that resided therein. The center-periphery division of labor cre-ated by modern colonialism reflected a particular spatial configuration in the law of uneven development, which is gradually being transformed by global-ization. The transnational geographic dispersal of the full range of world pro-duction processes suggests that core and peripheral production activities are less geographically bounded than previously. Furthermore, new financial cir-cuits allow wealth to be moved instantaneously around the world through cyberspace, just as easily as it is generated, so that the exact location where wealth is produced becomes less important for the issue of development.

While the global South is increasingly dispersed across the planet, so too is the global North. Rapid economic growth in India and China has created hundreds of millions of new middle-class consumers who are integrated into the global cornucopia, even as it has thrown other hundreds of millions into destitution. The cohesive structures of nations and their civil societies disinte-grate as populations become divided into core and peripheral labor pools and as local economic expansion results in the advancement of some (delocalized) groups and deepening poverty for others. We find that an affluent developed population, including a privileged sector among segmented labor markets linked to knowledge-intensive, professional, and managerial activities and high consumption, exists alongside a super-exploited secondary segment of flexibilized labor and a mass of supernumeraries constituting an underdevel-oped population within the same national borders. This social bifurcation seems to be a worldwide phenomenon, explained in part by the inability of national states to capture and redirect surpluses through interventionist mechanisms that were viable in the nation-state phase of capitalism. Development should be reconceived not as a national phenomenon, in which what develops is not a nation, but in terms of developed, underdeveloped, and intermediate population groups occupying contradictory or unstable locations in a transnational environment.

There remain, of course, very real regional differences in relation to global accumulation, and distinct regions have particular histories and configurations of social forces that shape distinct experiences under globalization. Moreover, these social forces operate through national and regional institutions. Hence there is variation in the process of globalization and in the concomitant processes of institutionalization of the new social relations and political structures of global capitalism. But this does not mean that national and regional competition are causal to processes of uneven accumulation. Instead, we want to see how transnational social forces from above are able to reproduce and utilize regional distinctions to serve global accumulation, and how transnational social forces from below continue to operate politically through local and national institutions in struggles against global capitalism.

The unequal exchanges—material, political, cultural—implied in a social division of labor on a world scale are not captured so much in the concept of an international division of labor as in a global division of labor, which implies differential participation in global production according to social standing and not necessarily geographic location. This global division of labor can then account for sweatshops in East Los Angeles and Northern Honduras, IT professional districts in Silicon Valley and Bangalore, and gated communities in Hollywood and São Paulo. The great geographic core-periphery divide, a product of the colonial and imperialist era in world capitalism, is gradually eroding, not because the periphery is "catching up" but because of the shift from an international to a global division of labor. For some, the international division of labor has merely permutated along the lines suggested by Fröbel, Heinrichs, and Kreye (1980). Manufacturing has shifted from North to South. The North specializes in high-skilled and better-paid labor, supplying advanced services and technology to the world market, while the South provides low-skilled and lower-paid labor for global manufacturing and primary commodity supply. But this analysis, as Harvard economist Richard Freeman observes, has become obsolete

> due to the massive investments that the large populous developing countries are making in human capital. China and India are producing millions of college graduates capable of doing the same work as the college graduates of the United States, Japan or Europe—at much lower pay. . . . The huge number of highly educated workers in India and

China threatens to undo the traditional pattern of trade between advanced and less developed countries. Historically, advanced countries have innovated high-tech products that require high-wage educated workers and extensive R&D, while developing countries specialize in old manufacturing products. The reason for this was that the advanced countries had a near monopoly on scientists and engineers and other highly educated workers. As China, India and other developing countries have increased their number of university graduates, this monopoly on high-tech innovative capacity has diminished. Today, most major multinationals have R&D centers in China or India, so that the locus of technological advance may shift. (2005, 3)

Processes of uneven accumulation increasingly unfold in accordance with a social and not a national logic. Different levels of social development adhere from the very sites of social productive activity, that is, from social, not geographic, space. Moreover, privileged groups have an increasing ability to manipulate space so as to create enclaves and insulate themselves through novel mechanisms of social control and new technologies for the built environment. The persistence, and in fact growth, of the North-South divide remains important for its theoretical and practical political implications. What is subject to debate is whether the divide is something innate to world capitalism or a particular spatial configuration of uneven capitalist development during a particular historic phase of world capitalism, and whether tendencies toward the self-reproduction of this configuration are increasingly offset by countertendencies emanating from the nature and dynamic of global capital accumulation.

To explain the movement of values between different nodes in globalized accumulation, we need to move beyond nation-state-centric approaches and apply a theory of value to transformations in world spatial and institutional structures (the nation-state being the central spatial and institutional structure in the history of world capitalism to the present time). The notion of development must take into account the deterritorialization of value creation, circulation, and appropriation and novel transnational institutional configurations through which these processes unfold. Capital no longer needs to pay for reproduction of labor power (production and social reproduction become severed), while the shift to global markets means that domestic markets are no longer strategic, or even necessary, for the reproduction (self-expansion) of capital. The notion of net social gain or loss used by development economists has little meaning if measured, as it traditionally is, in national terms, or even in geographic terms. The distribution of social costs and gains must be conceived in transnational social terms—not in terms of the nation-state vis-à-vis the world economy, but transnationally as social groups vis-à-vis other social groups in a global society. In reconceiving development, we need to move beyond the notion of an axial division of labor and consider replacing it with the conception of an emergent global social division of labor.

The Crisis of Global Capitalism

Since the 1980s, the TCC has been attempting to position itself as a new ruling class group worldwide and to bring some coherence and stability to its rule through an emergent TNS apparatus. The world politics of this would-be global ruling class is not driven, as it was for national ruling classes, by the flux of shifting rivalries and alliances played out through the interstate system, but by the new global social structure of accumulation. It appeared for a time in the 1990s that transnational elites would be able to establish a new global capitalist historic bloc. But in the 1980s and 1990s, such a globalist bloc achieved, at best, a certain restricted, as opposed to expansive, hegemony in global society, less through the internalization of the neoliberal worldview by popular classes worldwide than through the disorganization of these classes in the wake of the juggernaut of capitalist globalization (Robinson 2005b). Nonetheless, since the late 1990s, the globalist bloc has been unable to reproduce even this "restricted" hegemony, and its authority appeared to be fast collapsing as the global crisis deepened at breakneck speed in 2008.

The crisis, which exploded with the collapse of the global financial system, springs from contradictions in global capitalism that are expressed in immanent crisis tendencies and in a series of displacements over the past three decades that had served to postpone a day of reckoning. The global crisis involves four interrelated dimensions (Robinson 2004a, 2004b, 2008). The first is a crisis of social polarization. The system cannot meet the needs of a majority of humanity, or even assure minimal social reproduction. The second dimension is a structural crisis of overaccumulation. The system cannot expand because the marginalization of a significant portion of humanity from direct productive participation, the downward pressure on wages and popular consumption worldwide, and the polarization of income have reduced the ability of the world market to absorb world output. This is the structural underpinning of the series of lesser crises, including the Mexican peso crisis of 1995 and its effects elsewhere, followed by the Asian financial meltdown of 1997–98, which also spread around the world, and then the world recession of 2001. I will return momentarily to overaccumulation. The third dimension is a crisis of legitimacy and authority. National states face spiraling crises of legitimacy as they fail to meet the social grievances of local working classes experiencing downward mobility, unemployment, heightened insecurity, and greater hardships. The legitimacy of the system has increasingly been called into question by millions, perhaps even billions, of people around the world, and it is facing expanded counterhegemonic challenges. In the late 1990s, popular resistance forces in various parts of the world formed a critical mass, coalescing around agendas for global social justice, as in the case of the counterhegemonic regional bloc in the Andean region, led by Venezuela, or the transnational networks of the World Social Forum. In other instances, a counterhegemonic impulse has come from such reactionary forces as Christian or Islamic fundamentalism. It was clear that global elites were unable to counter the erosion of the system's authority in the face of worldwide pressures for a global moral economy. Finally, we face a crisis of sustainability—an ecological crisis expressed in climate change, peak oil, and the impending collapse of centralized agricultural systems in several regions of the world, among other indicators.

The global capitalism perspective put forth in this chapter offers a powerful explanatory framework for making sense of crisis. Following Marx, we must focus on the internal dynamics of capitalism to understand the crisis, and following the global capitalism perspective, we must also comprehend how capitalism has qualitatively changed in recent decades. The system-wide crisis that began with the collapse of the financial system in 2008 will not be a repeat of earlier crises, such as those in the 1930s or the 1970s, precisely because world capitalism is fundamentally different in the early twenty-first century. As we have seen, the globalization stage of world capitalism itself evolved out of the response of distinct agents to previous episodes of crisis. In particular, capital responded to the crisis of Fordism-Keynesianism in the 1970s by going global, which unleashed it from nation-state constraints on accumulation. The pursuant neoliberal counterrevolution opened up vast new opportunities for accumulation in the 1980s and 1990s. Major gains in productivity and the shedding of labor worldwide undercut wages and the social wage, transferring income to capital and to new high-consumption sectors around the world that provided new market segments, thus fueling growth; privatizations and intellectual property rights opened up public sectors, community spaces, and cultural and knowledge production to commodification, and hence facilitated new bursts of accumulation; deregulation and liberalization allowed for a new wave of foreign direct investment (FDI), transnational mergers and acquisitions, and so forth; the incorporation of the former socialist and Third World revolutionary countries provided vast new markets and investment outlets; and deregulation of the financial industry, together with the introduction of computer and information technology, made possible the creation of a globally integrated financial system and a global casino capitalism founded on financial speculation.

In sum, globalization unleashed a frenzied new round of accumulation worldwide that offset the 1970s crisis of declining profits and investment opportunities. But this period of restructuring remained fluid and indeterminate, and by the late twentieth century, the system was once again moving into crisis as the limits to expansion became clear. As privatizations ran their course and the former socialist and revolutionary countries were brought into the system, new opportunities for expansion began to dry up, global markets became saturated, and overcapacity increased. The system generated ever more massive surpluses as opportunities for the profitable absorption of those surpluses diminished. Overaccumulation historically follows periods of hyperaccumulation. The capitalist system faces the permanent challenge of how to profitably unload the surplus. Between the Asian financial meltdown of 1997–98 and the worldwide recession of 2001, global elites began to sound alarm bells. The more politically astute clamored for a post–Washington Consensus project of reform—a so-called globalization with a human face—in the interest of saving the system itself (Stiglitz 2002). But there were others from within and outside of the bloc who called for more radical responses. By the start of the new century, two major mechanisms for unloading surplus had taken over: financial speculation and militarized accumulation.

Transnational finance capital is the most mobile fraction of global capital and became the hegemonic fraction of capital on a world scale. Over the past thirty years, the revolution in finance has included all sorts of financial innovations and derivatives—mortgage-backed securities, swaps, futures markets, hedge funds, institutional investment funds, pyramiding assets, and so forth—and even turned debt into a tradable so that debt itself becomes a source of accumulation. Transnational finance capital has proved utterly predatory, seeking out one outlet after another for frenzied speculation. In the 1980s and 1990s, speculators invested massively in emerging global property markets, thereby inflating urban real estate values in global cities around the world. They also engaged in wild stock market speculation, which led to a succession of bubbles followed by busts, culminating in the bursting of the dot-com bubble at the turn of the century. Then there was the phenomenal escalation of hedge fund flows and pyramiding of assets, and later on the frantic speculation in global commodity markets, especially the energy and food markets, which pushed world prices up to unprecedented levels in 2007 and 2008 and sparked food riots around the world. Meanwhile, U.S. consumer debt climbed from $355 billion in 1980 to $1 trillion in 1994, $2 trillion in 2004, and $2.6 trillion in 2008, while the U.S. current account went from a surplus in 1992 to deficits of $100 billion in 1998, $700 billion in 2004, and $1.2 trillion in 2008, according to Federal Reserve data. The Federal Reserve decision to reduce interest rates to about 1 percent in an effort to overcome the 2001 recession led to a wave of speculation in the U.S. mortgage market. In this way, the U.S. market became the world's market of last resort for global capitalism. Consumption driven by U.S. consumer credit card and mortgage debt and state deficit financing sustained accumulation worldwide and momentarily displaced the crisis. In the perverse world of predatory transnational finance capital, debt and deficits themselves became new sources of financial speculation. Yet it must be stressed that it was trans-national—not U.S.—capital that relied on U.S. debt and deficits to sustain profit making around the world. The subprime mortgage market, for example, attracted trillions of dollars from individual, institutional, and corporate investors all around the world.

Global casino capitalism produced an ever greater expansion of fictitious capital—that is, money thrown into circulation without any base in commodities or in productive activity. The gap between the worldwide speculative economy and the real economy grew to an unfathomable chasm. In 2000, for instance, the worldwide trade in goods and services totaled less than $10 trillion for the entire year, according to IMF data, while daily movements in currency speculation stood at $3.5 trillion, so that in just a few days more currency circulated as speculation than the circulation of goods and services in an entire year! By the early years of the twenty-first century, massive concentrations of transnational finance capital were destabilizing the system and global capitalism ran up against the limits of financial fixes. The collapse of the subprime mortgage market in 2007 was merely the straw that broke the camel's back.

Meanwhile, the U.S. state militarized the global economy as the cutting edge of accumulation in the real economy worldwide shifted from computer and information technology, before the dot-com bust, to a military-security-industrial-construction-petroleum complex that also accrued enormous influence in the halls of power in Washington. Military spending skyrocketed into the trillions of dollars through the war on terrorism and the invasions and occupations of Iraq and Afghanistan, and the spin-off effects of this spending flowed through the open veins of the global economy. The war on terrorism resulted in numerous indicators of a global capitalism beset by structural, political, and ideological crises. It provided a seemingly endless military outlet for surplus capital, generated a colossal deficit that justified the ever deeper dismantling of the Keynesian welfare state and locked neoliberal austerity in place, and legitimated the creation of a police state to repress political dissent in the name of security.

Many interpreted militarization and renewed U.S. interventionism under the Bush administration through theories of a new imperialism, in which the United States was attempting to renew its empire and offset the decline in its hegemony amid heightened interimperialist rivalry (Wood 2003; Harvey 2005; Foster 2006; Appelbaum and Robinson 2005). These interpretations confused capitalist competition with state competition and conflated disarray, factionalism, and parochial and sectoral interests among transnational capitalist groups and global elites with nation-state rivalries. The hallmark of new imperialism theories is the assumption that world capitalism in the twenty-first century is made up of domestic capitals and distinct national economies that interact with one another, accompanied by a realist analysis of world politics as driven by governments' pursuit of their national interests. Once we belie the realist notion of a world of national economies and national capitals, then the logical sequence in new imperialism argumentation collapses like a house of cards, since the whole edifice is constructed on this notion (Robinson 2007a).

The U.S. state has attempted to play a leadership role on behalf of transnational capitalist interests, taking the lead in imposing a reorganization of world capitalism. But this does not mean that U.S. interventionism has sought to defend U.S. interests. As the most powerful component of the TNS, the U.S. state apparatus defends the interests of transnational investors and the overall system. The only military apparatus in the world capable of exercising global coercive authority is the U.S. military. The beneficiaries of U.S. military action around the world have been transnational, rather than U.S., capitalist groups. This is the underlying class relation between the TCC and the U.S. national state. Despite the rhetoric of neoliberalism, the U.S. state undertook an almost unprecedented role in creating profit-making opportunities for transnational capital and pushing forward an accumulation process that, left to its own devices, would have ground to a halt much earlier than 2008. The creative destruction of war (and natural and humanitarian disasters) generated new cycles of accumulation through reconstruction. As I have discussed elsewhere (Robinson 2008), the trillions of dollars invested by the U.S. state in war and "reconstruction" in Iraq and elsewhere have gone to a vast array of investors and subcontractors that span the globe (Phinney 2005); essentially, U.S. military spending has acted as fresh firewood being thrown on the embers of the global economy. For instance, Kuwaiti Trading and Contracting, Alargan Trading of Kuwait, and the Gulf Catering and Saudi Trading and Construction Company were just some of the Middle East–based companies that entered into multiple subcontracting relationships with Halliburton and Bechtel, sharing in the bonanza with companies and investor groups as far away as South Africa, Bosnia, the Philippines, and India (Phinney 2005). The picture that emerged was one in which the U.S. state mobilized the resources to feed a vast transnational network of profit making that passed through countless layers of outsourcing, subcontracting, alliances, and collaborative relations, benefiting transnationally oriented capitalists from many parts of the globe as the class relations of global capitalism became deeply internalized *within* every nation-state.

We can identify three types of crises: cyclical, structural, and systemic. It is clear that the current crisis is not merely cyclical, as were the recessions of the early 1980s, the early 1990s, and 2001. Cyclical crises of overproduction have appeared approximately once a decade over the past century and a half. Rather, the crisis that began in 2008 is structural. A structural crisis is a restructuring crisis, meaning that any resolution of the crisis must involve a major restructuring of the system. It was the early 1970s structural crisis that led, in the first place, to globalization and neoliberal restructuring, just as the 1930s structural crisis led to a restructuring of the system of Fordist-Keynesian redistributive capitalism, which prevailed through the middle decades of the twentieth century. A structural crisis opens up the possibility for a systemic crisis, meaning that the crisis is resolved by superseding the system itself and creating an alternative social order. Whether structural crises become systemic crises is not predetermined and depends entirely on the response of social forces to crisis and on historical contingencies that cannot be forecast.

Many global elites have responded to the crisis by pushing for a global neo-Keynesianism aimed at saving capitalism from itself and from potential radical challenges. The Obama administration appeared in its first two years to be attempting such a project, which entails a shift from neoclassical to institutionalist economics, a limited reregulation of global market forces, and state intervention to bail out transnational capital. A global reformism appeared to be the dominant response from elites in 2009, but there was no global elite consensus and it is entirely premature to predict or describe a new model of global capitalism, as social forces will be battling it out for a long time to come. Moreover, the prospects of such a project face the fundamental contradiction of a globalizing economy within a nation-state-based system of political authority and legal enforcement. "We now have global financial markets, global corporations, global financial flows," stated then British prime minister Gordon Brown at an emergency summit of the G20 countries in late 2008. "But what we do not have is anything other than national and regional regulation and supervision. We need a global way of supervising our financial system. . . . We need very large and very radical [political, institutional] changes" (quoted in Brecher, Costello, and Smith 2008).

Global reformism from above competes with resurgent left, radical, and anticapitalist forces worldwide that have placed socialism on the world political agenda once again. These forces call for the resolution of the crisis through a more far-reaching transformation of the global social order but lack a postmodern prince or political vehicles and concrete projects for reordering the world—deficiencies of which they seemed to be acutely aware. At the close of a 120,000-strong meeting of the World Social Forum in Belém, Brazil, in January 2009, representatives from social movements around the world declared,

> We are facing a global crisis which is a direct consequence of the capitalist system and therefore cannot find a solution within the system. . . .
> In order to overcome the crisis we have to grapple with the root of the problem and progress as fast as possible towards the construction of a radical alternative that would do away with the capitalist system and

patriarchal domination. We, the social movements, are faced with an historic opportunity to develop emancipatory initiatives on a global scale. . . . The challenge of social movements is to achieve a convergence of global mobilization. (World Social Forum 2009)

Their declaration raises the question: Could such a global mobilization from below push reformist-minded elites further to the left?

But reformist and radical responses compete with far-right forces from both above and below, in what I refer to as the impulse toward a twenty-first-century fascism (Robinson 2008). Such a project would involve the fusion of reactionary political power with transnational capital, would develop a mass social base among those traditionally more privileged sectors of the working and middle classes experiencing mounting insecurity and downward mobility in the face of the crisis, and would have targeted scapegoats, the most apparent being immigrant worker populations. It would also involve racism, militarization, and extreme masculinization. The outlines of such a project became visible during the Bush administration and have spread to an increasing number of countries as the crisis has deepened. The need for widespread, organized social control to contain the surplus population and potential rebellion from below certainly gives an impulse to twenty-first-century fascist responses to the global crisis. And global neo-Keynesianism programs are not mutually exclusive with authoritarian responses, which could take the form of oppressive right-wing populisms.

It is at times of crisis rather than equilibrium in a system that space opens up for new ideas and for collective agency to influence the course of structural change. At the structural level, crisis means that the system's capacity for surplus absorption is exhausted and that we have entered a phase of the destruction of value or devaluation of capital. Historically, dominant groups attempt to transfer the cost of crisis onto the mass of popular and working classes, and in turn these classes resist such attempts. This is the global political moment. We are entering a period of turbulence, upheavals, collapse of states, political vacuums, and prolonged conflict as we step into the unknown. In my view, the resolution of the crisis must involve a radical redistribution of wealth and power to poor majorities. Social justice requires, at the minimum, reintroducing a redistributive component into the global accumulation process. That being said, what would such a new redistributive component involve and how would it come about?

This raises the question of what the forces in favor of social justice can hope to achieve if and when poor people and popular sectors are able to win state power in particular countries or at least place people in state agencies who are responsive to their plight, aware of their needs, and willing to challenge the prerogatives of transnational capital. Yet this brings us full circle—back to globalization and to what makes the early twenty-first century distinct from previous moments in the history of world capitalism. In this qualitatively new stage of global capitalism, there are clear limitations to the reintroduction of a redistributive project at the nation-state level. It is not clear how effective national alternatives alone might be in transforming social structures and resolving the crisis. If the (capitalist) state as a class relation is becoming transnationalized, then any challenge to (global) capitalist state power must involve a major transnational component. Struggles at the nation-state level are far from futile. They remain central to the prospects for social justice and progressive social change. But any such struggles must be part of a more expansive transnational counterhegemonic project, including transnational trade unionism, transnational social movements, transnational political organizations, and so on. And they must strive to establish sets of transnational institutions and practices that can place controls on the global market and rein in some of global capital's power as the first step in a resolution of the crisis.

On the other hand, it seems to me that the flip side to progressive reform—if not an outright transformation—of the global order can only be successful when linked to the transformation of class and property relations in specific sets of countries. And absent such transformation, efforts at global reform will be frustrated. Local class and property relations have global implications. Webs of interdependence and causal sequences in social change link the global to the local, so that change at either level is dependent on change at the other level. An alternative to global capitalism must therefore take the form of a transnational popular project. In its struggle for social justice, the popular mass of humanity must develop a transnational class consciousness and concomitant global political protagonism, involving strategies, programs, organizations, and institutions that link local to national, and national to global.

REFERENCES

Aglietta, Michel. 1979. *A Theory of Capitalist Regulation: The US Experience*. London: Verso.

Appelbaum, Richard, and William I. Robinson. 2005. *Critical Globalization Studies*. New York: Routledge.

Arrighi, Giovanni. 1994. *The Long Twentieth Century: Money, Power, and the Origins of Our Time*. London: Verso.

Brecher, Jeremy, Tim Costello, and Brendan Smith. 2008. "The G-20 vs. The G-6 Billion." ZNet. November 20. http://www.zmag.org/znet/viewArticle/19707.

Carroll, William K., and Colin Carson. 2003. "The Network of Global Corporations and Elite Policy Groups: A Structure for Transnational Capitalist Class Formation?" *Global Networks* 3 (1): 29–57.

Caroll, William K., and Meindert Fennema. 2002. "Is There a Transnational Business Community?" *International Sociology* 17 (3): 393–419.

Castells, Manuel. 2000. *The Rise of the Network Society*. Vol. 1 of *The Information Age: Economy, Society, and Culture*. 2nd ed. Oxford: Blackwell.

Chossudovsky, Michel. 1997. *The Globalisation of Poverty: Impacts of IMF and World Bank Reform*. London: Zed Books.

Cox, Robert W. 1987. *Production, Power, and World Order: Social Forces in the Making of History*. New York: Columbia University Press.

Crozier, Michel, Samuel P. Huntington, and Joji Watanuki. 1975. *The Crisis of Democracy: Report on the Governability of Democracies to the Trilateral Commission*. New York: New York University Press.

Dicken, Peter. 1998. *Global Shift: Transforming the World Economy*. 3rd ed. London: Guilford Press.

Fishlow, Albert, Carlos F. Diáz Alejandro, Richard R. Fagen, and Roger D. Hansen. 1978. *Rich and Poor Nations in the World Economy*. New York: McGraw Hill.

Foster, John Bellamy. 2006. *Naked Imperialism: U.S. Pursuit of Global Dominance*. New York: Monthly Review.

Fourtou, Jean-Rene, and Marcus Wallenberg. 2005. "Last and Best Chance to Move Doha Round to a Successful Conclusion." *Financial Times*, November 8. http://news.ft .com/cms/s/328b4362-4ffd-11da-8b72-0000779e2340.htm l.

Freeman, Richard. 2005. "China, India, and the Doubling of the Global Labor Force: Who Pays the Price of Globalization?" *Globalist*, June 3. http://www.japanfocus.org/arti cle.asp?id = 377 (page discontinued).

Fröbel, Folker, Jürgen Heinrichs, and Otto Kreye. 1980. *The New International Division of Labour: Structural Unemployment in Industrialised Countries and Industrialisation in Developing Countries*. Cambridge: Cambridge University Press.

George, Susan. 1992. *The Debt Boomerang: How Third World Debt Harms Us All*. Boulder, Colo.: Westview Press.

Gill, Stephen, and David Law. 1993. "Global Hegemony and the Structural Power of Capital." In *Gramsci, Historical Materialism, and International Relations*, edited by Stephen Gill, 93–124. Cambridge: Cambridge University Press.

Harvey, David. 1982. *The Limits to Capital*. Chicago: University of Chicago Press.

———. 1990. *The Condition of Postmodernity: An Enquiry into the Origins of Cultural Change*. London: Blackwell.

———. 2005. *The New Imperialism*. 2nd ed. Oxford: Oxford University Press.

Hoogvelt, Ankie. 1997. *Globalization and the Post-Colonial World: The New Political Economy of Development*. Baltimore: Johns Hopkins University Press.

Horn, John. 2005. "Filmmakers Are Swept Away by Romania." *Los Angeles Times*, October 2.

Iritani, Evelyn. 2000. "High-Paid Jobs Latest U.S. Export." *Los Angeles Times*, April 2.

Kentor, Jeffrey. 2005. "The Growth of Transnational Corporate Networks, 1962 to 1998." *Journal of World-Systems Research* 11 (2): 262–86.

Kentor, Jeffrey, and Yong Suk Jang. 2004. "Yes, There Is a (Growing) Transnational Business Community." *International Sociology* 19 (3): 355–68.

Kolko, Joyce. 1988. *Restructuring the World Economy*. New York: Pantheon Books.

Kotz, David M., Terrence McDonough, and Michael Reich, eds. 1994. *Social Structures of Accumulation: The Political Economy of Growth and Crisis*. Cambridge: Cambridge University Press.

Lipietz, Alain. 1987. *Mirages and Miracles: The Crisis of Global Fordism*. London: Verso.

Marglin, Stephen A., and Juliet B. Schor, eds. 1990. *The Golden Age of Capitalism: Reinterpreting the Postwar Experience*. Oxford: Clarendon Press.

McMichael, Philip. 1996. *Development and Social Change: A Global Perspective*. Thousand Oaks, Calif.: Pine Forge.

Overbeek, Henk, ed. 1993. *Restructuring Hegemony in the Global Political Economy: The Rise of Transnational Neoliberalism in the 1980s*. London: Routledge.

Palmisano, Samuel, F. 2006. "The Globally Integrated Enterprise." *Foreign Affairs* 85 (3): 127–36.

Phinney, David. 2005. "Blood, Sweat, and Tears: Asia's Poor Build U.S. Bases in Iraq." *CorpWatch*. October 3. http://www.corpwatch.org/article.php?id = 12675.

Robinson, William I. 1996. *Promoting Polyarchy: Globalization, Hegemony, and U.S. Intervention.* Cambridge: Cambridge University Press.

———. 1998. "Beyond Nation-State Paradigms: Globalization, Sociology, and the Challenge of Transnational Studies." *Sociological Forum* 13 (4): 561–94.

———. 2001. "Social Theory and Globalization: The Rise of a Transnational State." *Theory and Society* 30 (2): 157–200.

———. 2002. "Remapping Development in Light of Globalization: From a Territorial to a Social Cartography." *Third World Quarterly* 23 (6): 1047–71.

———. 2003. *Transnational Conflicts: Central America, Globalization, and Social Change.* London: Verso.

———. 2004a. *A Theory of Global Capitalism: Production, Class, and State in a Transnational World.* Baltimore: Johns Hopkins University Press.

———. 2004b. "What to Expect from U.S. 'Democracy Promotion' in Iraq." *New Political Science* 26 (3): 441–47.

———. 2005a. "Global Capitalism: The New Transnationalism and the Folly of Conventional Thinking." *Science and Society* 69 (3): 316–18.

———. 2005b. "Gramsci and Globalization: From Nation-State to Transnational Hegemony." *Critical Review of International Social and Political Philosophy* 8 (4): 1–16.

———. 2006a. "'Aqui estamos y no nos vamos!': Global Capital and Immigrant Rights." *Race and Class* 48 (2): 77–91.

———. 2006b. "Reification and Theoreticism in the Study of Globalisation, Imperialism, and Hegemony: Response to Kiely, Pozo-Martin, and Valladao." *Cambridge Review of International Affairs* 19 (3): 529–33.

———. 2007a. "Beyond the Theory of Imperialism: Global Capitalism and the Transnational State." *Societies Without Borders* 2 (1): 5–26.

———. 2007b. "The Pitfall of Realist Analysis of Global Capitalism: A Critique of Ellen Meiksins Wood's *Empire of Capital.*" *Historical Materialism* 15 (3): 71–93.

———. 2008. *Global Capitalism and Latin America: A Globalization Perspective.* Baltimore: Johns Hopkins University Press.

Rothkopf, David. 1997. "In Praise of Cultural Imperialism." *Foreign Policy* 107 (Summer): 38–53.

Sassen, Saskia. 1991. *The Global City: New York, London, Tokyo.* Princeton: Princeton University Press.

———. 2006. *Territory Authority Rights: From Medieval to Global Assemblages.* Princeton: Princeton University Press.

Sklair, Leslie. 2002. *Globalization: Capitalism and Its Alternatives.* Oxford: Oxford University Press.

Stiglitz, Joseph E. 2002. *Globalization and Its Discontents.* New York: W. W. Norton.

United Nations Development Programme. 2005. *Human Development Report 2005.* New York: Oxford University Press and UNDP.

Williamson, John, ed. 1990. *Latin American Adjustment: How Much Has Happened?* Washington, D.C.: Institute for International Economics.

———. 1993. "Democracy and the 'Washington Consensus.'" *World Development* 21 (8): 1329–36.

Wood, Ellen Meiksins. 2003. *Empire of Capital.* London: Verso.

World Social Forum. 2009. "Declaration of the Assembly of Social Movements at the World Social Forum 2009." February 4. Global Research. http://www.globalresearch.ca/index.php?context=va&aid=12160.

6

POPULAR POWER IN A NEOLIBERAL WORLD:
HOW GLOBAL INTERDEPENDENCE CAN FOSTER
DEMOCRATIC EMPOWERMENT

Frances Fox Piven

What are the prospects for the effective exercise of power from below as the process of globalization dominated by market actors continues? My argument in this chapter is that the potential for popular power increases as the complex and fragile relations underlying neoliberal globalization proliferate and expand. The reasoning underlying this view is not obvious at first glance. It rests partly on an exploration of the very nature of popular power and perennial obstacles to its actualization. It also rests on a characterization of features of neoliberal globalization that may increase the vulnerability of economic and political elites to challenges from below.

But first, just what does our experience so far tell us about popular power under neoliberal globalization? At a glance, the evidence is contradictory. On the one hand, it appears that democratic institutions as we have known them are gravely undermined. The electoral representative arrangements that have come to be seen as the virtual definition of democracy gain their significance because they are vehicles through which the population exercises some control over elites based in the nation-state. But what use is such control when the nation-state itself appears to have lost the ability to control crucial market actors, including multinational corporations and international financiers? Moreover, as the state's capacity to regulate the economy diminishes, so does its ability to honor the labor and welfare state rights of the twentieth-century social compact. Soaring inequality is treated as evidence of this convulsive power shift. The indicators are numerous, but a headline from the *London Times* on December 6, 2006, captures the trend: "Richest Tenth Own 85 Per Cent of World's Assets."

On the other hand, these purported weaknesses in electoral representative democracy notwithstanding, people on the street seem to think that they have power, maybe even more power than they have had in the past. Protest movements are resurgent, especially in the global South, in China, Nigeria, Nepal, India, and across Latin America. Moreover, in Latin America, protest movements have played a key role in toppling governments that acted as the willing instruments of neoliberalism and bringing populists or social democrats to power in their place. The rich world is not exempt from protest movements either, as evident in recent immigrant riots and public sector strikes in France, the rise of an immigrant rights movement in the United States, and the recent protests in Greece.

The traditional explanations for the eruption of protests do not provide entirely satisfactory explanations. True, the economic trends associated with neoliberal globalization have increased hardship for many people, but efforts to correlate hardship with protests have never been entirely satisfactory. Sometimes hardship seems to provoke popular outbreaks, but certainly not always, and maybe not usually.[1] Alternatively, perhaps it is that globalization has weakened the social infrastructure that usually regulates collective life, whether the traditional family or the village or the stable residential community. Here again, the historical evidence for the proposition that social disorganization causes protest is uneven. And then there is the now familiar proposition offered by Karl Polanyi, the idea that the advance of the unregulated market triggers a countermovement, a double movement in his terminology, of resistance and reaction.

Perhaps, however, such explanations assume that the translation of hardship or social disorganization, or the impact of predatory markets on popular protest, is somehow natural or automatic. In fact, it is far from automatic. Whatever the source of their suffering or anguish, much of the time people simply endure; they resign themselves to their circumstances because they see no other way. When protest movements do emerge, they reflect the welling up of indignation, even outrage, at these circumstances. And if there is indignation, then there must also be some hope, because people imagine that it can be another way, and they even imagine that they can make it another way. As Rebecca Solnit (2007) puts it, "Hope is an orientation, a way of scanning the wall for cracks—or building ladders—rather than staring at its obdurate expanse. It's a worldview, but one informed by experience and the knowledge that people have power; that the power people possess matters; that change has been made by populist movements and dedicated individuals in the past; and that it will be again." Put another way, hope is a precondition for the anger and indignation that fuels protest. We do not become enraged at circumstances that we judge to be simply inevitable.

In other words, the eruption of protest across the globe argues that people think they have power, at least some power, and the often mild or even conciliatory responses to the protests argue that they are not entirely wrong. Moreover, the demands that are put forward by many of these movements are exceptionally bold and far reaching. Recall the large literature on the history of collective action by "the people out-of-doors" in Europe and the United States.[2] People gathered and, perhaps emboldened by their numbers, defied the authorities. But their demands were typically immediate and within reach, virtually inscribed in their actions, as they seized hoarded grain or looted the houses of the better-off or pulled down the "houses of industry" that had been established as workhouses for the poor.

In contrast, the demands of the Aymara Indians who blocked the roads into La Paz, or of the Ogoni and Ijaw peoples in the Nigerian delta, are pitched at national governments and distant multinationals, and they often purport to speak for collectivities much larger than the local community. For example, the 2000 uprising by the indigenous in Ecuador proclaimed, "Nothing just for the Indians" (Petras and Veltmeyer 2005, 173). A continental meeting of indigenous people in Guatemala in 2007 announced its slogan, "From resistance to power" (Becker 2007). And later in 2007, indigenous leaders concerned about deforestation protested that they were shut out of the UN Summit on Climate Change in Bali, Indonesia (Rizvi 2007). Consistently, the protestors typically demand far-reaching changes in the control and distribution of natural resources. And sometimes these contemporary protests have scored victories, as when local people protesting the privatization of water in Cochabamba, Bolivia, drove out the European multinational corporation with whom the government had signed a contract for the provision of water. This is surely historically extraordinary. At least as important is the remarkable restraint with which the authorities have responded to many of these popular mobilizations, in comparison to half a millennia of looting and massacre in the Southern hemisphere by European and American powers and their local allies.

So, why this growing sense of power from below? And why the evidence, albeit limited, that the people out-of-doors may indeed have some power, at least more power than in the past? I don't think that our usual way of understanding power offers much help in answering these questions. What I mean by the "usual way" is a tradition that roots the ability of some people to make others bend to their will in the control of diverse resources, especially in the control of wealth and force, and in domination of the institutional positions that yield control over wealth and force. To be sure, this view is consistent with much of our historical experience. The big landowner has power over small peasants, the media mogul over vast publics, the rich over the poor, armed troops over civilians, and so on. A vast theoretical literature elaborates variations of this view, along with assorted classifications and lists of the assets and positional advantages associated with wealth or force. For

instance, Randall Collins writes, "Look for the material things that affect interaction: the physical places, the modes of communication, the supply of
weapons, devices for staging one's public impression, tools and goods. . . .
The resources for conflict are complex" (1975, 60–61). C. Wright Mills emphasizes the resources for power available to the occupants of "top" institutional roles (1956, 9, 23).[3] And Charles Tilly points to "the economists' factors
of production: land, labor, capital, perhaps technical expertise as well" (Tilly
1978, 69).

Clearly, any of these variations of the widely held thesis that power is based
on control of wealth and force explains a good deal of our experience. Rural
overlords have wealth, social standing, and force of arms, and peasants have
none of these things. Most of the time, the overlords are the powerful, the
peasants are the powerless, and the distributional conception of power seems
confirmed. But sometimes peasants rise up against their overlords. They refuse to labor in the lord's fields, or they withhold their rents or taxes, take up
arms, or take to the hills. When they do, the outcome often goes against
them. But it does not inevitably go against them. Sometimes, in some places,
peasants prevail. Or they win at least something, perhaps some moderation
of the terms of their subjugation. And sometimes, whether in the end for
better or worse, their actions become part of the chain of events that transforms their society. However, when workers refuse to labor or take to the
streets or to the barricades, the outcome is not necessarily predictable. Insurgent workers sometimes win shorter hours or higher wages. More rarely still,
they might help set in motion the forces that topple governments. Even the
marginal poor—those on the fringes of social life who seem to play no role
in ongoing patterns of economic, social, or political activity—can become the
urban mobs of the American or French Revolutions or the urban rioters of
contemporary Latin America. And even rioters sometimes win something.[4]
If people without wealth or arms or status or technical skill sometimes prevail, then they must have some kind of power.

How are we to understand that power? In the contemporary era, we have
generally relied on two suggestive theories to explain the periodic exercise of
popular power—theories that are variously elaborated in the arguments of
intellectuals and are deeply imprinted in popular belief. One is simply the
theory of political democracy as it has developed since the seventeenth century. Ordinary people have power over state elites through electoral representative institutions that mediate between the citizenry and the state. This sort
of power is institutionalized in elaborate arrangements, including elections,
representation, and political parties. But the crucial element that gives these
arrangements their democratic cast is the widely distributed vote and the
periodic elections that determine the occupants of positions of state authority.
People, or at least many of them, exercise the right to vote, and the periodic
elections in which their votes are tallied make political officials dependent on

popular majorities to remain in command of government. Elections thus anchor state leaders to the voters. In other words, the vote means that people have power—at least, some power—because political elites depend on them.

The other theory is that of labor power, which is also expressed in both intellectual and folk versions but is most eloquently presented by Karl Marx and Friedrich Engels in *The Communist Manifesto*. The development of capitalism, they argue, gives rise to mass production industries and to the vast numbers of factory workers on whose labor power those industries rely. Because factory production depends on them, workers can exercise leverage by striking, or "shutting it down." Moreover, the growth of mass production industries steadily increases the numbers of workers who have this kind of power; it creates solidarity among them, even while the experience of mass production generates ever deeper divisions between capital and labor, singling out the former as the target for worker anger. Furthermore, labor power has an institutionalized expression in the formation of unions and in the panoply of labor rights incorporated in law and regulation.

The episodic and complex history of the expansion of political and labor rights in Europe, the United States, Latin America, and other parts of the world can be told as the history of state responses to the mobilization of both the popular power yielded by the development of electoral representative institutions and the power yielded by the industrial workplace. Each kind of power can affect the other. Workplace strikes are far more likely to be met with a degree of conciliation, as state elites are restrained from using force to suppress the strikers because they worry about the electoral repercussions among sympathetic voting constituencies. Of course, the reverse is also true. When elites feel free to summon the troops, strikes are far less likely to be successful, as demonstrated by the history of defeated nineteenth- and early twentieth-century strikes in the United States (Piven and Cloward 1977).

However, the state's monopoly on the legitimate use of violence is not the only factor that can make labor power conditional on electoral power. The recent success of the Service Employees International Union (SEIU) in organizing home health care workers in California followed a long electoral campaign to first create a public authority that would be the employer of record for these workers, replacing numerous and fragmented for-profit and nonprofit agencies—the previous official employers with whom the state had contracted (Holgate and Shea 2007). Thus, electoral influence can be deployed to facilitate the exercise of labor power, in this case by eliminating the difficult organizing problem created by multiple small employers. In turn, the heavy investment of American unions in electoral campaigns over the past quarter-century is an obvious example of the effort to use resources yielded by labor power to increase electoral power.

Similarly, the history of the welfare state can be told as a history of successive concessions made necessary by eruptions of both labor power and electoral power. I think that the story is unreasonably simplified when more unruly expressions of popular power are ignored. Nevertheless, there is truth in the big-picture characterization of the economic security afforded to working and poor people by public income supports and service programs as the price that political and economic elites must pay for the integration and cooperation of large swaths of the population—a price made necessary by periodic eruptions of democratic and labor power, separately and together.

Neoliberal globalization seems to undermine both of these forms of popular power, at least in the West, where these beliefs and the institutions that undergird them have been most developed. Democratic aspirations are not simply aspirations for abstract rights, but rather aspirations for a measure of influence over an otherwise often cruel and powerful state with great control over the lives of ordinary people. In other words, the passion for democracy evident in many popular struggles in the past depended critically on the authority of the nation-state over its territory and its people. If the state is itself helpless, elections and the paraphernalia of elections become mere ritual. In fact, the decisive authority of the nation-state is said to be compromised by the emergence of supranational authorities like the European Union (EU), the International Monetary Fund (IMF), the World Bank, the World Trade Organization (WTO), and so on. Except for the limited electoral exposure of the EU, these new agencies are all cut off from electoral representative institutions.

State authority is being compromised again by the rise of multinational corporations and international financial dealers; these are not firmly rooted in the sovereign territory of any state and are capable of pitting one state against another in the competition for investment. In other words, the new world order seems to replicate, on an international level, the democratic vulnerabilities apparent in the federal structure of the American government, which gives investors great leverage over the subnational governments that provide significant infrastructure and services. Federalism means that state and local governments must compete for investment, as well as the jobs and tax revenues that investment brings. Just as state and local governments are held hostage by investors on a national scale, who pick and choose the most favorable package that these governments have to offer, so are national governments held hostage in a global order. In both cases, the arrangement greatly reduces the influence of the voters, on whom political officials presumably depend. Or, as Steve Lerner, lead organizer of the SEIU says, "For 150 years, trade unionists and progressives have viewed influencing and trying to gain control of the state as central to any strategy of winning a more just society. National governments still have enormous influence, but their power is diminishing every day" (2007, 24).

The creeping privatization associated with neoliberal globalization has a similar effect. The ideological celebration of the market, now writ large as markets become international, justifies spinning off public functions to for-profit firms. And, of course, once governmental responsibilities are shifted to the private sector, they become more susceptible to the demands of investors and less susceptible to the demands of voters. None of this is to deny the deep imperfections in democratic practices that have little to do with neoliberal globalization. The democratic idea posits an unreal world in which the vote is the sole currency of power. Unlike other resources for influence, such as wealth or arms, the vote can in principle be widely and equally distributed. And viewed abstractly, electoral representative arrangements are indeed a re-markable institutional construction. Think of it: a new resource is created and widely and equally distributed, and in principle that equal resource over-rides all of the inequalities of social life in the selection of state leaders. No wonder the democratic idea has always been so magically compelling!

In the real world, however, these other inequalities are translated into cur-rencies that penetrate electoral spheres and distort the fundamental interde-pendence between equal voters and state leaders on which the democratic idea depends. Thus, contemporary critiques of American politics rightly em-phasize the corrupting influence of money, which makes politicians seeking election at least as beholden to the business contributors who pay for their campaigns as to the voters whom these campaigns are intended to persuade. And with the rise of television as the main medium of campaigning, not only does the capacity for voter manipulation grow, but so does the need for contributions, and therefore the influence of big money. Because money buys the means to reach and persuade voters, it buys votes today as surely as the two-dollar bribe once did. Still, all of this acknowledged, it is widely agreed that globalization will add to the catalogue of democratic woes, maybe fatally.

Labor power also seems eviscerated by neoliberal globalization. Capital mobility and accelerated trade lead to the shift of the mass production indus-tries to the global South and Asia, where wages and welfare state costs are lower. Privatization weakens the public sector unions whose growth seemed, for a time, to offset the contraction of industrial unions. In this weakened state, industrial workers in the First and Second Worlds are exposed to both intensified wage competition and fiercely anti-union employers who press for deregulation and lean production methods, using the specter of capital exit as leverage. And union density declines everywhere, seemingly inexorably, though it occurs the most in the United States, England, and Latin America, and less in Western Europe. Moreover, the weakening of the unions is re-flected in the weakness of labor political parties, which themselves adopt elements of the neoliberal agenda and replace the class-oriented political platforms that emerged at the dawn of the twentieth century with so-called catch-all party appeals.

In sum, neoliberal globalization seems to puncture the century-old confidence in popular power. Whereas working people in the mother countries of industrial capitalism were once thought to have economic power over employers because they could withdraw their labor, now they have to worry about the virtually boundless army of workers across the globe that is ready to replace them or to replace at lower cost the goods and services they once produced. And whereas ordinary people once thought that they had political power because state decision makers needed their votes, now the nation-state itself seems to have become weak, its policy options dictated more by the rulings of supranational agencies, international bankers and currency dealers, or the threat of disinvestment or trade competition than by voter preferences.

There is much to think about in the diverse analyses I have briefly summarized. Neoliberal globalization has weakened familiar patterns of popular power, and it is important to understand these shifts. However, I do not believe that the deep pessimism with which they conclude is justified. Underlying both democratic and labor theories of power is a set of propositions that suggests a far more sweeping theory, and that theory in turn is the basis for a more promising perspective on the possibility of popular power in a global era.

The power of people we ordinarily consider powerless derives from the patterns of cooperation and interdependence that constitute social life, and from the leverage embedded in interdependent relations. There is no production and no surplus for the overlord without peasant labor, and even the feudal lord struck a kind of compact with his serfs in the form of a guarantee of subsistence in times of scarcity. That compact was a tacit acknowledgment of peasant power. Not only do peasants need overlords in a feudal system of production, but overlords need peasants. Similarly, not only does labor need capital in an industrial system of production; just as land is not a means of production without those who work it, so is capital not capital without labor. And not only do the poor need contributions from the rich; in a society of densely interdependent relations, the rich also need contributions from the poor. If nothing else, they need the poor to be quiescent. Even apart from the electoral representative arrangements that we call democracy, history is dotted with those occasions when people without wealth or coercive resources exercised at least some power, at least for a time.

Obviously, the pattern of interdependent and cooperative relations that constitute a society, any society, is both intricate and sweeping. It includes family relations, educational relations, church relations, commercial relations, and so on. The relations between doctor and patient, beautician and client, merchant and customer, guru and acolyte are all relations of interdependence and cooperation, and all are susceptible to the exercise of power by parties to the relationship. I take for granted, however, that some relationships are much more important than others, and because they are, the threat or actuality of their disruption can yield both more substantial reforms to conciliate the disruptors and more substantial efforts to suppress them. The dominant interdependencies, and the power contests they make possible, develop within economic relationships and within the political relationships that anchor state elites to the societies they rule. Thus, the important interdependencies are rooted in the cooperative activities that generate the material bases for social life and that sustain the force and authority of the state. Economic relations are, of course, intertwined with political relations—markets always depend on political authority—helping to explain why state elites ordinarily buttress patterns of economic domination, and also why they sometimes intervene to modify them.[5] However, I should note here that people's ability to act on the central economic and political axes of interdependence is likely to be influenced by other relations in which they are enmeshed—a point to which I will return.

Because people are bound together in the economic and political activities to which they make contributions, their cooperation, even when it only means their quiescence, is necessary to what we call normal institutional life. It follows that people can disrupt these institutions by withdrawing their cooperation. We receive hints of this kind of social interdependence and the power it can yield from the model of political democracy, which can be understood as a deliberately constructed system of interdependence. Obviously, people depend on the government to provide the basic infrastructure of physical security, services, and regulation that modern societies require. But so do electoral representative arrangements force the politicians who run governments into relations of dependence on voters. At least in principle, if people withdraw their votes, the politician falls.

The compelling idea that workers have potential power is also based on recognition that the industrial enterprise is a system of cooperation to which workers make a key contribution. If capital fails to invest or disinvests, there is no enterprise. But the enterprise will also shut down if workers withdraw their labor. In other words, undergirding our convictions about the potential for democratic power or worker power is the idea that ordinary people can tame state and corporate elites because those elites are lodged in institutions that depend on these ordinary people. I am proposing that the power rooted in interdependent relations is not limited to the familiar forms of political democracy or mass production, and in fact never was. History is replete with episodes in which menacing mobs, aroused parishioners, boycotting consumers, or deserting soldiers exercised power.

In principle, interdependent power increases with centralization and specialization, for the obvious reason that as the division of labor advances, and as webs of cooperation grow wider and more intricate, the cooperative project involves more and diverse contributions from more and diverse people. And globalization, neoliberal or not, means just this: increased specialization and integration in complex and far-reaching systems of cooperation and interdependence. Throughout most of our history, isolated villagers have ordinarily had little power over distant imperial centers. But when, in recent years, indigenous highlanders repeatedly blocked the roads to La Paz, successive Bolivian governments fell and multinational energy corporations took notice, as did the world. Similarly, when militants from the Ogoni and Ijaw peoples of the oil-rich Nigerian Delta repeatedly protested the ruinous depredations of the international oil companies, holding oil workers hostage and blowing up oil and gas facilities, the consequences were a sharp reduction of oil production and a run-up of oil prices, and again the world took notice (Mouawad 2007a).[6] In other words, while we are acutely aware of the wide reverberations of the actions of multinational investors and currency speculators, many ordinary people also play an important part in the complex and fragile exchanges that constitute neoliberal globalization, and because they do, they also have potential power.

These observations suggest a very different perspective than the usual wisdom about neoliberal globalization and the decline of democratic and labor power. To be sure, globalization enormously expands investor opportunities for exit from relations with any particular group of working people. With the click of a mouse, capital can be moved to low-wage and low-cost parts of the world, and then moved again to places where wages and costs are lower still. This is what has happened in the case of factories that first moved from the United States to Mexico, and then moved again to take advantage of the docility bred by extreme poverty in Bangladesh or China.

But there is another side to these new and complex chains of production. The arrangements that make exit easier also create new and more fragile interdependencies. Outsourcing is two-sided. On the one hand, it reduces the dependence of employers on domestic workers. On the other hand, it binds them to many other workers in far-flung and extended chains of production. These chains in turn depend on complex systems of electronic communication and transportation, which are themselves acutely vulnerable to disruption. The old idea that logistical workers located at the key nodes of industrial systems of production had great potential labor power has, in a sense, been writ large. Many workers—those who run the far-flung transportation systems or the Internet, or are lodged at all the points in vastly extended chains of production, as well as those in "just-in-time" systems of production facilitated by the Internet—may have potential logistical power.

And this applies not only to workers. In a scenario that has become familiar in China and India, farmers recently refused to sell their land to make way for a petrochemical plant in a special economic zone south of Calcutta. They forced the Indian authorities to shelve the plan, which was intended to lure foreign investors, at least for the time being. The conflict left fourteen farmers shot dead. Nevertheless, the head of the Muslim group leading the protests announced triumphantly, "We have taught the government a lesson they will never forget" (Page 2007). Tens of thousands of similar farmer protests in China, and the bloody clashes they have produced, have reportedly prompted the national government to launch some ninety thousand investigations and to impose "administrative punishments" on some local governments that have evicted farmers and householders because they are greedy for new investment (Cheng 2007).[7] Overall, the much-touted number of seventy-four thousand mass protests, officially acknowledged in 2004, has prompted a new concern with social inequality in ruling circles, as well as some new programs to moderate inequalities.[8]

The widespread reverberations of such local protests can be remarkable. When people from the Argentine town of Gualeguaychú blocked the international bridge linking Uruguay with Argentina, they were protesting against the construction of a paper mill, which, they argued, would pollute the environment and hurt tourism and fishing along the Uruguay River. The plant was to be built by a Finnish company with a loan from the World Bank. The protests threatened not only the plant but also the Uruguayan economy, exposed fissures in the Mercosur trade alliance, activated international NGOs, and prompted Spain's King Juan Carlos to offer himself as a mediator (Futures and Commodity Market News 2006).[9]

I expect readers to be skeptical, but notice that I say *potential* power. Two major qualifications demand attention. First, the latent potential for interdependent power does not mean that the power based on wealth and force is superseded. To the contrary, wealth, and especially force, can be mobilized to suppress the mobilization of interdependent power. The co-optation that wealth makes possible usually works, and so does repression, at least for a time. The protest movements that have spread across much of Latin America have not erupted in Guatemala and Colombia, for example, and this may well be the brutal result of death squads, torture, illegal detention centers, and disappearances deployed by governments and paramilitaries. With the election in Guatemala of centrist Álvaro Colom, who was supported by the indigenous highlanders, popular movements that attempt to mobilize interdependent power may reemerge (Goldman 2007). We might also think of the bloody crackdown on protesting monks by the ruling Burmese junta in 2007. The international media were momentarily shocked by the repression, to be sure, but the media's attention span is short. Even while the protests were going on, India negotiated a major gas exploration deal with the

Burmese generals, and China, with huge economic stakes in Burmese gas, declined to use its influence to curb the generals (Ramachandran 2006). The power based on wealth and force can neutralize interdependent power, and most of the time, it probably does.[10]

The second qualification has to do with the restraints on the mobilization of interdependent power that are embedded in social life itself. The actualization of interdependent power typically requires that people break the rules that govern the institutions in which they participate, if only because those rules are designed to suppress interdependent power. People must also recognize that they possess some power on which elites depend. They must organize and contrive ways of acting in concert, at least insofar as concerted action is necessary to make their power effective. The inhibiting effects of other relationships, with family or church or party, must be suppressed or overcome. And the protesting group must be able to endure the interruption of cooperative relationships on which they also depend.

To actualize interdependent power, it is necessary to develop strategies to cope with all of these obstacles. Over time, as strategies become familiar and available, they are in effect scripts that can be drawn upon in subsequent challenges from below. In this sense, they are similar to what Charles Tilly called "repertoires." But I need to note how my viewpoint differs from that of Tilly, who defined repertoire as the "inventory of available means" of collective action (Tilly 1982, 21–51; 1984, 308). Tilly's great interest is in accounting for the way that power strategies change as institutional arrangements change—that is, as the "logic of the situation" that people confront changes. But institutions also have features that suppress the power potential they create. As a consequence, the leverage generated by changing institutional arrangements may or may not be realized, or it may be realized later rather than sooner. The relationship between the logic of the situation and the emergence of strategies to actualize popular power is always problematic, partly for the reasons I have just named, which have to do with the ability to defy the rules and routines to which people customarily conform, to recognize new levers of interdependent power, to coordinate the actions necessary to act on those levers, to withstand the pressures for conformity and cooperation exerted by other relationships, and to endure the interruptions and exit threats that disruptions entail. The realization of potential power under new conditions is also difficult, because the strategy scripts that solved these problems in the past have staying power; they persist because they are imprinted on memory and habit, reinforced by memories of past victories, and reiterated by the organizations and leaders thrust up in past conflicts.[11]

First, the activation of disruptive power typically requires that people break some of the rules that govern the cooperative relations in which they are enmeshed. In other words, rather than simply being a reflection of institutional arrangements, the actualization of interdependent power requires that

people defy the rules generated by institutions. After all, if patterned cooperation is the stuff of social life, it is not invented anew by the people who engage
in it. Most cooperative relations are to a greater or lesser extent institutionalized, meaning that they are governed by rule. The rules governing behavior
in cooperative activities are not neutral. To the extent that they are formed in
the context of the power inequalities resulting from concentrations of wealth
and force, rules work to suppress the actualization of interdependent power
inherent in social cooperation by subordinate groups. Rules do this by speci-
fying the permissible behaviors of different parties in interdependent relations. And since the rules are fashioned to reflect prevailing patterns of
domination made possible by concentrated force, wealth, and institutional
position, they typically prohibit some people but not others from using the
leverage yielded by social interdependence.

Over time, rules also become intertwined with deep interpretations of social life that justify conformity, despite the power disadvantage that results.
However, the force of the interpretations associated with market-dominated
globalization is likely to be weakened by the very fact of these arrangements'
newness, and also by the fact that they are imposed in the face of traditional
social arrangements and the traditional ideas that legitimate them. In other
words, the clash with tradition provides people with alternative ideas about
how life should be lived, as well as alternative ideas about how to exercise
influence over one's circumstances. However, consider how regularly social
movements charge that the actions or policies they are protesting are wrong
because they violate the rules prescribed by law or custom. In April 2007, a
number of indigenous subsistence communities in northern Guatemala held
a *consulta popular* on two issues: the construction of the Xalala Dam, which
would displace eighteen local communities, and permission to explore for oil
in the Quiché Department (Kern 2007). The consulta is a traditional decision-
making process, and 91 percent of attendees voted no. If the construction on
the dam goes forward anyway, the local communities may well break the
rules prescribed by law and custom—for example, by blocking highways, a
tactic that seems to have become ubiquitous in the global South.

Second, consider the problem of recognizing the fact of interdependence,
and therefore the potential for power from below, in the face of ruling-class
definitions that privilege the contributions of dominant groups to social life,
and may indeed even eradicate the contributions of lower-status groups. Economic and political interdependencies are real in the sense that they have
real ramifications in the material bases of social life and in the exercise of
coercive force. But they are also cultural constructions. Thus, the monetary
contributions of husbands to family relations have always been given much
more emphasis than the domestic services of wives, the contributions of entrepreneurial capital more weight than the productive labor of workers, and
so on. Before people are likely to withdraw their contributions as a strategy

for exercising power, they must recognize the large role that those contributions play in mating, economic, political, or religious relationships. Thus, this step in the mobilization of interdependent power is contingent on how people understand the social relations in which they are enmeshed. For instance, the development of the industrial workers' movement in Europe and North America was conditional on the emergence of a worker subculture that recognized its centrality to economic growth. "We have fed you all, for a thousand years. . . . Go reckon our dead by the forges red, and the factories where we spin," went the old Wobbly song (Industrial Workers of the World 1989, 28).

The neo-laissez-faire doctrine that justifies market-led globalization can be seen as the revival of a species of natural law that obliterates worker power by reducing it to market exchange. Like nineteenth-century laissez faire, it asserts the inevitable preeminence of market calculations and warns of the potentially hazardous consequences of interference in the dynamics of markets or market law. However, the exploitation of natural resources by multinational corporations has triggered a rash of protests across the global South, perhaps because abstracted arguments about markets and market law are outweighed by the palpable reality of customary uses of the land and traditional cultural justifications. Increasingly, protests in the global South are directed against the destruction of the basic elements that make human life possible—for example, the pollution of air or water, the privatization of water, or the destruction of the forests. The strongest and most successful protests against neoliberal globalization have been precipitated by multinational extractions of Southern countries' natural resources. In Nigeria, Ecuador, Bolivia, and Venezuela, the contest is over oil and gas; in Peru and Chile, over copper. Indeed, when Peruvian copper miners struck in early May 2007, copper prices in New York jumped to their highest level in eleven months.

Third, ongoing economic and political activities often receive contributions from many individuals, and these must be coordinated for the effective mobilization of disruptive power. Workers, villagers, parishioners, or consumers must act in concert if the withdrawal of their contributions is to have a disruptive effect on the factory, the church, or the merchant. This is the old problem of building solidarity, of organizing for joint action, confronted by workers, voters, or community residents when they try to exercise leverage over those who depend on them for their labor, their votes, or their acquiescence in the normal patterns of civic life.

As has often been pointed out, the social relations created by a stable institutional context may go a long way toward solving the coordination problem. The classic Marxist analysis of worker power argued that worker solidarity was created by the mines and factories of industrial capitalism, which drew people together in a shared setting where they would develop common grievances and common antagonists. Now, however, at least in the mother countries of industrial capitalism that inspired this argument, the numbers of miners and industrial workers are shrinking, along with their fabled power, as corporations shift production to low-wage countries in the global South.

Strategists from the old unions are searching for ways to overcome this weakness by coordinating labor action across borders. A good deal of these efforts seems to take the form of proclamations and wishful thinking, but a few examples of fledgling alliances may have more solidity. In April 2007, the International Association of Machinists and the International Metalworkers' Federation announced an agreement to form a Global Union Alliance representing Boeing workers in the United States, Canada, Australia, Germany, Italy, Sweden, and Japan. The United Steelworkers recently announced merger negotiations with two of Britain's largest unions (Meyerson 2007). SEIU's internationalist plans emphasize a strategy in which strong unions in one country will use their bargaining power or their treasuries to win organizing rights from multinational firms for workers in other countries (Lerner 2007; Bronfenbrenner 2007; Moody 1997; Piven and Cloward 2000). The pitfall in many of these efforts, also reflected in the American debate between the majority of the American Federation of Labor and Congress of Industrial Organizations (AFL-CIO) unions and the Change to Win coalition, is the typical separation of questions about organizing—specifically, about enlarging and consolidating or coordinating the ranks—from the power strategy in which those consolidated ranks are to be deployed. Slogans like "Organizing the unorganized," however appealing, reflect a mystical faith in numbers, as if enlarging ranks will automatically yield power. Enlarging ranks may or may not be important. From the viewpoint of my argument, just who is to be "organized," and how many people must be organized, should be determined by who and how many are needed to exercise interdependent power.

The new emerging collectivities are more localized than the old industrial unions, which, while they were not "international" (their names notwithstanding), were in fact national in scope. Many of the new protest groupings seem to have more in common with the village social organizations that, as Barrington Moore has argued, sometimes provided the solidarity that enabled people to act against the impositions associated with the fall of the ancien régime (1966, 470–74). However, the new local collectivities may have an advantage denied to European villagers living through the transition from feudalism to commercial capitalism. They are connected to one another, as well as to world audiences, in networks that rely on the Internet. The campaigns of the Ijaw and Ogoni militants in the Niger Delta rely on $2 and $3 phones, and the official spokesman for the Movement for the Emancipation of the Niger Delta, known as Jomo Gbomo, communicates with foreign journalists by e-mail (Junger 2007). The Zapatista protests in Chiapas that began in 1992 were also widely communicated through the Internet and resonated among indigenous peoples across the globe. Shefner concludes that while the protests had limited direct influence, they helped catalyze a broad democratization movement in Mexico (Shefner 2007).

Even the unions are exploring new structures. What their diverse efforts have in common, says Alan Howard, writing about the future of global unions, is that "the structures . . . do not resemble traditional union structures. They are fluid networks in which the agenda is set by participants directly linked to the shop floor. They include organizations that are not unions but are integral to the process. They can turn on a dime. . . . What their relationship will be to the existing global union federations or even their own national centers remains to be seen, but these organizing networks are the seeds of the global unions of the future" (2007, 66). There are also new organizational forms developing that take account of the informal character of work in much of the global South and eschew organizing drives against multiple small employers in favor of campaigns targeting government and demanding government regulation of the workplace (Agarwala 2006). This is clearly an attempt to avoid the dissipation of efforts, to which organizing in the informal sector would likely lead.

As a number of these examples suggest, it may also be the case that too much importance has been given to the solidarities created by underlying and preexisting social organization.[12] Street mobs can mobilize quickly, taking advantage of public gatherings such as markets, hangings, or simply crowded streets, and the participants may not know one another personally, although they are likely to be able to read the signs of group, class, or neighborhood identity displayed by the crowd. Many of the protests against neoliberal globalization have just this character of the instantly formed crowd or mob. Speaking of protests in Latin America, Adolfo Gilly recently commented on this: "These movements are made up of young people, many of them from the informal sector. They have no unions built by their fathers; they live in the slums instead of the village or the working-class neighborhood. They have to organize in a different way. And they are freer than we were!"[13] Marina Sitrin, writing about the Argentinean protests of 2001, says that "it was a rebellion without leadership, either by established parties or by a newly emerged elite. . . . People didn't know where they were marching, or why they were marching, they were just so fed up with this typically neoliberal system that Menem implemented. . . . There was no communication, no organization" (2996, 6). The chapters of a new Students for a Democratic Society that have sprung up recently in the United States display a similar stance. The group is deliberately antibureaucratic and antihierarchical, with no national leaders, and this freedom from centralized control is part of its appeal (Phelps 2007). More generally, the global justice movement has stridently disavowed the organizational forms associated particularly with the labor movement, opting for the forms of more spontaneous direct action

sometimes called horizontalism, or for looser methods of coordinating collective action as "spokes and wheels" rather than as pyramids (Sitrin 2006,
10–31).

Fourth, as noted earlier, social life is complicated, and political action takes
form within a matrix of social relations. Those who try to mobilize interdependent power must overcome the constraints typically imposed by their
multiple relations with others, as when would-be peasant insurgents are constrained by the threat of religious excommunication, or when labor insurgents are constrained by family responsibilities. English Methodist preachers
invoked for their parishioners the awesome threat of everlasting punishment
in hell that would be visited on Luddite insurgents in the early nineteenth
century. However, under some conditions, multiple ties may facilitate disruptive power challenges.[14] The church that ordinarily preaches obedience to
worldly authority may sometimes, perhaps simply in order to hold the allegiance of discontented parishioners, encourage the rebels, as occurred during
the course of the Solidarity movement in Poland, or during the Civil Rights
Movement in the United States, or in Chiapas when Bishop Samuel Ruiz and
his diocese lent support to the emerging indigenous insurgency. The financial and political aid that Hugo Chávez has extended to the new left governments in Ecuador and Bolivia is also a multilateral intervention, once
removed, since it influences the governments with which the movements are
entangled.[15]

Fifth, when people attempt to exercise disruptive or interdependent power,
they have to find ways to endure the suspension of the cooperative relationships on which they depend, and to withstand any reprisals they may incur.
This is less evident for the participants in mobs or riots, where the action is
usually short-lived and the participants are likely to remain anonymous. But
when workers strike, they still need to feed their families and pay the rent;
likewise, consumer boycotters need to be able to get by for a time without the
goods or services they are refusing to purchase. They may even have to face
down the threat of exit, which is often provoked by disruption. Husbands
confronting rebellious wives may threaten to walk out, employers confronting
striking workers may threaten to relocate or to replace workers, and so on.
Even rioters risk precipitating the exit of partners in cooperative relationships,
as when small businesses fled from slum neighborhoods in the wake of the
American ghetto riots of the 1960s.

However, the natural resource wars in Latin America and Africa sparked
by local protests seem to have fewer repercussions of this kind. To be sure,
foreign payments may fall, but since a main grievance of the protestors is
typically that they receive few benefits from these payments, there may be
little lost to local people by the suspension. In any case, in the only slightly
longer run, there are likely to be alternative bidders for these resources, and

in Africa and South America, Chinese bidders have in fact been quick to appear.[16]

To argue that the potential of popular power has increased rather than diminished as a result of neoliberal globalization does not, of course, guarantee us a happy ending. I argue the real possibility that interdependent power matters, and matters more as a consequence of the complex web of relations spun by neoliberal globalization. But the power yielded by wealth and force also continues to matter. The fourteen farmers shot dead in the Indian incident recounted above will inevitably have a restraining influence on future protests. On a larger scale, the years-long crackdowns in Guatemala and Colombia by government and paramilitary forces have turned those countries into murderous hellholes, with the consequence that not much effective insurgency has emerged. Protest movements can also be stifled when they are overtaken by electoral politics, which many observers think has occurred in South Africa, Argentina, and Brazil, and perhaps in Bolivia as well.[17] My point is not that interdependent power is singularly triumphant; my point is only that it has always played an important but largely hidden role in political development, and may play a larger role in the unfolding pattern of globalization. Much will depend on the ability of movements to develop strategies that overcome the perennial obstructions to the actualization of interdependent power. But so far the news is encouraging. Notice that when George W. Bush toured Latin America in the early spring of 2007, he was cautious and conciliatory and even promised American action to do something about Latin American poverty. That remains to be seen, of course. By the end of his terms, he had not sent in the Marines.

NOTES

Portions of this chapter were first published in 2008 as "Can Power from Below Change the World?" *American Sociological Review* 73 (February): 1–14. They have been reprinted with permission from the American Sociological Association.

1. Jon Shefner (2006) suggests that hardship is significant when it is widespread, thus providing political opportunities for the mobilization of large cross sections of the public, and also weakening state legitimacy.

2. The literature on crowd or mob actions is huge. On European crowds, see, for example, Hobsbawm (1965); Hobsbawm and Rudé (1968); Rudé (1964); Thompson (1963); and Tilly (1986). On American mob actions, particularly at the time of the Revolutionary War, see Maier (1972); Raphael (2001); Countryman (2003); Nash (2005); Zinn (1980); Piven and Cloward (1977); and Piven (2006).

3. This point about the organizational bases of power was later developed by Presthus (1964).

4. The literature on the reverberations of challenges from below is, of course, enormous. "Social movements based on power resources," Janoski asserts boldly, "provide the *pressure for change* in citizenship rights" (1998, 160). For a series of studies on contemporary protest movements and their outcomes in Latin America, see Eckstein and Wickham-Crowley (2002).

5. For a discussion of societies as overlapping, intersecting power networks that generate "promiscuous" sources of power, see Mann (1986, chap. 1).

6. Similar occurrences are spreading to other oil-rich regions. See Mouawad (2007b).

7. There are also plans afoot for heavier fines for illegal developments. See *Channel NewsAsia* (2007).

8. Daniel Bell writes, "In October 2006, for the first time in twenty-five years, a plenary session of the CCP's [Chinese Communist Party's] Central Committee devoted itself specifically to the study of social issues . . . [signaling] a shift from no-holds-barred growth to a more sustainable model that would boost social and economic equality (2007, 21).

9. See also *Financial Times* coverage by Benedict Mander, who was stationed in Montevideo in the first months of 2007.

10. Adolfo Gilly argues that in Bolivia the Aymaran protests of 2003 were effective because they too employed a kind of force, bringing down a hated president "with the violence of their dead . . . with the violence of their bodies." But it was, in fact, the government that deployed the force that resulted in so many deaths, even though the use of force had the effect of stripping the reigning powers of legitimacy (Gilly 2005, 43).

11. Others have also made this point. Jasper (1997), for example, talks about groups' tendency to draw on familiar and limited tactics from among the broader range of choices open to them.

12. Writing with Richard Cloward, I have argued in the past that the importance of institutionally created solidarities is often overstated: "Riots require little more by way of organization than numbers, propinquity, and some communication. Most patterns of human settlement . . . supply these structural requirements" (Piven and Cloward 1992, 310).

13. I am reproducing Gilly's comments from my notes, taken during a panel at the Left Forum meeting at Cooper Union in New York City on March 11, 2007.

14. Stathis N. Kalyvas's discussion of civil wars provides a useful analogy. Civil wars, says Kalyvas, "are not binary conflicts but complex and ambiguous processes that foster an apparently massive, though variable, mix of identities and actions" (2003, 475).

15. And, famously, Chávez offered subsidized heating oil to low-income people in the United States through CITGO, the wholly owned American subsidiary of the Venezuelan oil conglomerate.

16. However, the Chinese are likely to be subject to the same protests. In Ethiopia, a Chinese-run oil field was stormed by the Ogaden National Liberation Front in April 2007 (Gettleman 2007).

17. This is one of the main points of the analysis of developments in Argentina, Brazil, Bolivia, and Ecuador offered by Petras and Veltmeyer (2005).

REFERENCES

Agarwala, Rina. 2006. "Struggling with Informality: A New Class Movement in India." *Critical Asian Studies* 38 (4): 419–44.

Becker, Marc. 2007. "Continental Summit of Indigenous Peoples Meets in Guatemala." Upside Down World. April 4. http://upsidedownworld.org/main/index2.php?option=com_content&task=view&id=687&It.

Bell, Daniel. 2007. "From Marx to Confucius." *Dissent* 54 (2): 20–28.

Bronfenbrenner, Kate, ed. 2007. *Global Unions: Challenging Transnational Capital Through Cross-Border Campaigns*. Ithaca: Cornell University Press.

Channel NewsAsia. 2007. "China Plans Heavier Fines to Rein in the Property Sector." April 25. http://www.channelnewsasia.com/stories/afp_asiapacific_business/view/272388/1/.html.

Cheng, Eva. 2007. "Eviction Resisters Test Property Rights." *Green Left Weekly*, May 7. http://www.greenleft.org.au/2007/708/36761.

Collins, Randall. 1975. *Conflict Sociology: Toward an Explanatory Social Science*. New York: Academic Press.

Countryman, Edward. 2003. *The American Revolution*. Revised ed. New York: Hill and Wang.

Eckstein, Susan Eva, and Timothy P. Wickham-Crowley, eds. 2002. *Struggles for Social Rights in Latin America*. New York: Routledge.

Futures and Commodity Market News. 2006. "Uruguay/Argentina: Pulp Mill Protest Again Blocks Bridges." November 22. http://news.tradingcharts.com/futures/5/0/86216005.html (page discontinued).

Gettleman, Jeffrey. 2007. "Ethiopian Rebels Kill 70 at Chinese-Run Oil Field." *New York Times*, April 25.

Gilly, Adolfo. 2005. "Bolivia: A Twenty-First-Century Revolution." *Socialism and Democracy* 19 (3): 41–54.

Goldman, Francisco. 2007. Interview by Amy Goodman. *Democracy Now!* November 6. Transcript available at http://www.democracynow.org/2007/11/6/guatemalas_indigenous_countryside_drives_election_victory.

Hobsbawm, E. J. 1965. *Primitive Rebels: Studies in Archaic Forms of Social Movement in the Nineteenth and Twentieth Centuries*. New York: W. W. Norton.

Hobsbawm, E. J., and George Rudé. 1968. *Captain Swing*. New York: Pantheon Books.

Holgate, Brandynn, and Jennifer Shea. 2007. "SEIU Confronts the Home Care Crisis in California." *New Politics* 11 (2). http://ww3.wpunj.edu/newpol/issue42/SheaHolgate42.htm.

Howard, Alan. 2007. "The Future of Global Unions: Is Solidarity Still Forever?" *Dissent* 11 (4): 62–70.

Industrial Workers of the World. 1989. *I.W.W. Songs to Fan the Flames of Discontent*. Facsimile of the nineteenth edition (1923). Chicago: Charles H. Kerr.

Janoski, Thomas. 1998. *Citizenship and Civil Society: A Framework of Rights and Obligations in Liberal, Traditional, and Social Democratic Regimes*. Cambridge: Cambridge University Press.

Jasper, James. 1997. *The Art of Moral Protest: Culture, Biography, and Creativity in Social Movements*. Chicago: University of Chicago Press.

Junger, Sebastian. 2007. "Blood Oil." *Vanity Fair*, February. http://www.vanityfair.com/politics/features/2007/02/junger200702.

Kalyvas, Stathis N. 2003. "The Ontology of 'Political Violence': Action and Identity in Civil Wars." *Perspectives on Politics* 1 (3): 475–94.

Kern, Kimberly. 2007. "Ixcan, Guatemala Says NO to Xalala Dam." *Upside Down World*, May 2. http://upsidedownworld.org/main/index2.php?option=com_content&task=view&id=719&It.

Lerner, Steve. 2007. "Global Unions: A Solution to Labor's Worldwide Decline." *New Labor Forum* 16 (1): 23–37.

Maier, Pauline. 1972. *From Resistance to Revolution: Colonial Radicals and the Development of American Opposition to Britain, 1763–1776*. New York: Alfred A. Knopf.

Mann, Michael. 1986. *A History of Power from the Beginning to A.D. 1760*. Vol. 1 of *The Sources of Social Power*. Cambridge: Cambridge University Press.

Meyerson, Harold. 2007. "Unions Gone Global." *The American Prospect*, April 26. http://www.prospect.org/cs/articles?article=unions_gone_global.

Mills, C. Wright. 1956. *The Power Elite*. New York: Oxford University Press.

Moody, Kim. 1997. *Workers in a Lean World: Unions in the International Economy*. London: Verso.

Moore, Barrington. 1966. *The Social Origins of Dictatorship and Democracy: Lord and Peasant in the Making of the Modern World*. Boston: Beacon Press.

Mouawad, Jad. 2007a. "Growing Unrest Posing a Threat to Nigerian Oil." *New York Times*, April 21.

———. 2007b. "Nowadays Angola Is Oil's Topic A." *New York Times*, March 20.

Munshi, Millie. 2007. "Copper Futures Climb on U.S. Economic Data, Peruvian Strike." *Bloomberg*, May 6. www.bloomberg.com/apps/news?pid=20601086&sid=aF8jlsc5ySYw&refer=latin_am.

Nash, Gary B. 2005. *The Unknown American Revolution: The Unruly Birth of Democracy and the Struggle to Create America*. New York: Viking.

Page, Jeremy. 2007. "Farmers Put India's Growth in Doubt as They Win Battle of the Boom Zones." *Times*, March 19. http://www.timesonline.co.uk/tol/news/world/asia/article1533799.ece.

Petras, James, and Henry Veltmeyer. 2005. *Social Movements and State Power: Argentina, Brazil, Bolivia, Ecuador*. Ann Arbor, Mich.: Pluto Press.

Phelps, Christopher. 2007. "The New SDS." *Nation*, April 16.

Piven, Frances Fox. 2006. *Challenging Authority: How Ordinary People Change America*. Lanham, Md.: Rowman and Littlefield.

Piven, Frances Fox, and Richard A. Cloward. 1977. *Poor People's Movements: Why They Succeed, How They Fail*. New York: Pantheon Books.

———. 1992. "Normalizing Collective Protest." In *Frontiers in Social Movement Theory*, edited by Aldon D. Morris and Carol McClurg Mueller, 301–25. New Haven: Yale University Press.

———. 2000. "Power Repertoires and Globalization." *Politics and Society* 28 (3): 413–30.

———. 2005. "Rules, Rulebreaking, and Power." In *The Handbook of Political Sociology: States, Civil Societies, and Globalization*, edited by Thomas Janoski, 33–53. New York: Oxford University Press.

Presthus, Robert. 1964. *Men at the Top: A Study in Community Power*. New York: Oxford University Press.

Ramachandran, Sudha. 2006. "India Bends over for Myanmar's Generals." *Asia Times*, November 6.

Raphael, Ray. 2001. *A People's History of the American Revolution: How Common People Shaped the Fight for Independence*. New York: New Press.

Rizvi, Haider. 2007. "Indigenous Peoples Shut Out of Climate Talks, Plans." OneWorld. December 12. http://us.oneworld.net/article/indigenous-peoples-shut-out-climate-talks-plans.

Rudé, George. 1964. *The Crowd in History: A Study of Popular Disturbances in France and England, 1730–1848*. New York: John Wiley and Sons.

Shefner, Jon. 2006. "Do You Think Democracy Is a Magical Thing? From Basic Needs to Democratization in Informal Politics." In *Out of the Shadows: Political Action and the Informal Economy in Latin America*, edited by Patricia Fernández-Kelly and John Shefner, 241–67. University Park: Pennsylvania State University Press.

———. 2007. "Rethinking Civil Society in the Age of NAFTA: The Case of Mexico." *ANNALS of the American Academy of Political and Social Science* 610 (1): 182–220.

Sitrin, Marina, ed. 2006. *Horizontalism: Voices of Popular Power in Argentina*. Oakland, Calif.: AK Press.

Solnit, Rebecca. 2007. "The Secret Library of Hope: 12 Books to Stiffen Your Resolve." TomDispatch. December 17. http://www.tomdispatch.com/post/174875.

Thompson, E. P. 1963. *The Making of the English Working Class*. New York: Vintage Books.

Tilly, Charles. 1978. *Mobilization to Revolution*. Reading, Mass.: Addison-Wesley.

———. 1982. "Britain Creates the Social Movements." In *Social Conflict and the Political Order in Modern Britain*, edited by James E. Cronin and Jonathan Schneer, 21–51. New Brunswick: Rutgers University Press.

———. 1984. "Social Movements and National Politics." In *Statemaking and Social Movements: Essays in History and Theory*, edited by Charles Bright and Susan Harding, 297–317. Ann Arbor: University of Michigan Press.

———. 1986. *The Contentious French: Four Centuries of Popular Struggle*. Cambridge: Harvard University Press.

Zinn, Howard. 1980. *A People's History of the United States*. New York: Harper and Row.

7

IMMIGRANT TRANSNATIONAL ORGANIZATIONS AND DEVELOPMENT:
A COMPARATIVE STUDY

*Alejandro Portes, Cristina Escobar, and
Alexandria Walton Radford*

Conexión Colombia is a public/private partnership in the Republic of Colombia that aims both to diffuse information about the country among its emigrants all over the world and to channel their contributions to established charities and philanthropic initiatives throughout the nation. "With a simple click," says Conexión Colombia's attractive brochure, "any person in the world can donate and contribute to the country's development. Connect yourself now!"[1] According to the young, dynamic former executive director of the organization, Diana Sanchez-Rey, thousands of Colombians all over the world visit Conexión Colombia's website every day, looking for news and stories about their country and leaving their own statements. In her words, these visitors are "mostly the older, better-off migrants in Europe and the U.S. for whom nostalgia weighs heavier . . . but also the younger professionals who have left recently and feel an obligation toward the country that educated them."[2]

Not two miles away from the plush offices of Conexión Colombia, Sor Irene of the Vicentine Sisters of Charity operates a refuge for the homeless of Bogotá, mostly mentally disturbed and developmentally challenged persons or drug addicts. Every night, Sor Irene and her brave helpers roam the dangerous neighborhood surrounding the convent in search of the "inhabitants of the street." The refuge not only offers them shelter, food, and clothing, but also rehabilitation in the form of counseling and occupational therapy. All of the equipment for learning new work skills—from manufacturing and selling paper made from recycled waste to baking and selling bread—has been acquired through donations from Colombians abroad.[3]

In the same convent lives Sor Isabel, a vigorous middle-aged nun who helped create an asylum and school for orphans in the city of Tunja fifteen years ago. The funds for buying the land for the asylum and building the dormitories and the school were provided, in large part, by the Foundation of the Divine Child (Fundación del Divino Nino), a charity established by a Colombian priest, a journalist born in Tunja, and a network of immigrant volunteers in New York and New Jersey. The school's computers were donated by IBM through the good offices of the foundation.[4]

The examples could be multiplied. All over the hemisphere, countries and local communities that serve as sources of immigrants to the developed world have come to rely on the solidarity of these persons and on their sense of obligation to those left behind, not only for the survival of families but also for the implementation of a whole array of philanthropic and civic projects. By now, it is well known that the level of remittances sent by immigrants in the advanced countries to their respective nations easily surpasses the foreign aid that these nations receive and even matches their hard currency earnings from exports.

Less well known is the wide variety of collective organizations among immigrants pursuing a number of diverse projects in their respective countries and communities of origin, as well as the initiatives undertaken by these communities and even nation-states to motivate and channel the material contributions of their expatriates. Rising migration from the global South to the global North has become acknowledged as one of the trademarks of the contemporary capitalist world economy and of its relentless process of integration (Zolberg 1989; Castles 2004; Portes and DeWind 2004). Also less well recognized, until recently, is that this massive displacement is not a one-way process but rather has reciprocal influence, with rising force, becoming an important factor in the development of sending nations and regions. Immigrant communities have become an unexpected but increasingly visible actor in the politics of their hometowns and countries (Vertovec 2004; Levitt and Glick Schiller 2004).

"Transnationalism" is the term used to describe these activities and their effects in the recent sociological literature (Portes, Haller, and Guarnizo 2002; Guarnizo, Portes, and Haller 2003). While there have been some dissenting voices concerning the novelty and importance of the phenomenon (e.g., Waldinger and Fitzgerald 2004), the weight of the empirical evidence provides strong proof of the novel character of these practices and of their structural importance for sending regions and for immigrant communities themselves (Smith 2003; Vertovec 2004). Most of this evidence, however, comes from case studies of specific communities or from surveys of immigrants (Levitt 2001; Kyle 2000; Guarnizo, Portes, and Haller 2003; Portes 2003). So far, there have been few systematic studies of *organizations* involved in the transnational field, their origins, and their effects.[5]

This study aims to contribute to filling this knowledge gap with a systematic survey of immigrant organizations among three Latin American–origin immigrant groups along the East Coast of the United States. The data gathered over the course of the survey allow us to better understand the forces creating and sustaining these organizations and to test several preliminary hypotheses about the effects of contexts of exit and modes of incorporation in receiving countries on the character of immigrant transnationalism. This study focuses primarily on the implications of the phenomenon for local and national development in sending countries. Hence, interviews with leaders of organization in the United States were supplemented with visits and interviews with government officials, community activists, and counterpart organizations in each nation of origin.

This double perspective provides a far more comprehensive understanding of the social and political dynamics at play and of the different forces impinging on the phenomenon. The brochure of Conexión Colombia, one of the organizations identified and studied in the course of the project, illustrates some of these dynamics well: the organization's stated purpose is "to provide emotional, useful, and up-to-date information so that Colombians abroad remain in contact with their country. For that reason, the web page of Conexión Colombia has become the corner of nostalgia [sic] where it is possible to see the goals in the local futbol tournament, listen to the latest music, travel through the most beautiful areas of our geography, and locate the closest Colombian restaurants the world over."

Research Design

The first challenge confronted by the study was building an inventory of organizations created by the target immigrant groups in their respective areas of concentration. Fortunately, several circumstances made a near-complete enumeration, especially of organizations with transnational ties, possible. First, the consulates of the respective countries generally maintain lists of these organizations as part of their efforts to keep in touch and influence their communities abroad; second, umbrella confederations based on nationality or panethnicity (i.e., "Hispanic") make it their business to identify and bring together the relevant organizations, thereby increasing their visibility and power; and third, leaders of organizations are generally interested in advertising their goals and achievements as a means to attract both new members and donations. Organizations are *not* individuals, and unlike the latter, most seek public exposure; their leaders are generally willing to grant interviews and provide detailed information. Due to these circumstances, the research team was able to build a database of transnational organizations in the principal areas of concentration of each national group, including all but the most fleeting and smaller associations.

Colombians, Dominicans, and Mexicans were the groups selected for study. While these immigrant nationalities share a common language and culture, they are very different in terms of exit and reception. Colombians are a relatively recent inflow, now exceeding one million persons and concentrated in New York City and Miami.[6] Colombians tend to be urban in origin and to have higher levels of education than other Latin immigrants. Their departure has been motivated by growing violence and deteriorating economic and political conditions in their country. While the majority of Colombians are legal immigrants, the number of political asylees is growing. Phenotypically, Colombian immigrants are mostly white or light mestizo and thus tend to escape the worst forms of discrimination experienced by nonwhite groups in American society (Guarnizo, Sanchez, and Roach 1999; Escobar 2004).

Dominicans have been arriving in New York City and in smaller cities along the New York–Boston corridor since the 1960s. They now comprise over one million people and represent the largest immigrant group in New York City (Itzigsohn et al. 1999).[7] New York is second only to the capital city of Santo Domingo in the size of its Dominican population. This is mostly a working-class migration, but with a sizable component of middle-class professionals and entrepreneurs. Motivations for departure are mostly economic since the country of origin is at peace, and there is a dense traffic between the Dominican Republic and New York due to family and political reasons. All major Dominican parties have representatives in New York and in cities along the New York–Boston corridor, especially Providence. The current president of the country, Leonel Fernández, was himself born and educated in New York City. The Dominican Republic is predominantly a mulatto country, with a white upper-class elite that does not emigrate, and most Dominican immigrants are phenotypically black or mulatto. In America, they are generally regarded as part of the black population and have suffered discrimination accordingly (Portes and Guarnizo 1991; Grasmuck and Pessar 1991).

Mexicans are, by far, the largest immigrant group in the United States, numbering over ten million persons and representing close to one-third of the foreign-born population of the United States.[8] Historically, and at present, Mexico has effectively functioned as the principal manual labor reservoir for its powerful northern neighbor. The end of the Bracero program in 1964 led to the criminalization of this labor inflow and to the rapid increase in illegal or unauthorized immigrants among the U.S. Mexican population. As is well known, Mexican immigration has traditionally been concentrated in the Southwest and secondarily in the Midwest. Its principal areas of urban/metropolitan concentration are in Los Angeles, San Diego, Houston, Dallas, and Chicago. More recently, the flow of immigrants has moved steadily east in search of stable agricultural and urban employment in agriculture and services. As a consequence, the Mexican-origin population of states such as Georgia tripled during the last intercensal period (1990–2000) and grew from an insignificant number in New York City in the 1980s to an estimated 250,000 persons in 2000 (Massey, Durand, and Malone 2002; U.S. Census Bureau 2001; Delgado Wise and Márquez Covarrubias 2009).

Phenotypically, Mexican immigrants are identifiable by their darker skin and mestizo or indigenous features. These traits, added to their low average levels of education and frequently illegal status, have led to pervasive discrimination against them by the U.S. government and by American society at large. In the Southwest and Midwest, Mexicans have been traditionally confined to impoverished and isolated neighborhoods and, like blacks, treated as an inferior caste. In response to these conditions, Mexican American ethnic politics has pivoted around struggles to overcome discrimination and to gain a measure of dignity and economic advancement for members of this minority. In contrast, Mexican transnational organizations, created by first-generation rural immigrants, have aimed primarily at improving material and political conditions in their places of origin (Goldring 2002; Smith 2005).

Table 7.1 summarizes the characteristics of the three selected immigrant groups and their countries of origin. Their cultural similarities and systematic structural differences provide a suitable background for analyzing both the forms that transnational activities can take and their potential impact on sending countries and communities. As indicated previously, data collection on these organizations focused on their principal areas of concentration along the East Coast of the United States, as follows:

Colombians: New York, New Jersey suburbs, and Miami
Dominicans: New York, New Jersey suburbs, Boston, and Providence
Mexicans: New York, New Jersey suburbs, New England, Philadelphia, and North Carolina

For each target nationality, we selected the thirty principal organizations identified in the process of building the inventory and interviewed their leaders. For budget reasons, the study was limited to the East Coast. This is not a serious limitation in the case of Colombians and Dominicans, since their principal areas of concentration are known to be located in the East; however, it means that Mexican organizations interviewed for the study mostly represent a recently established population, since the larger and much older Mexican immigrant concentrations are located in cities in the West. The Mexican organizations included in the survey may be viewed as representative of the population's early associational efforts in its new areas of settlement and, as such, are likely to differ in size, age, and goals from those identified and

Table 7.1   Characteristics of countries of origin and immigrant communities

Characteristics	Colombia	Dominican Republic	Mexico
Country of origin			
Population (in millions, ca. 2000)	43.0	8.5	97.5
GDP per capita ($)	2254	1862	4574
Gini coefficient	0.57	0.47	0.47
Income share of top quintile (%)	60.9	53.3	60.2
Income share of bottom quintile (%)	3.0	5.1	5.4
Average years of education[a]	8.6	8.2	8.6
Open unemployment (%)[a]	19.8	13.8	3.7
Informal employment (%)[a]	46.3	44.0	44.1
Households below poverty line (%)	45.0	32.0	43.0
Capital city	Bogotá	Santo Domingo	Mexico D.F.
Political situation	Democracy; multiple civil wars	Democracy; no armed insurgencies	Democracy; localized rebellions
Immigrants in the United States			
Total number[b]	470,684	764,945	9,177,487
Percentage of U.S. Hispanic population	1.3	2.1	58.5
Legal immigrants (2001)	16,730	21,313	206,426
Percentage of total legal U.S. immigrants	1.6	2.0	19.4
Rank in total legal U.S. immigrants	16	14	1
Professional specialty occupation (%)	16.1	9.4	4.7
High school graduates (%)	72.0	48.1	29.7
College graduates (%)	21.8	9.5	4.2
Median household income ($)	43,242	34,311	36,004
Types of immigration	Mostly legal; increasing numbers of unauthorized immigrants and political asylees	Legal and unauthorized	Mostly unauthorized, but sizable number of legal immigrants
Principal cities of destination	Miami (15.8%) New York (12.3%)	New York (45.9%) Bergen-Passaic (5.9%)	Los Angeles (16.0%) Chicago (5.3%) Houston (4.8%)
Characteristics of settled U.S. population	Mostly first generation	Mostly first generation with rising second generation	Mostly second generation and higher

SOURCE: Data from United Nations Department of Economic and Social Development (2002), table A-2; Economic Commission for Latin America and the Caribbean (2002); International Labour Organization (2010); Department of Homeland Security (2004); U.S. Census Bureau (2003); World Bank Indicators Database (http://data.worldbank.org/indicator), data for 2003.

[a] Figures refer to the economically active population (ages 25–59) in urban areas.

[b] The number of immigrants is based on U.S. census figures. Estimates from sending country governments put resident Colombian and Dominican populations in the United States at over one million each and the Mexican population at over twelve million.

studied in the West (Goldring 2002; Roberts, Frank, and Lozano-Asencio 1999).

During one-and-a-half-hour face-to-face interviews with immigrant leaders, we gathered information on the origins of the organizations, their members, and the leaders themselves. These interviews were supplemented by meetings with consular officials and other informants knowledgeable about each immigrant community, as well as several visits to sending countries. During these visits, the project team established contact with the government departments responsible for their countries' respective immigrant populations; with private entities pursuing relationships with these populations; and with recipients of donations and assistance from the civic and philanthropic groups interviewed in the United States.

The Institute of Mexicans Abroad (IME) and the program Colombia Nos Une (Colombia Brings Us Together), established by the Colombian Ministry of Foreign Relations, are examples of official initiatives in this field. Conexión Colombia provides an illustration of a powerful private initiative supplementing official efforts. By contacting local municipalities, established philanthropies, and religious orders, the research team was able to ascertain the existence and effects of the civic and philanthropic projects organized by immigrants abroad. While the aggregate impact of such efforts is difficult to quantify, their existence and the attention they receive from government agencies and large private institutions in sending countries offer prima facie evidence of their importance.

Theoretical Overview

The concept of transnationalism was coined in the early 1990s by an enterprising group of social anthropologists to refer to the "multistranded" activities undertaken by immigrants across national borders (Basch, Glick Schiller, and Blanc-Szanton 1994; Glick Schiller 1999; Glick Schiller and Fouron 1999). The flurry of case studies that followed documented the many forms that these activities could take and advanced the notion that immigrant assimilation, as conventionally defined, was a thing of the past. Instead of a gradual process of acculturation and integration into the host society, as described by classical assimilation theory, transnationalism evoked the imagery of a permanent back-and-forth movement in which immigrants lived simultaneously in two or more societies and cultures, thus tying them together in "deterritorialized" communities (Basch, Glick Schiller, and Blanc-Szanton 1994).

The excessive claims of this literature led more scientifically oriented students of immigration to reject the concept altogether and stay within the

framework of conventional assimilation theory. Apart from the broad pro-
nouncements to which it led, the concept of transnationalism had the additional difficulty of having been applied to a number of disparate phenomena
in the past, obscuring and confusing its meaning. As early as 1916, a public
intellectual, Randolph Bourne, used the term in his oft-quoted essay "Transnational America" to deplore the process of immigrant assimilation, which,
in his view, "create[d] hordes of men and women without a spiritual country,
cultural outlaws, without taste, without standards but those of the mob. . . .
They become the flotsam of American life" (1916, 90–91).

Despite these difficulties, and seeing heuristic value in the concept as applied to contemporary immigrants, another group of social scientists set out
to define it more rigorously so that it could be empirically measured (Portes,
Guarnizo, and Landolt 1999; Guarnizo, Portes, and Haller 2003; Portes and
Smith 2008). These researchers adopted a definition of transnationalism as
the grassroots activities conducted across national borders by actors in civil
society, independent of and sometimes in opposition to official directives and
rules. Transnationalism thus encompassed, among other things, the efforts
of activists concerned with such matters as the environment, human and
labor rights, and political democracy (Evans 2000; Keck and Sikkink 1998).
Immigrant transnationalism is a subset of this universe, defined by regular
activities across national borders conducted by the foreign-born as part of
their daily lives abroad.

This definition sought to distinguish regular involvement in such activities
from the occasional sending of a remittance or a once-in-a-while trip to the
home country, things that immigrants have always done and which, by themselves, do not justify the coining of a new term. The novel element at present,
which the concept of transnationalism seeks to capture, is the frequent and
enduring participation of immigrants in the economic, political, and cultural
life of their countries, which requires regular and frequent contact across
national borders. Such contact is made possible by innovations in transportation and communications technology unavailable to earlier generations of
immigrants (Levitt 2001; Guarnizo 2003). By extension, transnational organizations are those whose goals and activities are partially or totally located in
countries other than where their members reside.

Thus defined, transnationalism is not assumed to characterize all immigrants or to be inimical to their assimilation. However, such questions may
be addressed by empirical research. Earlier characterizations of all immigrants as "transmigrants" and of transnationalism as an alternative to assimilation were based on extrapolation from case studies. The methodology of
these studies sampled on the dependent variable by focusing on transnational
entrepreneurs or political activists, to the exclusion of other immigrants not
involved in cross-border activities (Portes 2003).

The more restricted definition of the concept adopted by more recent studies aims to investigate the actual extent of the phenomenon among different groups of immigrants. It is accompanied by a typology that seeks to distinguish among the *international* activities conducted by governments and other nationally based institutions; the *multinational* initiatives of UN agencies, global churches, and corporate actors operating in multiple countries; and the *transnational* world of grassroots enterprises and initiatives undertaken by actors in civil society, immigrants included. The purpose of this typology is to delimit the scope of transnationalism and to clearly differentiate it from other phenomena also anchored in cross-border interactions but conducted by more institutionalized and far more powerful actors. Absent this distinction, the concept of transnationalism becomes a catchall devoid of any heuristic value.

This typology does additional service by highlighting the possible interactions and mutual influence of the three types of cross-border activities distinguished above. It turns out that governments—in particular those of sending nations—have not remained indifferent to the presence and initiatives of their expatriates and have increasingly sought to influence them. Reasons for governments' involvement are easy to understand: the rising volume of immigrant remittances; the investments of expatriates in housing, land, and businesses at home; and their cross-border civic and philanthropic activities. Taken together, these activities have "structural" importance for the development of local communities and even nations (Guarnizo 2003; Vertovec 2004).

Sending country governments have responded to immigrants' activity by passing laws allowing them to retain their nationality even if they naturalize abroad. Those who remain citizens of their home country have been granted the right to vote and even to run for office while living in another country. Consulates have been instructed to take a more proactive stance toward immigrant communities and have started to provide a number of services to their co-nationals, including legal representation, health assistance, identification cards, and English and home-country language training (Escobar 2003, 2004; Smith 2003; Itzigsohn et al. 1999).

Through these various initiatives, governments are seeking to preserve the loyalty of their expatriates and to increase and channel their remittances, investments, and charitable contributions. The significance of official initiatives is evident in the fact that almost every sending country government has undertaken them—from Mexico, Colombia, and the Dominican Republic to Turkey, Eritrea, and the Philippines (Portes 2003). In terms of the three-part typology outlined above, this means that the international activities of these countries' diplomats and government officials have become increasingly oriented toward promoting and guiding the transnational initiatives of their emigrant communities.

However, the flurry of official programs has fostered the impression that immigrant transnationalism is nothing but a reflection on and a response to these initiatives. Nothing could be further from the truth: all of the empirical evidence indicates that economic, political, and sociocultural activities linking expatriate communities with their countries of origin have emerged through the initiative of the immigrants themselves, with governments jumping on the bandwagon only when the importance and economic potential of their initiatives became evident (Landolt 2001; Guarnizo, Sanchez, and Roach 1999; Smith 2005). Still, the increasingly active presence of sending country governments in the transnational field cannot but have a bearing on the form and the goals adopted by these grassroots initiatives. Depending on the reach and the material resources committed by governments and the purposes for which they are used, immigrant organizations may come to accept and toe the official line, remain independent of it, or actively resist it as unwanted interference. We will return to these varying interactions between international and transnational activities below.

Waldinger and Fitzgerald (2004) have charged that there is really nothing new about the concept of transnationalism. Immigrants have always engaged with their countries and communities of origin, and abundant examples of what today is called transnationalism may be found in the literature on European immigrants to America written by the turn of the twentieth century. Indeed, multiple historical instances of grassroots cross-border activities exist. Yet, until the concept of transnationalism was coined and refined, the common character and significance of this phenomenon remained obscure. For instance, the theoretical linkage between Russian or Polish émigré political activism and the trading activities of the Chinese diaspora could not have been seen because there was no theoretical lens that connected them and pointed to their convergence. In this sense, Waldinger and Fitzgerald step into what Merton (1968) long ago identified as the "fallacy of adumbration," which consists of negating the value of a scientific discovery by pointing to earlier instances of it. Robert Smith drives the point home by noting, "If transnational life existed in the past, but was not seen as such, then the transnational lens does the new analytical work of providing a way of seeing what was there that could not be seen before" (2003, 725).

In line with Smith's statement, the concept of transnationalism has given rise to a fertile research literature and to the formulation of subsidiary ideas and hypotheses that did not exist previously in the field of immigration. Some of these hypotheses concern individual participation in transnational enterprises and activities, and others deal with the character of these organizations. The only quantitative survey conducted in this field so far, the Comparative Immigrant Entrepreneurship Project (CIEP), discovered that education was positively associated with participation in transnational activities—economic, political, and cultural—as were occupational and marital status. Married men were far more likely to take part. Furthermore, years of residence abroad actually *increased* the probability of transnationalism (Portes, Haller, Guarnizo 2002; Guarnizo, Portes, and Haller 2003).

Results from the CIEP study indicate that, contrary to the conventional assimilation story, the maintenance and cultivation of ties to the home nation do not decline with time since immigration, nor are they the preserve of marginal sectors within immigrant communities. To the contrary, these activities are more common among better-established, better-educated, and wealthier immigrants. The reason seems to be that these are the persons with the wherewithal to involve themselves in frequently complex and demanding cross-border ventures, something that is typically beyond the reach of more recent, and poorer, arrivals. In light of these findings, we hypothesize that assimilation to the host country and participation in transnational activities are not necessarily at odds with each other, as assumed earlier by both schools (Guarnizo, Portes, and Haller 2003; Portes, Haller, Guarnizo 2002; Portes 2003).

The CIEP study also found significant differences in transnational participation depending on contexts of exit and reception of different immigrant groups: those coming from rural areas, whether immigrants or refugees, tend to form nonpolitical hometown civic committees to support the localities left behind; immigrants with more urban origins commonly become involved in the politics and the cultural life of their countries as a whole, especially if political parties, churches, and cultural institutions there seek to maintain an active presence among their expatriates (Itzigsohn and Saucedo 2002; Guarnizo, Portes, and Haller 2003). Programs initiated by home country governments can also play a significant role, especially if they go beyond symbolic appeals and provide real help for their immigrants abroad. In such cases, official directives can heavily influence the direction and goals of grassroots transnational activities (Escobar 2003; Smith 2003). Based on these results, we hypothesize that differences in the sociopolitical context of exit and in the character of involvement of sending country governments will significantly influence the form and activities of organizations created by different immigrant groups.

Lastly, contexts of reception—specifically, the level of discrimination meted out on the newcomers—can affect the onset of activities. When, for reasons of low human capital or racial stereotypes, an immigrant group finds itself discriminated against, there is every reason to expect that it will band together and adopt a defensive stance toward the host country, appealing to symbols of cultural pride brought from home. When these conditions are absent, transnational initiatives may become more individualized and organizations, when they exist, may adopt "middle-class" forms recognizable and acceptable to mainstream society. Lions Clubs, Kiwanis Clubs, and charitable ladies' associations are examples of this alternative mode of transnationalism.

This third hypothesis, based on prior empirical results, will be examined with the others below, on the basis of data from our study.

Results

The Global Foundation for Democracy and Development (FUNGLODE) is a private nongovernmental organization that was set up by Leonel Fernández, president of the Dominican Republic, prior to his reelection in 2004. The foundation established a "strategic alliance" with the Institute of Dominican Studies at the City University of New York as a means to hold a number of conferences, appoint joint task forces, and explore other avenues to give Dominicans in the United States a greater voice in the affairs of their home country. This type of activity operates at a high level of formalization and, in terms of our typology, may be more properly termed "international" than "transnational." The latter element is present, however, because of the large number of Dominican immigrants taking part in this alliance and because its founder, Fernández, got the idea while growing up as an immigrant in New York.[9]

At the other extreme of formalization is the Canafisteros de Bani en Boston, a grassroots association created by Dominican immigrants in New England to help their hometown and province. A counterpart committee in the town of Canafistol receives and distributes the regular donations in money and kind. So far, the Canafistero immigrants have bought an ambulance and funeral car for their town, provided uniforms for the local baseball team, bought an electrical generator for the clinic, acquired various kinds of medical and school equipment, and created a fund to give $100 a month to needy families in Canafistol. They have literally transformed the town, which has grown increasingly reliant on the loyalty and generosity of its emigrants to meet a number of needs unattended by the national government.[10]

These contrasting Dominican examples serve as a good introduction to our data, for they highlight the notable range of transnational activities, even among immigrants from the same small country. Table 7.2 presents an initial profile of our sample of immigrant organizations. The predominant type are those that define themselves as "civic" entities pursuing an agenda of national scope. The examples of civic transnational organizations that appear in table 7.3 include such immigrant-created organizations as the Miami Colombian Lions Club and the Association of Dominican Provinces of New York. The Mexican example, which is regional in scope, is an association of immigrants in North Carolina that emerged under the sponsorship of the government of their home state, Guanajuato.

Second in importance are hometown committees, whose scope of action is primarily local. The examples provided in table 7.3 include the previously

Table 7.2 A profile of immigrant transnational organizations

Variable	%
National origin	
Colombian	36.0
Dominican	35.0
Mexican	29.0
Location	
New York/New Jersey	54.0
Miami	20.2
Philadelphia	4.5
Other	21.3
Type of organization	
Civic	40.4
Hometown committee	18.0
Social agency	12.4
Cultural	7.9
Political	6.7
Professional	4.6
Religious	3.4
Educational	2.2
Sports	2.2
Economic	2.2
Scope of projects in country of origin	
Local	26.0
Regional	13.0
National	61.0
Focus of activity in country of origin[a]	
Education/schools	53.9
Health	40.4
Children/old people	30.3
Church	13.5
Political parties	7.9
Legal status	
Formal nonprofit organization	45.0
Informal/other	55.0
Frequency of civic events sponsored by organization	
Occasionally	24.4
Yearly	36.6
Several times a year	26.8
Once a month or more	12.2
Frequency of festivals sponsored by organization	
Occasionally	19.0
Yearly	52.4
Several times a year	28.6
Sources of funds[b]	
Members' dues	59.0
Private companies	60.3
Churches	12.8
Foundations	9.2
Home country government	9.1
Home country political parties	2.6
N	90

SOURCE: Comparative Immigrant Transnational Organization Project (CIOP).

[a] Percentages do not add up to 100 because organizations may be engaged in multiple projects.

[b] Percentages do not add up to 100 because organizations may receive multiple sources of funds.

Table 7.3   Examples of transnational organizations

Type	Name	Nationality	Location	Number of members
Civic	Miami Colombian Lions Club	Colombian	Miami	32
	Association of Dominican Provinces	Dominican	New York/New Jersey	48
	Casa Guanajuato	Mexican	Carrboro, North Carolina	26
Hometown committee	Fundación Quimbaya	Colombian	New York/New Jersey	28
	Cañafisteros de Bani en Boston	Dominican	Boston	25
	San Miguel Comitipla (Xochihuehuetlan, Guerrero)	Mexican	New York/New Jersey	260
Social agency	Las Americas Community Center	Colombian	Miami	95
	Hermanas Mirabal Family Center and Child Care Network	Dominican	New York/New Jersey	20
	Mexican House of New Jersey— Development Corporation	Mexican	New Jersey	20
Religious	Committee of the Divine Child	Colombian	New York/New Jersey	11
	Dominican Sunday	Dominican	New York/New Jersey	9
Political	Colombian-American Political Action Committee	Colombian	Miami	25
	Dominican Revolutionary Party (PRD)	Dominican	New York/New Jersey	23,000
	Dominican Liberation Party (PLD)	Dominican	Boston	1,500

Source: Comparative Immigrant Transnational Organization Project (CIOP).

mentioned Canafisteros of Boston and a strong New York–based set of well-organized committees formed by Mexicans from Xochihuehuetlan, a town in the municipality of Guerrero. Next are social agencies that provide health, educational, and other services to immigrants in the United States, but which are also engaged in projects in their home country. These organizations are typically better funded, since their budgets include monies for social services provided by U.S. municipal, county, and state governments.

Transnational political organizations represent a small minority of the sample, and they do not exist at all among Mexican immigrants whose focus of interest is primarily their home communities. Among Dominicans, however, political party representation is quite important. As seen in table 7.3, the Dominican Revolutionary Party of New York (PRD) claims 23,000 affiliates in the metropolitan area, and the Dominican Liberation Party (PLD) of Massachusetts claims 1,500. While these figures are probably exaggerated, they signal the significance of party politics for this specific immigrant group.

Table 7.2 shows that most of these organizations operate informally, although 45 percent have registered their status as formal, nonprofit entities.

Regardless of status, the prime philanthropic concerns of the majority of these groups pertain to education and health in their home communities and countries, followed by care of children and the elderly. The data reveal vast differences in the funds available to organizations to implement these initiatives, ranging from a few thousand dollars to close to a million. As mentioned previously, social agencies are the better-funded organizations and are also most common in our sample of Dominican organizations. This accounts for the very sizable differences in average monetary resources among organizations of the three nationalities, as shown in table 7.4.

In actuality, these differences are due to only a few well-funded organizations, a fact that becomes evident when we examine the median of financial resources rather than the mean. The median is influenced by frequencies and not extreme values; hence, differences among nationalities in this indicator become much smaller. Still, Dominican organizations remain the best funded, with Mexican organizations trailing far behind. This story repeats itself when we consider monthly budgets or the number of salaried employees. Four-fifths of immigrant transnational organizations do not have paid staff, but 25 percent of Dominican organizations employ five salaried workers or more. No organization among the other two nationalities falls into this category.

By and large, these transnational organizations consist of volunteers, with an average of thirty-five regular members. This number is inflated to almost

Table 7.4 Quantitative characteristics of transnational organizations

Variable	Colombian	Dominican	Mexican	Total
Mean number of members	44	939	69	356
Median number of members	25	34	23	26
Mean number of occasional members	65	1061	144	492
Median number of occasional members	23	20	25	20
Mean monetary funds ($)	24,056	695,737	24,470	247,493
Median monetary funds ($)	20,000	24,000	5,000	20,000
Monthly expenses				
No expenses (%)	46.7	10.0	60.0	37.7
Less than $1,000 (%)	33.3	23.3	20.0	25.9
Less than $5,000 (%)	16.7	43.3	16.0	24.8
$5,000 or more (%)	3.3	23.4	4.0	10.6
Salaried employees				
None (%)	87.1	70.0	82.6	79.8
Less than 5 (%)	12.9	3.3	17.4	10.7
Less than 10 (%)	0.0	16.7	0.0	6.0
10 or more (%)	0.0	10.0	0.0	3.5
N	31	30	29	90

Source: Comparative Immigrant Transnational Organizations Project (CIOP).

one thousand among Dominicans. In this case, it is not social agencies but political party affiliates that are the outliers. The fact that political party organizations are few in number is reflected in the median, which discounts extreme values. Differences in membership size become much smaller, though Dominican organizations still preserve some advantage. Like figures on monetary resources, the data on membership (both regular and occasional) indicate wide dispersal, with organizations ranging from a handful of committed activists to hundreds of members.

We asked leaders of each selected organization to report on characteristics of their regular members. These data are important because they bear on opposite hypotheses concerning determinants of transnationalism. As seen previously, an orthodox assimilation perspective would regard as proper such activities of more recent immigrants who have not yet severed their ties with their home countries and cultures and who are keener to assist those left behind. As time passes, these ties should weaken; when immigrants become more settled, better able to speak English, and more comfortable in their new environments, they should gradually abandon active involvement in their home countries (Alba and Nee 2003; Gordon 1964; Warner and Srole 1945). To the contrary, results from the CIEP study summarized above indicate that older, better-educated, and more established immigrants are more prone to participate in these ventures. These are the individuals with the information, the security, and resources of time and money to dedicate to these initiatives (Portes, Haller, and Guarnizo 2002; Guarnizo, Portes, and Haller 2003).

The organizations included in the present project have an estimated membership of 9,040 immigrants, or 32,040 if affiliates to the PRD of New York are counted. Table 7.5 presents relevant data on their average sociodemographic characteristics. Results consistently support the hypothesis that transnational organizations are backed by older, better-educated, and more established immigrants. About half of regular organization members are forty years of age or older and have at least a college degree, in contrast to a fifth or fewer who are under thirty and have less than a high school education. The only exceptions are Mexican organizations, which attract a larger proportion of young people and have as many poorly educated as well-educated members. This result is in line with the well-known youth and low average human capital of the Mexican immigrant population as a whole (Cornelius 1998; López and Stanton-Salazar 2001; Massey, Durand, and Malone 2002; Portes and Fernández-Kelly 2008).

The figures on occupational status tell a similar story, with professionals and business owners doubling the proportion of manual laborers among organization members. Again, the exceptions are Mexican associations, where the proportion of high- and low-status participants is about the same. However, the figures that most decisively contradict the orthodox assimilation hypothesis pertain to knowledge of English, legal status, and length of U.S.

Table 7.5 Characteristics of members of transnational organizations (%)

Characteristic	Colombian	Dominican	Mexican	Total
Age				
30 years or younger	12.1	11.1	24.8	15.2
40 years or older	53.2	53.8	33.6	48.3
Education				
Less than high school	7.4	29.7	28.7	20.9
College degree or more	52.3	50.5	27.0	45.7
Occupation				
Manual laborer	18.0	26.4	40.1	26.6
Professional/business owner	49.8	61.5	36.0	50.3
Knowledge of English				
Very little	11.9	18.7	5.0	12.4
Good or very good	64.2	49.7	60.9	58.5
Legal status				
Does not have entry visa	6.3	3.5	27.9	10.7
U.S. citizen	56.3	48.5	38.4	49.1
Length of U.S. residence				
Less than 5 years	10.1	5.8	10.4	8.7
10 years or more	68.9	66.8	69.5	69.3
Average trips to home country for organizational matters				
Never or rarely	6.7	3.6	30.0	11.5
At least 3 trips a year	40.0	35.7	20.0	33.3

SOURCE: Comparative Immigrant Transnational Organizations Project (CIOP).

residence. As shown in table 7.5, about 60 percent of immigrants actively supporting transnational organizations speak English well or very well, as opposed to just 12 percent who speak it poorly. This pattern is clear among all nationalities, Mexicans included. Similarly, close to 70 percent of these organizations' members have lived in the United States for ten years or more, and half are already U.S. citizens. Only one-tenth are relatively recent arrivals or are in the country without a legal visa. Once again, Mexican organizations are a partial exception, as they draw about one-fourth of their regular members from immigrants without papers, but even then naturalized U.S. citizens outnumber the undocumented.

From these data, we conclude that the motivation to engage in civic, philanthropic, political, and other activities in the home country is primarily found among better-educated, higher-status members of Latin American immigrant communities and among those with longer periods of U.S. residence and secure legal status. Apparently, the process at play is one in which recent immigrants concentrate on carving a niche in the host country rather than concerning themselves with collective organization. Transnational initiatives emerge and begin to influence the home localities and countries of origin only after the initial stages of adaptation have been successfully completed. Since half of participants in these organizations are already U.S. citizens and

70 percent have been in the country for ten years or more, we conclude that assimilation and transnationalism are not at odds but can actually occur simultaneously. Even Mexican organizations do not contradict this conclusion; though many members of their *clubes de oriundos* (hometown committees) are still undocumented, the vast majority of participants have been in the United States for a significant amount of time.

Using the data at hand, it is possible to investigate further the characteristics and origins of transnational organizations. This analysis bears directly on hypotheses concerning the effects of contexts of exit and incorporation on the emergence of these organizations. The dependent variables in this analysis are type of organization, whether or not it has achieved formal status, the causes of its creation, the sources of its funds, and the scope of its action. Our predictors are the nationality of the organizations, and our controls are the size of their membership and the financial resources and characteristics of members—age, education, visa status, and length of U.S. residence. With the exception of nationality, which stands as a proxy for the characteristics of origin and reception of each immigrant group, no implication of causality is made for results involving these control variables.

Table 7.6 presents the results of both a multinomial logistic regression of type of organization and a binomial logistic regression of whether the organization is formally incorporated as a nonprofit or operates informally. Only the three main types of organizations—civic/cultural, hometown committees, and social service agencies—are included. These regressions are nested, with the first model including characteristics of the organization—location, national origin, size of membership (logged), and size of financial resources (logged). The second equation adds the characteristics of members. Only coefficients significant at the .10 level or lower are presented. With a sample size of just eighty-nine cases, coefficients at this level of significance can be reasonably interpreted as important.

Civic/cultural organizations, by far the main type, are not well accounted for by this set of predictors. National origins do not have a significant effect, and neither does geographic location or the characteristics of members. These results indicate that civic/cultural organizations are the normative form of immigrant transnationalism and that they emerge *regardless* of the origins of the group, how it is received, or where it happens to be concentrated. The single significant result is the logarithm of membership size, which shows that, relative to other types of organizations such as social service agencies or branches of political parties, civic/cultural entities tend to be smaller.

On the other hand, the findings reinforce the conclusion that hometown committees are the normative form of transnationalism among Mexican immigrants. Relative to the reference category (Dominicans), the odds of a Mexican organization being a hometown committee are forty-six to one. The fact

Table 7.6 Characteristics defining principal transnational organizations

	Type of organization[a]							
	Civic/cultural		Hometown committees		Social service agencies		Formal nonprofits[b]	
Predictors	Model I	Model II	Model I	Model II	Model I	Model II[c]	Model I	Model II
Nationality[d]								
Colombian	—	—	—	—	—	—	—	—
Mexican	—	—	3.83** (2.8)	4.49* (2.3)	4.10** (2.6)	7.51* (2.1)	−2.26** (3.2)	−4.07*** (3.5)
Location[e]								
New York/New Jersey	—	—	—	—	—	—	—	—
Philadelphia	—	—	—	—	—	—	—	—
Characteristics of organizations								
Financial resources (logged)	—	—	—	—	1.25** (3.0)	2.24* (2.0)	—	—
Number of members (logged)	—	−0.635* (2.2)	—	—	—	—	—	—
Characteristics of members								
% younger than 20 years of age	—	—	—	—	—	—	—	−0.027* (2.2)
% 40 years of age or older	—	—	—	—	—	—	—	—
% with less than high school education	—	—	—	—	—	—	—	—
% with college degree or more	—	—	—	−0.071* (2.3)	—	—	—	—
% without legal entry visa	—	—	—	—	—	—	—	0.052* (2.5)
% U.S. citizens	—	—	—	—	—	—	—	—
% with less than 5 years of U.S. residence	—	—	—	—	—	—	—	—
% with 10 or more years of U.S. residence	—	—	—	—	—	—	—	—
Constant	2.10	3.94	−3.77	−1.01	−10.92	−24.36	1.60	2.05
N		89		89	89		89	
Pseudo R^2	.234***	.450***	.234***	.450***	.234***	.450***	.124*	.257**

NOTE: Columns refer to different regression models. A dash represents a variable that was nonsignificant, while a blank cell signifies that the variable was not part of the model.
[a] Multinomial logistic coefficients. Z-ratios in parentheses. Coefficients not significant at the .10 level are excluded.
[b] Binomial logistic coefficients. Z-ratios in parentheses. Coefficients not significant at the .10 level are excluded.
[c] Maximum likelihood iterations did not converge due to limited degrees of freedom.
[d] "Dominican" is the reference category.
[e] "Elsewhere" is the reference category.

$*p < .05$; $**p < .01$; $***p < .001$

that these committees are mostly the creation of immigrants of modest origins is reflected in the negative effect of higher education: the higher the proportion of college graduates among members, the less likely that a transnational organization will be a hometown committee.

Social service agencies are also significantly less common among Colombian and Dominican immigrants, relative to Mexicans. The odds of a social service agency engaging in transnational activities among Mexicans in the first model are sixty to one, relative to the reference nationality. On the other hand, the fact that these are the best financially endowed organizations is reflected in the positive and significant coefficient of financial resources. This is not a causal effect but a direct reflection of the fact that these organizations are more likely to receive funds from the cities and states in which they are located.

National origin also affects the likelihood of a transnational organization becoming a formal nonprofit, rather than operating informally. Reflecting their grassroots character and their creation by immigrants of more modest background, Mexican associations tend to operate informally; their net odds of achieving formal status, relative to Dominican associations, are less than one in ten. With nationality controlled, organizations with a higher proportion of younger members and those without papers tend to operate more formally. This unexpected result is explained, in part, as a consequence of the formal character of social service agencies attending these needier populations, and as a residual effect after controlling for Mexican origin—Mexico being the largest source of younger and undocumented immigrants.

Additional regressions supply further useful information on the reasons for each organization's creation and on its scope of action in the respective home country. The results are presented in table 7.7. Transnational associations initiated by "groups of friends" are undifferentiated by nationality and most other collective and individual characteristics. This reflects the fact that such spontaneous efforts are found among *all* types of immigrants, regardless of national origin, age, or education, and that the organizations thus created are not significantly smaller or poorer than those stemming from more institutional sources. The only other noteworthy result is that immigrants with longer periods of U.S. residence tend to be less common among the members of these organizations, as shown by the second model. This is arguably a consequence of established immigrants' preference for more formal and more institutionalized initiatives.

As the prior descriptive results have indicated, organizations created by the initiative of sending country governments tend to be exceptional, but those that have emerged this way are concentrated in just one national group. As table 7.7 shows, Mexican organizations are far more likely to fall into this

Table 7.7 Origins and scope of transnational organizations

Predictors	Origins[a] Group of friends Model I	Group of friends Model II	Government sponsorship Model I	Government sponsorship Model II	Natural disasters Model I	Natural disasters Model II[c]	Scope[b] Nationwide Model I	Nationwide Model II
Nationality[d]								
Colombian	—	—	—	—	24.778** (2.7)	—	—	—
Mexican	—	—	22.901*** (7.2)	45.036** (3.3)	—	—	—	—
Location[e]								
New York/New Jersey	—	—	—	—	—	—	—	—
Philadelphia	—	—	—	—	—	—	—	—
Characteristics of organizations								
Financial resources (logged)	—	—	—	—	—	—	—	—
Number of members (logged)	—	—	—	—	—	—	—	—
Characteristics of members								
% younger than 20 years of age	—	—	—	—	—	—	—	—
% 40 years of age or older	—	—	—	—	—	—	—	—
% with less than high school education	—	—	—	—	—	—	—	—
% with college degree or more	—	—	—	—	—	—	—	0.033* (2.5)
% without legal entry visa	—	—	—	—	—	—	—	—
% U.S. citizens	—	—	—	—	—	—	—	—
% with less than 5 years of U.S. residence	—	0.034* (2.1)	—	—	—	—	—	—
% with 10 or more years of U.S. residence	—	—	—	—	—	—	—	—
Constant	0.409	−0.193	18.343	59.493	−34.633	—	−0.717	−4.770
N	89		89		89		89	
Pseudo R²	.293***	.530***	.293***	.530***	.293***		.068	.316***

NOTE: Columns refer to different regression models. A dash represents a variable that was nonsignificant, while a blank cell signifies that the variable was not part of the model.

[a] Multinomial logistic coefficients. Z-ratios in parentheses. Coefficients not significant at the .10 level are excluded.

[b] Binomial logistic coefficients. Z-ratios in parentheses. Coefficients not significant at the .10 level are excluded.

[c] Maximum likelihood iterations did not converge due to limited cases.

[d] "Dominican" is the reference category.

[e] "Elsewhere" is the reference category.

*p < .05; **p < .01; ***p < .001

category. The corresponding coefficient is very strong, making the corresponding odds of a Mexican transnational organization being created by government initiative far higher than among Dominicans (the reference category).[11] This result reflects the proactive stance of the Mexican government relative to its large expatriate population, a topic to be discussed in greater detail in the following section.

Organizations created in response to natural disasters are significantly more common among Colombians. The corresponding coefficient is again quite strong, indicating a higher probability that Colombian organizations will emerge this way. This result reflects the more urban origins of Colombians and their more individualistic patterns of settlement, due to which the prodding of major national or regional emergencies may be necessary to galvanize them into collective action (Guarnizo and Diaz 1999).[12]

Lastly, table 7.7 answers the question of what factors are associated with transnational activism of a national scope, as opposed to an exclusively local or regional one. The binomial model in the second column indicates that national scope of action is primarily associated with a college-educated and older membership. Organizations that bring together younger immigrants and those of more modest origins tend to focus primarily on local issues. Mexican organizations are overrepresented among those with a low-education membership, so this result is essentially a restatement of their dominance among hometown committees.

Overall, these results reveal patterned differences among immigrant communities in the types of organizations that they create, their motivations for doing so, and their intended scope of action. These patterns correspond well to known differences in the human capital composition of these immigrant flows and in their contexts of exit and incorporation. A clear divide emerges in the forms of transnationalism adopted by Mexican immigrants—focused on the welfare of mostly rural communities, with a heavy dose of governmental intervention—and those of Dominicans and Colombians, whose organizations tend to be broader in scope, more formalized, and more often created by spontaneous grassroots initiatives in response to disasters and other national emergencies. The net impact of these different forms of transnationalism on the home countries is examined next.

Impact on Sending Nations

As mentioned above, our survey of transnational organizations in the United States was complemented by visits to each of the sending countries in order to assess, on the ground, the effects of this form of activism. This part of the study was qualitative, but the balance of the interviews left no doubt as to the actual and potential significance of transnational initiatives. Since it is impossible to present the information obtained from these interviews in detail, we summarize the results obtained in each country and illustrate them with representative examples below.

As mentioned previously, the Colombian state's principal initiative in this field is Colombia Nos Une, established within the Foreign Affairs Ministry in 2003 with direct support from the current president of the republic, Álvaro Uribe. The program has organized a series of seminars about international migration in Colombia, sponsored an empirical study of remittances, and brought together Colombian consular personnel in the United States and Europe to explore ways of taking a more proactive stance toward the respective expatriate communities. However, budget limitations have prevented Colombia Nos Une from offering actual assistance to immigrants or contacting them directly. The latter role has been assumed by the privately sponsored Conexión Colombia, which uses its web page and slick advertising materials to solicit contributions from expatriates and channel them into selected philanthropies throughout the country.

Neither Colombia Nos Une nor Conexión Colombia has thus far provided a major channel linking immigrant organizations to their home country; such efforts have mainly focused on reaching expatriates individually through such means as Internet sites. In this context, transnational immigrant organizations have established their own direct lines of communication with charities, asylums, and churches in Colombia. Fig. 7.1 presents examples of the ways in which these connections are established. As the best educated and most urban of the three groups studied, Colombians have created forms of transnationalism similar to well-known philanthropic institutions in the developed world. These are exemplified in the United States by the emergence of Lions and Kiwanis Clubs, whose leaders travel to Colombia to establish formal agreements for programmatic assistance with local charities.

The Colombian Lions Clubs of Miami and New York have donated equipment, supplies, and money to orphanages in the towns of Quindío and Valle, and provided direct assistance in the wake of natural disasters in these regions through their counterpart clubs in cities like Armenia and Cali. The Kiwanis Club of Miami has done likewise, supporting, among other programs, an asylum and school for handicapped children in the city of Calarcá, Quindío. Religious ties are exemplified by the projects of the Vicentine Sisters of Charity in Bogotá and their vital connection to a New Jersey parish. Another case is that of a group of Colombian immigrants in New York and New Jersey who helped create, consistently support, and frequently visit a school and refuge for handicapped children in their hometown of La Tebaida, Quindío. The director of the school had this to say about the Sons of La Tebaida in New York:

> They have been here twenty years and have been helping us since we started. First, they gave us a donation of 900,000 pesos, which was a

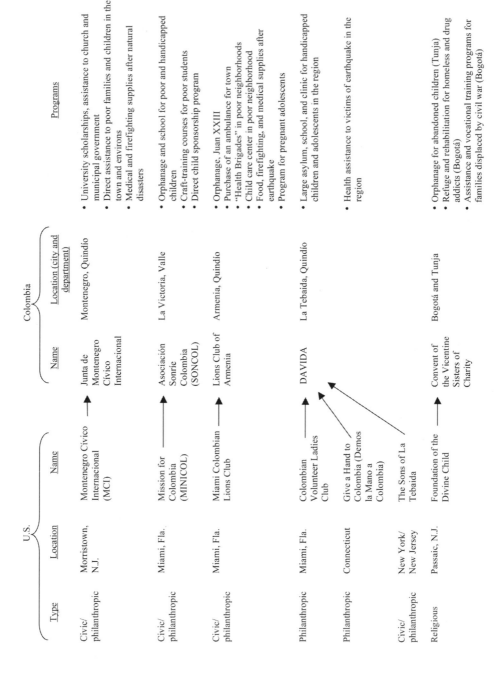

	U.S.			Colombia		Programs
Type	Location	Name		Name	Location (city and department)	
Civic/philanthropic	Morristown, N.J.	Montenegro Cívico Internacional (MCI) →		Junta de Montenegro Cívico Internacional	Montenegro, Quindío	• University scholarships, assistance to church and municipal government • Direct assistance to poor families and children in the town and environs • Medical and firefighting supplies after natural disasters
Civic/philanthropic	Miami, Fla.	Mission for Colombia (MINICOL) →		Asociación Sonríe Colombia (SONCOL)	La Victoria, Valle	• Orphanage and school for poor and handicapped children • Craft-training courses for poor students • Direct child sponsorship program
Civic/philanthropic	Miami, Fla.	Miami Colombian Lions Club →		Lions Club of Armenia	Armenia, Quindío	• Orphanage, Juan XXIII • Purchase of an ambulance for town • "Health Brigades" in poor neighborhoods • Child care center in poor neighborhood • Food, firefighting, and medical supplies after earthquake • Program for pregnant adolescents
Philanthropic	Miami, Fla.	Colombian Volunteer Ladies Club →		DAVIDA	La Tebaida, Quindío	• Large asylum, school, and clinic for handicapped children and adolescents in the region
Philanthropic	Connecticut	Give a Hand to Colombia (Demos la Mano a Colombia)				• Health assistance to victims of earthquake in the region
Civic/philanthropic	New York/New Jersey	The Sons of La Tebaida				
Religious	Passaic, N.J.	Foundation of the Divine Child →		Convent of the Vicentine Sisters of Charity	Bogotá and Tunja	• Orphanage for abandoned children (Tunja) • Refuge and rehabilitation for homeless and drug addicts (Bogotá) • Assistance and vocational training programs for families displaced by civil war (Bogotá)

Fig. 7.1 International and transnational connections of Colombian immigrant organizations

lot of money at that time. We did a lot with that money. Afterwards, the Sons have supported many programs: lunch for the children, electric fans, and many other things. The floor and roof of this building were built with another donation. I send them letters telling them what we need. Sometimes I send three a year. I'm always asking because I also feel that they are part of us and we're part of them.[13]

In line with our expectations, Colombian transnationalism occurs primarily among relatively educated, urban immigrants whose philanthropic activities are either conducted individually or through secular and religious organizations that are both familiar and compatible with those of the developed world. These organizations emerge through grassroots efforts, often in response to emergencies or dire poverty in places of origin.

Like Colombia, the Dominican state has enacted legislation granting its emigrants the right to nationalize abroad without losing their Dominican citizenship or the right to vote in national elections. Political parties and associations involved in political activities have been most visible and most successful at attracting a large number of immigrants. This tendency is shaped, in part, by the heavy influence of political parties in the home country and by the political nature of the early waves of Dominican migration. Even if subsequent migration has taken place for economic reasons, the political character of early arrivals has continued to shape the associative development of this collectivity (Escobar 2006). President Leonel Fernández has given priority to the development of relations with the expatriate community, appointing a secretary of Dominicans abroad and designing a program (yet to be implemented) to better integrate them into the social and political life of the country.[14]

Immigrant initiatives in this field have taken two forms: emergency assistance following natural disasters and hometown civic associations. The largest Dominican agency in New York, Alianza Dominicana, is primarily concerned with providing social services to immigrants, but it has also been active in offering assistance to municipalities and provinces in the wake of emergencies. The most recent occasion for Alianza's charitable activities on the island was the river flooding of the town of Jimaní in 2004, where upward of seven hundred people lost their lives. Local churches are commonly used as conduits of this kind of assistance in order to avoid official corruption.

Grassroots hometown associations created by expatriates have adopted forms and goals quite similar to those found among Colombians. A prominent example is the previously mentioned Canafisteros de Bani en Boston, which has created its own representative group in the town and provided it with all kinds of equipment, supplies, and assistance programs for the poor and elderly. A parallel example is the Association of Jimanenses of Massachusetts (ASOJIMA), which has also given its town an ambulance, a funeral car, a clinic, and school supplies, as well as generous financial assistance after the 2004 flood. Women's groups fighting for women's rights and against domestic violence in cities of the interior have received support from churches in New York and from immigrant agencies, such as the Hermanas Mirabal Family Center and Child Care Network of the Bronx. Fig. 7.2 presents a summary of these international and transnational ties.

The case of Mexican immigrant transnationalism is different from the others in several key respects. Not only is the Mexican immigrant population larger than all other Latin American groups combined, but it is predominantly rural in origin. Traditional loyalties to local birthplaces translate into a proliferation of hometown civic associations, which are far more numerous and durable than those created by other immigrant groups. For example, while Colombian and Dominican associations depend on raffles, dances, and similar events for fund-raising, Mexican immigrants commonly contribute regularly to their associations as a continuation of their traditional duties to their hometowns.

Equally important is the strong and proactive presence of the state in the transnational field. As noted previously, the Mexican case is one in which the international activities of government interact with the transnational initiatives of immigrants. Several Mexican states, starting with the well-studied case of Zacatecas (Goldring 2002; Gonzalez Gutierrez 1999), have moved to create federations of their hometown committees and promote new ones. The governor of Zacatecas, mayors, and legislators travel frequently to Los Angeles to build ties with leaders of the immigrant federations, who, in turn, visit the state regularly. Zacatecas has been a strong supporter of the Dos-por-Uno (now Tres-por-Uno) program, in which each dollar donated by immigrant organizations for public works in Mexico is matched by contributions from the Mexican federal and state governments (Smith 2003; Goldring 2002).

Other states that have experienced high levels of emigration, such as Jalisco and Michoacán, have adopted the Zacatecan model; during the 1990s, they promoted the creation of federations in centers of Mexican immigration such as Los Angeles, Chicago, and Houston. This example has been followed more recently (in most cases with the help of the Mexican consulates and the states' governments) by immigrants from nontraditional migration states. On the East Coast, where the Mexican immigrant population comes predominantly from Puebla, community organizations received strong support from the New York consulate and the state government to establish Casa Puebla during the 1990s. Since 1994, the State of Guanajuato has supported the establishment of forty-five Casas Guanajuato in fourteen U.S. states; this includes five recently created on the East Coast (Escobar 2006).

Still more important has been the Mexican federal presence in this field. This has taken the form of matching programs for immigrant contributions, most recently the Tres-por-Uno program launched in 2002; the creation of *plazas comunitarias,* which provide library services, information, and language training (in English and Spanish) for Mexicans in a number of U.S. cities; the strengthening of legal defense programs for immigrants through forty-five consulates in the United States and Canada; and the creation of "health windows" in several of these consulates, which provide basic medical services. The creation of the Institute of Mexicans Abroad (IME) represents the culmination of these efforts. IME is housed in the federal Secretariat of Foreign Relations and includes a Consultative Council consisting of 105 representatives of immigrant organizations in the United States and Canada, elected in the forty-five consular districts, plus delegates from each of the thirty-two states of the Mexican Union (Gonzalez Gutierrez 2005; Escobar 2006).

While this system of representation is new and a number of problems remain to be solved, it clearly signals the commitment of the Mexican government to establish an active presence among its huge expatriate population. The state seeks to demonstrate, with concrete actions, its interest in the immigrants' welfare and, by the same token, stimulate their loyalty and their contributions. Together with the activities of the Mexican state governments, this proactive stance is transforming the character of immigrant transnationalism from a grassroots phenomenon to one guided and supported by the international policies and programs of the home state. Following well-established political practice in Mexico, government officials are thus seeking to incorporate immigrants and their organizations into state-sponsored structures. In this vein, former president Vicente Fox spoke of his governing mandate as for *todos los Mejicanos* (all Mexicans), regardless of where they reside.

Mexican transnationalism is thus quite distinct from that of other immigrant groups, and the differences can be traced back to the immigrants' contexts of exit and incorporation. As part of a mostly rural and frequently indigenous labor flow, Mexican immigrants' low human capital prevents them from joining more middle-class forms of organization. No Lions or Kiwanis Clubs can be expected to emerge from immigrants of such modest origins, who occupy positions at the bottom of the American labor market. Instead, traditional loyalties and duties bring immigrants together and sustain vibrant ties with their places of origin. In some cases, these ties are so strong that immigrants seem to have never really left the places from which they came. Even unauthorized immigrants are willing to lead hometown committees and dedicate many hours and hard-earned dollars to them (Smith 2005; Roberts, Frank, and Lozano-Asencio 1999).

A relevant example is the town of San Miguel Comitlipa, in the state of Guerrero, whose hometown committee in New York/New Jersey was included in our sample. In a subsequent visit to Mexico, members of the research team traveled to Guerrero to visit the town and the surrounding area

	U.S.		Dominican Republic			Programs
Type	Location	Name	Name	Location	Type	
Education and research	New York	Institute of Dominican Studies, CUNY	Global Foundation for Democracy and Development (FUNGLODE)	Santo Domingo	Educational/civic	• Conferences • Joint task forces and steering committees • Promotion of civic and political participation by expatriates in home country
Political	New York	Dominican Revolutionary Party, local branch	Dominican Revolutionary Party (PRD), Department for Dominicans Abroad	Santo Domingo	Political	• Fund-raising for party candidates • Mobilization and campaigns for votes abroad
Political	Boston, Mass.	Dominican Liberation Party, local branch	Dominican Liberation Party (PLD), Foreign Affairs Department	Santo Domingo	Political	• Fund-raising for party candidates • Mobilization and campaigns for votes abroad
Social agency	New York	Alianza Dominicana	National Emergency Council	Santo Domingo	Government agency	• Emergency assistance after natural disasters • Health and educational projects
			Local parishes and NGOs	Affected towns and provinces	Religious/ philanthropic	

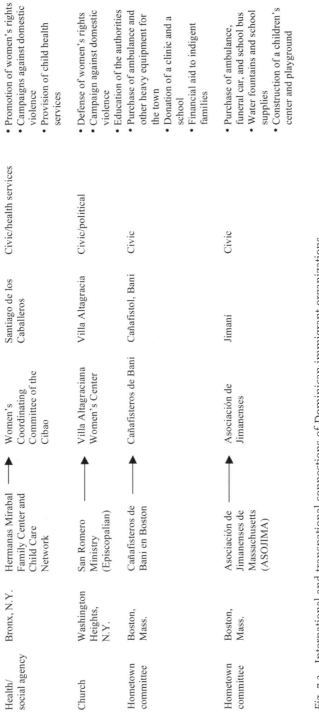

Health/social agency	Bronx, N.Y.	Hermanas Mirabal Family Center and Child Care Network →	Women's Coordinating Committee of the Cibao	Santiago de los Caballeros	Civic/health services	• Promotion of women's rights • Campaigns against domestic violence • Provision of child health services
Church	Washington Heights, N.Y.	San Romero Ministry (Episcopalian) →	Villa Altagraciana Women's Center	Villa Altagracia	Civic/political	• Defense of women's rights • Campaign against domestic violence • Education of the authorities
Hometown committee	Boston, Mass.	Cañafisteros de Baní en Boston →	Cañafisteros de Baní	Cañafistol, Baní	Civic	• Purchase of ambulance and other heavy equipment for the town • Donation of a clinic and a school • Financial aid to indigent families
Hometown committee	Boston, Mass.	Asociación de Jimanenses de Massachusetts (ASOJIMA) →	Asociación de Jimanenses	Jimaní	Civic	• Purchase of ambulance, funeral car, and school bus • Water fountains and school supplies • Construction of a children's center and playground

Fig. 7.2 International and transnational connections of Dominican immigrant organizations

and interview its authorities. The first concrete result of immigrant transnational assistance was the impressive kiosk built in the town's central plaza; then the town church was repaired and redecorated, and a big clock was later bought for its tower. Most of these projects were accomplished with immigrant monetary contributions and local voluntary labor, following long-standing indigenous tradition. The more ambitious current project is the expansion of the plaza to make room for annual festivities. It is expected to cost about US$80,000; this figure will rise to $260,000 with the addition of a roof. Immigrants from the center of Xochihuehuetlan, the municipality to which the town of San Miguel Comitlipa belongs, have also carried out their own projects. The municipal president of Xochihuehuetlan described the beginnings of this transnational collaboration as follows:

> More or less in 1985, works began that benefited our town. . . . They were of a religious character to improve the sanctuary of San Diego de Alcalá, which is the most respected patron saint around here; then we bought streetlights for the avenue leading to it . . . the avenue where the procession takes place. Today and with the help of the migrants in the United States, public works are very advanced. The church is in good shape, redecorated and with gold leaf in the altars. . . . Now we are looking at rebuilding the school with support from the municipality, [over] which I preside, and the people that we have in the United States, with whom we always have good relations.[15]

Figure 7.3 presents an overview of Mexican international and transnational ties.

Conclusion

This study has sought to present an account of the phenomenon of immigrant transnationalism as it takes place *on the ground*—that is, in the daily experience of immigrants and their home country counterparts. We find that, while by no means universal, transnational civic, philanthropic, cultural, and political activities are common among immigrants in the United States, and on the aggregate, they possess sufficient weight to affect the development prospects of localities and regions and to attract the attention of sending governments. Initiators and leaders of these activities tend to be older and better-established immigrants with above-average levels of education. This finding, which supports those from prior quantitative studies based on the CIEP surveys, indicates that home loyalties and nostalgia endure and, hence, that such activities can be expected to continue as immigrant communities mature. Whatever else it may be, transnationalism is not a phenomenon associated

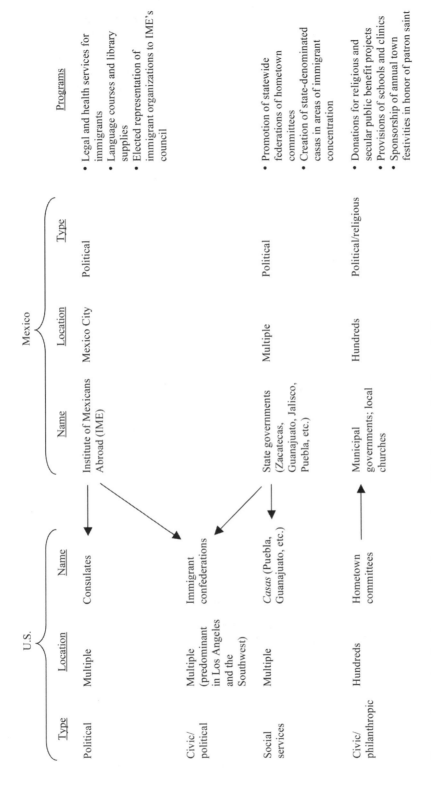

Fig. 7.3 International and transnational connections of Mexican immigrant organizations

The table in the figure contains the following information:

U.S.

Type	Location	Name
Political	Multiple	Consulates
Civic/political	Multiple (predominant in Los Angeles and the Southwest)	Immigrant confederations
Social services	Multiple	*Casas* (Puebla, Guanajuato, etc.)
Civic/philanthropic	Hundreds	Hometown committees

Mexico

Name	Location	Type	Programs
Institute of Mexicans Abroad (IME)	Mexico City	Political	• Legal and health services for immigrants • Language courses and library supplies • Elected representation of immigrant organizations to IME's council
State governments (Zacatecas, Guanajuato, Jalisco, Puebla, etc.)	Multiple	Political	• Promotion of statewide federations of hometown committees • Creation of state-denominated casas in areas of immigrant concentration
Municipal governments; local churches	Hundreds	Political/religious	• Donations for religious and secular public benefit projects • Provisions of schools and clinics • Sponsorship of annual town festivities in honor of patron saint

with recency of arrival and destined to disappear as part of an inexorable process of assimilation (Guarnizo, Portes, and Haller 2003).

That being said, however, the study's major finding is the very different forms that these activities take across immigrant nationalities. Our results amply support the proposition that contexts of exit and reception determine the origin, strength, and character of transnational organizations. However, they go well beyond this assertion to document, in detail, the forms that these initiatives take among the three nationalities under study. To summarize, Colombian transnationalism includes a number of hometown committees, but, by and large, it is a middle-class phenomenon spearheaded by immigrant Lions and Kiwanis Clubs, professional associations, and Catholic philanthropies in the United States. Dominican organizations also include hometown committees and professional associations, but their defining profile is political, marked by the strong presence of Dominican parties in major areas of immigrant settlement and by the politically well-connected nature of social service agencies in this community. Lastly, the hometown committee is the norm among Mexican immigrants, who have created hundreds of these organizations, supported them with regular contributions and voluntary work, and, in the process, generated durable and important developmental effects in their sending localities. The bonds linking the hometown with its people abroad are much stronger in the case of these rural, frequently indigenous immigrants. They tend to create "transnational communities" in the full sense of the term (Levitt 2001).

National differences are apparent in both qualitative and multivariate regression results, where they are resilient predictors of the origin and type of transnational organizations, as well as their scope of action. These differences reflect, in part, the entrance of sending country governments into the transnational field and the policies that they have implemented so far. All governments have shown growing interest in their expatriate communities, and all have legislated concessions and programs designed to renew their loyalties and make them feel like part of a common imagined national community (Smith 2005). But then the differences begin. Colombian and Dominican state efforts seldom transcend the realm of the symbolic. Both governments seem too weak and too poor to implement large-scale programs that would provide their expatriates with concrete benefits or reorganize and give new direction to their transnational initiatives. Given this situation, the main impulse for the continuation and expansion of these activities comes from other actors in the sending country—a private sector corporate partnership in the case of Colombia and the foreign affairs departments of political parties in the case of the Dominican Republic.

The Mexican experience is different, for it features a much stronger and more proactive presence of the state, which, at both the national and regional levels, seeks to incorporate and guide the already strong links between a large immigrant population and their places of origin. Since the Mexican federal and state governments have no authority over their citizens living in the United States, they have sought to induce their participation in official programs by providing a series of benefits that extend beyond those of a purely symbolic nature. The result has been the progressive incorporation of many hometown committees and federations into officially designed structures, although, as noted before, others remain independent of these plans.

If transnational organizations and activism can be so different among three immigrant nationalities that share the same historical roots and language, we can expect that such variations will be magnified among immigrants from other lands, religions, and cultures. It is impossible, with the data at hand, to construct an exhaustive typology of immigrant transnational organizations, precisely because the study of the phenomenon is still in its infancy. Nevertheless, it seems clear from the existing evidence that the manifold activities of immigrants and their home country counterparts hold the potential for coalescing into an important feature of contemporary processes of globalization running opposite to the "multinational" logic of corporate capitalism. This logic exacerbates inequalities among nations and remains largely indifferent to the plight of inhabitants of the global South. On the contrary, the activities of hometown committees and other immigrant organizations vigorously seek to alleviate these problems. As a young Salvadoran sociologist trenchantly put it, "Migration and remittances are the true adjustment programs of the poor in these countries" (Ramos 2002, 35).

The dialectics by which people who are driven from their countries by poverty, violence, and lack of opportunities turn around and seek to reverse these conditions by using the resources acquired abroad need to be further investigated. They offer the promise of at least slowing down the partition of the world into the increasingly rich and the desperately poor, which capitalist globalization has done little to reduce. In this context, the migrating poor have had no alternative but to take matters into their own hands, seeking a better future for themselves and for those left behind.

NOTES

This chapter is a revised version of the 2007 article "Immigrant Transnational Organizations and Development: A Comparative Study," *International Migration Review* 41 (1): 242–81. The authors wish to thank *IMR* for permission to use this material. The data on which the chapter is based were collected under a research and writing grant to Alejandro Portes from the MacArthur Foundation and a supplementary faculty research grant from Princeton's Institute for International and Regional Research (PIIRS). Rosario Espinal from Temple University and Lilian Bovea were co-researchers, taking responsibility for fieldwork among Dominican organizations in the United States and the Dominican Republic. Maria Jesús Criado from the Instituto Universitario de Investigación Ortega y Gasset in Madrid, Spain, provided valuable support in the initial stages of the project. We are grateful for comments from Raúl Delgado Wise, Carlos Gonzalez Gutierrez, and Scott Lynch. Responsibility is solely ours.

1. This brochure and similar materials were gathered during field interviews. See also Conexión Colombia's website at www.conexioncolombia.com.

2. Field interview conducted by Alejandro Portes in Bogotá, Colombia, March 15, 2005. Throughout this chapter, the personal names of interviewees are either fictitious or have been withheld by mutual consent.

3. Field interview conducted by Alejandro Portes in Bogotá, Colombia, March 16, 2005.

4. Field interview conducted by Alejandro Portes in Bogotá, Colombia, March 16, 2005.

5. An exception is the detailed study of Mexican hometown associations by Manuel Orozco (2003). The study is based on interviews with one hundred such associations and field visits to more than twenty communities in Mexico receiving assistance from these groups.

6. The U.S. census count for 2000 is less than half of this figure. Based on figures from the Colombian government and independent calculations from various specialists, we believe that this is a serious underestimate resulting from the failure to count unauthorized immigrants and potential asylees. We report the census estimate in table 7.2.

7. The U.S. census puts the number of Dominicans at less than eight hundred thousand in 2000. However, estimates from the Dominican government and specialized research centers indicate that the number of immigrants, including the unauthorized, easily exceeds one million. See table 7.2.

8. The U.S. census puts the resident Mexican population in 2000 at 9 million. The Mexican government, on the other hand, estimates 12 million based on the latest Mexican census. We opt for an intermediate estimate, which, based on the U.S. census's likely undercount, appears conservative (see Rumbaut 2005 and Passel, Caps, and Fix 2004).

9. Field interviews conducted by the research team in New York and the Dominican Republic, 2004.

10. Ibid.

11. The corresponding odds are higher than what would be credible, due to the limited number of cases and the consequent difficulty of using the maximum likelihood iterative routine to estimate the models. For this reason, results should be interpreted with caution as preliminary figures.

12. The possibility cannot be ruled out, however, that a greater relative frequency of such emergencies in Colombia in recent years may also (partially) account for this result.

13. Field interviews conducted by the research team in New York and Colombia, 2004.

14. Field interviews conducted by the research team in the Dominican Republic, 2004.

15. Field interview conducted by the research team in Mexico, 2005.

REFERENCES

Alba, Richard, and Victor Nee. 2003. *Remaking the American Mainstream: Assimilation and Contemporary Immigration.* Cambridge: Harvard University Press.

Basch, Linda G., Nina Glick Schiller, and Cristina Blanc-Szanton. 1994. *Nations Unbound: Transnational Projects, Post-Colonial Predicaments, and De-Territorialized Nation-States.* Langhorne, Pa.: Gordon and Breach.

Bourne, Randolph S. 1916. "Trans-national America." *Atlantic Monthly,* July, 86–97.

Castles, Stephen. 2004. "The Factors That Make and Unmake Migration Policies." *International Migration Review* 38 (3): 852–84.

Cornelius, Wayne A. 1998. "The Structural Embeddedness of Demand for Mexican Immigrant Labor: New Evidence from California." In *Crossings: Mexican Immigration in*

Interdisciplinary Perspective, edited by M. Suarez-Orozco, 115–55. Cambridge: Center for Latin American Studies, Harvard University.

Cortina, Jeronimo, and Rodolfo de la Garza. 2004. *Immigrant Remitting Behavior and Its Developmental Consequences for Mexico and El Salvador.* Los Angeles: Tomás Rivera Policy Institute.

Delgado Wise, Raúl, and Humberto Márquez Covarrubias. 2009. "A Mexican Perspective on the Role of Mass Labor Migration Under NAFTA." In *Global Connections and Local Receptions: New Latino Immigration to the Southeastern United States*, edited by F. Ansley and J. Shefner, 35–64. Knoxville: University of Tennessee Press.

Department of Homeland Security, Office of Immigration Statistics. 2004. "Estimates of the Legal Permanent Resident Population and Population Eligible to Naturalize in 2002." http://www.dhs.gov/xlibrary/assets/statistics/publications/lprest2002.pdf.

Economic Commission for Latin America and the Caribbean. 2002. *Indicadores de desarrollo social.* Santiago: United Nations.

Escobar, Cristina. 2003. "Various Routes to Dual Citizenship and Extraterritorial Political Rights: The Colombian Experience in the Latin American and Caribbean Context." Paper presented at the 2003 meeting of the American Sociological Association, Atlanta, August 16–19.

———. 2004. "Dual Citizenship and Political Participation: Migrants in the Interplay of United States and Colombian Politics." *Latino Studies* 2 (1): 45–69.

———. 2006. "Migration and Citizen Rights: The Mexican Case." *Citizenship Studies* 10 (5): 503–22.

Evans, Peter. 2000. "Fighting Marginalization with Transnational Networks: Counter-Hegemonic Globalization." *Contemporary Sociology* 29 (1): 230–41.

Glick Schiller, Nina. 1999. "Transmigrants and Nation States: Something Old and Something New in the U.S. Immigrant Experience." In *The Handbook of International Migration: The American Experience*, edited by C. Hirschman, P. Kasinitz, and J. DeWind, 94–119. New York: Russell Sage Foundation.

Glick Schiller, Nina, and Georges Fouron. 1999. "Terrains of Blood and Nation: Haitian Transnational Social Fields." *Ethnic and Racial Studies* 22 (2): 340–66.

Goldring, Luin. 2002. "The Mexican State and Transmigrant Organizations: Negotiating the Boundaries of Membership and Participation." *Latin American Research Review* 37 (3): 55–99.

Gonzalez Gutierrez, Carlos. 1999. "Fostering Identities: Mexico's Relations with Its Diaspora." *Journal of American History* 86 (2): 545–67.

———. 2005. "Mexico's Relation to Its Diaspora." Keynote address to the Hispanic Summit of the Plains conference, sponsored by the Office of Latin and Latino Affairs (OLLAS), University of Nebraska–Omaha, April.

Gordon, Milton M. 1964. *Assimilation in American Life: The Role of Race, Religion, and National Origins.* New York: Oxford University Press.

Grasmuck, Sherri, and Patricia Pessar. 1991. *Between Two Islands: Dominican International Migration.* Berkeley: University of California Press.

Guarnizo, Luis E. 2003. "The Economics of Transnational Living." *International Migration Review* 37 (3): 666–99.

Guarnizo, Luis E., and Luz M. Diaz. 1999. "Transnational Migration: A View from Colombia." *Ethnic and Racial Studies* 22 (2): 397–421.

Guarnizo, Luis E., Alejandro Portes, and William Haller. 2003. "Assimilation and Transnationalism: Determinants of Transnational Political Action Among Contemporary Immigrants." *American Journal of Sociology* 108 (6): 1211–48.

Guarnizo, Luis E., Arturo I. Sanchez, and Elizabeth Roach. 1999. "Mistrust, Fragmented Solidarity, and Transnational Migration: Colombians in New York and Los Angeles." *Ethnic and Racial Studies* 22 (2): 367–96.

International Labour Organization (ILO). 2010. "Overview of Labor Statistics." http://www.ilo.org/global/statistics-and-databases/statistics-overview-and-topics/lang—en/index.htm.

Itzigsohn, Jose, and Silvia G. Saucedo. 2002. "Immigrant Incorporation and Sociocultural Transnationalism." *International Migration Review* 36 (3): 766–98.

Itzigsohn, Jose, Carlos Dore, Esther Fernández, and Obed Vazquez. 1999. "Mapping Dominican Transnationalism: Narrow and Broad Transnational Practices." *Ethnic and Racial Studies* 22 (2): 316–39.

Keck, Margaret, and Kathryn Sikkink. 1998. *Activists Beyond Borders: Advocacy Networks in International Politics.* Ithaca: Cornell University Press.

Kyle, David. 2000. *Transnational Peasants: Migration, Networks, and Ethnicity in Andean Ecuador.* Baltimore: Johns Hopkins University Press.

Landolt, Patricia. 2001. "Salvadoran Economic Transnationalism: Embedded Strategies for Household Maintenance, Immigrant Incorporation, and Entrepreneurial Expansion." *Global Networks* 1 (3): 217–42.

Latin American Weekly Report. 2003. "Remittances: Year's Total to Exceed Forecast." Report No. WR-03-43. November 4.

Levitt, Peggy. 2001. *The Transnational Villagers.* Berkeley: University of California Press.

Levitt, Peggy, and Nina Glick Schiller. 2004. "Conceptualizing Simultaneity: A Transnational Social Field Perspective on Society." *International Migration Review* 38 (3): 1002–39.

López, David E., and Ricardo D. Stanton-Salazar. 2001. "Mexican-Americans: A Second Generation at Risk." In *Ethnicities: Children of Immigrants in America,* edited by R. G. Rumbaut and A. Portes, 57–90. Berkeley: University of California Press and Russell Sage Foundation.

Massey, Douglas S., Jorge Durand, and Nolan J. Malone. 2002. *Beyond Smoke and Mirrors: Mexican Immigration in an Era of Economic Integration.* New York: Russell Sage Foundation.

Merton, Robert K. 1968. *Social Theory and Social Structure.* New York: Free Press.

Orozco, Manuel. 2003. *Hometown Associations and Their Present and Future Partnerships: New Development Opportunities.* Washington, D.C.: U.S. Agency for International Development.

Passel, Jeffrey S., Randy Capps, and Michael Fix. 2004. "Undocumented Immigrants: Facts and Figures." Urban Institute Immigration Studies Program. January 12. http://www.urban.org/uploadedPDF/1000587_undoc_immigrants_facts.pdf.

Portes, Alejandro. 2003. "Theoretical Convergences and Empirical Evidence in the Study of Immigrant Transnationalism." *International Migration Review* 37 (3): 874–92.

Portes, Alejandro, and Josh DeWind. 2004. "A Cross-Atlantic Dialogue: The Progress of Research and Theory in the Study of International Migration." *International Migration Review* 38 (3): 828–51.

Portes, Alejandro, and Patricia Fernández-Kelly. 2008. "No Margin for Error: Educational and Occupational Achievement Among Disadvantaged Children of Immigrants." *ANNALS of the American Academy of Political and Social Science* 620 (1): 12–36.

Portes, Alejandro, and Luis E. Guarnizo. 1991. "Tropical Capitalists: U.S.-Bound Immigration and Small Enterprise Development in the Dominican Republic." In *Migration, Remittances, and Small Business Development: Mexico and Caribbean Basin Countries,* edited by S. Diaz-Briquets and S. Weintraub, 101–31. Boulder, Colo.: Westview Press.

Portes, Alejandro, Luis E. Guarnizo, and Patricia Landolt. 1999. "The Study of Transnationalism: Pitfalls and Promise of an Emergent Research Field." *Ethnic and Racial Studies* 22 (2): 217–37.

Portes, Alejandro, William Haller, and Luis E. Guarnizo. 2002. "Transnational Entrepreneurs: An Alternative Form of Immigrant Adaptation." *American Sociological Review* 67 (2): 278–98.

Portes, Alejandro, and Lori D. Smith. 2008. "Institutions and Development in Latin America: A Comparative Analysis." *Studies in Comparative and International Development* 43 (Summer): 101–28.

Ramos, Carlos Guillermo. 2002. "Rapporteurs' Comments." Delivered at the Conference on Immigrant Transnationalism and Its Impact on Sending Nations, sponsored by the Center for Migration and Development, Princeton University, and the Latin American School of Social Science (FLACSO), Santo Domingo, Dominican Republic, January.

Roberts, Bryan R., Reanne Frank, and Fernando Lozano-Asencio. 1999. "Transnational Migrant Communities and Mexican Migration to the United States." *Ethnic and Racial Studies* 22 (2): 238–66.

Rumbaut, Rubén. 2005. "Turning Points in the Transition to Adulthood: Determinants of Educational Attainment, Incarceration, and Early Childbearing Among Children of Immigrants." *Ethnic and Racial Studies* 28 (6): 1041–86.

Smith, Robert C. 2003. "Diasporic Memberships in Historical Perspective: Comparative Insights from the Mexican, Italian, and Polish Cases." *International Migration Review* 37 (3): 724–59.

———. 2005. *Mexican New York: Transnational Lives of New Immigrants.* Berkeley: University of California Press.

United Nations Department of Economic and Social Development. 2002. *World Urbanization Prospects: The 2001 Revision.* New York: United Nations.

U.S. Census Bureau. 2001. *The Hispanic Population 2000.* Census Brief No. C2KBR/01-3. Washington, D.C.: U.S. Department of Commerce.

———. 2003. "Census 2000." Public-Use Microdata Sample. http://www.census.gov/census2000/PUMS5.html.

Vertovec, Steven. 2004. "Migrant Transnationalism and Modes of Transformation." *International Migration Review* 38 (3): 970–1001.

Waldinger, Roger, and David Fitzgerald. 2004. "Transnationalism in Question." *American Journal of Sociology* 109 (5): 1177–96.

Warner, W. Lloyd, and Leo Srole. 1945. *The Social Systems of American Ethnic Groups.* New Haven: Yale University Press.

Zolberg, Aristide. 1989. "The Next Waves: Migration Theory for a Changing World." *International Migration Review* 23 (3): 403–30.

8

BREAKING WITH MARKET FUNDAMENTALISM: TOWARD DOMESTIC AND GLOBAL REFORM

Fred Block

For almost thirty years, politics in the United States and around the world have been kept hostage to market fundamentalism—a vastly exaggerated faith in the capacity of self-regulating markets to solve economic and social problems (Block 2007; Klein 2007). This commitment to market fundamentalism has allowed globalization to proceed in a chaotic and turbulent fashion that has put billions of people at the mercy of fickle and irrational markets. Over the last decade, social thinkers and a global social justice movement have advanced powerful critiques of this quasi-religious faith in self-regulating markets (Klein 2007; de Sousa Santos 2008; Stiglitz 2002), and there is mounting evidence of the deep failures of market fundamentalist policies. Recently, the lax regulation of the U.S. home mortgage market resulted in a global financial crisis, leaving financial institutions around the world holding vast quantities of bonds whose value has fallen sharply.

Nevertheless, the administration of George W. Bush turned toward unilateralism and military force as a means to shut down any negotiations about global reform or change (Block 2003a). After the United States walked away from the Kyoto Accord on global climate change and defied international conventions against torture and the illegal detention of foreigners, it became utopian to imagine that the United States would agree to any orderly process of revising global governance rules. Whatever might be said about the irrationality of the U.S. military interventions in Afghanistan and Iraq, they successfully blunted drives by activists and governments for global reform.

In the United States itself, the combination of thirty years of market fundamentalism and two terms of George W. Bush's unilateralist foreign policy has had a shattering impact on the social imagination. In contrast to the 1960s and 1970s, when a multitude of radical visions jockeyed for position on the political left, few people bother to lay out radical alternatives any more. On the contrary, the goals proposed by mainstream Democratic Party politicians—health care reform and slightly less economic inequality—appear to be the outer limit of the possible. In foreign policy, the pattern is similar. Democratic politicians favor a slightly less unilateral foreign policy and the incorporation of environmental and labor clauses into free trade agreements; relatively few voices propose more radical demands than these.

History, however, does not proceed in a linear fashion. After long periods of stasis, there can be sudden moments in which seemingly durable structures totter and fall, as did the Berlin Wall in 1989. In such moments, changes that were previously inconceivable become not only possible but inevitable. It is in this spirit that this chapter is written. The goal is to lay out a reform agenda for both U.S. domestic and foreign policy that goes well beyond ideas in the current political mainstream. The claim is not that this agenda is currently practical and achievable, but that with a certain realignment of political forces and circumstances, it could become relevant.

But this kind of exercise of social imagination inevitably confronts two familiar kinds of objection. The first is that even in an era in which the imagination of alternatives has been stifled, any reform agenda remains vulnerable to attack for doing too little to challenge the multiple shortcomings of the existing global status quo. The proverbial question is why we should bother to mobilize people for a difficult battle to win half a loaf when they could win the whole loaf instead. Why simply reform the existing structures of a market economy when they could be replaced altogether by a new and radical type of economy? But when people have been getting only crumbs, it is difficult to persuade them that *any* change is possible. Winning part of the loaf is a way to restore confidence in the capacity of popular mobilization to win real changes. So the reform agenda advanced here is not conceived as an "end to history," but as a framework that might open the way to more radical demands in the future.

The second objection is that the tools of scholarship are ill suited to illuminate such normative questions as what type of reforms are desirable and politically achievable over the next several decades. According to this view, social scientists should focus their energies on describing and analyzing that which already exists. But while there are risks in this kind of project, there are also potential rewards, because the boundary line between empirical and normative questions is far less certain than imagined by those who make this objection.

The most rigorous science cannot understand any particular reality without contrast and comparison. But since there is only one global economy, only one International Monetary Fund (IMF), and only one World Trade Organization (WTO), our only comparative cases are those that existed in earlier historical periods or the alternative institutional possibilities that we might envision. Hence, the exercise of social imagination, including the envisioning of alternative paths, is indispensable to understanding the world as it currently exists. In short, social science that crosses the line into normative questions is a necessary part of the way that we make sense of that which exists in the present.

This chapter proceeds in three parts. The first lays out the reasons that a significant shift in U.S. domestic politics might occur over the next decade. The second proposes a domestic reform agenda that could take advantage of this moment of social and political discontinuity. The final section explores a new U.S. approach to global politics that would complement that domestic reform agenda.

The Potential for Discontinuity

Through 2011, politics in the United States operated like a broken record stuck in the groove of the 1960s, endlessly repeating the same familiar notes. The Republican right has been preoccupied with reversing what it views as the mistakes or excesses of the 1960s, especially cultural permissiveness, the questioning of authority, and the belief in the responsibility of government to solve social problems that was exemplified by Lyndon Johnson's "war on poverty." Every election cycle, Republicans attack Democrats as big spenders who are soft on criminals, welfare recipients, and traditional values. Even when Jimmy Carter, Bill Clinton, and Barack Obama were able to withstand these attacks and win the presidency, they were unable to initiate a new and different political conversation.

The same pattern has been equally pronounced in foreign policy. The architects of George W. Bush's war policies self-consciously tried to reverse the "lessons" of Vietnam and the restrictions on executive power that dated back to the Watergate era (Suskind 2006). In fact, the wounds of the Vietnam era remain so close to the surface that the 2004 presidential election centered on what John Kerry and, to a lesser degree, George W. Bush had been doing during that polarizing conflict.

The causes of the broken record phenomenon are complex, but one way to understand this pattern is through the idea of "postindustrial transition" (Block 1990; Brick 2006). The intense conflicts of the 1960s were manifestations of the shifts from an industrial to a postindustrial society. Three particular trends were central to the transition: the growing importance of service sector employment as manufacturing declines, the rise of computer-based

automation in both blue-collar and white-collar settings, and the interconnected decline of the patriarchal family and the linear life course.[1] These
postindustrial trends began to push older social arrangements into crisis in
the 1960s, and the turmoil of that decade marked the beginnings of a scramble for new understandings and new institutional arrangements that would
replace those of the industrial era.

However, the Republican political coalition that formed in response to the
upheavals of the 1960s has steadfastly refused to engage this postindustrial
problematic. It has sought instead to suppress and avoid debate about postindustrial transition by endlessly repeating two very old ideas. The first is "market fundamentalism," a contemporary recycling of the free market ideas of
Malthus and Ricardo (Somers and Block 2005). The second is a neotradition-
alist defense of those forms of authority that were put into question in the
1960s—exemplified by church, flag, and CEO. So instead of debating and
managing a postindustrial transition, society has been locked into a set of
sterile arguments about the genius of markets and the importance of obeying
established authorities.

Market fundamentalism has worked to freeze political debate on the question of whether society should rely more on the market or the state to solve
economic and social problems. But successful postindustrial policies are not
a question of moving toward either greater reliance on the market or greater
reliance on the state. They require new ways of combining states and markets. In innovation policy, for example, highly decentralized and flexible initiatives by government agencies in various countries, including the United
States, have played a key role in helping private firms accelerate technological
change (Block 2008; O'Riain 2004). Similarly, defending or attacking traditional authority is irrelevant; the postindustrial challenge is to construct new
forms of legitimate authority that are both bounded and flexible (Block 1989).

While the right has been extraordinarily successful in keeping the debate
within the same grooves for a very long time, a number of issues have produced recent shifts. One is the growing concern over global climate change.
When the administration of George W. Bush first came into office in 2001,
it paid little price for its repudiation of the Kyoto Accord and its insistence
on market-oriented solutions to energy problems. By 2005, even Bush was
speaking of the national "addiction to oil" in negative terms, and pressures
were building in both parties for systematic initiatives to slow the production
of greenhouse gases.

In addition, the subprime lending crisis might finally discredit market fundamentalist ideas. To be sure, the era of market fundamentalism has produced a long series of financial disasters, including the Third World debt
crisis, the savings and loan debacle in the 1980s, the overbuilding of commercial real estate, and the Internet-driven stock market bubble of the 1990s. All
of these crises and the subprime mortgage lending boom have followed a

similar pattern of herd behavior in search of higher rates of return and seemingly unstoppable increases in asset prices. And all have imposed huge economic and social costs once the bubble burst. Since the current mortgage crisis is having a direct and destructive impact on millions of homeowners in the United States, it could finally swing the pendulum in favor of effective regulation of the financial sector.

Nonetheless, up until now, the advocates of market fundamentalism have been remarkably successful in containing such disruptive issues through their insistence that "there is no alternative" to increased reliance on markets. By pointing out the failures of Soviet socialism and exaggerating the problems of Scandinavian social democracies, they have battered people into accepting greater income and wealth inequalities as inevitable and necessary. If progressives are to take advantage of current opportunities, they must persuade people by advancing an attractive and coherent vision of how the economy could be organized.

The major example available to us of a successful reform epoch in U.S. history is Franklin Roosevelt's New Deal. FDR framed his alternative vision as an incremental and pragmatic advance on existing institutions rather than a radical break with current practices (MacArthur 2003). Since it is unreasonable to expect that public disillusionment with self-regulating markets will again reach the levels of the 1930s, we would do well to emulate FDR's approach. A few analysts have suggested the broad outlines of such an alternative (Greider 2003; Alperovitz 2005), but thus far, few of their reform proposals have caught on. But I will follow William Greider in labeling the alternative the construction of a "moral economy," in order to emphasize the centrality of cooperation and ethical behavior as key sources of productivity, efficiency, and social cohesion under postindustrial conditions (Block 2006a).[2]

Envisioning a Moral Economy

Emphasizing the economic value of ethical principles has deep roots in the history of economic thought. While market fundamentalists have wrapped themselves in the mantle of Adam Smith, much of what he wrote in *The Wealth of Nations* built on arguments in an earlier book, *The Theory of Moral Sentiments*. In that book, he repeatedly emphasizes that justice is a necessary precondition for a well-functioning society and economy: "Justice, on the contrary, is the main pillar that upholds the whole edifice. If it is removed, the great, the immense fabric of human society, that fabric which to raise and support seems in this world, if I may say so, to have been the peculiar and darling care of Nature, must in a moment crumble into atoms" ([1759] 2002, 86). Smith was even more specific in using the athletic metaphor to stress that participants in economic competition must obey the "rules of the game": "In the race for wealth, and honours, and preferments, [the individual] may run as hard as he can, and strain every nerve and every muscle, in order to outstrip all his competitors. But if he should justle, or throw down any of them, the indulgence of the spectators is entirely at an end. It is a violation of fair play, which they cannot admit of" ([1759] 2002, 92).

Contemporary analysts who emphasize the centrality of trust and reciprocity as critical lubricants of market transactions are returning to Smith's insights (Putnam 2001; Kay 2003; Ringmar 2005). When participants in market transactions are fearful of violations of fair play, transaction costs rise dramatically and fewer deals are likely to be made. So the willingness of participants in markets to obey norms of reciprocity is not some kind of luxury, but rather a key precondition for efficient markets to work.

Yet it is also indisputable that unethical activities have been central to profit making over the last two centuries of industrialization. Fair play was irrelevant to those who built great fortunes extracting raw materials from the earth with little regard for the environment or the interests of indigenous communities. Reciprocity means little to those who run factories that exploit workers and foul the air and water. Justice cannot be reconciled with financial practices that shift resources from the weak and poor to the rich and powerful. And certainly these forms of "accumulation by dispossession" continue right down to the present moment (Harvey 2003).

However, a renewal of interest in Adam Smith's formulations in *The Theory of Moral Sentiments* reflects the current postindustrial conjuncture, in which partial or total disregard of the Golden Rule has become economically problematic for several reasons. First, as expanding productivity and wealth becomes dependent on the appropriation of scientific and technological advances, the economy depends on a broader culture of cooperation and collaboration. Both scientific breakthroughs and their transfer to commercial products require the free flow of knowledge and collective problem solving by teams that are often assembled across organizational boundaries. Norms of reciprocity and fair play are indispensable for the effective functioning of these communities (Heckscher and Adler 2006).

The problem, of course, is that the potential rewards of both wealth and status to individuals who ruthlessly pursue their self-interest in these settings are enormous. As the example of Bill Gates has shown, the sky is the limit for those who are the first to commercialize new technologies. But if all participants are continually asking, "What's in this for me?" or "How do I use what I know to make a killing?," then collaboration and information sharing suddenly disappear (Benkler 2006). The norms of a moral economy become indispensable to effective functioning of these innovative teams.

Second, the dispossession that results from unconstrained market practices has become a threat to future economic development. For a long time,

it was possible to accept growing inequality and social exclusion within societies as the inevitable price paid for continuing economic growth. But now
there are increasing signs that societies that are relatively more egalitarian
will have distinct advantages with the new communications and information
technologies. Although the United States pioneered many of these advances,
its global lead is being undermined by the "digital divide" that has been created by pervasive inequalities of wealth and income. For example, more than
a dozen of the more egalitarian developed societies in both Asia and Europe
have jumped ahead of the United States in the percentage of households that
have access to high-speed Internet services. This creates the distinct possibility that they will also outpace the United States in developing the next generation of applications that take advantage of an almost universally wired
population (Turner 2007).

Third, the tighter integration of the globe through communication and
transportation means that profit-oriented assaults on ecosystems and people,
even if they happen on the other side of the world, are likely to have boomerang effects. The most obvious instance is global climate change. For decades,
it was possible to ignore the negative environmental impacts of economic
activity by concentrating the damage in areas that would then be abandoned
by anyone who had options. But the strategy of moving elsewhere no longer
works as we approach and exceed the carrying capacity of the planet. Another
example is the threat of a global health crisis through the rapid diffusion of a
new virus. In earlier decades, it was a matter of indifference to Western elites
that millions of people lacked access to modern health care. Now, however, it
is impossible to protect the health of one's own population if one neglects
potential threats from areas of the world that have underdeveloped systems
for monitoring and managing epidemics.

In short, Adam Smith's insights about the dependence of economic advance on justice have become particularly relevant for our contemporary situation. Ongoing scientific and technological advances and heightened global
interdependence make it both possible and necessary to construct a moral
economy in which economic actors are continually questioning whether their
treatment of others meets an ethical standard. The functioning of this moral
economy can be understood in terms of a three-sector model. The core of the
economy consists of scientists and technologists working in high-tech firms,
universities, and the public sector. They are continually developing new products and more efficient ways to produce older products that save on labor,
capital, and raw materials. The technological frontier toward which they are
working is a zero-waste economy in which the by-products of production
processes are either directly useful or recyclable.

Surrounding this core, we can conceive of the "thing economy," which
supplies people with food, energy, products, and the built environment. The
efficiency with which this economy operates would be steadily improving as

a consequence of the innovations in the core. But precisely because of its increasing efficiency, this sector would employ only a steadily declining share of the population. Most people would be employed in an outer ring, which can be termed the "care economy." The activity here would involve producing and maintaining human beings who are knowledgeable, healthy, creative, and energetic. Activities in the care economy encompass health, education, child care, elder care, social services, and tourism and leisure services.

In this three-sector model of the economy, the inner sector is the wealth-producing arena, whose continuous stream of innovative products ensures that the entire economy maintains a healthy balance of trade and payments. Moreover, the ideas generated in the inner core ensure the continued strength of the thing economy. Yet the role of the care economy is also critical, because it provides a continuous inflow of new scientific and engineering talent to the core, as well as skilled, flexible employees with a high capacity to learn to the rest of the economy.

In many respects, this new economy looks very much like the economy we have now. It would continue to consist of profit-oriented firms, nonprofits, and a public sector, but the understanding of how the parts function together would be quite different. The definitions of wealth-creating and wealth-destroying activities would be revised. Measures to ensure that children from low-income families can access higher education would be understood as wealth-creating activities. Corporate maneuvers to shift costs onto other groups would be perceived as wealth-destroying activities. Getting to this new economy involves six separate—but interrelated—reform projects, discussed below.

Creating ethical corporations. Corporate governance in the United States is in crisis. Boards of directors have failed to rein in executive compensation; top managers continue to be strongly tempted to pursue shortcuts to enrich their firms and themselves; firms are often myopically fixated on short term-objectives; and the rewards for deals, such as taking firms private, are often greater than the incentives for improved performance (Bogle 2005). Moreover, corporate governance must be redesigned for an era that is dependent on scientific and technological advances. Firms that have embraced "best practices" in board functioning and management have pointed the way toward creating highly effective firms that are built around communities of learning. But within the current legal and financial structures, there are too many obstacles that block the diffusion of these positive models. Thus, a concerted program of reform is necessary to make the ethical corporation the dominant model. This will involve creating stakeholder boards of directors that represent both employees and shareholders, have a stronger focus on the long term, and systematically incorporate environmental, labor, and community impacts into their decision making (Block 2006b).

Prioritizing social inclusion. While our society's rhetoric promotes the notion of leaving no child behind, the reality is that both poverty and inequality continue to deepen. Moreover, greater employment insecurity, a shrinking of the safety net, and the problems of the health care sector place millions of families at risk of downward mobility (Hacker 2006). These problems must be addressed by new social policies that redistribute income to the poor, provide middle-income families with greater protection from economic shocks, and universalize access to health care, child care, and higher education. Reform of the educational system is also urgent, but it is far more likely to be successful in the context of broader initiatives to reduce poverty and economic insecurity (Block and Manza 1997).

Democratic developmentalism. The great engine of technological advance in the United States over the past half century has been a three-sided collaboration among government, the scientific community, and private industry. Government has funded the basic and applied research that has generated important breakthroughs in computer technology, bioscience, materials science, and other fields. The key research takes place in university and government laboratories, and private firms usually enter the process at the final stage to bring the new technology to the market and reap most of the profits. Within the prevailing framework of market fundamentalism, the performance of this developmental engine is suboptimal. Market fundamentalism makes it possible for firms to insist that they alone are responsible for the key innovations and to monopolize the resulting profit streams. Funding levels for the government are far below what they could be, and there is insufficient public discussion about the direction of technological change (Block 2008).

The democratization of this state-led process of technological development would require several changes. One would be to ensure that a larger portion of the profits that firms earn on publicly funded research be recycled to pay for the next generation of basic research. Another would be to develop procedures for much more extensive public involvement in discussions about which technological paths will be pursued. An obvious example that demonstrates the need for change is genetic engineering, as government agencies have helped prioritize research on seeds that provide greater benefits to agribusiness firms than to the public. To be sure, questions of scientific fact cannot be decided by public referenda, but there are still significant advantages to creating a broader public dialogue on technological priorities.

Green design and production. In both the organization of the built environment and the production of goods and services, environmental sustainability must become a central priority. This involves accelerating the shift away from fossil fuels and a drive toward zero waste in production processes (McDonough and Braungart 2002). This priority intersects with several of the other reform initiatives. A major focus of democratic developmentalism would be accelerating the development and diffusion of green technologies. Ethical corporations would play a far more aggressive role in advancing environmental sustainability than traditional firms, which have often been indifferent to the environmental costs of profit-making activity.

Rebuilding the care economy. Human services are increasingly central to our economy, but the organizational structures that have continued to yield productivity gains for manufactured goods have often been counterproductive when it comes to care services, such as health care, child care, elder care, and a variety of social services. The results are continuous shortages of quality care and sustained upward trends in prices that put even low-quality care out of reach for many. Quality care ultimately depends on caregivers who provide the kind of assistance that they would wish to receive. But building these norms of reciprocity back into our care economy will require considerable reorganization of delivery systems, employment structures, and funding mechanisms.

Restructuring finance. The severity of the 2007–9 financial crisis has made clear the urgency of shifting the financial system away from its focus on destabilizing speculation. This requires a combination of regulations designed to discourage highly leveraged speculative activity and the creation of new channels that expand the flow of private capital into financing socially and economically productive activities that have been chronically starved for funding. Three areas are particularly important. The first is infrastructure spending, which includes rebuilding decaying bridges, sewers, and water treatment facilities. The second is the massive investments that are needed to transition the economy away from its dependence on carbon-based energy. This includes building a new "smart" electricity grid and the rapid deployment of alternative energy technologies. Finally, the thousands of small high-technology firms require patient capital to allow them to move new technologies into the marketplace. The precise mechanisms for constructing new channels will vary across these different areas, but some combination of favorable tax treatment, government loan guarantees, and the creation of new hybrid institutions can work to redirect capital flows. Just as FDR's New Deal successfully redirected vast quantities of private capital to finance the post–World War II suburban housing boom, a new period of financial reform can lay the basis for a far stronger domestic economy.

The Global Dimensions of the Reform Agenda

Taken together, these six projects suggest the broad outline of a new era of domestic reform in which the United States would renew and rebuild its core institutions. But any domestically oriented reform agenda is doomed to defeat if it is not linked to a persuasive vision of the role played by the United States in global politics. For the entire forty-year period from Vietnam to Iraq, the United States has been locked into a sterile and polarized political debate over the best strategy for protecting U.S. security in an increasingly dangerous world.

Throughout this period, progressives have lacked a positive vision for U.S. foreign policy. In mobilizing opposition to high levels of military spending and the aggressive use of U.S. military power in Southeast Asia, Central America, and now the Middle East, progressives tend to argue that domestic politics should have priority over global adventures. Similarly, in debates over U.S. trade policy, progressives have emphasized that the country's support for "economic globalization" has exposed its workforce to greater insecurity, and they have advocated measures to protect groups in the United States from the impact of global competition. To be sure, an important "global justice" current of the progressive movement has criticized the impact of "free trade" and financial liberalization on the populations of developing countries. But this current has been politically weak, and it has not had a significant impact on national debates.

In consequence, the left in the United States is often seen as urging the country to pull back from the rest of the world and focus on tending its own garden. Segments of the right, in contrast, maintain a significant internationalist focus, seeking to make the world a better place by exporting the U.S. economic model both through trade negotiations and, when necessary, through the exercise of military force.[3] In the run-up to both the Afghan and the Iraq wars, George W. Bush very skillfully took advantage of this discursive alignment. He was able to tap into strong currents of Wilsonian internationalism in the United States by insisting that our military interventions were designed to liberate women in Afghanistan and bring democracy and freedom to the Middle East. This rhetoric was extremely important in gaining support from many liberal internationalists who believe that U.S. power should be used in the pursuit of global human rights.

The actual policies that the United States has pursued in both Afghanistan and Iraq belie the president's rhetoric. But the main lesson should be obvious. When progressives cede the moral high ground of internationalism and idealism, their position in foreign policy debates is greatly weakened. It is not enough to simply say "no" to the misguided foreign policies of Republican or Democratic presidents; progressives need a positive vision for U.S. foreign policy. This is the niche that ethical globalization is designed to fill. Below, I offer some visions of alternatives that fit within a new and increasingly forceful conversation (Chang 2008; Evans 2008; Stiglitz and Charlton 2005; Unger 2007).

Ethical Globalization

Ethical globalization means that the United States would seek to make the moral economy a global phenomenon. Just as we attempt to create opportunity and inclusion for the "poorest of the poor" at home, so we would seek to do the same for the "poorest of the poor" globally. In the same way that we hold corporations to the highest ethical standards in West Virginia and Nevada, so we would seek to hold them to the same standards in Jakarta and the Niger Delta. And just as we pursue environmental sustainability at home, so we would seek to do the same on a global basis. This foreign policy vision is consistent with domestic reform, because when science and technology are the basis for economic growth, a "positive-sum" global economy can be created in which expanding trade "raises all boats." But getting to this more benevolent global economy will require significant changes in global institutions and practices.

Ethical globalization identifies the principles and goals for U.S. foreign policy, but it provides little guidance on questions of the pace of transformation. This is evident in the example of global climate change. The U.S. interest in creating environmental sustainability on a global level means that it will work with other nations to establish benchmarks for achieving reductions in the production of greenhouse gases. Such negotiations will necessarily include incentives for nations such as China and India to accelerate their efforts to shift to alternative energy sources. The negotiations will also inevitably produce significant disputes about the timing of change. On one side, more radical groups will argue for benchmarks that produce dramatic shifts in the initial years of the agreement. They will insist on a serious initial down payment to prove that the global community is taking the climate change crisis seriously. On the other side will be groups that favor more modest, short-term goals as a way to build confidence in the global process, which will lead to more ambitious benchmarks ten or twenty years into the future.

These strategic dilemmas cannot be resolved by abstract principles or theoretical formulations. Rather, they must be worked out through political conflict and debate that will determine which global commitments are feasible in the present and sustainable over time. With this caveat in mind, it is possible to identify the four core ideas of ethical globalization, which are detailed in the following sections.

Reforming the Ground Rules for the Global Economy

The most urgent task is to restructure the ground rules for the global economy in a way that facilitates balanced, equitable, and sustainable growth across all parts of the global economy. Since the existing rules were written to consolidate the privileged position of the richest nations, they must be revised to expand the opportunities for real economic growth in the global South. But the goal is not just redistribution; it is to create a positive-sum global economy in which development in the South supports and reinforces economic growth in the North. The first step is to create effective global standards for corporations and effective enforcement mechanisms to police those standards. Historically, European and U.S. corporations, whether engaged in resource extraction, production, or sales, have taken advantage of weak regulatory regimes in the developing world to profit through unethical or unsustainable means. Firms that operate within strict rules in their home country are often careless about worker health or the environment in their foreign operations. Today, these questionable practices are being emulated by international corporations based in Japan, China, and numerous other nations. Moreover, these unethical business practices play a major role in sustaining civil conflicts in a number of resource-rich areas of the world.

Activists and nongovernmental organizations (NGOs) have fought for labor, environmental, and human rights standards to cover some of these practices, but it is now time for corporations to be brought under an effective global legal regime. This regime would define legitimate and illegitimate corporate practices with standards that could be ratcheted up as conditions warranted. But just as the emergence of national regulatory structures provided both costs and benefits to corporations, so this global regulatory structure would provide firms with some protections that they currently lack, such as legal recourse in the face of capricious regulations and the illegitimate appropriation of their intellectual property (Evans 2008).

A second step is to make key changes in the global regimes for trade and finance. Both the rules and the enforcement mechanisms that currently exist under the World Trade Organization (WTO) are in need of dramatic revision (Stiglitz and Charlton 2005; Unger 2007). Similarly, in the financial arena, current rules and institutions have worked to the disadvantage of developing nations in two critical respects. First, governments in developing nations need to have mechanisms that will insulate their populations from external economic shocks. Individuals and firms cannot make effective decisions in environments in which income fluctuates wildly from year to year, and existing procedures have intensified those shocks. Under the existing rules, the only way to avoid shocks has been to accumulate enormous currency reserves, which block more productive use of those resources (Eatwell and Taylor 2000; Teunissen and Akkerman 2007).

Third, the global financial institutions should be providing a stable and predictable flow of financial resources that would allow developing societies to make productive investments at all levels of the economy. Under the current regime, flows have been irregular and unpredictable, and have often involved net shifts of resources from developing to developed nations. There needs to be a large, sustained, and growing net transfer of resources to those places where the most disadvantaged people live.

A Global Sustainability Initiative

A global sustainability initiative must be a key element of a program of ethical globalization. In the context of systematic efforts by the richer nations to address global inequality, it should be considerably easier to negotiate new global environmental standards. Rather than lecturing poorer nations that they should not waste resources the way that rich nations have, adopting stricter environmental rules in the global South can be part of a global bargain in which the developing world receives greater benefits. Moreover, the world faces too many interconnected environmental challenges to continue with piecemeal and partial strategies, which can sometimes prove ineffective or counterproductive. For example, in the current rush to provide alternatives to oil, there is a danger that accelerated production of certain crops for ethanol and biodiesel might cause even greater environmental damage than benefits. The global sustainability initiative would set key priorities for meeting the full range of global environmental challenges, and it would target public and private funding at key intervention points in both the richer and the poorer countries. Obviously, the most urgent challenge is global climate change, but the initiative would also address other key issues, such as the protection and enhancement of supplies of safe drinking water, the restoration of the health of the oceans and coastal wetlands, and the preservation of farmland.

Cooperative Efforts to Repair Failed States

The main threats to national security in the twenty-first century require a fundamental shift in U.S. foreign policy. The dangers today are not military confrontations with another major nation, but international terrorism, the increased availability and diffusion of weapons of mass destruction, environmental catastrophes, the spread of infectious diseases, and the potential for widespread death from famine or environmental degradation in parts of the developing world. Citizens of the world's richer nations cannot protect themselves from this kind of disorder by building walls; it is too easy for weapons, germs, or masses of migrants to find ways around walls and fortified borders.

All of this points to failed states as a core danger. When governments are unable to provide for their citizens, it creates opportunities for social movements that are willing to engage in terror tactics, as we have seen in Somalia, Afghanistan, and post-Hussein Iraq. Just as serious, however, are the potential health threats. As we have learned from avian flu, the world is only a few mutations away from a global pandemic that could kill tens of millions of people. Societies in which the state is too weak to support a public health infrastructure provide an opportunity for such viruses to become firmly established in the human population, and the porousness of global boundaries assures that the danger will not be contained in the poorer nations.

During the last quarter century of market fundamentalist orthodoxy, the number of these failed states throughout the developing world has risen dramatically. This was not accidental; policy makers and global institutions preached an ethic of "tough love," telling leaders in poor nations that they could no longer rely on handouts and that their societies would have to pull themselves up by their bootstraps if they were to make it in a competitive global marketplace. But the bootstraps had to come from the private sector, since the new orthodoxy insisted that the government's role in the economy should be kept to a minimum. To make matters worse, the rules of the game in this global marketplace were written by the rich nations, who often either blocked agricultural imports from poor nations or assured that their commodities received rock-bottom prices (Harvey 2005).

For these reasons, the exercise in tough love pushed many societies into hopeless poverty. Governments that no longer had any effective tools for making a difference lost legitimacy, and dissatisfied groups increasingly turned to violent means to pursue their ends. The downward cycle is familiar. Many honest civil servants leave in disgust, and the ones who are left behind are often driven by revenge or greed. Sometimes the result is full-scale civil war; sometimes it is just a government whose writ does not extend beyond the capital city. Reversing this process and replacing failed states with effective states is an enormous challenge for the global community. It cannot be done simply by imposing order militarily from the outside. It requires a sustained cooperative effort among governments, public and private aid agencies, and the people who live in the territories where states have failed.

The way forward has already been charted by those engaged in global campaigns against poverty and disease. The starting point has to be the promise of universal human rights. Since human beings have the right to be secure in their person, to be protected from disease, and to develop their capacities through education, the global community has to begin building the capacity of public agencies in these countries to provide order and security and working systems of public health and education.

This will require an initiative on the scale of a Global Marshall Plan, drawing on both public and private resources. The targets must not be limited to those societies in which states have already failed; they must include those societies at serious risk of such failures. The process must also include negotiations of peace agreements in societies divided by civil conflict and will, in certain cases, require multilateral military forces to maintain the peace. But the key is an infusion of resources that immediately make a difference in the health, education, and life chances of the people.

Strengthening the Global Human Rights Regime

The first three initiatives are all efforts to fulfill the basic human right to live with dignity in an environment that is safe and secure. But making progress on this front requires strengthening global institutions so that they can make the rule of law and justice a global reality. As suggested above, existing global economic institutions, such as the IMF, World Bank, and WTO, must be reformed or replaced so that they put a much greater emphasis on overcoming the unsustainable gap in income and wealth between rich and poor nations.

At the same time, there must be considerable progress made in creating better global regulatory and enforcement mechanisms. Recent efforts to bring war criminals to justice in the International Court of Justice in The Hague are just a first step in constructing a global framework that could effectively deter human rights abuses within countries by individuals and corporate entities. Similarly, current efforts to create global peacekeeping missions need to be enhanced and developed, so that the world community can quickly intervene if genocide or systematic human rights abuses are taking place.

Conclusion

Ethical globalization represents a significant break with the dominant perspectives in U.S. foreign policy debates. In the tradition of foreign policy realism, helping the bottom line of U.S. corporations is in the national interest and should be a major policy objective. Ethical globalization clearly distinguishes between two different ways that firms can earn profits abroad: those that shift costs onto foreigners and those that result from innovation and efficiency. Since the former source of profits is unsustainable, the United States should focus on creating the conditions in which U.S. firms can profit internationally while providing real benefits to foreigners.

At the same time, ethical globalization is different from the internationalism that has inspired neoconservative thinkers to advocate an aggressive U.S. campaign to export democracy, even by military means. While ethical globalization shares the view that the fullest realization of human rights occurs in societies that are governed democratically, it rejects the idea that simply having elections is an end in itself. As the example of Afghanistan poignantly suggests, elections are neither a substitute for nor a guarantee that citizens will have personal safety or legitimate ways to pursue their livelihoods. Real democracy requires economic development, and that is something that the market fundamentalist policies favored by these neoconservatives have not been able to provide.

Most important, ethical globalization represents a way for the United States to chart a transition away from its global role as guarantor of the international order, which it has played ever since World War II. This role, in which the United States serves as "global hegemon" or the "indispensable nation," is no longer sustainable. Despite its overwhelming military superiority over other nations, the United States lacks the economic and human resources and the political will to exercise dominance over the globe. As the failures of the Bush administration's foreign policy have amply demonstrated, the clock cannot be turned back to an imperial past in which a single nation dominates the global economy.

Yet accepting this reality does not mean either retreat from the globe or a precipitous decline in the American standard of living. The domestic reform program outlined here points a way to a more broadly shared domestic prosperity, even as the United States abandons its imperial ambitions. And ethical globalization provides a framework in which the United States would continue to play a global leadership role, albeit through cooperative relationships with other nations, to create a global order that would truly meet the needs of all of the world's people.

NOTES

1. The linear life course is the idea that people move through the life course—education, marriage, child rearing, and careers—in a predictable and relatively uniform fashion (Block 1990).

2. In using the term "moral economy," I am also drawing on the intellectual legacy of Karl Polanyi (1968, [1944] 2001). See also Booth (1994) and Block (2003b).

3. Significant parts of the religious right are deeply suspicious of globalization. This has helped push the Bush foreign policy toward unilateralism and militarization (Block 2007).

REFERENCES

Alperovitz, Gar. 2005. *America Beyond Capitalism: Reclaiming Our Wealth, Our Liberty, and Our Democracy.* New York: John Wiley.

Benkler, Yochai. 2006. *The Wealth of Networks: How Social Production Transforms Markets and Freedom.* New Haven: Yale University Press.

Block, Fred. 1989. "Modernity, Democracy, and the Problem of Authority." In *Social Class and Democratic Leadership: Essays in Honor of E. Digby Baltzell,* edited by Harold Bershady, 216–30. Philadelphia: University of Pennsylvania Press.

———. 1990. *Postindustrial Possibilities: A Critique of Economic Discourse.* Berkeley: University of California Press.

———. 2003a. "The Global Economy in the Bush Era." *Socio-Economic Review* 1 (3): 439–56.

———. 2003b. "Karl Polanyi and the Writing of *The Great Transformation.*" *Theory and Society* 32 (3): 275–306.

———. 2006a. "A Corporation with a Conscience?" *New Labor Forum* 15 (2): 75–83.

———. 2006b. "A Moral Economy." *Nation,* March 20, 16–19.

———. 2007. "Understanding the Diverging Trajectories of the United States and Western Europe: A Neo-Polanyian Analysis." *Politics and Society* 35 (1): 3–33.

———. 2008. "Swimming Against the Current: The Rise of a Hidden Developmental State in the United States." *Politics and Society* 36 (2): 169–206.

Block, Fred, and Jeff Manza. 1997. "Could We End Poverty in a Postindustrial Society? The Case for a Progressive Negative Income Tax." *Politics and Society* 25 (4): 473–511.

Bogle, John C. 2005. *The Battle for the Soul of Capitalism.* New Haven: Yale University Press.

Booth, William James. 1994. "On the Idea of Moral Economy." *American Political Science Review* 88 (3): 653–67.

Brick, Howard. 2006. *Transcending Capitalism: Visions of a New Society in Modern American Thought*. Ithaca: Cornell University Press.

Chang, Ha Joon. 2008. *Bad Samaritans: The Myth of Free Trade and the Secret History of Capitalism*. New York: Bloomsbury.

de Sousa Santos, Boaventura. 2008. "The World Social Forum and the Global Left." *Politics and Society* 36 (2): 247–70.

Eatwell, John, and Lance Taylor. 2000. *Global Finance at Risk: The Case for International Regulation*. New York: New Press.

Evans, Peter. 2008. "Is an Alternative Globalization Possible?" *Politics and Society* 36 (2): 271–305.

Greider, William. 2003. *The Soul of Capitalism: Opening Paths to a Moral Economy*. New York: Simon and Schuster.

Hacker, Jacob. 2006. *The Great Risk Shift: The Assault on American Jobs, Families, Health Care, and Retirement—and How You Can Fight Back*. New York: Oxford University Press.

Harvey, David. 2003. *The New Imperialism*. Oxford: Oxford University Press.

———. 2005. *A Brief History of Neoliberalism*. Oxford: Oxford University Press.

Heckscher, Charles, and Paul S. Adler, eds. 2006. *The Firm as a Collaborative Community: Reconstructing Trust in the Knowledge Economy*. New York: Oxford University Press.

Kay, John. 2003. *The Truth About Markets: Why Some Nations Are Rich but Most Remain Poor*. London: Penguin.

Klein, Naomi. 2007. *The Shock Doctrine: The Rise of Disaster Capitalism*. New York: Metropolitan Books.

MacArthur, John Burritt. 2003. "The Great Depression and the Limits of Market-Based Policy." Ph.D. dissertation, School of Public Policy, University of California, Berkeley.

McDonough, William, and Michael Braungart. 2002. *Cradle to Cradle: Remaking the Way We Make Things*. New York: North Point Press.

O'Riain, Sean. 2004. *The Politics of High-Tech Growth*. New York: Cambridge University Press.

Polanyi, Karl. [1944] 2001. *The Great Transformation*. Boston: Beacon Press.

———. 1968. *Primitive, Archaic, and Modern Economies: Essays of Karl Polanyi*. Edited by George Dalton. Boston: Beacon Press.

Putnam, Robert D. 2001. *Bowling Alone: The Collapse and Revival of American Community*. New York: Touchstone.

Ringmar, Erik. 2005. *Surviving Capitalism: How We Learned to Live with the Market and Remained Almost Human*. London: Anthem Press.

Smith, Adam. [1759] 2002. *The Theory of Moral Sentiments*. Cambridge: Cambridge University Press.

———. [1776] 1976. *The Wealth of Nations*. Chicago: University of Chicago Press.

Somers, Margaret, and Fred Block. 2005. "From Poverty to Perversity: Ideas, Markets, and Institutions over 200 Years of Welfare Debate." *American Sociological Review* 70 (2): 260–87.

Stiglitz, Joseph E. 2002. *Globalization and Its Discontents*. New York: W. W. Norton.

Stiglitz, Joseph E., and Andrew Charlton. 2005. *Fair Trade for All: How Trade Can Promote Development*. New York: Oxford.

Suskind, Ron. 2006. *The One Percent Doctrine: Deep Inside America's Pursuit of Its Enemies Since 9/11*. New York: Simon and Schuster.

Teunissen, Jan Joost, and Age Akkerman. 2007. *Global Imbalances and Developing Countries: Remedies for a Failing International Monetary System*. The Hague: FONDAD.

Turner, S. Derek. 2007. *Shooting the Messenger: Myth vs. Reality: U.S. Broadband Policy and International Broadband Rankings*. Free Press. http://www.freepress.net/docs/shooting_the_messenger.pdf.

Unger, Roberto Mangabeira. 2007. *Free Trade Reimagined: The World Division of Labor and the Method of Economics*. Princeton: Princeton University Press.

9

THE (DE)COLONIALITY OF KNOWLEDGE, LIFE, AND NATURE: THE NORTH AMERICAN–ANDEAN FREE TRADE AGREEMENT, INDIGENOUS MOVEMENTS, AND REGIONAL ALTERNATIVES

Catherine Walsh

For the indigenous peoples and nations of Abya Yala,[1] the North American–Andean Free Trade Agreement was not simply a new economic policy but rather "a Christopher Columbus disguised . . . a new form of invasion and colonization."[2] Notably, this free trade agreement (FTA) is referred to in Spanish as the Tratado de Libre Colonización (the Agreement of Free Colonization, TLC). In Ecuador, these words have appeared as graffiti on various city walls; they are also present in the declarations and documents of numerous South American indigenous organizations.

How might we understand this correlation of free trade and colonization? What is the perspective it affords in terms of modernity, neoliberal capitalism, and "development"? Or, asked differently, how do these new and ongoing manifestations of colonialism—what Quijano (2000) has termed coloniality—reflect modernity's other face, that not readily seen but which has been and continues to be instrumental to the development of global capitalism and to the control of knowledge, life, and nature? And what are the emergent resistances and insurgencies in the region that not only confront this new form of invasion and colonization but also propose and construct alternatives?

Such questions, seldom evidenced in the emergent literature in the United States on free trade and the North American Free Trade Agreement (NAFTA) but central to debates within the Andean region, provide a foundation for the discussion presented in this chapter. They offer an important perspective for understanding not only present-day imperial, hemispheric, and continental strategies and politics, but also the growing force of an insurgent offensive rooted in what Arturo Escobar (2005) refers to as "politics based in place." Such reference to "place" challenges the dislocalization perpetuated by both globalization and "universal" Eurocentric analyses of culture, economy, and modern thought. At the same time, it works to highlight the location of struggle and experience, as well as the links among practice, politics, territory, and place that have long governed the thought and action of Latin American social movements. In the context of this chapter, the idea of politics based in place also gives attention to the particularity of the Andean region of South America, a place where social movement politics, particularly those of indigenous peoples, and imperial-colonial interests clearly collide.

In fact, the "place" of the Andean region could probably not be more pivotal to U.S imperial interests and designs. Plan Colombia and its regional manifestation, Plan Patriota, as well as the U.S. military base in Manta, Ecuador (1999–2009),[3] are tied not just to drug control but, more importantly, to the control and appropriation of natural resources. These policies are part and parcel of the "new form of invasion and colonization" that "pretend[s] to convert the Andean community into part of the military strategy of the United States" (Moreano 2006, 67). Yet it is also in this region that the challenges to invasion and colonization are most apparent, evidenced in not only the resistance but also the insurgence of indigenous movements, and in the national-regional politics led by Hugo Chávez in Venezuela, Evo Morales in Bolivia, and, more recently, Rafael Correa in Ecuador.

This chapter presents a reflection in terms of this politics based in place. Its intent is severalfold. First, the chapter will analyze the geopolitics of free trade in the Andean region from the perspective of coloniality, making clear how neoliberal politics and free trade are pivotal components of a contemporary framework of power that extends beyond economics to the spheres of knowledge, life, and nature. Second, it will examine the struggles waged by indigenous peoples in the region with regard to the North American–Andean FTA, and the manner in which these struggles construct and reflect decolonial proposals, strategies, and positioning, which have at their center existence and life. Finally, the chapter explores emergent regional alternatives, including Venezuela's Bolivarian Alternative for the Americas (ALBA) and Evo Morales's proposal for a People's Trade Agreement (PTA), as well as the philosophical and practical premises of *suma qamaña* in Bolivia and *sumak kawsay* in Ecuador (understood as "to live well"); these alternatives are based in a defense of place, providing a way to confront and counteract "the new strategy of colonization brought forth by Free Trade Agreements and the Free Trade Agreement of the Americas . . . mechanisms not to regulate commercial exchange, but rather to impose politics of extermination" (Red Erbol 2006).

The Geopolitics of Free Trade in the Andean Region

The association of colonialism with the negation of future has long defined indigenous struggle in the Andean region—a struggle intimately tied to concerns of identity and territory or land, including the inextricable elements of knowledge and being. From this perspective, the North American–Andean FTA, neoliberal policies, and other emergent imperial impositions represent a geopolitical threat not just to economic stability but, more importantly, to the prospect of life itself.

It is precisely in this problem of the future of humanity and life that the real concern resides. From the perspective of colonial-imperial powers such as the United States, the problem—seen as an economic, social, and political problem of governance and "development"—requires a remodeling of the region based, in part, on the establishment of Western models of democracy and the expansion of hemispheric, economic, and global ties, including free trade. Such reshaping, according to the CIA report *Global Trends 2015*, could help weed out the weak nations that, in the global sphere, are unlikely to survive, leaving the stronger ones to forge alliances in which the United States and the global North, naturally, maintain their superiority (National Intelligence Council 2000). Of course, it is of little surprise that in this remodeling of the Andean region, the countries that would simply disappear are those with a powerful indigenous presence and resistance. Interestingly enough, it is in these same countries that the politics of neoliberal adjustment and liberalization have not, principally because of indigenous opposition, been able to fully take hold. And precisely for this reason, the United States now identifies indigenous peoples as factors of destabilization and terrorism, and as threats to security and hegemony (González 2005).

While it is clear that a strengthening and deepening of the neoliberal project is at the center of U.S.-controlled free trade, it is not always apparent or understood that this project is not just economic and political but also social, cultural, and epistemic in nature. That is to say, in its dogmatic reaffirmation of Western "universalism"—including its lineal conceptions of progress and development, its view of the central countries as models to which all others must turn, its indifference toward "others" who cannot find a place in the utopia of market and liberal democracy, and its monolithic precepts of "science" (Lander 2000)—neoliberalism, in essence, crosses almost all elements of life.

As such, it is no wonder that the ambitions and interests (as well as the effects) of FTAs and neoliberal policies in the region are multiple, interlaced, and far-reaching. They include economic regional control, particularly the control of natural resources,[4] the majority of which are located in the ancestral lands of indigenous and Afro-descendant communities. Such control would serve as a stepping-stone to securing the United States' hegemonic position in the hemisphere, as a counterforce to the growing power of the European Union. This ambition was substantiated by Colin Powell during his time as secretary of state: Washington intended, he said, "to guarantee for North American companies the control of the territory from the Arctic Pole to Antarctica and free access without any obstacle or difficulty to products, services, and technology, and capital in all of the Hemisphere" (quoted in Acosta et al. 2006, 55).

Indigenous leaders refer to this hemispheric plan as recolonization.[5] While such territorial control denotes political and economic dominion, it also represents, from the perspective of indigenous communities, a dominion over culture, nature, and being. In Andean cosmology, these elements are inextricably entwined in a world where the living occupy three interrelated spaces: "*Kay pacha* is the space where we currently are and where identity, culture, and organization develop along with our means of life. *Hanan pacha* is the space above where life also exists. *Uku pacha* is the subsoil. And all of these three spaces belong to and are part of us. In essence, territory is our thought, actions, and life in our Mother Earth; . . . it is what unites us and gives us life" (Minga Informativa de Movimientos Sociales 2007).

Seen from this "other" logic, rationality, and perspective, the success of U.S.-controlled free trade resides in part in its ability to eliminate indigenous cosmologies and peoples (or at least to relegate them nonexistent), physically or by other means, including through their "modernization" and incorporation into the market. As I have argued elsewhere (Walsh 2002), this modernization and incorporation of indigenous peoples and Afro-descendants is an integral part of neoliberal multiculturalism—what Zizek (1997) refers to as the "cultural logic of multinational capitalism." This is clearly reflected in the constitutional reforms of Latin America in the 1990s and the multilateral policies that, in large part, have governed and oriented them. These reforms and policies, which recognized indigenous and black peoples and their ancestral rights in nations like Colombia and Ecuador, were essentially a double-edged sword (Van Cott 2000). On the one hand, they gave status to historical demands, and on the other, they used these "officialized" demands to include, co-opt, manipulate, and control opposition—particularly opposition related to the protection of land and natural resources. However, as I will discuss later, the new constitutions adopted by Ecuador (September 2008) and Bolivia (January 2009) turn this logic of neoliberal multiculturalism on its head.

In this sense, the geopolitics of U.S.-controlled free trade is not only about capitalism; it is also, and in a totally related way, about the control of culture, nature, knowledge, and being within and central to capitalism. The effect and effectiveness of such politics can be witnessed in the increasing individualization of indigenous and Afro leaders; in these leaders' co-optation and corruption; in the ruptures, divisions, and debilitation within organizations and movements; and in communities' concession of lands to transnational companies for the exploitation of oil and other natural resources. Such processes are particularly evident in Ecuador, where, since the mid-1990s, successive governments have worked to break the force of the indigenous movement, which was until recently the strongest in Latin America. This strategy of disintegration was, in essence, achieved in 2003 with the presidential election of Colonel Lucio Gutiérrez and an ostensible military-indigenous government alliance that lasted for eight months. Through these events, the indigenous movement lost its critical force as an oppositional movement that had historically worked outside of and against the hegemony of the nation-state structure (Walsh 2002). Also lost, or at least greatly weakened, was its capacity for national mobilization, its positioning as a major social and political actor, and its effectiveness in building ties between the national leadership and the community bases.[6]

The strategy of disintegration and division, in fact, is integral to the geopolitics of neoliberalism and to the overall success of FTAs, not only in terms of indigenous organizations and movements, but also in terms of nation-states. In its operation of negotiations throughout the region, the North American–Andean FTA's apparent aim is to establish dominance over each individual nation and thereby rupture integration among Andean countries, including the regional integration conceived in the Andean Community of Nations, leaving each country to negotiate on its own and, in effect, to compete against its neighbors. By breaking up a potential regional political-economic-social force, the United States can secure the field for its own model of integration.

In the Andes, the emergence of such a model is evident in U.S.-controlled regional militarization, justified by the so-called war on drugs, and most especially in relation to Plan Colombia, in which the role of FTAs is strategic and fundamental. The link between the North American–Andean FTA and Plan Colombia was made clear in a November 2003 letter written by former U.S. commercial representative Robert Zoellick to J. Dennis Hastert, then Speaker of the House of Representatives. In the letter, Zoellick argued that an "FTA with the Andean countries . . . will serve as a natural complement to Plan Colombia, to which the Congress, over the years, has given significant support" (quoted in Acosta et al. 2006, 94). It is in this context that the FTA between Colombia and the United States appears particularly strategic for both nations. The Colombian government has worked, with the Bush administration's backing, to get the needed support in its own congress as well as that of the United States. In the first half of 2007, Colombia spent $100,000 on lobbying each month, and it contracted prestigious U.S. public relations firms and pressure groups, many of which have strong ties to former president Bill Clinton, to assist in the effort to persuade democratic legislators to vote in favor of the North American–Andean FTA (*El Hoy* 2007).

How are we to understand this geopolitics of free trade in the Andean region in all of its multiple dimensions? Are the frameworks anchored in Western modernity and in models of late capitalism—including those evoked by authors like Fredric Jameson, Anthony Giddens, Michael Hardt, Antonio Negri, and Immanuel Wallerstein, among others—sufficient? What might it mean instead (or at least additionally) to take seriously the arguments and thought of indigenous movements—that is, that free trade is "a new form of invasion and colonization"? How might this perspective on the struggles and ongoing reality of coloniality, as lived by indigenous peoples (and, in different ways, as lived by Afro-descendants), afford an "other" view that reveals modernity's hidden face of domination, instrumental to the emerging global capitalism?

Free Trade and Coloniality

As the United States has made increasingly clear, indigenous peoples are an obstacle to FTAs and to the full implementation of neoliberal policies. Such a perception is not new; Indians in Latin America have always been viewed as a hindrance to modernization. Domingo Faustino Sarmiento, considered one of the most important Latin American thinkers of the nineteenth century, made this evident when he said, "The Indian represents barbarism and, as such, it is necessary to eliminate him in order to open the way to progress and civilization" (quoted in Sacoto 1994, 54).

Indigenous peoples' perception of the correlation between U.S.-controlled free trade and colonization is, in fact, grounded in the history of Abya Yala (the Americas) and in the establishment of certain models of power that have remained constant over the last 515 years. For Anibal Quijano, "globalization is the culmination of this process that began with the constitution of America and colonial/modern Eurocentered capitalism as a new global power" (2000, 533). The fundamental base of this power is the relationship that it constructs between race and capitalism, thus forming a structure for the control of labor as well as knowledge, being, and nature. Quijano writes,

America was constituted as the first space/time of a new model of power of global vocation, and both in this way and by it became the first identity of modernity. Two historical processes associated in the production of that space/time converged and established the two fundamental axles of the new model of power. One was the codification of the differences between conquerors and conquered in the idea of "race," a supposedly different biological structure that placed some in a natural situation of inferiority to the others. The other process was the constitution of a new structure of control of labor and its resources and products

. . . together around and upon the basis of capitalism and the world
market. (2000, 533–34)

In this way, race and the new social identities it produced in the Americas
(Indians, blacks, and mestizos) became fundamental criteria for the distribution of the population into ranks, places, and social roles that were both necessary for the development and maintenance of the structure of power and
useful in the control, exploitation, and division of labor.[7] This specific model
of global hegemonic power—the coloniality of power—not only bestowed
white Europeans with superiority but also positioned European or Western
hegemony at the center of an emergent global capitalism and global cultural
order. Europe had control of the world market. Slavery was established to
produce goods for this market and to serve the needs of capitalism; the serf-
dom of Indians was organized for the same ends. Europe also had control
over subjectivity, culture, and the production of knowledge in the Americas.
In this process of domination, the colonizers

> expropriated the cultural discoveries of the colonized most apt for the
> development of capitalism to the profit of the European center.
> . . . [They] repressed as much as possible the colonized forms of knowl-
> edge production, the models of the production of meaning, their sym-
> bolic universe, the model of expression and of objectification and
> subjectivity. . . . [And] they forced the colonized to learn the dominant
> culture in any way that would be useful to the reproduction of domina-
> tion. (Quijano 2000, 541)

It is this history to which indigenous people refer when they draw the connection between free trade and colonization—a history that has worked to reproduce and maintain the inferiority of Indians and blacks, while allowing
colonizers to expropriate their knowledge, exploit their labor, invade their
lands, and work to draw them into the capitalist system.

Of course, this model of power also extends to the construction and configuration of Latin America, in which the countries of the Southern Cone
(Argentina, Chile, and Uruguay) are considered the Europe of the South,
while the Andes (particularly Ecuador, Peru, and Bolivia) are the backward
nations, due in large part to their indigenous composition. The use of race as
a basic category through which to establish superiority in the social and material realms was particularly evident in Alcides Arguedas's well-known text
Pueblo enfermo, written about his native Bolivia: "If there hadn't been a predominance of indigenous blood, from the beginning it would have been possible to give the country a conscious orientation of its life, adopting every
form of perfections in the material and moral order. If this had happened,
today we would be at the same level as other societies, favored by waves

of immigration from the old continent (e.g., Chile, Argentina, Uruguay)" (1909, 8).

Coloniality and modernity go hand in hand (Mignolo 2001). And the effects of both extend to the very concerns of being, knowledge, and nature. The development of science and knowledge among white men in Europe, for instance, reflects coloniality's operation. Eurocentrism became the only perspective of knowledge—a perspective that Latin American elites have long worked to adopt. In this frame, Indians and blacks were viewed as intellectually incapable, inferior, and even childlike. Such perceptions persist today, locating these groups in the realm of tradition and folklore, never in the realms of intellectual leadership, knowledge, and science. Of course, the manifestation of such Cartesian perceptions is clearly observed in present-day Bolivia; the representations and criticisms of President Evo Morales voiced by national elites continue to find ground in references to savagery, barbarism, and backwardness—that is, to the racialized category of "not modern."

The promotion of a relationship between race and knowledge is what the African philosopher Emmanuel Chukwudi Eze (2001) refers to as "the color of reason," a position that has clearly oriented Western philosophy and contemporary social thought since the eighteenth century. Probably the most evident representation of such thinking can be found in the philosophic anthropology of Kant: "Humanity exists in its perfection in the white race. . . . The blacks are inferior, and the most inferior are the [native] American peoples" (quoted in Eze 2001, 231). This bond between humanity and reason marks a third dimension: the coloniality of being, which points not so much to an ontological violence but more to the preferential character of the violence implicated in and by the coloniality of power—that is to say, the "colonized being," who has his or her roots in and with history, and in and with space or place (Maldonado-Torres 2004).

But we can also identify a fourth dimension of coloniality, which, particularly in the Andes, is integrally related to the other three. I refer to this dimension as the coloniality of Mother Nature; it finds its foundation in the Cartesian binary division of nature and society. Such a binary division completely negates the millennial relationship among humans, plants, and animals, as well as the relationship between these living beings and the spiritual world, including that of the ancestors—understood as also living. The coloniality of Mother Nature has worked to erase and eliminate the relationality and complementarity that is central to life, cosmology, and thought in most indigenous and Afro-descendant communities of the Andes. It is this rationalist logic that, as Noboa (2006) maintains, denies both the notion that the earth—the "body of nature"—is a living being with its own forms of intelligence, feelings, and spirituality, and the belief that human beings are elements of earth-nature.

As such, the coloniality of Mother Nature adds a fundamental element to the models of power discussed in this chapter: this is the dominion over the cultural rationalities that, in essence, form the foundations of being and knowledge in the Andes. It is the continual relationship of being with thought, and with knowledge and knowing, that finds its ground in the fluid connection among three worlds: the biophysical world below, the spiritual or supernatural world above, and the human world of now. In exerting its dominion, the coloniality of Mother Nature "mythicizes" this connection and relationship. That is to say, it converts it into myth, legend, and folklore. At the same time, it positions the connection and relationship as nonrational—as the invention of nonmodern or premodern beings. In this way, the coloniality of Mother Nature works to eliminate and control the sustenance, meanings, and understandings of life itself—that is, of place, territory, and *pachamama*—replacing them with a delocated, Western, modern rationality that endeavors to govern everyone.

In a similar vein, Leff (2000, 2004) argues that the relationship among nature, knowledge, and being is, in essence, what we might understand as "environment." For him, environment represents

> the field of relations between nature and culture, of the material and the symbolic, of the complexity of being and thought; a knowledge about the strategies of appropriation of the world and nature through/ by means of the power relations that are inscribed in the dominant forms of knowledge. It is environmental knowledge that weaves, in a complex weft, knowledges, thoughts, cosmovisions, and discursive formations, going beyond the limits of the scientific logos and opening a dialogue of knowledges in which diverse rationalities and traditions are made to confront. (2004, 4–5)

Both the environmental knowledge of which Leff speaks and Mother Nature as I have posed it here open other routes to understand and confront the problem of modernity/coloniality and its ties to the current geopolitics of free trade. These avenues are based in social experience and the epistemologies that are built from it, and in the ancestral cosmology and philosophy of existence that give meaning to this experience and to life. As the next section makes clear, the struggles of indigenous movements against the North American–Andean FTA have everything to do with this cosmology, philosophy, and way of life-being. More than a simple discord with state politics and the capitalist-imperial imposition of market control, these struggles are grounded in a historical resistance in defense of existence and life, in which the nature-knowledge-being relationship is primordial.

The North American–Andean FTA and Indigenous Movements

In the Andean region, the indigenous-led opposition to neoliberal policies and to the North American–Andean FTA is part and parcel of centuries of struggle that, in the present, are moving beyond resistance toward the creation and construction of an improved way and form of life. This is what Evo Morales refers to in Aymara as *suma qamaña* or in Spanish as *vivir bien* (to live well), a key principle also incorporated into the new Ecuadorian Constitution as *sumak kawsay* (in Kichwa) or *buen vivir,* understood, in both cases, not in terms of per capita income and "living better" than others, but in terms of cultural identity, community, and harmony with Mother Earth, or Nature, and all of her species.[8] This opposition is distinct from those conceived primarily from the perspective of economy, politics, and the market; it has a different and much wider base, with existence and humanity at its core. Imperialism, including the North American–Andean FTA, represents the "culture of death," as opposed to the "culture of life" that indigenous nations defend. It is in this context that the peoples and nations of Abya Yala have begun to declare themselves the "watchmen of the future of humanity" (Continental Encounter of Indigenous Pueblos and Nations of Abya Yala 2006).

The struggle against imperialism, neoliberalism, and the new forms of colonization reflected in the North American–Andean FTA serves as the foundation for emergent efforts to consolidate a continental indigenous movement, and for the re-creation of societies and states in which the millenary principles of complementarity, reciprocity, and duality, and the ancestral rights of territory, Mother Nature, autonomy, and free determination, occupy a central, contemporary role. Such elements constituted the *manifiesto* of the Third Indigenous Summit held in Guatemala in March 2007. In ratifying their rejection of FTAs and other imposed trade mechanisms, promising continued vigilance against future agreements of so-called free trade, and delineating steps toward a political platform that would oppose neoliberal policies that annihilate Mother Nature, the sons and daughters of the indigenous peoples and first nations of the continent announced "the continental resurgence of *Pachakutik* (the return), the closure of *Oxlajuj Baq'tun,* the long account of 5,200 years, and the approach of the new *Baq'tun,* directing us toward the making of *Abya Yala,* a 'land full of life.'"[9] This association of neoliberalism and free trade with the struggle for existence and life—a struggle clearly decolonial in nature—marks a logic and rationality quite distinct from that of most treatises against free trade.

In Ecuador, more than any other nation, the indigenous movement has, over the last twenty years, taken the lead in placing the neoliberal project in constant tension, limiting privatizations to the lowest level in Latin America, alerting the populace to the dangers of free trade, and assuring that the governments in turn do not sign the country off to U.S. interests. As one of the smallest nations in the region, Ecuador is famous for its popular overthrow of presidents (three since 1997) and for its dollarization; it is the only Latin American country other than Panama in which the U.S. dollar is the only currency (since 2000). Dollarization was the "response" to the deep economic crisis that resulted, in large part, from the growth of a massive public debt over three decades, the taking of money from the Central Bank by a succession of presidents, and the complicity of governments with multinational banks, corporations, and foreign aid missions as part of what Perkins (2004) refers to as a "corporatocracy." During these three decades, official poverty rose from 50 to 70 percent (reaching 90 percent in rural indigenous and black communities). Furthermore, the share of natural resources allocated to the poorest sectors of the population declined from 20 to 6 percent (Perkins 2004).

Despite the devastating effects that the North American–Andean FTA could have in Ecuador, particularly in agriculture—close to 4 million persons (almost a third of the national population) depend on farming activities—no other sector of society has demonstrated the determined opposition of the indigenous movement. Among the so-called left, up until the election of Rafael Correa, there was little debate, discussion, or comprehension of the North American–Andean FTA. In fact, in March 2006, progressive sectors strongly criticized indigenous mobilizations and actions opposing then president Alfredo Palacios's potential negotiations with the commissions of free trade, claiming that these actions were "antidemocratic," caused chaos, and blocked the "progress" of the nation.[10] The interpretation by those in power was that the indigenous movement was unwilling to negotiate with the state. Of course, the supposition here is that indigenous peoples are not part of society; they only destabilize and impede government and the social order.

Yet, in this context of opposition, what remains unrecognized is that what is really at stake with the North American–Andean FTA are national sovereignty and the defense of life for all Ecuadorians. In the Confederation of Indigenous Nationalities of Ecuador's (CONAIE's) declaration, presented to the nation and to the world on March 23, 2006, in anticipation of social protests, the organization stated,

> We have manifested to the government our indeclinable willingness to obey the mandates of our organizations to defend national sovereignty; the mobilization in defense of life and of sovereignty is not negotiable. The indigenous nationalities and peoples . . . have once again given an example of resistance to neoliberalism. . . . We wish to stress that the country does not belong to four or five big businessmen who have kidnapped the government of Alfredo Palacios, as the president of a

regimen that pursues the surrender of the country's resources to foreign interests. (CONAIE 2006, 97)

What followed were protest marches that virtually paralyzed the country for a three-week period, reestablishing the force of the movement after the serious fragmentation and debilitation that had resulted in 2003 from its alliance with the Gutiérrez government. The protests were based on a platform of four demands: the cessation of the government's FTA negotiations with the United States and the holding of a public consultation; the decision not to renew the contract with Occidental Oil; the nation's refusal to be involved in Plan Colombia and the return of the military base in Manta to Ecuadorians; and the convocation of a National Constituent Assembly to reform the political constitution (Larrea Maldonado 2006).[11] However, while these demands represented issues of deep concern for the entire nation, the opposition and government responded by using the race card. They accused indigenous people of ethnic-racial and national division, employed the military to pull every person who looked indigenous or had an indigenous surname off the buses traveling to the capital, placed key indigenous leaders in jail, and called for a national mestizo countermobilization.[12]

Of course, as has been true since colonial times, it is assumed that indigenous leaders are incapable of such massive mobilization and organization. In fact, one article in El Comercio referenced the "intellectual incapacity" of CONAIE's then president Luis Macas—a lawyer, former congressman, former minister of agriculture, and former chancellor of the Indigenous Intercultural University.[13] Such a comment reconstructs, once again, the coloniality of knowledge and of power. The press and national authorities proclaimed that there must be others behind the protest, accusing Chávez and the Venezuelan government along with Spanish nongovernmental organizations (NGOs) of Basque origin. On television and in the written press, large business owners, particularly those tied to the flower industry, were positioned as speakers of the real truth in the name of modernity, national progress, and future advancement. In the dominant discourse and rhetoric, as well as in the racial confrontations between white-mestizos and Indians in the provinces, the colonial dichotomy of civilization and barbarism regained centrality.

Yet, despite the organized opposition, the mobilizations won out. The signing of the North American–Andean FTA was placed on hold until the next presidential election, then permanently detained in 2007 with the election of Correa (an election made possible, in large part, by the 2006 indigenous mobilizations and their evidencing of the dangers of the FTA).[14] But again, what is notable is not only the victory against the North American–Andean FTA as such, but also how and by whom it was achieved. That is to say, as has been true since the first massive indigenous uprising in 1990, it has been the indigenous movement and its organizations in Ecuador that have slowed neoliberal privatizations and made evident the political negotiations and dynamics of free trade, including its colonial-imperial intentions.[15] Due to the movement's agency, today we are witnessing the exhaustion of neoliberalism, as an alliance of forces and interests (the result of the 2006 mobilizations) make it apparent that the dominant elite no longer have the capacity to build, govern, and control the country (Moreano 2006). Certainly, this alliance is now operating on a regional scale, as evidenced in an emergent continental indigenous force and in the new regional anti-imperial politics led by Hugo Chávez in Venezuela, Evo Morales in Bolivia, and Rafael Correa in Ecuador.

Regional Alternatives

In May 2007, more than seven hundred social and popular movement leaders gathered in Havana at the Sixth Hemispheric Encounter against FTAs and for integration to continue their assessment of the struggles surrounding free trade and to strengthen efforts toward a common articulation and regional alternative. The event's coordinators argued that processes like the Bolivarian Alternative for the Americas (ALBA), the People's Trade Agreement (PTA), the Union of South American Nations, and other initiatives helped configure a new, more just, and rational economic map.

The urgency of regional alternatives had been stressed several months earlier by South American indigenous movement leaders: "We are alerted to the incoherence of a 'South American Community of Nations,' where some opt for self-development and others for an outside-controlled subordination; we demand the implementation of regional sovereign proposals such as ALBA, the People's Trade Agreement, and the proposal to 'live well'" (García Mérida 2006). These manifestos make evident the broader nature of the struggle—a struggle not just against imperial/colonial free trade but, more important, for cooperation, social justice, and life. It is a struggle that has worked to weaken the unipolar nature of U.S. hegemony while building a regional integration that enables a multipolar world (Sader 2007). ALBA is a clear example of a regional integration process and a revolutionary alternative that transcends the Free Trade Area of the Americas (ALCA).

ALBA began in late 2004 as a joint initiative of Hugo Chávez and Fidel Castro. It focused on fair trade and the notion that each country could trade what it had: in the case of Venezuela, crude oil, and in the case of Cuba, highly trained personnel in the areas of medicine, education, and sports. Later, the initiative came to include structural and strategic integration toward an anticapitalist model of twenty-first-century socialism that emphasizes political, social, and economic complementarity and collaboration, as a counterproposal to U.S.-sponsored free trade. Bolivia joined ALBA in April 2006, followed by Nicaragua in 2007, Dominica and Honduras in 2008, and Ecuador in 2009.

In contrast to the market gains that ALCA seeks, ALBA constructs a model based on the application of just trade, solidarity, and cooperation. This model advocates a socially oriented trade block rather than a trade block based on the logic of deregulated profit maximization; it appeals to the egalitarian principles of justice and equality, focusing on the well-being of the most dispossessed sectors of society and promoting a reinvigorated sense of solidarity with undeveloped societies so that they can enter into trade negotiations on more favorable terms. Additionally, ALBA seeks to achieve a regional integration that transcends the prerogatives of the transnational corporations (TNCs), and it pushes for solidarity with the economically weakest countries, aiming to achieve a free trade area in which all of its members benefit. Finally, it provides a compensatory fund for structural convergence as a way to manage and distribute financial aid to the most economically vulnerable nations, thus encouraging endogenous development; prioritizing agriculture and food self-sufficiency over profit-making processes; protecting genetic biodiversity and traditional knowledge against intellectual property rights regimes; and providing public services aimed at fulfilling basic needs instead of the interests of business and profit.

ALBA's conceptualization is based on key elements that are unthinkable within the parameters of capitalism: complementarity based on national potential, cooperation, solidarity, and respect for the sovereignty of each country. It also conceives a form of integration that does not derive from the commercial, but rather from the political and the social, implying popular mobilization. By including a Council of Social Movements along with the Council of Presidents and the Council of Ministers in its structure, ALBA seeks to build an "other" notion of governance and participation:

> ALBA has become the new historical horizon of Latin America and the Caribbean, from which progressive forces have to think [about] their identity, objectives, and forms of action. It constitutes an exemplary model of the application of "just trade," of solidarity, of cooperation. [It is] an alternative space of free trade, of dominion of the market, revealing concretely how it is that in the exchange between necessities and possibilities that ends in illiteracy, family agriculture and food security can be strengthened and the power of vision can be returned to millions of people. In sum, it is where the needs of the population are placed above those of the market and the accumulation of capital. (Sader 2007, 2)

As such, ALBA is much more than an agreement of free trade. It is a process of integration shaped by cooperation, not for market gain. In the fight against illiteracy, for attention to health, and for access to education—together with concrete actions to reach integration in the areas of energy, infrastructure, and culture—ALBA shows its essential difference from the anemic and commercialist integration practiced until now. Its advances are already evident. They include the tripling of internal trade among members and the securing of energy stability; an increase in agricultural production; and, with the help of Cuba, the reduction of illiteracy in Venezuela, Bolivia, and Nicaragua. The creation of a regional monetary zone that will entail a unified common account, enabling and facilitating homologous transactions, compensatory funds, and a common currency has begun.

ALBA also includes a bank housed in Caracas with branch offices in member countries. It began with a sum of $100 million contributed by member countries based on their individual financial capacities. The ALBA Bank has been charged with the financing of multinational regional projects of member countries, the granting of soft credit, and the settling of economic disputes. Furthermore, in line with ALBA and proposals for an "other" integration, is the Bank of the South (Banco del Sur), an effort formally agreed upon in June 2008 by Venezuela, Bolivia, Argentina, Paraguay, Brazil, Uruguay, and Ecuador. The Bank of the South is based on the need for the creation of a different financial structure, with deposits coming principally from the public banks and the federal reserves of the Southern countries. As Ecuador's former minister of economy Ricardo Patino indicated in 2007,

> Our countries have all this money deposited [in U.S. and European banks], earning low rates of interest. However, we are asking the World Bank, the International Monetary Fund, and the International Development Bank to help us solve our financial problems, when, in reality, we have an immense wealth of savings that could be used for these same aims without having to fall into the conditionalities that these organisms impose. . . . In 2005, IDB loaned $4.898 billion, the World Bank $5.087 billion, and the Andean Corporation of Promotion $1.337 billion. Adding up everything, we have $11.322 billion and another $164 million in reserves. That is ten times more than the credits we receive with all kinds of conditions attached to them. (Quoted in Tamayo 2007)

According to the Ecuadorian economist Pablo Dávalos, the creation of the Bank of the South should be seen not only from a financial perspective but also from a geopolitical and epistemic perspective. That is to say, it represents a vision that implies the reformulation of the content of financing for development, a rethinking of integration from the criteria of complementarity and subsidizing, and a thinking of "our own" (*pensamiento propio*) outside the frames of neoliberalism (Tamayo 2007).

The PTA is another example of a regional alternative to the neoliberal model of deregulation, privatization, and an indiscriminate opening of markets. The PTA, conceived by Bolivian president Evo Morales and signed by Venezuela, Cuba, and Nicaragua, poses trade and investment not as ends in themselves but as means of satisfying basic needs and promoting a notion of productive development for the benefit of people. It is primarily based on the principle of "just trade," creating a model of trade integration among peoples that limits and regulates foreign investors and TNCs. It recognizes the right of peoples to define their own agriculture and alimentary politics, and to protect and regulate national farming production in order to avoid a flooding of the domestic market with other nations' surplus goods. It seeks to assure nations that basic services will not be turned over to the market but rather will be dependent on public companies regulated by the state. Further, the model prioritizes complementarity over competition, and coexistence with nature in contraposition to the irrational exploitation of resources, including the defense of social property over external privatization. The PTA urges its members to pursue solidarity-based integration that gives priority to national businesses as the exclusive providers for public institutions. In sum, it promotes an integration that transcends commerce and economics and finds its ground in a philosophy of just, endogenous, and sustainable development based on communitarian and indigenous principals, including complementarity and reciprocity, and it takes both national and cultural differences into account (United Nations Research Institute for Social Development [UNRISD] 2006).

In its formulation and intention, PTA puts forward an "other" logic of coexistence that seeks equity and complementarity among countries and peoples and with nature. As such, it intentionally differs from the neoliberal model of free trade organized around competition, accumulation, privatization, the indiscriminate and irrational exploitation of natural resources and labor, and the uniformity of the market. Its philosophical base reflects and constructs what Andean indigenous peoples refer to as *vivir bien* (to live well), the cosmological paradigm that orients the present Bolivian government led by Morales as well as his proposal for a real South American Community of Nations:[16]

> Our integration is and should be an integration of and for the people. Trade, energy, infrastructure, and finance should be in function of resolving the great problems of poverty and the destruction of nature in our region. We cannot reduce the South American Community to an association that promotes highway projects or credit that ends up favoring sectors tied to the world market. Our goal is to forge a true integration to "live well." We say "live well" because we do not aspire to live

better than others. We do not believe in the line of progress and development without limits and at the cost of others and of nature. We need to complement one another and not compete. We need to share and not take advantage of our neighbour. To "live well" is to think not only in terms of per capita income but rather in terms of cultural identity, of community, of harmony between us and our mother earth. (Morales, quoted in Agencia Latinoamericana de Información 2006)

In this sense, *vivir bien* denotes a very different paradigm of life and civilization grounded in indigenous cosmological principals that not only challenge the neoliberal paradigm but, more importantly, turn it on its face. The option here is for life, not for death and destruction.

Taken together, ALBA, the Bank of the South, and PTA afford real regional alternatives and innovations. The alternative and innovation of the Bank of the South rest in its proposed egalitarian and democratic governance and design, which purport to disrupt the hegemonic dominion and unilateral power of credit systems operated by Western multilateral institutions. Similarly, ALBA and PTA construct models of integration, cooperation, and commerce that are the antitheses of the FTAs and the free trade zones of the Americas. But more than just affording alternatives, these new emergent models are indicative of a broader social, political, and epistemic force—a force that is engendered by indigenous and social movements and popular sectors, and is working to decolonize and refound knowledge, life, and nature, as well as the state. Herein lies the challenge and opportunity.

Conclusion

As this chapter has endeavored to show, the FTAs proposed by the United States for Andean nations are part and parcel of a new colonial-imperial strategy. It is a strategy that goes way beyond the regulation of commercial exchange, encompassing, in a much more critical sense, the control of knowledge, life, and nature.

Free trade and colonization clearly correlate. And, as I have argued here, it is this correlation that enables a very different perspective of the aims and effects of development and global trade, and of the reaccommodation and reconcentration of political and economic power—that is, of global capitalism. Such a perspective, grounded in the lived reality of coloniality as modernity's other, hidden side, is made manifest in the political-historical and epistemic agency of the region's indigenous movements. These movements are providing the challenge to the North American–Andean FTA, but more important, they are making its disrobement possible. Again, the significance of such challenge and intervention lies in an "other" perspective, one that is distinct from the resistance and compliance typically associated with social movements and "civil" society (concepts that clearly depart from a Euro-American logic and perspective).

Such significance also prompts a consideration of what it might mean to engage and dialogue *with* (not study *about*) indigenous logics and perspectives of "others"—to make visible and understand not only the actions of social and political opposition but also the "other" thinking and rationalities, and the "other" decolonial paradigms of civilization and of life that these movements, communities, and peoples enable and construct for both themselves and the planet. It is these paradigms—together with the alternatives to neoliberalism and free trade that are emerging in the region—and the creation of new designs of society and state that offer fresh promises of existence and life. These promises are rooted not in Western modernity's "well-being," or the "good life" for some, but in the integral harmony of all the living: *sumak kawsay* or *suma qamaña*.

NOTES

1. Abya Yala, meaning "land in full maturity," is the name coined by the Kunas in Panama to refer to the territory and indigenous nations of the Americas. For Muyulema (2001), this naming has double significance, as a political positioning and as a way to confront the colonial weight present in "Latin America," understood as a cultural project of westernization and ideologically articulated in *mestizaje*. As Ticona (2005) points out, "The 'recategorizing' of names, such as *Abya Yala*, means a rethinking of decolonialization from the experience of kichua and aymara peoples and from their ethical-political values." Of course, the problem is that while Abya Yala recuperates indigenous roots, it leaves out the presence and struggles of African descendants, who, particularly in the Andean region, continue to be treated as nonexistent (see Walsh and León, 2007).

2. Jairo Chicamá, indigenous ethnoeducator in the Department of Risaralda, Colombia, quoted in Díaz (2005).

3. On March 31, 1999, the Ecuadorian government signed a ten-year agreement with the United States for the leasing of logistical facilities in Manta, on Ecuador's Pacific coast. This made Manta one of four U.S. cooperative security centers; the other three are located in El Salvador, Aruba, and Curacao. The Manta agreement involved an air base, a naval base, the port, and all of the areas neighboring this infrastructure. Initially proposed as a base focused on fighting the drug trade, numerous reports have revealed that the Manta Base's real purpose was to provide logistical support for the counterinsurgency war in Colombia. This was in fact corroborated by Javier Delucca, the former commander of the U.S. Advanced Security Operations Site at the base: "The Manta Base is very important within Plan Colombia. We are very well situated to operate in this area" (quoted in Serrano 2008). The base also exercises immigration control by locating boats carrying people who are trying to reach the United States in search of the so-called American dream. Furthermore, Ecuadorian media uncovered several attempts by the U.S. company DynCorp to convert Manta into a center for recruiting mercenaries (Saavedra 2007). The base was closed in 2009.

4. Such interest was clearly established in the First International Conference of American States held in Washington, D.C. at the end of the nineteenth century; in Nelson Rockefeller's and the U.S. Security Commission's attempt to gain control of oil and other natural resources in Latin America in the first half of the twentieth century; and in George H. W.

Bush's initiative for the Americas in 1990, including the subsequent Free Trade Area of the Americas (see Acosta et al. 2006 and Colby 1995).

5. Interview with Eduardo Cholango, president of the Confederation of Peoples of Kichwa Nationality (ECUARUNARI), January 2005.

6. Similar processes are evident in black movements in Colombia. Álvaro Uribe's appointment of a black woman (a former consultant to the United States Agency for International Development [USAID]) as minister of culture in 2007 reflects the same kind of strategy. This strategy also included ties between the Uribe government and republican Afro-American legislators during George W. Bush's presidency. In this case, "blackness" became a tool for establishing relations with black communities along the Pacific coast of Colombia—relations that involved the offer of financial support for "development" projects. Of course, the fact that this region is strategically key for the North American–Andean FTA and part of the Plan Puebla, which includes the biogeographical region of Chocó, extending from Panama to the north of Ecuador, is no mere coincidence.

7. These new social identities, in effect, aimed to eliminate the diversity in histories, languages, memories, and identities, as well as the articulation of such differences with ancestral lands. All of these differences were merged into single, homogeneous, and negative identities: "Indians" or "Indios," and "blacks" or "Negros."

8. This notion of "living well" is at the core of both Bolivia's and Ecuador's new constitutions.

9. See the "Declaración de Iximche" of the III Cumbre Continental de Pueblos y Nacionalidades Indígenas del Abya Yala: De la Resistencia al Poder, Iximulew, Guatemala, March 30, 2007.

10. Of course, one might ask about the meanings of "democracy" and "progress" in operation here. This question would also apply to "chaos," particularly given the fact that over the course of eleven months of governance, the Palacios government faced fifty-two strikes by multiple sectors of society.

11. While none of these demands were initially met in 2006, all were achieved by 2007 with the election of Correa.

12. In Ecuador, the term "mestizo" is part of a discourse of power that has been used historically to mark national identity, subalternizing indigenous peoples, negating or folklorizing indigenous heritage, and strengthening the coloniality of power. It is interesting to note that in times of indigenous mobilizations, uprisings, and demands for change, "mestizo-ness" becomes the rallying cry of conservative sectors (see Walsh 2009).

13. This occurred on the same day that El Comercio named Macas the "person of the week" for his rehabilitation of the indigenous movement. In the newspaper as well as a public announcement on national television, the secretaries of communication and state attacked Macas, questioning his knowledge of agriculture and challenging him to a televised debate so that "he can tell us how much he knows about agriculture and so that he can show to the people that what he is building is a plot against the nation" (El Comercio 2006a, 6).

14. Such dangers include (1) the dismantling and destruction of the small domestic economy and indigenous and peasants' agricultural production; (2) the destruction and privatization of natural resources (flora, fauna, water), biodiversity, and ancestral knowledge, and related issues of intellectual property rights; (3) transnational oil exploitation resulting in contamination, displacement, disease, and death; (4) an increase in the price of medications and the disappearance of generic drugs from the market; and (5) drastic increases in poverty, undernutrition, and unemployment.

15. While the actual implementation of neoliberal policy has occurred to a lesser degree in Ecuador than in neighboring countries, its impact is still significant. For example, between 1980 and 1996, the minimum salary was reduced by 48 percent; unemployment figures between 1990 and 2004 increased from 6 to 11 percent; and expenditures in education, health, and agriculture were greatly reduced, together accounting for less than 10.5 percent of the national budget in 2004. In the period 2000–2001, Ecuador was one of the

lowest-ranking Latin American countries with regard to social expenditure—at $131 per capita—followed only by Guatemala, El Salvador, Honduras, and Nicaragua (Moreano 2006).

16. As previously mentioned, it is also the principle that orients the new Ecuadorian Constitution, approved by a wide margin in the popular referendum held on September 28, 2008. What in Ecuador is referred to as *buen vivir*, or *sumak kawsay* in Kichwa, is explicitly reflected in seventy-five articles of the Constitution, including in such diverse areas as education, health, social security, housing, culture, social communication, science, technology, ancestral knowledge, biodiversity, ecological systems, alternative energy, labor, and Latin American integration, among others. See Walsh (2009).

REFERENCES

Acosta, Alberto, Fander Falcón, Hugo Jácome, and René Ramírez. 2006. *El rostro oculto del TLC*. Quito: Abya Yala.

Agencia Latinoamericana de Información. 2006. "Evo Morales propone CSN para 'vivir bien.'" *América Latina en Movimiento*. October 5. http://alainet.org/active/13718& lang = es.

Arguedas, Alcides. 1909. *Pueblo enfermo*. La Paz: Juventud.

Colby, Gerard. 1995. *Thy Will Be Done: The Conquest of the Amazon: Nelson Rockefeller and Evangelism in the Age of Oil*. New York: HarperCollins.

El Comercio. 2006a. "La Conaie insiste en el bloqueo." March 18.

———. 2006b. "Provocan una reacción represiva?" Opinión. March 22, 4.

Confederación de Nacionalidades Indígenas del Ecuador (CONAIE). 2006. "Declaración de la CONAIE al país y al mundo." *Revista del Observatorio Social de América Latina* 19 (July): 95–97.

Continental Encounter of Indigenous Pueblos and Nations of Abya Yala. 2006. "Declaration of La Paz: Continental Encounter of Indigenous Pueblos and Nations of Abya Yala." October 12. http://www.internationalfunders.org/images2/Declarationof LaPaz.pdf.

Diario HOY. 2007. "Colombia hace lobby en favor del TLC." Dinero. June 5, 2.

Díaz, Christian. 2005. "El TLC y su incidencia sobre los pueblos indígenas de Colombia." February 28. http://www.bilaterals.org/article.php3?id_article = 1370.

Escobar, Arturo. 2005. *Más allá del tercer mundo: Globalización y diferencia*. Bogotá: Instituto Colombiano de Antropología e Historia and Universidad del Cauca.

Eze, Emmanuel Chukwudi. 2001. "El color de la razón: Las ideas de 'raza' en la antropología de Kant." In *Capitalismo y geopolítica del conocimiento: El eurocentrismo y la filosofía de la liberación en el debate intelectual contemporaneo*, edited by W. Mignolo, 201–52. Buenos Aires: Ediciones del Signo.

García Mérida, Wilson. 2006. "Movimiento indígena sudamericano cierra filas en defensa de Evo Morales." August 12. www.adipal.com.br/site/noticia_imp.asp?cod = 25797& lang = ES (page discontinued).

González, Gustavo. 2005. "América Latina: Indígenas en el 'Eje del Mal.'" *Tintaji*, June.

Lander, Edgardo. 2000. "Eurocentrism and Colonialism in Latin American Social Thought." *Nepantla: Views from South* 1 (3): 519–32.

Larrea Maldonado, Ana María. 2006. "Movimiento indígena, lucha contra el TLC y racismo en el Ecuador." *Revista del Observatorio Social de América Latina* 19:75–84.

Leff, Enrique. 2000. *Saber ambiental: Sustentabilidad, racionalidad, complejidad, poder*. Mexico City: Siglo XXI.

———. 2004. "Más allá de la interdisciplinariedad: Racionalidad ambiental y diálogo de saberes." Seminario Internacional Diálogo Sobre la Interdisciplina, Guadalajara, Mexico, September 27–28.

Maldonado-Torres, Nelson. 2004. "The Topology of Being and the Geopolitics of Knowledge: Modernity, Empire, Coloniality." *City* 8 (1): 29–56.

Mignolo, Walter. 2001. *Local Histories, Global Designs: Coloniality, Subaltern Knowledges, and Border Thinking.* Princeton: Princeton University Press.

Minga Informativa de Movimientos Sociales. 2007. "Pueblos indígenas: La lucha por el territorio es la lucha por la vida." March 27. http://movimientos.org/show_text .php3?key=9569.

Moreano, Alejandro. 2006. "Ecuador en la encrucijada." *Revista del Observatorio Social de América Latina* 19:65–74.

Muyulema, Armando. 2001. "De la 'cuestión indígena' a lo 'indígena' como cuestionamiento." In *Convergencia de tiempos: Estudios subalternos/contextos latinoamericanos estado, cultura y subalternidad,* edited by I. Rodríguez, 327–64. Atlanta: Rodopi.

National Intelligence Council. 2000. *Global Trends 2015: A Dialogue About the Future with Nongovernment Experts.* Washington, D.C.: National Intelligence Council.

Noboa, Patricio. 2006. "Representaciones del 'corpus' de la naturaleza: De la Pre a la Postmodernidad." In *Texiendo textos y saberes: Cinco hilos para pensar los estudios culturales, la colonialidad y la interculturalidad,* edited by A. Albán, 83–104. Popayán, Colombia: Editorial Universidad de Cauca.

Perkins, John. 2004. *Confessions of an Economic Hit Man.* New York: Penguin.

Quijano, Anibal. 2000. "Coloniality of Power, Eurocentrism, and Latin America." *Nepantla: Views from South* 1 (3): 533–80.

Ramos, Hernán. 2007. "A qué Vino John Negroponte." *El Comercio,* May 13, 2.

Red Erbol. 2006. "Evo Morales organiza una cumbre indígena para oponerse a los TLC y recordar al 'Che.'" News release, August 28. http://www.bilaterals.org/spip .php?article5689.

Saavedra, Luis Ángel. 2007. "The Manta Base: A U.S. Military Fort in Ecuador." In *Winter 2007: Closing Bases, Supporting Communities,* by the Fellowship of Reconciliation. http://forusa.org/winter-2007-closing-bases-supporting-communities.

Sacoto, Antonio. 1994. *El indio en el ensayo de la América Española.* Quito: Universidad Andina Simón Bolívar.

Sader, Emir. 2007. "ALBA: Del sueno a la realidad." *La Jornada,* May 19. http://www.jornada .unam.mx/2007/05/19/index.php?section=opinion&article=024a1mun.

Serrano, Helga. 2008. "Anti-Bases Coalition Pushes U.S. Military Base out of Ecuador." Americas Program, Center for International Policy (CIP). November 5. http://americas .irc-online.org/am/5652 (page discontinued).

Tamayo, Eduardo. 2007. "El Banco Sur en debate." *America Latina en Movimiento.* April 26. http://www.uruguay.attac.org/Documentos/sfinanciero/banco_del_esur.htm.

Ticona, Esteban. 2005. "El estado, el poder y la dominación y el pensamiento occidental: Una crítica desde Abya Yala-América." Unpublished essay, Doctoral Program in Latin American Cultural Studies, Universidad Andina Simón Bolívar, Quito, Ecuador.

United Nations Research Institute for Social Development (UNRISD). 2006. "Comercio justo en Bolivia: De las iniciativas en pequena escala al tratado de comercio de los pueblos." In *Temas globales en Bolivia,* Report No. 2, May 17–30.

Van Cott, Donna Lee. 2000. *The Friendly Liquidation of the Past: The Politics of Diversity in Latin America.* Pittsburgh: University of Pittsburgh Press.

Walsh, Catherine. 2002. "The (Re)articulation of Political Subjectivities and Colonial Difference in Ecuador: Reflections on Capitalism and the Geopolitics of Knowledge." *Nepantla: Views from South* 3 (1): 61–98.

———. 2009. *Interculturalidad, estado, sociedad: Luchas (de)coloniales de nuestra época.* Quito: Universidad Andina Simón Bolívar/Abya Yala.

Walsh, Catherine, and Edizon León. 2007. "Afro Andean Thought and Diasporic Ancestrality." In *Shifting the Geography of Reason: Gender, Science, and Religion,* edited by Marina Banchetti-Robino and Clevis Headley, 211–24. London: Cambridge Scholars.

Žižek, Slavoj. 1997. "Multiculturalism, or The Cultural Logic of Multinational Capitalism." *New Left Review* I/225 (September–October): 29–49.

10

FROM CRISIS TO OPPORTUNITY:
GLOBALIZATION'S BEYOND

Jon Shefner and Patricia Fernández-Kelly

This book brings us to a moment in which we can look beyond the globalization that has been—a neoliberal globalization that has exacerbated economic inequalities, centralized political power, and had destructive and homogenizing cultural effects. Building on a series of possibilities suggested by the authors of this volume, we look toward a globalization that may support multiple poles of political and economic power with resulting diminution of poverty and inequality, and in which cultural differences may be understood as a source of strength rather than only as a constraint on market freedom. We are not foolish enough to predict that such a humane outcome is inevitable or around the corner. In fact, we are not convinced that the neoliberal era is entirely behind us. The argument we posed in the introduction regarding the uneven and incomplete application of neoliberal policy suggests that neoliberalism may be as flexible in its decline as in its ascent, and that the hegemony of the market over other human institutions may not be over. But something is clearly changing as a result of the global financial crisis, and it is the purpose of this chapter to contribute to discussions about what the next phase of globalization might look like.

The utopian exercise of imagining alternatives to neoliberal globalization preceded the crisis (George 2004; Held and McGrew 2007; Fisher and Ponniah 2003; Glatzer and Rueschmeyer 2005; Hershberg and Rosen 2006; Block 2008; de Sousa Santos 2008; Evans 2008). In a recent contribution to this debate, Chase-Dunn and Lawrence (2009) examine three different possibilities as the neoliberal model unravels: a revival of U.S. economic and political hegemony, yet with a decline in dominance; a collapse of U.S.

hegemony leading to violent and disruptive globalization, including military, economic, and political crises; and the evolution of multipolar power driven by progressive movements aimed at resolving global economic and environmental problems. We do not disregard the possibility of deglobalization, but we take heart in the current recognition that one of the characteristics distinguishing this economic crisis from the Great Depression is the vast number of global institutions and regulations that, although co-opted by neoliberalism, still offer a venue for discussion and possess sufficient power to offset the worst affects this crisis might otherwise have posed.

It is commonplace in current sociology to argue that out of crisis comes opportunity. However, we cannot understand the parameters of those opportunities or anticipate the alternative futures on which we may be embarking without understanding how we got to this moment of global crisis. To this consideration we now turn.

How Did We Get Here?

Given that a significant amount of the changes we've discussed are rooted in U.S. economic, political, and military hegemony, our version of this story begins in the United States. In the post–World War II era, U.S. economic production and profits were the envy of the world (Foster and Magdoff 2009). Until the 1970s, U.S. production was nurtured by high wages for many U.S. workers, which fed into the consumption, production, and profit loop. By the mid-1970s, profits began to sink, and U.S. industrialists were confronted by choices. One of those choices could have been reinvestment in the bricks and mortar of U.S. production, updating factories that would have continued to drive production and consumption, even at lower profit rates.

For the most part, U.S. capital made choices that contradicted that earlier industrial policy (Bluestone and Harrison 1982; Harrison and Bluestone 1988). Instead of updating and innovating production, U.S. corporations disinvested in U.S. industry, relying on new technologies and flexible specialization to shutter factories and send many of the Rust Belt jobs to the southern United States and the global South. This process was lengthy, but over time, much of the production process formerly conducted in the United States shifted to Mexico, Honduras, Bangladesh, China, and Vietnam, to name just a few countries.

The choice to deindustrialize and move to offshore production led corporations to further economic choices: What to do with the money that was no longer being fed back into traditional production in the United States? Certainly some of that investment capital pursued new high-tech industries as communication technology became an increasingly profitable business. An increasing share of the investment capital sought new places to invest and new financial instruments to generate profit. Financialization became both a structural imperative and corporate strategy as U.S. manufacturing declined (Foster 2008; Krippner 2005).

Organized labor in the United States, never as strong as its European counterparts, weakened over the course of the following decades. Faced with the increasing threat of exit, unions agreed to limit the wages and diminish benefits that had made middle-class families out of blue-collar workers. Many jobs disappeared, leaving workers and their families at a disadvantage while also imposing mounting pressure on local governments. Here, too, capital gained further leverage, as the threat of exit increased its power in negotiations that forced local governments to lower taxes and pay for land and infrastructure. In effect, the post-WWII capital-labor accord was broken because of the new geography of production. Corporations found ready, capable, and cheaper labor forces abroad, in locales where governments were willing to repress labor and ignore both environmental standards and quality of work regulations. Consequently, the pressure on both U.S. labor and local governments escalated. The neoliberal race to the bottom was on.

In the developing world, the power shift was facilitated by debt and the new predominance of the international financial institutions (IFIs). Debt grew enormously, driven in large part by international banks seeking profitable investments for the burgeoning deposits of oil monies. The story of the too-readily available money is widely known, as developing and socialist nations borrowed in unprecedented amounts. In short order, faced by increasing interest rates and declining prices for many of its export commodities, nation after nation was forced to negotiate with the International Monetary Fund (IMF), accepting neoliberal-inspired conditions that diminished the size of states as employers and service providers, and opening protected markets of all kinds (Harris and Seid 2000; MacEwan 1990; Onimode 1989; Pastor 1987). Thirty years of structural adjustment leveled great damage on the populations of Africa, Asia, and Latin America (Portes and Hoffman 2003; Structural Adjustment Participatory Review International Network [SAPRIN] 2005).

But the neoliberal economic framework also provided a series of new investment opportunities: ownership restrictions were abolished concurrently with privatization of many state-owned industries; capital mobility increased as industrial protection policies were reduced; and new financial markets opened wider to international investors (SAPRIN 2005; Stiglitz 2002, 2006). Indeed, the debt of developing nations itself became a commodity for sale in ways that benefited capital. As capital mobility increased and new financial instruments became available, the flurry of corporate gambling escalated, leaving nations vulnerable to huge and speedy flights of money at the first signs of financial downturn.

Corporate profits increased with the offshoring of production, and with deregulation of markets of all kinds. But deregulation also opened opportunities for risky investments that became riskier, with fewer monitors in place and the market-first ideology hampering those that remained. Increased profit drove the process even closer to the precipice, as these increases generated expectations of even greater profit growth. So standard investment opportunities—U.S. bricks and mortar—became less likely to be pursued, even where they may still have existed. And global bricks and mortar—production facilities in the developing world—proved unstable compared to their earlier counterparts in the developed world, as capital consistently pursued the lowest-cost sites of production. Mexico, for example, long an aggregate beneficiary of the new production model, began to deindustrialize in the 2000s as other locales, such as China, proved cheaper.[1]

As profits from financial speculation accrued, and traditional investment opportunities failed to keep pace, a new dynamic occurred among U.S. households. Housing values increased, pushing people—both individuals and brokers—to turn even more to real estate as locales of investment. The housing bubble grew as investment capital pursued real estate, driving prices above and beyond reasonable expectations of return. When bundled mortgages became investment sites, a vicious cycle ensued in which inflated values further inflated profit returns and expectation of returns. The immediate outcome of this cycle was increasing debt, as more homeowners put more money into, and took more money out of, houses that could not sustain the expected increase in value. The illusory value surge had additional damaging outcomes, as the expectations that values would continue to be ever-increasing led investors to pursue more risky investments, and homeowners to spend their seeming gains on more consumption.

Internationally, deregulation of investment and ownership in other nations meant increased mobility of investment, as we have noted. But these additional financial interrelationships also created increased vulnerability. One manifestation of that greater vulnerability is the extensive foreign purchase of U.S. debt, especially by China. China's purchase of US$1 trillion has alarmed both Chinese and U.S. political figures (Wines and Bradsher 2009).

The worries of those who cautioned against the increasing global financial interrelationships amid a climate of deregulation proved prescient.[2] When the U.S. housing bubble burst, the result was the devaluation of a chain of loans, each linked to the other and all risky. The foundation of wealth on which these loans were built became recognized as mere sand, and shifting sand at that. Added to the financial meltdown, decades of deindustrialization meant that the nuts-and-bolts economy, newly called the "real economy," was no longer able to protect the United States. Industrialization in other nations proved no more solid a foundation of development, as low-wage flexible specialization failed to build either complementary industries or internal consumption markets. Thus, new globalized production remained dependent on bust-and-boom cycles among consumers in wealthy nations. The increased interrelatedness of national economies within a global economy means that vulnerability is contagious, as is crisis.

Various elements of this story are likely to be familiar to many. We do not claim to articulate a new theory of the current crisis, but instead to offer a synthesis that we believe brings a fuller set of elements under consideration. There are two basic problems with recent literature that has warned of the coming crisis, then sought to explain it. First, theorists of financialization (Foster and Magdoff 2009) and other overreaches of the global capitalist model (Panitch et al. 2004) fail to address the globe; they focus instead on the global North. The financialization thesis finds the increasing predominance of financial capital in Western economies to be the origin of the current crisis. But Foster and Magdoff, and to a lesser extent Panitch et al., bracket the rest of the world. As the debt crisis, the peso crash of 1995, and the Asian financial crisis of 1997 demonstrated, the links to the developing world constitute a crucial element of U.S. and Western capital financialization. The increased opening to speculative investment that could move across national borders with the click of a computer mouse provided huge investment opportunities. Scholars of Latin America, Africa, Asia, and Eastern Europe have long identified capital mobility and new venues for foreign investment—with subsequent repatriation of profit in good times and disinvestment in bad—as financial dynamics that have accompanied the neoliberal turn. One cannot explain a global crisis without integrating the globe.

Second, the increase of financialization does not mean that material production—the so-called real economy—ceases. To put it simply, people still produce stuff. The questions about the new geography of production are where it goes, with what result for nations and workers, and what kind of investment drives it. Again, scholars of both the neoliberal shift and flexible and segmented production have much to teach the scholars of financialization in this regard. Stuff is still produced, but in ways that disadvantage many of the new producers, and with results that fail to provide stability for many of the new producing locales. That is, to situate financialization in a global economy, rather than a national one, requires the recognition of new production relations in addition to an understanding of the way that economic and political powers have acted to eliminate much of the material and national progress that accompanied preceding periods of global industrial growth.

This story, now familiar to many, documents the origin of the global financial crisis. As we noted earlier, crisis is often followed by opportunity.

Despite neoliberalism's demonizing of the state, it is the state that has become the focus of attention for those seeking the route out of crisis.

The Return of the State

What will the current crisis mean for states? One clear outcome of the current crisis is the rethinking of the state by both academics and policy makers. The "disappearance" of the state under neoliberalism was always oversold; the state did not disappear, and that was not the neoliberal intent. The intent instead was to shift its policy from developmentalism to facilitating market competition, from welfare provision to the embrace of capital. In many ways, even the notion of the thinning of the state did not capture the crux of neoliberal policy. Although many states did diminish as regulators, as employers, and as service providers, the most significant outcome of the uneven and incomplete application of neoliberal policy has been the shifting of constituencies. Despite the important contributions of many Marxist-oriented theories of the state (Aronowitz and Bratsis 2002; Carnoy 1984; Jessop 1982, 2002), it is indisputable that states prior to neoliberalism were willing to address the needs of their popular constituencies, to greater and lesser extents, whether these were labor, the middle class, peasantries, or the urban poor. These constituencies were, of course, never as well attended as were capitalist classes. But neither were they as neglected as they became in places where neoliberalism was applied most fully. The novelty of the neoliberal state was to dramatically reduce any policy that provided for noncapital constituencies. The deregulation of a variety of markets was a direct result of the shift in prioritization of constituencies.

It now appears that the policy of deregulation will be rethought, which marks a clear movement away from neoliberal orthodoxy. Importantly, it is not just academics who are looking to theorize the new state; policy makers are actively redesigning policy that will renovate the relationship of government to economy. The recognition that deregulation facilitated the ascension of those who prioritized personal gain over societal need, leading to disastrous global consequences, seems to have shaken those who held dearly to the illusion of the self-sustaining market. Alan Greenspan, one of the architects of deregulation, put it this way when speaking to the House Committee on Oversight and Government Reform: "Those of us who have looked to the self-interest of lending institutions to protect shareholders' equity, myself included, are in a state of shocked disbelief" (quoted in Andrews 2008).

More important than the architects of disaster admitting their errors are the policy changes that have followed the crisis. The United States, the European Union (EU), China, and other affected nations and regions scurried to control the damage, increasing regulation and spending heavily in order to forestall further damage. The state has, by default, reemerged as the singular actor that can ameliorate the damage caused by free marketers. The depth of the damage leads us to believe that this resorting to state action is not a short-term policy shift.

So what will states look like following the crisis? At this point in the Great Recession, there appears to be substantial conflict over national and global state policy. One possibility is the resurgence of the developmentalist state. The United States, among others, designed a stimulus package aimed at jump-starting the economy, reinforcing a role for states in providing employment rooted in Keynesian economics and New Deal politics. Some who preached the gospel of open markets and free trade now recognized the need for greater regulation. We believe that the ravages of neoliberalism have demonstrated, once again, the necessity for states to regulate the economy and provide some protection for the vulnerable.

Indeed, the uneven application of neoliberalism may provide opportunities for its rollback. Block (2008) reinforces the possibility of the reemergence of developmentalist states, as he finds such state entities flourishing in the context of U.S. research and development, even while we have exhorted the world to diminish the role of states in economies. Block's argument that state developmentalism cannot be effective by staying hidden fits well into current policy makers' and academic reflections on how to revive the state. The fact that such structures are in place offers the United States a way to reveal the important contributions that the state has made. Such revelations can then serve to advocate for greater resources while providing ideological justification for a rebuilding of states.

For Block, one of the keys to an alternative globalization continues to be innovation and technological solutions to social injustice. Such resolutions are best suited to address neoliberal globalization if they emerge from governments and universities, as opposed to institutions focused on profit making. These are important insights into ways to combat inequity among knowledge-based economies. However, the hallmark of globalization, as compared to earlier moments of international development, is the movement of manufacturing offshore. How can we pursue equity in places still defined by labor exploitation and natural resource extraction? That is, where are the new models of state activity founded in places that are not postindustrial?

Various states preceded the crises in their responses to the ravages of neoliberalism; those responses demonstrate a continuum of depth of interventions that provide clues for future policy. Brazil has focused largely on poverty alleviation, while Venezuela has pursued much more active interventions in social welfare based on oil wealth. Ecuador and Bolivia are both pursuing greater state regulation of, and control over, their natural resources. The new constitutions in both of those nations suggest very different possibilities with regard to the use of natural resources for public well-being, simultaneously restricting the previously unlimited prerogatives of capital.

Additionally, it appears possible that states will assume greater planning functions. The EU's neoliberalism has always included greater elements of planning and regulation than that imposed in the developing world or in the United States, as policy has been coordinated on issues such as immigration, green production, and national wealth redistribution to lessen inequalities among union members. The propensity to plan is likely to increase globally as states are forced to confront questions of investment, production, climate change, and the legacy of neoliberalism's inequalities.

All three of these possibilities—the further recognition of the wrongheadedness of neoliberal policy, the greater intervention of states in economies, and the push for greater planning—provide some challenge to neoliberal hegemony. Can neodevelopmentalism coexist with neoliberalism? In theory, probably not. But if we are to equally apply the incomplete and uneven nature of neoliberal policy to neodevelopmentalism, it may be that states find niches to act, while markets remain predominant in other areas.

As we noted at the beginning of this chapter, however, neoliberalism is not likely to go quietly. It is clear from recent G8 and G20 talks that Keynesian-inspired stimulus policies will meet opposition among deficit hawks. The irony of Washington's argument that stimulus spending must be maintained was overshadowed by European and other developing nations' concern over deficit spending. At the G20 meeting in April 2010, most nations expressed concern over debt and planned for austerity. The United States ended up agreeing to the "goal of cutting government deficits in half by 2013 and stabilizing the ratio of public debt to gross domestic product by 2016." Yet the G20 leaders did not display the fervor so long voiced by the Washington Consensus, as the statement released at the meeting's end recognized that "there is also a risk that the failure to implement consolidation where necessary would undermine confidence and hamper growth" (Chan and Calmes 2010). We can hope that, at the least, Keynesian tools have been added to neoliberal ones as the toolbox of the state is redesigned.

The resurgence of states will not necessarily disrupt current hierarchies of global power, of course. Actors may switch roles without changing the script. Arrighi (2007, 2009) has been unequivocal in his argument that the United States is declining as a hegemonic actor, with China emerging as a political and economic leader pursuing noncapitalist interests. Sources as diverse as the U.S. National Intelligence Council (2008) agree that the United States is facing, at the least, a multipolar world in which not only China's power is ascendant, but that of India as well. The U.S. intelligence community, however, believes that the United States will remain the globe's most powerful nation, even if its relative dominance diminishes. That assumption ignores the potential for change emerging from transitions in global governance. One important factor on which the United States has relied for its exercise of power in the recent past has been its relative control over the IFIs.

Reforms in the International Financial Institutions

As we wrote in the introduction, the IFIs, which have been key to imposing neoliberal polices across the globe, are currently in a state of flux. The World Trade Organization (WTO) has been effectively paralyzed, as the Group of 22's efforts to disrupt the uneven and incomplete application of neoliberalism have stymied accords. That is, the efforts of those coalesced nations did not challenge neoliberalism itself but rather its incomplete application in the United States, Japan, and the EU. It was not only reformist trade policy requested by the Group of 22; it was instead a demand that neoliberalism be applied in the dominant nations in ways similar to recent applications in the developing world.[3] The developing nations' desire to further open markets was fully consistent with neoliberalism. Thus, the WTO became the playground where nations tried to out-market others.

Current reductions in trade resulting from the global crisis suggest that nations will be no more flexible than they have been in the past regarding these disputes. Cries for protection may come from developing nations, but it is hard to imagine the West offering favorable responses to those demands. It is possible that some of the less wealthy nations of the Organisation for Economic Co-operation and Development (OECD) may provide a counterbloc, thus posing an alternative that would bring some level of protection to national markets. And the potential increase in power of organized labor in the West may bring some protectionist calls, as the early "Buy American" provisions of the economic stimulus package demonstrate. Yet the Obama administration quickly articulated its opposition to the inclusion of any language that would contradict current trade policy (Sanger 2009). It is entirely possible that the WTO will diminish in importance as trade negotiations remain paralyzed.

In contrast, the IMF has made a dramatic reappearance, lending to various nations hurt by the credit-freeze component of the current crisis. Recent meetings of the G20 nations (November 2008, March 2009, and April 2010) suggest that they are looking to the IMF to play a role in alleviating the current crisis (European Network on Debt and Development [Eurodad] 2009; Paletta and Fidler 2009). G20 nations favor rebuilding the IMF's resources so that it can play a larger role in providing credit to strapped nations. Indeed, the G20 nations demonstrated a breathtaking inability to conceive of new policy in their 2009 meetings, increasing IMF capital by $500 billion rather than creating another tool by which the needs of struggling nations might be addressed. The G20 leaders further demonstrated the inconsistent thinking characteristic of the uneven application of neoliberalism as they continued to hold firmly to their critique of protectionism while urging greater regulation of financial markets and more state spending (Paletta and Fidler 2009).

Interestingly, the IMF may provide less of an ideological resource to the United States if that nation continues down the neoliberal path. The IMF appears willing to reexamine its Keynesian roots. The institution's leaders argued, even before the depths of the current crisis became apparent, that global economic problems required global fiscal stimulus packages, despite the increased governmental budget deficits that would result (*International Herald Tribune* 2008).

Perhaps most important is the potential for change in governance at the IMF. As early as 2006, the IMF increased the voting rights of China, South Korea, Mexico, and Turkey, a move that then managing director Rodrigo Rato said reflected those nations' growing economic power (*Indian Express* 2006). This shift in voting power away from the hegemony of the United States, Western Europe, and Japan was minimal, but it demonstrated some recognition of change in global economic and political power (Weisman 2006). Further changes were limited, with the developing world's share of the vote in the body increasing by only 1.6 percent, while wealthy nations continued to hold almost 60 percent of the votes (Bretton Woods Project 2008). However, the power of the BRIC nations (Brazil, Russia, India, and China) on the IMF board may increase with the current crisis, as they hold significant foreign exchange reserves on which the IMF may rely to make loans, while other developed nations are under financial strain. Nevertheless, the current ability of these nations to exert power over the IMF, and thus over international financial architecture, will continue to be stymied by the disproportionate voting power of developed nations and the veto power of the United States (Lifei 2008).

Additional demands for change have come with Indian Deputy Chairman of Planning Commission Montek Singh Ahluwalia's suggestion that further restructuring of the IMF will be necessary due to its inability to stop the hemorrhaging of capital outflows from developing nations. Moreover, the accumulation of vast foreign reserves by several developing countries demonstrated their lack of trust in the IMF, due to their belief "that the IMF was neither adequately equipped nor had sufficient operational flexibility to deal with the global financial problem" (*Hindustan Times* 2009).

Regional Power

The question of the ongoing power of the IFIs must be contrasted with the potential emergence of new institutions, or changes among preexisting ones. The nascent Bank of the South is one of those emerging institutions and has the potential to displace the traditional IFIs in Latin America, posing a new, alternative source of investment capital, infrastructure development, balance-of-payments financing, and monetary policy. The bank's capacity is as yet untested, and there is disagreement among the founder nations (Venezuela, Argentina, Brazil, Uruguay, Paraguay, Bolivia, and Ecuador) as to which of its varied policy areas is the most important. The Bank of the South is also a source of political contention, as Latin American leaders use it to search for allies to support different visions of development. Indeed, the early articulated commitment to equivalent power over policy making, a crucial difference from the IFIs, is already being tested by suggestions that the source of capital donations will help determine policy (Romero and Bedoya 2008).

Despite the current lack of clarity as to its direction, the Bank of the South holds the potential to provide capital with fewer conditions than the traditional IFIs. The creation of the bank is notably different in the participation in its design by members of the global debt relief movement, such as Latindadd, Jubilee South, and Rede Brasil. Independent critics of neoliberalism have not achieved as prominent a voice in current discussions of IMF or WTO restructuring. Additionally, the ongoing importance of oil, water, and newly important natural resources like lithium suggests that the bank's member economies are well placed to withstand some of the damage of the current crisis. Whether it will become an institution that can genuinely champion an alternative vision of development is as yet unknown.

A further implication of the resurgence of states, as well as the decreasing profile of the IFIs and the emergence of other institutions, is the increased power of regions. This trend is perhaps most likely to appear in trade blocs. We hesitate to suggest that these will be free trade blocs, as it is unclear which elements of neoliberalism are likely to survive the current crisis. But institutions like the Bank of the South and the Bolivarian Alternative for the Americas (ALBA) add to the Bush administration's failures to pass new free trade accords, and suggest that the substitution of trade policy for development policy may diminish. Trade regimes may retreat from the sole focus of destroying barriers to open markets and refocus on comparative advantages of various nations.

Although it appears for now to be subordinated to the current crisis, the search for new energy policies and resources suggests that new trade policy may reflect natural resource wealth rather than neoliberal antiprotectionism. Thus, resource wealth manifested by oil reserves in Venezuela, Mexico, Ecuador, and Brazil, reinforced by Bolivian lithium and vast freshwater supplies across Latin America, may mean that these nations have more highly valued commodities than they have possessed since the conquest. The heightened value of these commodities, concurrent with global political economic shifts, may increase both these nations' attractiveness and leverage as trade partners. Certainly, much of the region is recovering more quickly from the crisis than most developed nations. Indeed, a recent World Bank forecast suggested that the region's economy will grow by 4.5 percent in 2010 (Romero 2010). Increasing economic trade with Asia has been driven in large part by high demand for various commodities. The regional concentration of these resources, along with the emergence of new geographically focused institutions, means that the Latin American region may have greater power than it has seen in the past.

Asian nations affiliated with the Association of Southeast Asian Nations (ASEAN) are also active in ways that may defy U.S. hegemony. A November 2008 meeting of Japanese, Chinese, and South Korean finance ministers called for greater Asian collaboration in response to fears of slowed economies and financial instability. The ministers called for increased funding to the Asian Development Bank (ADB) to provide aid to the strapped Asian economies, as well as for reform of the IFIs (Ministry of Finance, Japan 2008). As the crisis deepened, the ASEAN +3 nations (South Korea, China, and Japan) met in Thailand in February 2009 and outlined a plan to address regional challenges posed by the global crisis. Like most policy makers, the regional bloc finance ministers articulated their staunch opposition to anything but the freest of markets. However, the outflow of capital and general economic instability raised alarm, and they echoed the calls of many for global economic coordination that would reinstall market predictability. One of their resolutions was to increase the size, from US$80 billion to US$120 billion, of the Multilateralised Chiang Mai Initiative (CMIM), an agreement created during the 1997 Asian financial crisis to increase short-term liquidity and provide credit. The agreement recognized the greater economic strength of the +3 nations, as 80 percent of the increased fund was to be financed by those three nations alone. The finance ministers hoped to activate the cooperative lending institution as soon as possible, making credit available with the aid of the IMF. This latter part of the agreement means that funds will be disbursed under IMF conditionality, although what those conditions will look like is unclear (Finance Ministers of the ASEAN +3 2009; Chaitrong 2009).

The ASEAN +3 nations also announced the strengthening of the Asian Bond Markets Initiative in ways that would increase the sales of bonds in national currencies. The finance ministers called for the growth of the ADB by 200 percent (Chaitrong 2009). In general, ASEAN and other Asian nations are clearly pushing the resurgence of the state, both by cooperating in regional agreements and by undertaking national polices of stabilization, regulation, and economic stimulus. For example, Thailand, Singapore, Malaysia, and the Philippines all implemented multibillion-dollar stimulus packages that include a mix of infrastructure projects, cash handouts, or tax cuts aimed at creating jobs and boosting consumer demand (Associated Press 2009).

Many of the changes identified throughout this volume preceded the crisis. For example, the Pink Tide—the leftist electoral transition that has encompassed so much of Latin America—began long before the developed nations were shaken by the crisis. In much of Latin America, as well as other locales of the global South, popular action generated electoral movement. Thus, two more issues bear examination: implications of the economic crisis for expressions of popular action, and the emergence of alternative values around markets, production and consumption, and work and natural resources.

Popular Action and the Search for Alternatives

U.S. social movement theory pays little attention to the hardships that drive collective action, focusing more on issues as diverse as organization and emotions. But across the globe, it has been demonstrated that people turn out to protest when their collective interests are threatened. The surge in discussion of "civil society" was concurrent with a great deal of material harm imposed on popular sectors due to neoliberal policies. As subsidies for food, transportation, or other basic necessities were removed, citizens across the globe responded with protest. The "emergence of civil society" is in no way reducible to anti-neoliberal protest, of course, but enough of the two trends was contemporaneous to be suggestive of how material harm can trigger popular protest. The work on austerity protests pioneered by John Walton (Walton 1989; Walton and Ragin 1990; Walton and Shefner 1994) made it entirely clear that when IMF stabilization programs threatened to push poor people off their knife-edge of survival, they protested loudly. Structural adjustment affected middle classes as well, as Walton and others document (Shefner, Pasdirtz, and Blad 2006; Johnston and Almeida 2006; Nef and Robles 2000; Onimode 1989; Bradshaw and Huang 1991). Furthermore, popular protest has significantly impacted states. In some cases, protestors were able to roll back the offending reforms, and in others, long-standing neoliberal policies provided political targets for successful electoral transitions. Such examples of material harm driving protest are given further credence by postcrisis protests in Russia, Mexico, Britain, Greece, and elsewhere.

What does this mean for global political change? One of Piven and Cloward's (1977) many enduring contributions is the recognition that when poor people's movements emerge, their greatest power is in the disruption of current economic and political order. These are not mechanistic responses, induced at some critical point of hardship, but rather they are contingent on historical circumstances, state activity, and culture. At this point, we might build on these insights to recognize that hardship-driven protests have been characteristic of the global response to neoliberalism, and those affected have spread well beyond the poor to include many middle-class sectors also harmed by economic decline.

Latin America is currently the site where we can note the most dramatic influence of protest on state transition, as leftist administrations have been ushered into Argentina, Bolivia, Brazil, Chile, Ecuador, El Salvador, Nicaragua, Paraguay, Uruguay, and Venezuela. All of these nations suffered the damage of neoliberal policy, and all of them experienced waves of protest that coalesced popular forces—the urban poor, indigenous movements, the working class, peasants, and middle-class professionals, among others—in support of leftist candidates. Although the damage to which these nations responded occurred well before the current crisis, it gives an indication of the depth of political contention that we may witness with the current crisis.

Popular protests, however, are likely to have a greater effect on politics if they are grounded in some consistent set of ideologies. Neoliberalism's great success has been due not only to its reconfiguring of the global economy and state functions, but also, as Harvey (2005) demonstrated, to its ideological power. For a time, as former British prime minister Margaret Thatcher famously intoned, there was no alternative. The fall of the Soviet Union appeared to be the final straw in the ideological failure of planned economies and state interventions. Not only was there no alternative, but the alternatives that previously existed showed their inability to function.

The data from the developing world regarding the negative consequences of neoliberalism were available early in its history. But the tenacity of the economic model, in the face of so much evidence revealing its savage effects, demonstrates its ideological hold. Now, it appears, the door has opened for new thinking about economies and their place in society. Collective action leads to the sociological imagination—the recognition that our public issues have structural and collective roots. But collective action will be less episodic and more transformative if it is founded on coherent articulations of alternatives that build on the current moment of crisis to unveil opportunities for a more socially responsible, environmentally sustainable, and politically participatory political and economic system. What currents of thought might find purchase if neoliberal ideology continues to wane?

There are many possibilities, but few are fully coherent. De Sousa Santos (2008) directs our attention to the diverse yet inclusive alternative represented by the World Social Forum. The forum, according to him, offers an interpretation that alternatives do exist, even while refusing to define what those alternatives look like. Instead, it espouses a "radically democratic utopia" that, at this point, is diverse yet nonprogrammatic, anti-neoliberal without being necessarily postcapitalist. Thus, shared hardships give movements ways to unite, but they have yet to articulate new directions.

Like many, Evans (2008) celebrates the tools of globalization as applicable to counterhegemonic movements, just as they have been used by those imposing hegemony. Globalization supplies resources to those pursuing both domination and resistance. Yet Evans, like Chase-Dunn and Lawrence, de Sousa Santos, and countless others who espouse the counterhegemonic potential of opposition movements, underestimates the differentiation among global movements. Movements, like other expressions of organized society, vary greatly in the kind and amount of resources they can marshal, the status and legitimacy they possess, and the ideologies on which they rely. We don't believe that a common position of disagreement—contesting neoliberalism—provides a sufficient foundation for the unified creation of a coherent alternative ideology.

There are too many utopian alternatives to fully discuss them in this volume. However, we want to touch on two from largely different sources. One, *buen vivir*, is being articulated by global South indigenous movements; the other, Polanyian institutional equivalence, is being voiced by global North academicians. Buen vivir is one of the spiritual underpinnings of movements such as Bolivian president Evo Morales's Movement Toward Socialism and many Ecuadorian indigenous movements, including the Confederation of Indigenous Nationalities of Ecuador (CONAIE) and the Confederation of Peoples of Kichwa Nationality (ECUARUNARI). Based in ancient traditions that find life reliant on, and intertwined with, the natural world as opposed to economic growth, the notion of buen vivir advocates balance. Economically, balance is to be achieved by allowing extraction, production, and consumption without endangering nature. The commodification of nature has to be balanced by recognizing the cultural value of water, timber, and other resources. This latter process is achieved by a careful stewardship, which in many nations has been led by indigenous people but need not and cannot be solely their responsibility. Politically, balance is to be achieved by a genuine respect for diversity within equity. Thus, a variety of peoples defined by their own or emergent identities must have voice and participation in a political system. Diversity becomes more than a cultural category when groups are accorded political rights defined by their community membership. Finally, culture is key to buen vivir as the source of values regarding nature, community, work, family, and other components of human life that challenge the interpretation that human worth can be calculated only in economic terms.

Buen vivir poses a challenge to the neoliberal model in several ways. First, an important component of this way of thinking is the decommodification of nature and social life. While recognizing the pragmatic need to use natural resources for national gain, proponents of buen vivir advocate much more of a stewardship and conservationist ethic than full-scale exploitation. This decommodification then reasserts concepts of justice and community as

foundations of property rights, rather than the possession of the most efficient means of economic exploitation. Indeed, buen vivir provides an alternative economics, the adequacy of which may be measured by its ability to fulfill
production and distribution needs, as opposed to levels of growth and profit
rates. In this way, the concept of buen vivir re-embeds economy as one
human institution among many, in contrast to the neoliberal position that
the rights and needs of economic actors must stand above all others.[4]

In ways not yet explored, buen vivir is reconcilable with Polanyian institutional equivalence. One of Polanyi's great contributions was the recognition
that savagery is the clear result of humans prioritizing one human institution,
namely market economy, over political and cultural systems. The source of
the double movement, or political action by movements and states to control
the savagery of unrestrained capitalism, demonstrates the importance of political institutions. However, Polanyi's recognition moved beyond the critique
of the predominance of economics when post-Marxists recognized the similar error of relying too heavily on the state, and the savage consequences that
may stem from prioritizing that institution too highly. Rather than posing the
greater importance of politics over economics, or vice versa, Polanyi points to
the embeddedness of all human institutions. Increasingly, scholars such as
Block (2008) and Evans (2008) have suggested that some kind of balance is
necessary among economic, political, and cultural institutions. Empirical reality leads all of us to recognize that such a balance must also include the
carrying capacity of the environment.

The notion of institutional equivalence may appear too static for true Polanyian aficionados. But the articulation of such an ideological notion does not
deny that its pursuit will require struggle. Adherents of one institution or
another will continue to argue for that institution's priority. Such struggle is
true to a Polanyian analysis of a double movement, although we may find that
"quadruple movement" is a better descriptive term, as advocates of culture,
environment, politics, and economics conflict over priorities and subsequent
policy.

The current financial crisis has had contradictory effects. We in no way
seek to diminish the damage incurred by unemployment and loss of economic security, which are clear outcomes of this moment. But we refuse to
believe in any analysis that is founded on either overly optimistic or unduly
pessimistic versions of the end of history. Humans have devised institutions,
cultures, and politics that are bestial and subhuman. So too have we developed systems that increase emancipation. We refuse to prepare only for the
worst. There may be no totalizing response to the current crisis, as may be
derived from a synthesis of buen vivir and Polanyian institutional equivalence. Instead, there may be a fragmented set of responses that replicate ongoing hierarchies while lessening polarizations of privilege, poverty, and

inequality. Such a liberatory trend, we presume, will follow reformist precedents rather than revolutionary ones.

We continue to believe in the upward slope of human emancipation. But the trend, if history is a guide, will be slow and interrupted. The great advantage we see now is the potential to destroy another totalizing ideology, that of neoliberalism. To achieve post-neoliberalism, we need to think about multiple institutions and organizations that pose alternative possibilities—national neodevelopmentalist states in some areas, indigenous movements in others, and coalitions of states and movements in still others. The uneven application of neoliberalism may not be succeeded by a fully coherent liberatory ideology and set of practices, but that does not mean that efforts to remake the world are unsuccessful. It may mean instead that different schema continue to define certain areas and problems better than others.

NOTES

1. See chapters 3 and 4 of this volume.

2. Perhaps one of the most frustrating elements of the current crisis for academics has been policy makers' and journalists' insistence that "nobody saw the crisis coming." The ravages of neoliberalism have been documented in too many sources to be cited. The work of Panitch et al. (2004), Foster and Magdoff (2009), and Massey, Sanchez, and Behrman (2006) demonstrates that the unsustainability of the political economic model was likewise clear to many. Unfortunately, given the realities of political power, these authors may not have been preaching to the choir, but certainly to a small congregation.

3. In assessing global inequalities, Stiglitz (2006) makes similar suggestions for trade policy.

4. Much more can be said about buen vivir. See, for example, chapter 9 of this volume and Walsh (2009).

REFERENCES

Andrews, Edmund L. 2008. "Greenspan Concedes Error on Regulation." *New York Times*, October 30. http://www.nytimes.com/2008/10/24/business/economy/24panel.html?_r=1&hp&oref=slogin.

Aronowitz, Stanley, and Petere Bratsis, eds. 2002. *Paradigm Lost: State Theory Reconsidered*. Minneapolis: University of Minnesota Press.

Arrighi, Giovanni. 2007. *Adam Smith in Beijing: Lineages of the Twenty-First Century*. New York: Verso.

———. 2009. *The Long Twentieth Century: Money, Power, and the Origins of Our Time*. New York: Verso.

Associated Press. 2009. "ASEAN Agrees to Boost Regional Fund by $40 Billion." February 22. http://www.cnbc.com//id/29335457 (page discontinued).

Block, Fred. 2008. "Swimming Against the Current: The Rise of a Hidden Developmental State in the United States." *Politics and Society* 36 (2): 169–206.

Bluestone, Barry, and Bennett Harrison. 1982. *The Deindustrialization of America: Plant Closings, Community Abandonment, and the Dismantling of Basic Industry*. New York: Basic Books.

Bradshaw, York W., and J. Huang. 1991. "Intensifying Global Dependency: Foreign Debt, Structural Adjustment, and Third World Underdevelopment." *Sociological Quarterly* 32 (3): 321–42.

Bretton Woods Project. 2008. "IMF Governance Renovations: Fresh Paint While Foundations Rot." April 1. http://www.brettonwoodsproject.org/art-561041.

Carnoy, Martín. 1984. *The State and Political Theory.* Princeton: Princeton University Press.

Chaitrong, Wichit. 2009. "Finance Ministers Agree to Expand Currency Pool." *The Nation,* February 23. http://www.nationmultimedia.com/2009/02/23/business/business_30096352.php.

Chan, Sewell, and Jackie Calmes. 2010. "World Leaders Agree on Timetable for Cutting Deficits." *New York Times,* June 27. http://www.nytimes.com/2010/06/28/business/global/28summit.html.

Chase-Dunn, Chris, and Kirk Lawrence. 2009. "The Next Three Futures: Another U.S. Hegemony, Global Collapse, or Global Democracy?" Working paper, Institute for Research on World Systems, University of California–Riverside. http://www.irows.ucr.edu/papers/irows47/irows47.htm.

de Sousa Santos, Boaventura. 2008. "The World Social Forum and the Global Left." *Politics and Society* 36 (2): 247–70.

European Network on Debt and Development (Eurodad). 2008. "IMF Back in Business as Bretton Woods II Conference Announced." *Eurodad Newsletter,* no. 15, October 23. http://www.eurodad.org/whatsnew/articles.aspx?id=3010.

Evans, Peter. 2008. "Is an Alternative Globalization Possible?" *Politics and Society* 36 (2): 271–305.

Finance Ministers of the ASEAN +3. 2009. "Joint Media Statement: Action Plan to Restore Economic and Financial Stability of the Asian Region." Phuket, Thailand, February 22. http://www.aseansec.org/22158.htm.

Fisher, William, and Thomas Ponniah, eds. 2003. *Another World Is Possible: Popular Alternatives to Globalization at the World Social Forum.* London: Zed Books.

Foster, John Bellamy. 2008. "The Financialization of Capital and the Crisis." *Monthly Review* 59 (11): 1–19.

Foster, John Bellamy, and Fred Magdoff. 2009. *The Great Financial Crisis: Causes and Consequences.* New York: Monthly Review Press.

George, Susan. 2004. *Another World Is Possible If . . .* London: Verso.

Glatzer, Miguel, and Dietrich Rueschmeyer. 2005. *Globalization and the Future of the Welfare State.* Pittsburgh: University of Pittsburgh Press.

Harris, Richard L., and Melinda J. Seid. 2000. "Critical Perspectives on Globalization and Neoliberalism in the Developing Countries." *Journal of Developing Societies* 16 (1): 1–26.

Harrison, Bennett, and Barry Bluestone. 1988. *The Great U-Turn: Corporate Restructuring and the Polarizing of America.* New York: Basic Books.

Harvey, David. 2005. *A Brief History of Neoliberalism.* Oxford: Oxford University Press.

Held, David, and Anthony McGrew. 2007. *Globalization/Anti-Globalization: Beyond the Great Divide.* Cambridge: Polity Press.

Hershberg, Eric, and Fred Rosen, eds. 2006. *Latin America After Neoliberalism: Turning the Tide in the Twenty-First Century?* New York: New Press.

Hindustan Times. 2009. "India Calls for IMF Restructuring, Reversal of Capital Outflow." January 31. http://www.hindustantimes.com/Homepage/Homepage.aspx (page discontinued).

Indian Express. 2006. "New Governance at IMF." September 19.

International Herald Tribune. 2008. "IMF Changes Stance on Deficits." January 28.

Jessop, Bob. 1982. *The Capitalist State: Marxist Theories and Methods.* New York: New York University Press.

———. 2002. *The Future of the Capitalist State.* Cambridge: Polity Press.

Johnston, Hank, and Paul Almeida. 2006. *Latin American Social Movements: Globalization, Democratization, and Transnational Networks.* Lanham, Md.: Rowman and Littlefield.

Krippner, Greta R. 2005. "The Financialization of the American Economy." *Socio-Economic Review* 3 (2): 173–208.

Lifei, Zheng. 2008. "Crisis May Increase China's Role in IMF." *China Daily,* December 22.

MacEwan, Arthur. 1990. *Debt and Disorder: International Economic Instability and U.S. Imperial Decline.* New York: Monthly Review Press.

Massey, Douglas, Magaly Sanchez R., and Jere R. Behrman. 2006. "Chronicle of a Myth Foretold: The Washington Consensus in Latin America." *ANNALS of the American Academy of Political and Social Science* 606 (1): 6–7.

Ministry of Finance, Japan. 2008. "Joint Message: The Ninth Trilateral Finance Ministers' Meeting Among China, Japan, and Korea." http://www.mof.go.jp/english/if/081115joint_message.htm.

Nef, Jorge, and Wilder Robles. 2000. "Globalization, Neoliberalism, and the State of Underdevelopment in the New Periphery." *Journal of Developing Societies* 16 (1): 27–48.

Onimode, Bade, ed. 1989. *The IMF, the World Bank, and the African Debt: The Economic Impact.* London: Zed Press.

Paletta, Damian, and Stephen Fidler. 2009. "Geithner Gets G-20 Earful About Need to Speed Reform." *Wall Street Journal,* March 16. http://online.wsj.com/article/SB123702789137730081.html.

Panitch, Leo, Colin Leys, Alan Zuege, and Martijn Konings, eds. 2004. *The Globalization Decade: A Critical Reader.* London: Merlin Press.

Pastor, Manuel. 1987. "The Effects of IMF Programs in the Third World: Debate and Evidence from Latin America." *World Development* 15 (2): 249–62.

Piven, Frances Fox, and Richard Cloward. 1977. *Poor People's Movements: Why They Succeed, How They Fail.* New York: Pantheon Books.

Portes, Alejandro, and Kelly Hoffman. 2003. "Latin American Class Structures: Their Composition and Change During the Neoliberal Era." *Latin American Research Review* 38 (1): 41–82.

Romero, Maria José, and Carlos Alonso Bedoya. 2008. "The Bank of the South: The Search for an Alternative to IFIs." Bretton Woods Project. September 26. http://www.brettonwoodsproject.org/art-562433.

Romero, Simon. 2010. "Economies in Latin America Race Ahead." *New York Times,* June 30. http://www.nytimes.com/2010/07/01/world/americas/01peru.html?r + 1&emc + etal.

Sanger, David E. 2009. "Senate Agrees to Dilute 'Buy America' Provisions." *New York Times,* February 4.

Shefner, Jon. 2008. *The Illusion of Civil Society: Democratization and Community Mobilization in Low-Income Mexico.* University Park: Pennsylvania State University Press.

Shefner, Jon, George Pasdirtz, and Cory Blad. 2006. "Austerity Protests and Social Immiseration: Evidence from Mexico and Argentina." In *Latin American Social Movements: Globalization, Democratization, and Transnational Networks,* edited by Hank Johnston and Paul Almeida, 19–42. Lanham, Md.: Rowman and Littlefield.

Stiglitz, Joseph E. 2002. *Globalization and Its Discontents.* New York: W. W. Norton.

———. 2006. *Making Globalization Work.* New York: W. W. Norton.

Structural Adjustment Participatory Review International Network (SAPRIN). 2005. *Structural Adjustment: The SAPRIN Report.* London: Zed Books.

Taylor, Paul. 2010. "Do-Little G20 Summit Cheers Spared Bankers." Reuters. June 28. http://www.reuters.com/article/idUSLDE65R0I720100628.

U.S. National Intelligence Council. 2008. *Global Trends 2025: The National Intelligence Council's 2025 Project.* http://www.dni.gov/nic/NIC_2025_project.html.

Walton, John. 1989. "Debt, Protest, and the State in Latin America." In *Power and Popular Protest: Latin American Social Movements,* edited by Susan Eckstein, 299–328. Berkeley: University of California Press.

Walton, John, and Charles Ragin. 1990. "The Debt Crisis and Political Protest in the Third World." *American Sociological Review* 55 (6): 876–90.

Walton, John, and David Seddon. 1994. *Free Markets and Food Riots: The Politics of Global Adjustment.* Cambridge, Mass.: Blackwell.

Walton, John, and Jon Shefner. 1994. "Latin America: Popular Protest and the State." In *Free Markets and Food Riots: The Politics of Global Adjustment,* edited by John Walton and David Seddon, 97–134. Cambridge, Mass.: Blackwell.

Weisman, Steven R. 2006. "IMF Changes Structure; Bank Backs Anti-graft Plan." *International Herald Tribune,* September 19.

Wines, Michael, and Keith Bradsher. 2009. "China's Leader Says He Is 'Worried' over U.S. Treasuries." *New York Times,* March 13.

Contributors

Giovanni Arrighi was Professor of Sociology at Johns Hopkins University. His main interests lay in the fields of comparative and historical sociology, world-systems analysis, and economic sociology. He conducted research on processes of labor-market formation and economic development in Southern Africa and Southern Europe; on the origins and transformations of the world capitalist system; and on the stratification of the global economy. He published extensively, and several of his books are regarded as classics. His last book, *Adam Smith in Beijing: Lineages of the Twenty-First Century* (2007), analyzes contemporary processes of development that may result in the rearrangement of international power hierarchies, with China emerging as a dominant nation. Giovanni Arrighi died in 2009.

Walden Bello is Professor of Sociology and Public Administration at the University of the Philippines and Executive Director of Focus on the Global South, a policy research institute based in Bangkok, Thailand, which he helped establish. Bello is currently a member of the Philippine Congress. He holds a doctoral degree in sociology from Princeton University and has taught at the University of California, Berkeley. In 2003, Bello was awarded the Right Livelihood Award. He is a fellow of the Transnational Institute in Amsterdam and a columnist for *Foreign Policy in Focus*. In March 2008, he was named Outstanding Public Scholar by the International Studies Association. He is a leading authority on economic internationalization.

Fred Block is Professor of Sociology at the University of California, Davis. He is a leading economic and political sociologist and the author of five major books: *The Vampire State and Other Myths and Fallacies About the U.S. Economy* (1996); *Postindustrial Possibilities: A Critique of Economic Discourse* (1990); *The Mean Season: The Attack on the Welfare State,* co-authored with Richard A. Cloward, Barbara Ehrenreich, and Frances Fox Piven (1987); *Revising State Theory: Essays in Politics and Postindustrialism* (1987); and *The Origins of International Economic Disorder: A Study of United States International Monetary Policy from World War II to the Present* (1977). Block has served on the Board of the Karl Polanyi Institute of Political Economy since 1989 and was a Distinguished Scientific Visitor to the Republic of China in 1995. He has also written for the *Nation,* the *American Prospect, In These Times, Commonweal, Boston Review,* and *Tikkun.*

James M. Cypher is Professor of Global Capital and Development in the Doctoral Program in Development Studies at the Universidad Autónoma de Zacatecas (Mexico). He is the co-author of *The Process of Economic Development* (2005) and two other books, including *State and Capital in Mexico: Development Policy Since 1940* (1990), along with approximately one hundred articles and book chapters. Since 1988, his research has been focused on questions of development, with particular emphasis on Latin America. Cypher has been a visiting professor and researcher at the American University (Washington, D.C.), the Universidad Nacional Autónoma de México (UNAM), the Universidad Autónoma Metropolitana, Iztapalapa (Mexico), and the Facultad Latinoamericana de Ciencias Sociales (FLACSO, Chile). He is a member of the editorial committee of several academic journals, including the *International Journal of Development Issues* (Australia), *Journal of Economic Issues* (United States), *Revista Oikos* (Chile), and *Latin American Perspectives* (United States).

Raúl Delgado Wise is Professor and Director of the Doctoral Program in Development Studies at the University of Zacatecas (Mexico) and Executive Secretary of the International Migration and Development Network. He is the author or editor of fourteen books and more than eighty essays, including book chapters and refereed articles. Delgado has been a guest lecturer in Canada, the United States, Germany, the Netherlands, Great Britain, Italy, Spain, and various Latin American countries. He received the annual prize for economics research, Maestro Jesús Silva Herzog, in 1993, and is a member of the Mexican Academy of Sciences, the National System of Researchers, and several scholarly associations in Canada, the United States, Latin America, and Europe. He is the chief editor of the journal *Migración y Desarrollo;* a member of the editorial committee of several academic journals, including *Latin American Perspectives* (United States), *AmeriQuests* (United States), *Revista Oikos* (Chile), *Revista Theomai* (Argentina), and *Quehacer Científico* (Mexico); and the editor of the book series Latin America and the New World Order for Miguel Angel Porrúa publishers.

Cristina Escobar is a research associate at the Center for Migration and Development at Princeton University. She received her Ph.D. in sociology from the University of California, San Diego. She has done research on citizenship and political participation in Latin America and among Latino immigrants in the United States. She is currently involved in a research project on Colombian, Dominican, and Mexican immigrant organizations in the United States and their impact in both the countries of origin and the United States.

Patricia Fernández-Kelly holds a joint appointment in the Sociology Department and the Office of Population Research at Princeton University. She is a social anthropologist with an interest in international development and an early student of export processing zones in Asia and Latin America. She has written on migration, economic restructuring, women in the labor force, and race and ethnicity. With Jon Shefner (University of Tennessee, Knoxville), she is the editor of *Out of the Shadows: Political Action and Informal Economy in Latin America* (Penn State Press, 2006) and *NAFTA and Beyond: Alternative Perspectives in the Study of Global Trade and Development* (2007). With Paul DiMaggio (Princeton University), she is editing a volume on art and immigration in the United States. With Alejandro Portes (Princeton University), she is the editor of *Exceptional Outcomes in Education and Employment Among Immigrant Children* (2008), a volume in the *ANNALS of the American Academy of Political and Social Science*. Her latest projects include ethnographic research on immigrant children, and immigration and health.

Frances Fox Piven is Distinguished Professor of Political Science and Sociology at The Graduate Center, City University of New York. She earned her Ph.D. from the University of Chicago in 1962. In 2006–7, she served as President of the American Sociological Association. She was co-founder of Human SERVE, an organization dedicated to encouraging people to register and vote. Piven has been honored with the American Sociological Association Career Award for the Practice of Sociology (2000); the Mary Lepper Award of the Women's Caucus of the American Political Science Association (1998); the Lifetime Achievement Award of the Political Sociology section of the American Sociology Association; the Tides Foundation Award for Excellence in Public Advocacy (1995); the Annual Award of the National Association of Secretaries of State (1994); the President's Award of the American Public Health Association (1993); the Lee Founders Award of the Society for the Study of Social Problems; the Eugene V. Debs Foundation Prize; and the C. Wright Mills Award.

Gary Gereffi is Professor of Sociology and Director of the Center on Globalization, Governance, and Competitiveness at Duke University. His research interests include social and environmental certification in global industries, the competitive strategies of global firms, and industrial upgrading in East Asia and Latin America. His three major ongoing research projects are industrial upgrading in East Asia, North America, and Eastern Europe/Central Asia; a comparative analysis of global restructuring in the apparel, automotive, computer, and retail sectors; and a study of the emergence of public and private governance systems in the Americas. Gereffi is writing a book on global value chains and industrial upgrading. His latest book, *The New Offshoring of Jobs and Global Development* (2008), reexamines and updates processes of economic internationalization.

Alejandro Portes is Howard Harrison and Gabrielle Snyder Beck Professor in the Department of Sociology and Director of the Center for Migration and Development at Princeton University. He has written extensively in several fields, including Latin American urbanization, international development, migration, the informal economy, and economic sociology. With Rubén Rumbaut, he spearheaded the Children of Immigrants Longitudinal Survey (CILS), the most ambitious project on the trajectories of second-generation immigrants in the United States. Portes is the author or editor of numerous influential books and hundreds of articles, a fellow of the American Academy of Arts and Sciences, a member of the National Academy of Sciences, and former president of the American Sociological Association.

William I. Robinson is Professor of Sociology at the University of California, Santa Barbara. He is also affiliated with the Latin American and Iberian Studies Program and the Global and International Studies Program at UCSB. His main research interests lie in the fields of macrosociology and comparative sociology, globalization, political economy, development, social change, political sociology, and Latin America and the Third World. Robinson is the author of numerous books and articles, including *Promoting Polyarchy: Globalization, U.S. Intervention, and Hegemony* (1996), *A Theory of Global Capitalism: Production, Class, and State in a Transnational World* (2004), and *Latin America and Global Capitalism: A Critical Globalization Perspective* (2008). He is a leading critical analyst of international globalization.

Jon Shefner is Professor and Head of the Sociology Department at the University of Tennessee, Knoxville. His work examines the relationship of economic deprivation and democratization in Mexico within a comparative study of IMF austerity policies, protest, and regime change. With Patricia Fernández-Kelly, he edited *Out of the Shadows: Political Action and Informal Economy in Latin America* (Penn State Press, 2006), a volume that examines for the first time the intersection of unregulated economic activities and political mobilization in various Latin American countries. More recently, Shefner has authored *The Illusion of Civil Society: Democratization and Community Mobilization in Low-Income Mexico* (Penn State Press, 2008) and, with Fran Ansley, co-edited a volume on new destination immigration, *Global Connections and Local Receptions: New Latino Immigration to the Southeastern United States* (2009).

Catherine Walsh is Professor and Director of the Doctoral Program in Latin American Cultural Studies at the Universidad Andina Símon Bolívar in Quito, Ecuador. Her research interests include the geopolitics of knowledge, interculturality, and concerns related to the Afro-Andean Diaspora and the production of decolonial thought. Walsh's publications include *Pensamiento *crítico y matriz (de)colonial* (2005); "Shifting the Geopolitics of Critical Knowledge: Decolonial Thought and Cultural Studies 'Others' in the Andes" in the journal *Cultural Studies* (2007); and "Interculturality and the Coloniality of Power: An 'Other' Thinking and Positioning from the Colonial Difference" in *Coloniality of Power, Transmodernity, and Border Thinking* (forthcoming from Duke University Press).

Alexandria Walton Radford completed her Ph.D. in sociology at Princeton University and is a research associate in postsecondary education with MPR Associates, Inc., in Washington, D.C.

Lu Zhang is Assistant Professor of Sociology at Temple University. She received her Ph.D. from Johns Hopkins University in 2010. Her research interests and teaching have focused on globalization, labor, and social movements, as well as the political economy of development in East Asia, especially China. She has published articles and book chapters on the evolving state-labor-business relationships, the dynamics of labor unrest, and the development path in reform China. Zhang is currently working on a book manuscript that examines the present conditions, subjectivity, and collection actions of Chinese autoworkers, and how the interplay of economic, social, and political processes at the global, national, regional, and shop-floor levels has produced specific labor relations and dynamics of labor unrest in the Chinese automobile industry. She has also started a second book-length project that explores the causes and impacts of capital relocation within China (from coastal to inland regions) and out of China to new low-cost countries (such as Vietnam).

Index